*The Romance
of Victorian
Natural History*

The Romance
of Victorian
Natural History

Lynn L. Merrill

New York   Oxford
OXFORD UNIVERSITY PRESS
1989

Oxford University Press

Oxford   New York   Toronto
Delhi   Bombay   Calcutta   Madras   Karachi
Petaling Jaya   Singapore   Hong Kong   Tokyo
Nairobi   Dar es Salaam   Cape Town
Melbourne   Auckland

and associated companies in
Berlin   Ibadan

Library of Congress Cataloging-in-Publication Data
Merrill, Lynn L.
The romance of Victorian natural history / Lynn L. Merrill.
p.   cm.
Bibliography: p.
Includes index.
ISBN 0-19-505203-X
1. English prose literature—19th century—History and criticism.
2. Natural history—Great Britain—History—19th century.
3. Natural history in literature.   4. Literature and science—Great
Britain—History—19th century.   I. Title.
PR756.N38M47   1989
828'.808'0936—dc19

9 8 7 6 5 4 3 2 1

Printed in the United States of America
on acid-free paper

For K.A.K.

"What a life of wonder—every object new."

TENNYSON

PREFACE

Imagine for a moment that you are embarked on a typical course of graduate study at an American university, specializing in Victorian literature. You expect, of course, to find among your assignments the agreed-on major writers: Dickens and Thackeray, Hardy and Hopkins, Trollope and Eliot, Tennyson, Browning, and Arnold. You anticipate encountering poets and novelists of perhaps somewhat lesser rank, too: Mrs. Gaskell, Disraeli, Butler, Clough, the Aesthetes and Pre-Raphaelites.

Since your tastes, presumably, are Victorian, you appreciate the prestige and quality of the nonfiction prose of the age; so finding Carlyle, Ruskin, Mill, and Newman on the reading list seems quite appropriate. *Sartor Resartus*, *The Stones of Venice*, Mill's *Autobiography*, *The Idea of a University*—Who would study Victorian literature without them? Their place in the canon is secure. From them, you would expect to learn something of the Victorian milieu, its politics, economics, religion, historiography, and art.

And science too, since science and technology scored such triumphs in the period. Naturally, you would dip into *The Origin of Species*, admire the argument of Huxley's "On the Physical Basis of Life," perhaps contemplate the humanist's counterpoint in Arnold's "Literature and Science." Ape or angel? Huxley or Bishop Wilberforce? Such notorious debates in biology surface irrepressibly. A course on "Victorian Literature and Science," a fairly common topic, might supplement Darwin and Huxley with the geologist Lyell, perhaps a snippet of Spencer or Tyndall, a mention of Herschel, Chambers, or Paley.

But unless your curriculum is extraordinary, you will not find the names of Philip Henry Gosse, Hugh Miller, Henry Walter Bates, Frank Buckland, Charles Waterson, J. L. Knapp, Arabella Buckley, W. H. Harvey, or Thomas Belt. You might read Kingsley's fiction, but not his *Glaucus*. You might hear of Wallace, vis-à-vis Darwin, but not read *The Malay Archipelago*. You might recognize the name of G. H. Lewes, but never realize that he had a connection to marine biology as well as to George Eliot. In short, you will not even glance at natural history. Alongside Victorian scientific, philosophical, political, economic, or religious prose, Victorian natural history prose will have no acknowledged place as an adjunct to the literature of the period. And it should.

Nineteenth-century natural history sparked no revolutions. It did not change the world, as Darwin arguably did. But it molded vision and put its stamp on language—the very things that should be most interesting to students of literature. For much of the nineteenth century, thousands of Britons of all social classes were avid amateur natural historians, collecting specimens, peering through microscopes, attending museums. Natural history was in the air. It was a topic of discussion and debate at social gatherings and in the periodical press. It generated fads and hobbies; it shaped decorative tastes. Naturalists appeared as characters in children's stories and in novels. And if that were not enough, natural history spawned some fascinating texts, many of them now quite unjustly condemned to oblivion. Blowing the dust off these volumes, a reader finds a lively, visual, particularized language, often accompanied by equally compelling illustrations. The discourse of Victorian natural history is marked by characteristic perceptions, motifs, tropes, tone, and style. In turn, its rhetorical strategies, metaphors, and diction influenced other forms of literature, just as the illustrations in natural history texts influenced art.

In intellectual circles, natural history is a curious orphan. Just as it has no stature in the literary canon, so too does it garner scant respect in the literature of science. The history of science for the nineteenth century is something of a glamour field of late, dominated as it is by Darwin's towering figure, and given the intense interest of contemporary biologists in evolution, genetics, and their powerful offshoot, genetic engineering. The dazzling research that makes headlines today—monoclonal antibodies, plasmids, gene-mapping—had its source in Victorian science. Victorian hard science, that is: biology, geology, chemistry, and physics. Not natural history, the older pursuit that these fields superseded. In consequence, there is a tendency to dismiss Victorian natural history as a dead end—quaint, frivolous, outmoded—to throw in one's lot with the Victorian sciences most like those valued today.

In fact, historians of science often take pains to dissociate the "important," "real" Victorian sciences from natural history, to make sure that Victorian biology, say, is accorded respect as a complex and difficult subject (like modern biology). It wasn't mere natural history, they say; it was better than that. Take Adrian Desmond, for example, who in a book about Victorian paleontology, called *Archetypes and Ancestors*, hastens to demarcate his subject from natural history. Victorian geologists, he assures us, were serious, rigorous scientists—as opposed to Victorian naturalists, whom he disparagingly labels "spider-stuffers, country parsons and the like" (p. 17).

Or, as another example, there is Martin Rudwick, who also discusses Victorian paleontology in his book *The Meaning of Fossils*. His difficult task, he states, is to convince historians of science that "a science like palaeontology is not to be dismissed as mere 'stamp-collecting'" (unpaginated preface). The stigma is strong: amateur naturalists, fossil collectors, contributed nothing but chaotic clutter to the field. Worse, their unsystematic bumbling marred the reputation of geology, then and now. All Victorian naturalists did was collect rocks or bugs in their spare time; thus they are easily dismissed as dabblers. They did not practice *science*. And if what they did was not good science, then how could it have been worth anything at all?

Desmond and Rudwick ally themselves with one strand of nineteenth-century science: professional, systematic, and specialized. No one would doubt its importance. And Desmond is right when he points out that many Victorians themselves, notably Huxley, championed science of this bent and eschewed "merely cataloguing collections" (p. 15). But natural history—amateur, descriptive, and encyclopedic—had its triumphs, too.

In this book, I come to the defense of "spider-stuffers" and "country parsons." Theirs was not the mainstream of Victorian science; it was more a leisurely meander, which in truth as the century wore on became something of an oxbow lake, cut off from the prevailing current. But for writers, artists, and the general public, it was by no means a backwater. The discourse of natural history was, and still remains, a powerful imaginative expression of the pleasures of the concrete world.

Set in the dual contexts of literature and science, Victorian natural history is a very large topic. Because my immersion in the subject has extended over many years, I fear that I cannot recount in detail every source of inspiration. Nevertheless, I am grateful to all those who have commented on the manuscript or my ideas, or who have suggested in conversation avenues for me to explore. Certainly I owe great intellectual debts to my predecessors in the field, particularly Allen, Ball, Barber, Christ, and Scourse, as my notes and Bibliography will show. More directly, I wish to thank J. Wallace Donald, Lewis Sawin, and Hobart Smith for reading and critiquing a version of the text, Caroline Hinkley for taking the photographs, and Cathy Preston for helping with the germination of the thesis. I particularly wish to thank Michael J. Preston, whose enthusiasm, encouragement, and sheer confidence were crucial to the project, and James R. Kincaid, whose unfailing cheerfulness, Victorian sense of eccentricity, and faith in my abilities did more than anything else to make me feel I should—and could—write this book. On a more personal level, I could not have written it without the help and forbearance of Kathy Kaiser and Michèle Barale, each of whom provided not only intellectual but also pragmatic and emotional support. They stood fast while subjected to endless drafts, editorial drudgery, and authorial tantrums, and for this I am deeply grateful.

Boulder, Colorado   L.L.M.
January 1988

CONTENTS

The Romance
of Victorian
Natural History

1

The Positive Force
of Natural History

Come with me, and lovingly study Nature, as she breathes, palpi-
tates, and works under myriad forms of Life—forms unseen, unsuspected, or unheeded by the mass of ordinary men. Our course may be
through park and meadow, garden and lane, over the swelling hills
and spacious heaths, beside the running and sequestered streams,
along the tawny coast, out on the dark and dangerous reefs, or under
dripping caves and slippery ledges. It matters little where we go:
everywhere—in the air above, in the earth beneath, and waters under
the earth—we are surrounded with Life.[1]

GEORGE HENRY LEWES, *Studies in Animal Life*

On a brilliant summer's day in 1854, a Victorian gentleman named Philip
Henry Gosse waded off the coast of Wales, knee-deep in the surf. Clad in
a somber black coat and fisherman's boots, the serious-minded member
of the Plymouth Brethren sect was spattered with mud and dashed with
brine. As might be expected, the other tourists in his party had long since
been deposited on the dry beach, where with grave decorum they strolled
along the sand, content to admire from a distance the picturesque coastal
view. What, then, was the estimable Mr. Gosse doing, clambering about
the oozy rocks, squeezing himself through sea-arches, seizing gelatinous
seaweed with his hands, imploring the rough fishermen to row him out to
the wildest surf-pounded crags? Forty-four years old, Gosse was a successful man of letters and the father of a son, Edmund, who would be a
writer as well. Yet here was this staid Victorian patriarch, laden with
buckets and glass vials and nets, poking about in tidepools and turning
over rocks for the worms they might conceal. Here roamed Mr. Gosse,
extolling to all who would listen the arcane beauties of anemones and
algae, starfish and seaweed, polypes and jellies, delighting over even the

3

least prepossessing of nature's oddities and collecting the squirming specimens for his saltwater tanks at home. Here was a Victorian completely caught up in the romance of natural history. And Philip Gosse was by no means alone in his enthusiasm.

It is quite surprising, in fact, how many eminent Victorians could be found at one time or another, turning over rocks in tidepools, or chipping at stones with hammers, pouncing on beetles and butterflies, or trolling dip-nets into ponds. George Henry Lewes, for example, although usually preoccupied with literary criticism and matters philosophical, spent two summers splashing, like Gosse, along the British coastline in search of curious marine creatures. The poet Tennyson, one acquaintance testified, could boast an intimate and loving knowledge of all the "wealth of minute animal and vegetable life" that filled the "limpid rock-pools" of Watcombe Bay.[2] The esteemed chronicler of Arthurian legend, classical myth, and human grief evinced an equally keen interest in the "life-history" of a single "tiny mollusc half-hidden in the short turf." And Charles Kingsley, too—novelist and social reformer—could be found happily beachcombing for invertebrate species, or even taking the trouble to pull a dredge behind a boat, eagerly snaring bottom-dwelling creatures and hauling them into the light.

As amateur naturalists, Lewes, Tennyson, and Kingsley dabbled in a pursuit that captivated a great many Victorians, famous and obscure, rich and poor, privileged and plebian. In the spread of this pastime, Philip Gosse was instrumental. By vividly recounting his passion for natural history, he motivated all sorts of people to grub for specimens in tidepools, ensconce them in displays, scrutinize their secrets with a microscope. Led by Gosse and other writers like him, many Victorians discovered that natural history as a pastime amounted almost to a creed. As a hobby it promised both endless diversion and endless education, cloaking amusement in the mantle of useful work. As one advocate put it: "The naturalist is more independent of circumstances than most men. Give him fields and hedges, the barren moor, or the quarry,—from each and all he will collect a store of useful and entertaining facts."[3]

Because it emphasized the collecting of specimens, natural history had the effect of focusing one's attention on diverse and fascinating natural forms. Of these there was a bountiful supply, with more being discovered daily. During the nineteenth century the total number of known species increased phenomenally, thanks to the exploratory efforts of scientific travelers who ventured into the tropics, such as Darwin, Belt, Wallace, and Bates; Bates alone collected over 14,000 insect species, more than half of them previously unknown.[4] Even in Britain itself, one writer confidently asserted in 1849, "New species and even new genera, are still continually being met with among both marine plants and animals . . . and this, not merely among the more minute and obscure kinds . . . but among the larger and more perfectly organised classes."[5]

The exciting revelations possible in natural history—of new species, new types of animals and plants, new modes of life—heightened one's sense of nature as boundless, inexhaustible. Face to face with the breathtaking plenitude of nature, the naturalist enjoyed an insatiable curiosity and sense of wonder. And one need not travel to Brazil to unearth amazing specimens; they were everywhere, in every humble hedgerow and puddle or, as Gosse revealed, tidepool and undercliff. All one had to do was look for them. With a microscope to expand the range of vision, a naturalist could pursue specimens even into the mysterious microcosm. The closer one looked, the more one saw; the microcosm teemed with details.

Collecting, microscopes, curiosity, wonder, and close vision—these were the hallmarks of natural history. Unfailingly, a Victorian naturalist brimmed with optimism. What could be more beautiful, more amazing, than nature's details? What could be more blessed than the hunt for them? Lewes, a captivated amateur, expressed the heady optimism of natural history very well when he described the "field" in which the naturalist labors: "It is truly inexhaustible. We may begin where we please, we shall never come to an end; our curiosity will never slacken."[6] With promises like that, Victorian natural history was well-nigh irresistible.

Once popularized, it gained strength until it could count legions of devotees. The manifestations of popular natural history are stories in themselves, infiltrating as they did every level of society, shaping Victorian attitudes and tastes. But more important, natural history lent itself well to expression in both prose and pictures. A thriving book industry ensured that this distinctive kind of discourse reached a wide audience. And the practice of natural history—collecting, microscopy, aquariums, and so on—was in itself a powerful stimulus to the imagination. It could indeed produce revelations—often described as such—a quasireligious sense of being privy to nature's secrets. The discourse of natural history, both verbal and pictorial, not only had imaginative power but took characteristic forms. Natural history books constituted a literary genre. The language they engendered emphasized meticulous detail, and their wide readership ensured that the language of natural history influenced other forms of literature as well. A love of concrete natural specimens created a demand for particularity and specificity in both language and art.

To understand the essential character of Victorian natural history and its particular discourse, it is first necessary to understand how "natural history" differs from nature in general, from nature simply as pretty scenery, or from nature images cast in poetic diction. Furthermore, it is important to understand how natural history differs from science. In the nineteenth century, the definitions of the terms *science, biology,* and *natural history* were in flux. But in practice, useful distinctions can be drawn between them, because they differed in attitude, scope, and effect. When modern scholars examine the Victorians' relationship to nature, Victorian science usually receives the most attention: the pure science that sought to understand the natural world, such as the theories of Darwin, the technological science that transformed the English country-side with its smoky mills and railroads, or science as it was described in texts, such as the essays of Thomas Henry Huxley. Critics and historians usually bury natural history under the rubric of science, and that is unfortunate. Treating it as science, expecting it to be scientific in the modern sense, does natural history a disservice and neglects its consider-able charms.

As in the eighteenth century, in the nineteenth *nature* was a word much talked about. Its connotations were many. Nature was the given world, created by God in all its variety and, as such, a norm of truth. Natural meant the opposite of artificial, a term frequently assigned to clumsy human creations. Moreover, in England's green and pleasant land, na-ture meant familiar, comforting scenery, country fields and well-tended gardens. Nature had also become a literary legacy enshrined in Romantic poetry. Wordsworth's daffodils and sweet lore of Nature, Shelley's Mont Blanc, west wind, and skylark, Keats' nightingale, autumn fruitfulness, and the poetry of earth never dead—these were exaltations of nature as a source of beauty or of Spirit. The post-Romantic tradition of nature poetry, the widespread assumption that lovely nature was one of the fittest subjects for verse, left Victorian poets with a mandate for explor-ing nature in very specific ways. Explore it they did; stripped of its nature subjects, Victorian poetry would be diminished indeed. In fact, as one critic points out, "Probably no term occurs as often in mid-century literature as *nature*."[7] What "nature" meant was highly inconsistent, but "truth to nature" was the rallying cry of the arts.

The preoccupation of the Victorians with Romantic nature poetry and contemporaneous versions of it, with nature as an "aesthetic norm," and with nature as a perennial source of beauty and delight can hardly be overstated. All cultures of necessity have some relation to nature; as John

Stuart Mill remarked, in his *Three Essays on Religion*, "Nature, natural, and the group of words derived from them . . . have at all times filled a great place in the thoughts and taken a strong hold on the feelings of mankind." But as Carl Dawson points out, Mill's contemporaries were especially engrossed in nature and definitions of "natural." As the rural face of England changed, the Victorians found their relationship to nature becoming more problematic and thus, in a curious way, more urgent.

Changeable though the term's meaning was, the ubiquity of nature in Victorian literature and culture is no surprise. But a poet's bird or flower is not the same as a naturalist's—not, at least, for a nature poet working in the Romantic tradition. Nature in such a poem may be specific, a particular species of bird, say. But this nature is not looked at *too* closely, because details about scaly feet or parasites would spoil the mood. Up close, nature may be fascinating, but it is not necessarily lovely. Nineteenth-century poets and their readers, by and large, preferred that descriptions of nature be beautiful, that is, in accord with accepted limits of poetic diction. The Victorian naturalist, on the other hand, felt no such constraints. For the naturalist, every fact mattered, every detail inspired amazement. A slimy black worm, a sticky cluster of sea-urchin eggs, a parasitic protozoan—these natural features rarely, if ever, appeared in poetry, but they quite comfortably inhabited the prose of natural history. Eventually, as they grew more familiar through their appearance in natural history books, details such as these did infiltrate poetry to some extent. At the very least, many Victorian poets found themselves compelled to respond to the popular demand for meticulous detail in descriptions of nature. The Pre-Raphaelite poets, and Tennyson and Browning to some extent, found natural history making inroads upon their imagery.

Natural history involved encountering nature in a new, direct way. Specialized naturalists had done this for some time; however, in the nineteenth century great numbers of people not only came eye to eye with nature, but more remarkably found the experience quite evocative. It was an acquired taste, natural history, but it transformed standards of descriptive beauty. During the nineteenth century, new habitats became accessible and, thus, new elements of nature. Explorers braved heretofore unknown territory. But on a more prosaic level, right within Britain, travel revealed new sights. For example, from the 1840s on, expanding railroads fostered a great deal of travel within England, hitherto impossible without great expenditures either of time or money or both. Cheap and efficient railway travel in itself helped make natural history a pastime for people of all classes, industrial workers as well as the wealthy. Most notably, the railroads increased the numbers of people who could spend their holidays on the coasts.

Seaside holidays, including brief, regimented dips in the bracing waters, had become attractive in the latter part of the eighteenth century. Like the Alps, the sea previously had held few charms. To a pre-Romantic sensibility it seemed unpredictable, unkempt, wild, if not downright dangerous. But cumbersome horse-drawn bathing machines provided decorum and safety. Entering these wheeled huts on dry land, swimmers undressed in private. Then, after the horses pulled the contraptions into the water, the bathers could modestly step out into the surf. Tentatively at first, then more boldly, a few took to the sea. In the nineteenth century, as the enthusiasm for ocean dips grew, and as seaside resorts rushed to erect pleasure piers and gay pavilions, the railroads opened up beaches to the multitudes. By 1850, the far stretches of the realm, such as Wales and Cornwall, were no longer remote—a fact that Philip Gosse exploited in his popular natural history books. Because new rail lines provided ready access to the coasts, and because natural history helped while away the hours when one was on vacation, the creatures of the littoral zone suddenly took on a new exotic aura. Once collectors had the opportunity to explore such locales, the definition of what constituted an attractive natural object changed radically.

The enthusiasm for natural history was abiding and passionate, fueling one nature fad after another. Not nature in the abstract, but nature in the hand: collected, identified, and displayed. Natural history was open to anyone, because it required few tools, and those most necessary could be made by hand or bought for little money. Knowledge of natural history could be gotten from books or from nature directly. Middle-class collectors could afford the latest volumes with which to compare their specimens; working-class collectors often were self-taught. Even children frequently participated in natural history at the urging of their elders; many books on the subject addressed themselves to young people, emphasizing the moral and educational benefits of its study. Sometimes its adherents got so carried away that their activities could be seen as eccentric, even a little bit silly. Amateur naturalists pounced on everything that moved, and much that didn't. As Lynn Barber points out,

> By the middle of the century there was hardly a middle-class drawingroom in the country that did not contain an aquarium, a fern-case, a butterfly cabinet, a seaweed album, a shell collection, or some other evidence of a

taste for natural history, and at the same time it was impossible to visit the seaside without tripping over parties of earnest ladies and gentlemen, armed with a book by Mr. Gosse and a collection of jamjars.[8]

Natural history increased in popularity until it could be called "a national obsession." Barber, who admirably surveys natural history as a cultural phenomenon, goes on to mention the ways in which the subject reached print. At the height of the obsession, she says, "Every newspaper ran a natural history section." Furthermore, natural history partisans clamored so for accounts of naturalists' adventures, that "books on the subject were only marginally less popular than the novels of Dickens."

How did the interest in natural history manifest itself? For one thing, around mid-century, among the newly prominent middle classes certain pastimes or hobbies became well entrenched. For example, in 1856 one manual of domestic advice mixed tips for amateur naturalists with instructions on more ordinary household chores. The book gives copious advice on such matters as cooking, cleaning, etiquette, and health. But quite matter-of-factly it also offers detailed instructions for nature hobbies: preserving curious insects, collecting and laying out seaweed, making skeleton leaves, preserving curious fish, preparing birds' eggs for cabinets, drying botanical specimens, preserving fungi, taking leaf impressions, modeling wax flowers, and keeping caged birds healthy.

The suggestions for laying out seaweed come by way of *Miss Gifford's Marine Botanist* and include a lengthy discussion of the relative merits of gumming dried algae onto scrapbook pages as opposed to inserting them into slits; in either case, of course, one would label each specimen with name, date, and locality. To preserve fungi requires exacting chemical preparations. First,

> take two ounces of sulphate of copper, or blue vitriol, and reduce it to powder, and pour upon it a pint of boiling water, and when cold, add half a pint of spirits of wine; cork it well, and call it "the pickle." To eight pints of water add one pint and a-half of spirits of wine, and call it "the liquor."[9]

Armed with an array of bottles, one can then proceed to dry the fungi, bathe them in the pickle, and finally entomb them in the liquor. And one must not fail to arrange the bottles "in order," with the name of each specimen prominently displayed. The steps for achieving perfectly preserved birds' eggs for one's cabinet are, if anything, even more arduous, involving the application of corrosive sublimate and gum-arabic if one is to keep the shells forever untainted by "corruption." Obviously, though, such procedures were not considered extraordinary. On the contrary, they were common sources of enjoyment—an instructive way to use one's leisure time and occupy idle hands.

Mid-century nature books reflected the popularity of such pastimes. Did one lack the patience or dexterity to dry and mount plants? Never mind—there were other ways to acquire them. Botany books could be purchased containing actual specimens, already pressed and neatly mounted on the pages. Amateur naturalists vexed by troublesome identifications could choose from a multitude of books on the most popular topics: British ferns, lichens, shrubs, birds, beetles, butterflies, and seaweed. Nearly every creature of "familiar haunts," every plant of the "waysides," every member of the animal "tribes" had its literary champion. Ladies' guides to botany or to the symbolic Language of Flowers abounded. Question-and-answer and conversational formats were popular; the tone frequently cozy. Illustrations, often beautifully hand-colored, aided identification of the most obstinate natural rarity.

Just as railroads stimulated travel and thus the yen for natural history, crowded railroad stations served as an important locus of dissemination for cheap editions of popular books. Books bought at the station stalls could be read aboard the train, whereas reading had been difficult or impossible in jerking, bouncing horse coaches. From the train stations, popular books of all kinds poured into England. Around mid-century, many books were produced specifically for "railway and seaside reading."[10] The traveling public's insatiable reading appetite favored travel accounts and natural history books as well as novels,[11] and many became huge best-sellers. As a vivid example of the craving for nature books, and the numbers of people who read them, one modest mid-century nature book, *Common Objects of the Country*, by the Reverend J. G. Wood, sold 100,000 copies in one week. In comparison, *Self-Help* by Samuel Smiles, often cited by cultural historians as a highly influential force in shaping the Victorian popular mind, managed to sell only 20,000 copies in its first year.[12]

Natural history held sway even in incongruous circumstances, so that, for example, it was not uncommon to find books with titles like "The Natural History of Cage-Birds." Cage-birds, in fact, were favorite companions, as can be seen in Walter Howell Deverell's painting *A Pet*. Exhibited in 1853, this painting in the Pre-Raphaelite style shows a young woman standing at the open door of a conservatory, cooing affectionately to her caged pet. Outside in the lush garden, its wild analogue, a vivid yellow-green bird, walks along the path. Keeping a tame bird in the house was a way to bring natural history indoors. Cage-birds, exotic plants in conservatories, anemones in aquariums, minerals in cabinets, even floral patterns on wallpaper—all testified to the popularity of natural history.

By participating in fads and hobbies like these, mid-Victorians learned to see nature in a more intent, closely focused way, especially with the aid of microscope or hand-lens, and to value objects of nature *as objects*, as material possessions with all the satisfying virtues of the concrete. From close contact with natural history, people came to value the specimen—the individual, concrete, particular chip or bit of nature. This ascendancy of the *specimen* dovetailed with the prodigious industrial production and the philosophical formulations that fostered the well-known Victorian materialism, the Victorian love of facts.

How can one explain the stupendous popularity of natural history in the nineteenth century? It had been gaining momentum during the preceding century, when aristocratic and wealthy collectors had amassed great private museums for their own amusement. Natural history in the nineteenth century simply filtered down to the middle and working classes, where it found a wider audience. The railroads and the ready availability of travel, as well as the stirring accounts of tropical explorers, gave people more nature to see, both in reality and in the imagination, pleasures unconstrained by money or class. Other reasons for the popularity of natural history include its religious foundations, specifically in natural theology, and how well it fit Victorian theories of education, morality, and duty—the implicit value of keeping the hands and mind busy. On nature walks, one could get outdoor exercise, as prescribed by the developing preoccupation with what Matthew Arnold disparagingly called "British muscularity." And certainly, natural history benefited from another irresistible social force in the nineteenth century: the juggernaut of science.

Science in its pure, theoretical form indelibly colors the image of the nineteenth century. The atomic theory, the discovery of thirty or so chemical elements and the proportional laws of chemical composition, the relationships of the periodic table, the birth of organic chemistry, oceanography, physiology, the elucidation of the cell as the basic living unit, the theory of natural selection, the step from electromagnetic induction to the electromagnetic theory of light—these are among the major scientific syntheses of the period. Applied science, of course, created the railroads that stung some Victorian eyes but opened others, as well as such potent triumphs as coal mines, textile mills, steam pumps, ship canals, wrought iron, the *Great Eastern* steamship, and the Crystal Palace. It was, as Carlyle pointed out, "The Age of Machinery, in every outward and inward sense of that word."[13] Science gained so much power that the nineteenth century saw the birth of "the two cultures," with writers lamenting the yawning gulf between the classical worldview and the upstart scientific one. One of natural history's great strengths was that for many people it served as a bridge between these two disparate views.

For centuries, natural history and science had meant pretty much the same thing: knowledge about the natural world. But gradually, in the nineteenth century, the two disciplines divided. In a sort of mitosis, they became two discrete entities, two cells spawned from a single progenitor. Or rather, from natural history, which had encompassed the study of all nature, various distinct sciences were born: geology, biology, biochemistry, physiology, and so on. A naturalist could still study all of nature (animal, vegetable, and mineral); a scientist studied only a certain part of it. In the study of living things, the naturalist was supplanted by the biologist. Natural history remained accessible to amateurs, while biology, like the other sciences, became the province of professionals. Furthermore, natural history and biology had different aims and appealed to different types of people. William Morton Wheeler, a zoologist whose career spanned the turn of the century, provides a clear definition of the two types. The naturalist, Wheeler says,

> is mentally oriented toward and controlled by objective, concrete reality, and probably because his senses, especially those of sight and touch, are highly developed, is powerfully affected by the esthetic appeal of natural objects. He is little interested in and may even be quite blind to abstract or theoretical considerations. He is primarily an observer and fond of outdoor life, a collector, a classifier, a describer, deeply impressed by the overwhelming intricacy of natural phenomena and revelling in their very complexity.[14]

The naturalist, then, prefers to observe rather than analyze, enjoys particulars more than abstractions. Finding natural objects beautiful and evocative, the naturalist responds to objects rather than examining them critically. Not so the true biologist, who, according to Wheeler,

> is oriented toward and dominated by ideas, and rather terrified or oppressed by the intricate hurly-burly of concrete, sensuous reality and its multiform and multi-colored individual manifestations. He often belongs to the motor rather than to the visual type and obtains his esthetic satisfaction from all kinds of analytical procedures and the cold desiccated beauty of logical and mathematical demonstration. His will to power takes the form of experimentation and the controlling of phenomena by capturing them in a net of abstract formulas and laws.[15]

Of course, Wheeler here oversimplifies to make a point. Clearly, not every naturalist or biologist would neatly fit into these categories, or agree with them (especially since Wheeler seems a bit prejudiced against the theoretical side of science). But in fact, Wheeler's definition of a naturalist fits Victorian natural history extremely well. In addition, the definition helps explain why natural history appealed to so many people. The naturalist's approach to nature (visual, tactile, and aesthetic) and activities (collecting, describing, taking pleasure in nature's multiplicity and complexity) would appeal far more readily to an ordinary person than would the biologist's generalizing and abstracting. The naturalist is concrete, specific, sensory, and colorful—precisely the rhetorical qualities that make a written description powerful. That is why natural history, as an activity, translates itself so readily and so successfully into the written word.

At about mid-century, ordinary people in Britain could hardly have failed to notice the technology around them, and they probably had heard, through the periodical press or perhaps public lectures, of startling scientific advances. But although they may have been aware of science, many of its arcane discoveries had little relevance to their lives. Yet even shoemakers and bakers, though perhaps illiterate and isolated from the intellectual issues of the day, could have direct contact with natural history, collecting beetles or stones, flowers or ferns on walks. If these objects gave people pleasure as they stooped to examine their colors or shapes, if they evoked other times, called up feelings and associations, or even seemed to mirror their moods, then nature was providing not fodder for science but rather, to use Philip Gosse's term, the romance of natural history.[16]

In literary terms, a *romance* may be thought of as an extravagant fiction, a pleasurable excursion into a lavish or fantastic realm; if something partakes of romance, it may be said to be adventurous or exotic. When Philip Henry Gosse chose to title one of his books *The Romance of Natural History*, he was thinking of natural history in all these senses. A product of his times, Gosse found natural history full of extravagant charm. Far from being dry or colorless, nature to the naturalist seemed exotic, endlessly entertaining. The complexity of nature's forms could range beyond the wildest poet's dreams—could seem, in fact, like the enchanted imaginings of an author in a medieval romance. Natural history appealed to the imagination—and therein lay its romance. A popular book from 1840 makes this connection clear for one facet of natural history, geology. Far from being dry or theoretically rigorous, amateur geology, according to the book, is "a romantic science."[17] Like other pursuits in natural history, geology "carries the imagination" and thus reveals a world as delightful as "the happy Valley in 'Rasselas.'"

Natural history was not a subject that, like science, could alter the course of history and change the world, but it was a subject that could deeply affect the individual, both mind and spirit. The "Victorian intelligentsia," as one critic has dubbed them, did not dwell on it, preferring weightier issues like evolutionary theory.[18] Natural history is aesthetic science, nature closely examined to enhance the pleasure that an ordinary person takes in it. It offers pleasures of detail, form, and complexity, as well as evocative connotation and human associations. For many reasons, it had strong appeal for the Victorians. But even in the very different computerized climate of the late twentieth century, natural history remains popular, as an abundance of widely read modern writers attests—Joseph Wood Krutch, Rachel Carson, Edwin Way Teale, Aldo Leopold, Henry Williamson, Gerald Durrell, Archie Carr, Annie Dillard, John McPhee, and David Attenborough, to name but a few.

Because the relationship of natural history to science is historically complex, it is not always possible to draw a sharp distinction between the two endeavors. The word *scientist* was not coined until 1834, by William Whewell (it became more widely known after 1840, when he used the term in his *Philosophy of the Inductive Sciences*), and of course the introduction of the word did not instantly clarify its domain. In popular usage, terms like *natural history*, *science*, *natural philosophy*, and *natural knowledge* remained muddled throughout the first half of the nineteenth century. As a result, a person might call himself a naturalist and yet, by my definition, still be primarily practicing science, and vice versa. Basically, a naturalist studied what a botanist, zoologist, biologist, and geologist studied—just not in the same way. In 1876, Thomas Henry Huxley acknowledged the problem of terminology when he gratefully accepted the new term *biology*, which, he said, "clear thinkers and lovers of consistent nomenclature" will prefer over "the old confusing name of 'Natural History,' which conveyed so many meanings."[19] When *natural history* appears in a Victorian text, then, one must take care to determine what its author's sense of the term is. One can, nevertheless, apart from slippery contemporaneous labels, identify an attitude, an aim, and a practice that is natural history: aesthetic science, personal science, evocative and connotative.

The breadth of natural history, really encompassing all field study of nature, gave it a great deal of synthesizing might. Not merely an intellectual power for discovering scientific laws or relationships, but a visual power, the power of appreciation of form that painters might use. Natural history covered a wide range of natural objects, not just plants, animals, and microscopic life, but rocks and fossils, mountains and oceans as well. By virtue of its all-inclusiveness, natural history embraced entire landscapes in addition to objects—the totality of impression, the long view—of landforms, weather, vegetation, color, and light. The aesthetic of natural history was thus dialectical, moving from particulars to panorama and back again. In this, the discourse of natural history parallels much of Victorian poetry, for instance that of Tennyson and the Pre-Raphaelites. Because so much of Victorian literature is dialectical, for example frequently expressing a tension and vacillation between affirmation and doubt, it is interesting that natural history contains so many dialectical tensions as well—not only between the microscopic and the wide view, but also between multiplicity and singularity. One pleasure of natural history was the perception that nature was inexhaustible, bountiful, endlessly variable; on the other hand, there was a great deal of pleasure to be found in the perception that much in nature was singular and unique.

Natural history bears a special relationship to Victorian literature and art precisely because it stands halfway between science and the arts. Its approach to nature partakes of both. Like science, it notes, identifies, and delineates details; like art, it arranges them in an overall composition, whether that be an illustration, a collection in a cabinet, an essay, or a book. It does in one genre (natural history writing) with words what Ruskin advocated that another (painting) do with line and color. In fact, the whole Ruskinian program, so influential among Victorian writers, closely parallels the naturalist's approach to nature.

Yet while Romantic legacies of nature, Ruskin's nature theories, and the treatment of nature in literature figure prominently in Victorian studies, direct Victorian contact with nature—in the form of natural history—is seldom mentioned. Great numbers of people studied, classified, and collected specimens from nature, and thereby established tangible and particular links with it, but curiously, this dedicated industry is overlooked by most general literary, cultural, or purely historical studies of Victorian times.

Richard D. Altick's *Victorian People and Ideas* is one of the few general guides to the Victorian period that takes note of natural history, and Altick mentions it but briefly, saying only that "the long English tradition of scientific amateurism came into full flower in the Victorian era" when "a host of avocational scientists were eager to help honor their hobby and promote its intellectual authority." Altick, however, only speaks of the "numerous spare-time ornithologists, botanists, geologists, and astronomers" because he wishes to emphasize their contributions to a process he considers far more important than natural history: the "acceptance" and increased prestige of science.[20]

Walter Houghton, in his *Victorian Frame of Mind*, mentions nature and the Victorian response to it in the context of industrialism and the growth of smoky cities. The number of people living in nonrural surroundings did increase dramatically, of course, in the first half of the nineteenth century. Urban dwellers (in towns of 5,000 or more) comprised just 13 percent of the population in 1700, but 25 percent in 1800, and more than 50 percent by 1851.[21] "In this environment," Houghton says,

> the romantic love of nature passed into a new phase. It became the nostalgia for a lost world of peace and companionship, of healthy bodies and quiet minds. The image had its basis in memory, for every Victorian in the city had either grown up in the country or in a town small enough for ready contact with the rural environment.[22]

This nostalgia for a lost rural past, Houghton says, "is the background against which one should read the nature poetry of the Victorians (and understand the popularity of Wordsworth), or look at their landscapes."[23]

Houghton has a valid point here, but this—one standard view of Victorian nature—is looking at nature as a negative force. Nostalgia is longing for something that is lost, gone, is no more. If the Victorians longed in this way for nature, then nature was to them a lack, an absence (except in memory), a void; a background, but no longer an active part of their lives. Such a view does not do justice to the large numbers of Victorians who actively sought contact with nature through collecting or excursions to the coasts or, in the imagination, through natural history books. Ensconced in cities, industrialized Victorians were no longer simply surrounded by nature; they had to seek it out. This process was more difficult, but also of necessity more deliberate, conscious, and active. The nostalgia for a lost rural past was real and may have served as an impetus for the vogue in natural history, but once the passion for natural history was kindled many Victorians responded to nature as a positive force.

Like Houghton, Buckley's *The Victorian Temper*, Young's *Victorian England: Portrait of an Age*, Himmelfarb's *Victorian Minds*, among many other well-known Victorian critiques, say nothing of natural history, little about any popular response to nature, except perhaps as filtered through Romantic poetry—not sales of nature books, nor fads for butterfly or fern collecting, nor the rage for seaside holidays. Darwin, of course, is mentioned; the change in human stature brought about by Darwin's shocking theory, the recession of God, the loss of human uniqueness and God-like form, the necessary but painful acknowledgment of apes and finches as our cousins, perhaps even grandfathers—all these things, without doubt, profoundly influenced Victorian (and modern) ideas. But Darwin, at least in his *Origin of Species*, and his oft-cited geological predecessor, Charles Lyell,[24] whose sweeping application of Hutton's uniformitarian theory radically expanded notions of time and landform-building processes, do not strictly belong to the realm of natural history, but instead to science. Thus most who study the Victorians do not mention natural history at all, much less dignify its prose as literature.

There are several possible reasons for this. The first is simple omission. Many of the books are, after all, long out of print and thus forgotten. A second reason is the fact that natural history is too often lumped with science, and so thought to be of interest only to historians of science. As far as the Victorians are concerned, such an approach is short-sighted in itself, but in addition, as I have pointed out, natural history displays some very unscientific qualities that draw it closer to literature: emotion, evocativeness, and connotation. Third, a question might be raised about the quality of the prose; perhaps it's simply not very good. Uneven it certainly can be, as one might expect when dealing with so many different authors of varying talents. No naturalist will displace Arnold or Carlyle in the pantheon of great writers. Yet at its best, as later chapters will demonstrate, natural history prose is extremely skillful, lively, and affecting—particularly in the case of P. H. Gosse. It can rise to the level of lyric; it can raise fundamental questions about one's place in nature, one's moment in time.

Perhaps so, a critic might say, but it is still nonfiction, another reason to exclude it from the literary critic's purview. If one considers, however, how many nonfiction writers inhabit the canon of Victorian literature, then an obvious precedent exists for treating natural history writing as a genre, or at least an ancillary subset, of literature. It is customary to read as Victorian literature the political science of Mill, the theology of Newman, the history of Macaulay, and the science of T. H. Huxley. Why should prose on such subjects rank as literature, while that of natural history does not? Clearly subject matter alone is no criterion. For the vast sea of Victorian nonfiction prose, strict definitions of "literature" versus "expository prose" are impossible to enforce. Categories blur. British Victorian writers were too omnivorous, too wide-ranging, to be constrained by the picket fences of any genre. Any topic could fall within the imaginative purview of belles-lettres. Since natural history writing may actually be closer to affective, aesthetic literature than are, say, Matthew Arnold's injunctions on culture and anarchy, I contend that natural history prose should take its place alongside them.

Perhaps the most intractable rationale for excluding natural history from the realm of Victorian literature is the canon itself. Natural history books had a very wide readership and appealed to people of all classes, even those of distinctly frivolous tastes. The very popularity of these books works against their serious consideration, for, as Leslie A. Fiedler suggests, twentieth-century English literary critics tend to feel that any "best-seller" is inherently suspect. If a book was popular, it must have been sentimental, sensational, shallow, kitsch. Even Dickens stirs misgivings. How could a writer that popular have been creating art? The literary canon resists lowbrow or previously uncanonized works.[25] So to a large extent natural history books are not in the canon now—because they haven't been there before. Thus the circle closes upon itself, but for the multifarious Victorians, such an approach is especially limiting.

The range of texts for the Victorianist to choose from is wide. One of the consummate stylists of the period is Philip Henry Gosse, and yet he is known to students of Victorian literature today only by virtue of his somewhat dubious fame as the repressively religious father in Edmund Gosse's *Father and Son*. Historians of science remember his misguided attempt to circumvent evolution in *Omphalos*. But he wrote dozens of natural history books that found a wide audience—for example, *The Romance of Natural History*, *Evenings at the Microscope*, and *Tenby: A Sea-Side Holiday*. Those three books alone reveal in their titles much about the components of this Victorian genre. Another natural history writer has a literary reputation: Charles Kingsley, the historical novelist and religious stalwart. His natural history book, *Glaucus; or, the Wonders of the Shore*, is, however, largely forgotten. Another enormously popular and rewarding work is *The Old Red Sandstone* of Hugh Miller, the pious, self-taught, working-class geologist. These are some representative primary works;[26] from them, one can get a good understanding of what natural history included, what sorts of language it employed, what kinds of objects it valued. With these books as a center, a study of Victorian natural history can ripple outward, with wider implications that concern Victorian language, perception (especially vision), art, and even the accepted literature of the canon.

When critics do study Victorian natural history, what approach do they take to it? One tactic is to simply study it as a social phenomenon, as do David Elliston Allen in *The Naturalist in Britain: A Social History*, Lynn Barber in *The Heyday of Natural History*, and Nicolette Scourse in *The Victorians and Their Flowers*. These books concern themselves with natural history as a social, not a literary or stylistic, issue. Other critics study the stylistic qualities typical of natural history writing—but they find these qualities only in literature, ignoring the natural history texts. For example, Carol T. Christ in *The Finer Optic: The Aesthetics of Particularity* and Patricia M. Ball in *The Science of Aspects: The Changing Role of Fact in the Work of Coleridge, Ruskin and Hopkins* study the Victorian preoccupation with closely observed facts. Both, however, concern themselves with literature as such—poetry or fiction, mainly— and touch only peripherally on the influence of natural history. Both notice the prevalence of "particularity" (the quality of valuing particular incidents or objects more than idealized or general ones) in Victorian literature, without proposing natural history as a source for it.

Natural history writing is the link that connects popular natural history—with its love of physical objects—to Victorian literature, with its lexicon of particularity. Yet few critical studies have examined natural history texts in terms of their language. Two studies that do are both somewhat out of date: Philip Marshall Hicks' *The Development of the Natural History Essay in American Literature* (1924) and Julian M. Drachman's *Studies in the Literature of Natural Science* (1930). The first of these pertains to American literature and is not particularly rigorous in its analysis. Drachman's study, like most that deal with British writing, sticks closely to writers of science, not natural history, covering the likes of Darwin,[27] Huxley, Lyell, Chambers (of *Vestiges of Creation* fame), Herschel, Tyndall, Hooker, and Owen. These are writers Drachman claims have never, or seldom, been acknowledged as literary; his task is proving that they should be. Drachman makes some mention of writers whom I would call naturalists, rather than scientists, such as Charles Waterton, Henry Walter Bates, and John Burroughs. But he clearly differentiates them from the core group of his study. Natural history essays, he proclaims, "are generally admitted to belong to literature."[28] Since that is manifestly the case, Drachman feels no need to bother with them.

I cannot agree with Drachman that works of natural history normally count as literature. What works of natural history appear with any regularity on the syllabus for a Victorian literature class? If they are "literature," they have that rank only in the loose, popular sense: natural history books are like novels in that they make for light reading, fun reading. One reads them by choice and for pleasure. They are not like a physics textbook—not intimidating, not a rigorous workout for the

brain. In other words, in the popular sense, natural history is like literature in that it is not "serious." But in a much deeper sense, this prose does
"belong to literature," as Drachman suggests. Look at some of his criteria
for natural history prose: a predominance of "outdoor observation, often
minutely detailed," "little attempt at constructing theories," descriptions
that are "quite literary in their emotional and pictorial quality," and a
"large element of personal narrative."[29] Such qualities do indeed sound
more like literature than like science. Drachman, however, concentrates
not on writers of such ilk but instead on scientists—who write to theorize,
systematize, and instruct.

The influence of science on Victorian literature has hardly gone unremarked. Critics frequently trace the stamp of Darwinism and evolutionary theory on novels and poems, as Gillian Beer does in *Darwin's Plots* or
Peter Morton in *The Vital Science*. The effect of scientific ideas on
literature intrigues critics like Tess Cosslett, who wrote *The "Scientific
Movement" and Victorian Literature*. Cosslett is primarily interested in
Victorian novelists and poets whose works were infiltrated by scientific
philosophies or theories: Tennyson, Eliot, Meredith, and Hardy (a pretty
standard list of the Victorian writers most interested in science). Natural
history, again, makes no appearance here.

The approach that Cosslett takes is instructive, for it typifies much of
the critical work done on the relationship between Victorian science and
literature. She introduces her analysis by taking the phrase "scientific
movement" from an 1877 essay by the literary critic Edward Dowden.
Dowden reconciles science and literature, but sanctions only some elements of science as catalysts for poetry. In his essay he says: "Such
passages as have been quoted from Byron and Goethe and Shelley make
clear to us what kind of scientific inquiry and scientific result is fruitful
for the feelings and imaginations of men. Not the details of the specialist,
but large *vues d'ensemble*."[30] What matters, in other words, is not scientific terminology, and certainly not closely observed details—such as the
naturalist describes—but scientific ideas, sweeping conceptions that
change people's sense of their place in the natural scheme.

Cosslett picks up on Dowden's angle of approach and analyzes how
Victorian literature is permeated by scientific ideas—the scientific meaning of truth or natural law, human kinship with nature, natural unity and
processes.[31] This is, in fact, the preponderant literary critical approach.
Most articles and books on Victorian science and literature concern
themselves either with theories and governing conceptions—such as natural selection, geological gradualism, atomism, thermodynamic behavior
of heat, or scientific epistemology—or with individual figures like Dar-

win, Lyell, Herschel, Hutton, Humboldt, I. K. Brunel, Geikie, or Tyndall. Studies of science and religion as well as science and education flourish. But not studies of natural history.

The omission of natural history from the concept of "Victorian nature" is perhaps most glaring in an otherwise excellent critical anthology devoted entirely to that idea: *Nature and the Victorian Imagination* edited by U. C. Knoepflmacher and G. B. Tennyson. Various essays within it range widely on topics from photography to art to literature, from science to exploration. But in a review of this collection of essays, David J. DeLaura complains that one type of nature is missing from the collection. The book, DeLaura says, deals with romantic, pastoral, transcendental, and philosophical nature, but fails to mention the "problematic kind of nature" that was "the kind perhaps of most interest to ordinary readers—the microscopic particulars recently studied by Patricia Ball and Carol Christ." From this collection, according to DeLaura, one would assume that Victorians had no interest in "the sticky, odoriferous experience of the actual out-of-doors."[32]

What DeLaura describes is precisely natural history. And yes, there is a dearth of discussion of Victorian "sticky particulars," because natural history has been overlooked in the glittering array of Victorian sciences.

If the canon of British nineteenth-century literature snubs natural history, American literature is somewhat more open to it. This is so for two main reasons. In the first place, the American experience of nature differed substantially from the English. While English nature had long been domesticated, subdued for the purposes of agriculture, American nature was savage, a wilderness, a frontier. Early settlers mainly applied themselves to taming it, but by the nineteenth century the beauties of dramatic natural features, many on a scale unprecedented in Great Britain—Niagara Falls, for example, which fascinated English visitors[33]—began to be appreciated for themselves. Nearness to wild nature and vast expanses was a fact of life for Americans and infiltrated the American character and American expectations. North America was wild enough that British naturalists toured it eagerly, just as they did South America. Bates and Wallace journeyed to the Amazon; Gosse sailed to Alabama. Their accounts share a similar tone of awe at the abundance of nature around them. Natural history flourished in nineteenth-century America and, in fact, paralleled the British (and Continental) experience in many ways. Collecting, museums, geological controversies, microscopes—all characterized American natural history just as they did British, although as a popular fad natural history captured the British imagination to a much greater degree.

The second reason for the recognition of nature literature in America is the existence of a powerful literary progenitor: Henry David Thoreau. Thoreau almost invented and certainly mastered a form of nature writing—particular, observant, exact, but also synthetic, musing, and connective—that others could emulate. The title of one critical work on Thoreau, James McIntosh's *Thoreau as Romantic Naturalist: His Shifting Stance toward Nature*,[34] serves as an example of the kind of stature Thoreau has in American literature. He is no scientist, but he is a naturalist fascinated by nature and equally fascinated by the reworking of nature's raw material into essays. McIntosh does not hesitate to think of Thoreau as both literary artist and naturalist, linking him both to the Romantic nature-study of Goethe and to the Romantic poetry of Wordsworth. Nature, in all its guises, mattered a great deal to the American Transcendentalists. Emerson, who of course explored the general topic, also found himself seduced for a while by practical natural history, collecting, and museums. Cloaked in dignity by the Transcendentalists, the nature essay established itself as an American genre.[35] One of its most industrious popularizers was John Burroughs. Often called Thoreau's disciple, Burroughs extended Thoreau's models in volume after volume of nature essays.[36] Burroughs' advocacy of the natural history approach to observation closely parallels that of Ruskin in England. Burroughs and Ruskin eloquently formulate the paradigmatic ideals, the theoretical underpinnings, of the field.

Victorian literature has no Thoreau, no naturalist-writer accepted into the canon (it does have Huxley, but he is a scientific essayist). If Thoreau has a counterpart in England, it is Gilbert White (1720–1793). No discussion of British natural history can neglect his contribution. White, a gentle curate in the parish of Selborne, published his accumulated observations of nature in 1789 as *The Natural History of Selborne*. Perennially popular, this book still ranks as a beloved nature classic. White's book had special pertinence to Victorian natural history for two reasons. First, although published in the late eighteenth century, it "remained more or less unknown outside the *cognoscenti* until its 1827 edition, when it became the vogue for the middle classes."[37] And second, White's *Natural History of Selborne* served as a model for a naturalist's approach to the world. Anyone could practice his humble but powerful method of empirical observation and learn, as he did, a great deal about the natural world in the process. One did not need wealth; only doggedness and an open mind. Like Thoreau, White made the most of observations within a small compass. He was keenly alert to the pleasures of the mundane; nothing was beneath his notice. White's meticulous approach to natural history had an incalculable effect on his nineteenth-century heirs.

With typical humility, White said of himself: "My little intelligence is confined to the narrow sphere of my own observations at home" (Pennant Letter XXVII). That, of course, is the secret of his power. With only a "narrow sphere" to move in, he notices small details that most would overlook. And, paradoxically, he finds that the smaller the sphere, the more there is to see: "It is, I find, in zoology as it is in botany: all nature is so full, that that district produces the greatest variety which is the most examined" (Pennant Letter XX). This assertion might almost be engraved as the credo for the Victorian naturalists who followed White.

Like them, White displays an inquiring, nearly infinite curiosity about the natural world. Although a clergyman, in the material realm White practices a strict empiricism. He cites many weighty authorities (such as Linnaeus, Ray, or Buffon) who claim one or another natural fact to be true, but always with skepticism; he prefers to be an "eye-witness," to verify the situation for himself. As he describes himself, White is "an *outdoor naturalist*, one that takes his observations from the subject itself, and not from the writings of others" (Barrington Letter I). Hearsay is dangerous: "There is such a propensity in mankind towards deceiving and being deceived, that one cannot safely relate any thing from common report, especially in print, without expressing some degree of doubt and suspicion" (Pennant Letter XXI). So scrupulous is he in his insistence on observed truth that he might have taken the motto of the Royal Society for his own: *Nullius in verba* (no one else's words).

Scientifically speaking, Gilbert White is a strict Baconian who inductively assembles facts, then crafts explanations from them. When in doubt, White experiments, always taking, as he says, "particular pains to clear up the matter" (Pennant Letter XXVI). He battles legend, hearsay, superstition, and analogy as modes of scientific explanation; he champions direct observation and evidence. In so doing, White resolutely turns his back on a long-standing tradition in natural history, honored in medieval and ancient times, of trusting authority rather than observation, and sets a tone for the natural history (and science) to come. Thus the Selborne naturalist establishes many of the prototypical characteristics of natural history writing later embraced by Victorian naturalists: a passion for quantification, an insistence on correct classification, inexhaustible particularity, and a fondness for Latin species names.

White cannot describe a mouse without measuring it exactly: "A full-grown *mus medius domesticus* weighs, I find, one ounce lumping weight,

. . . and measures from nose to rump four inches and a quarter, and the same in its tail" (Letter XIII). A stickler for precision, he cannot describe a bird without correcting its previous classification:

> I have taken a great deal of pains about your *salicaria*. . . . I have surveyed it alive and dead, and have procured several specimens; and am perfectly persuaded myself (and trust you will soon be convinced of the same) that it is no more nor less than the *passer arundinaceus minor* of Ray. . . . It is so strangely classed in Ray, who ranges it among his *picis affines*. It ought no doubt to have gone among his *aviculae cauda unicolore*. (Letter XXV)

Much of *The Natural History of Selborne* has this tone: measured, rational, precise—even persnickety. Every sort of creature powerfully attracts White, but he seldom waxes sentimental. Such was not always the case for Victorian naturalists.

The irrepressible Victorians put their own stylistic stamp on White's natural history. An 1864 edition of White's classic shows the Victorian approach. The Reverend J. G. Wood, well-known Victorian naturalist and author of the exceedingly popular encyclopedic work *The Illustrated Natural History*, supplied additional notes for White's original text, correcting and enlarging on his observations. The effect is to increase the level of specificity even more. White says that he knows of only two species of British bats; Wood informs the reader that there are in fact twenty-three known species; the British Museum boasts specimens of fourteen. Lest that information be insufficient, Wood lists all fourteen by common name, Latin name, and locality.[38] Many of Wood's notes are quite lengthy, a mixture of fact, anecdote, and personal report, including such gruesome details as how he found that newts fail to die expeditiously when immersed in corrosive sublimate, but struggle and go blind (p. 74n). He justifies these additions in his Preface, assuring the reader that "naturalists . . . are fully aware of the value of any observations, whether additional or merely corroborative" (p. v). And, he says, "with a view to rendering the work more accurate, the scientific name of every natural object has been appended" (p. vi). Accuracy is paramount, and one can never have a surfeit of details. Except that—well, certain details might not be suitable for all readers, especially the young. The judicious Reverend Wood has felt compelled to do a bit of protective pruning of White's text. As he puts it, "many passages have been omitted, which, although useful to the scientific naturalist, might possibly have given offence to those whose studies in Natural History are not of a rigidly scientific character" (p. v). The Reverend thus demonstrates a Victorian anxiousness to render lubricious nature "more fit" for the home.

Wood also has felt it an improvement to illustrate White's book with numerous pictures by a Mr. Harvey. Harvey also did the engravings for Wood's encyclopedia, and with much the same effect—they make the work into something of a field guide, handy for identification of species. Illustrations are appropriate, for as Wood points out, "it is well known that the eye is affected sooner than the ear, and that a good figure of any object conveys the idea better to the mind than the best and most accurate description" (p. vi). Wood's assertion accords well with the visual and pictorial emphases of Victorian natural history and reflects the increasing role played in the nineteenth century by natural history art.

Indeed, the most charming feature of Wood's Victorian edition is its illustrated cover, printed in gold on red cloth. The spine sports an elaborate rustic design. Surrounded by a spider web, flowers, and a trellis of leafy stems, White's title is set in letters that look like rough-hewn logs. The front cover picture mingles eighteenth-century elements with Victorian design. It shows a naturalist's desk and bench, with quill pen and flowers in a vase, a cat on the desk and a dog beneath it. Draped over the bench is a cloak and a quaint three-cornered hat. Tendrils bearing leaves grow up and down from the floor, enclosing the desk within a decorative, improbable bower. Most interesting of all are the emblems of natural history that dot the design: a geologist's hammer, a mouse, two butterflies, a turtle (representing, no doubt, the tortoise that White described), and, at the apex, a bird in a cage.

These emblems ably represent White's legacy and the mingled reverential and pragmatic feelings with which many Victorians approached natural history. In Victorian Britain, natural history was more than popular; it was a craze. To call it a craze in no way denigrates it. Popular natural history had some of the earmarks of a fad—it was fashionable, spread to all sorts of people, expressed itself in newspaper columns and other popular forums, and became quite "the thing" to do—but it was much more enduring than that. Signs of the passion for natural history proliferate over a span of sixty years or more. It was a craze in the sense that its adherents went to incredible lengths to pursue it, and in the sense that the excitement over natural objects infected people in droves. But silly though its expressions might sometimes be—like proper ladies petticoat deep in tidepools, led by Mr. Gosse—the effects of the natural history craze were very serious indeed. Far beyond being merely quaint or eccentric, the Victorian study of nature changed the way people regarded objects and their own relationship to the natural world, expanding their vision. The positive force of natural history spawned a discourse rooted in particularity, in the glorious singularity of things. For a heady half-century, before its own power ironically plundered the riches it so admired, natural history extolled the inexhaustibility of nature's forms. One could look where one pleased; one never saw them end. And where the naturalist's rapt attention went, there language followed.

Notes

1. George Henry Lewes, *Studies in Animal Life* (London: Smith, Elder and Co., 1862), p. 1.

2. Norman Page, ed., *Tennyson: Interviews and Recollections* (Totowa, NJ: Barnes & Noble Books, 1983), p. 38.

3. W. H. Harvey, *The Sea-Side Book; Being an Introduction to the Natural History of the British Coasts* (London: John Van Voorst, 1849), p. 7.

4. The figures of 14,712 species, 8,000 of them new, are given by Robert L. Ulsinger in the Foreword to Henry Walter Bates, *The Naturalist on the River Amazons* (1864; Berkeley: Univ. of California Press, 1962), p. vii. These figures are frequently cited as examples of the industriousness of Victorian naturalists.

5. Harvey, p. 18.

6. Lewes, p. 8.

7. Carl Dawson, *Victorian Noon: English Literature in 1850* (Baltimore: The Johns Hopkins Univ. Press, 1979), p. 32.

8. Lynn Barber, *The Heyday of Natural History: 1820–1870* (Garden City, NY: Doubleday and Company, Inc., 1980), pp. 13–14.

9. *Inquire Within Upon Everything* (1856; rpt. New York: Farrar, Straus and Giroux, 1978), p. 203.

10. Christopher Marsden, *The English at the Seaside* (London: Collins, 1947), p. 27.

11. For a discussion of the railroads' influence on popular science and reading habits, see David Elliston Allen, *The Naturalist in Britain: A Social History* (London: Allen Lane, 1976), pp. 122–126, 138–140. Cheap railway editions as a spur to wider reading of both fiction and nonfiction are also mentioned in Raymond Chapman, *The Victorian Debate: English Literature and Society 1832–1901* (London: Weidenfeld and Nicolson, 1968), p. 60.

12. The figures for Wood's and Smiles' books are cited in Allen, *Naturalist*, p. 139. The same statistic for Wood's sales appears in Barber, p. 14. Both these authors point out that Wood's book has little intrinsic merit to account for its popularity, Barber calling it "quite undistinguished" and Allen, "indifferent." For a discussion of Samuel Smiles and the doctrine of self-help, see Asa Briggs, *Victorian People: A Reassessment of Persons and Themes 1851–1867* (Chicago: Univ. of Chicago Press, 1955), chapter 5. Briggs notes that *Self-Help* went on to sell 55,000 copies in five years, and 150,000 copies by 1889, still selling beyond 1900, so it had an enduring popularity that Woods could not match.

13. In *Signs of the Times*. For a discussion of the influence of Victorian technology, see Herbert L. Sussman, *Victorians and the Machine: The Literary Response to Technology* (Cambridge, MA: Harvard Univ. Press, 1968).

14. Quoted in Charles P. Curtis, Jr., and Ferris Greenslet, eds., *The Practical Cogitator: The Thinker's Anthology*, 3rd ed. (Boston: Houghton Mifflin Company, 1962), p. 226. I have been unable to track down Wheeler's original, which is identified as an address to the Boston Society of Natural History in April 1931.

15. Curtis and Greenslet, p. 227.

16. P. H. Gosse, *The Romance of Natural History* (New York: A. L. Burt Company, Publishers, 1902). Gosse's book was first published in 1860. My Chapter 8 is devoted to Gosse and *The Romance of Natural History* in particular.

17. Granville Penn, *Conversations on Geology: Comprising a Familiar Explanation of the Huttonian and Wernerian Systems* (London: J. W. Southgate and Son, 1840), p. 5.

18. Robert M. Young, *Darwin's Metaphor: Nature's Place in Victorian Culture* (Cambridge: Cambridge Univ. Press, 1985), p. 1.

19. *Science and Education: Essays* (New York: D. Appleton and Company, 1896), p. 268.

20. Richard D. Altick, *Victorian People and Ideas* (New York: W. W. Norton and Company, Inc., 1973), p. 260.

21. Keith Thomas, *Man and the Natural World: A History of the Modern Sensibility* (New York: Pantheon Books, 1983), p. 243.

22. Walter E. Houghton, *The Victorian Frame of Mind: 1830–1870* (New Haven: Yale Univ. Press, 1957), p. 79.

23. Houghton, p. 80.

24. Lyell's *Principles of Geology, Being an Inquiry on How Far the Former Changes of the Earth's Surface Are Referable to Causes Now in Operation* appeared between 1830 and 1833, consolidating and more powerfully expressing ideas gleaned from James Hutton's *The Theory of the Earth* (1785), John Playfair's *Illustrations of the Huttonian Theory of the Earth* (1802), and William Smith's *English Strata Identified by Organized Remains* (1814).

25. See Fiedler's essay, "Literature as an Institution: The View from 1980," in Leslie A. Fiedler and Houston A. Baker, Jr., eds., *English Literature: Opening Up the Canon*, Selected Papers from the English Institute, 1979, New Series, no. 4 (Baltimore: The Johns Hopkins Univ. Press, 1981), pp. 73–91. For a discussion of how judgments of "literature" and "not literature" are made, see Raymond Williams, *Marxism and Literature* (Oxford: Oxford Univ. Press, 1977), pp. 45–54, 145–150.

26. Lynn Barber's book, *The Heyday of Natural History*, mentions more of these books than any other single source I know of, although it does not contain a bibliography as such. Nicolette Scourse gives a Select Bibliography in *The Victorians and Their Flowers* (London: Croom Helm; Portland, OR: Timber Press, 1983).

27. The critical material extant on Darwin is voluminous, to say the least, and ever-growing. I make no attempt here to summarize it, because as a scientist Darwin is on the periphery of my study, not at the center. In Chaper 3 I deal briefly with Darwin as a naturalist—that is, as a stylist rather than an evolutionary theorist—and mention some studies taking that approach.

28. Julian M. Drachman, *Studies in the Literature of Natural Science* (New York: The Macmillan Company, 1930), p. 395.

29. Drachman, p. 396.

30. Edward Dowden, *Studies in Literature, 1789-1877* (London: Kegan Paul, Trench, Trübner and Co., Ltd., 1892), p. 103.

31. Tess Cosslett, *The "Scientific Movement" and Victorian Literature* (Sussex: The Harvester Press, 1982), chapter 1, "The Values of Science."

32. David J. DeLaura, "Nature Naturing: Literary Natural History," *Victorian Studies*, 22, No. 2 (1979), 194.

33. On differences between American and British views of nature and scenery, see Christopher Mulvey, *Anglo-American Landscapes: A Study of Nineteenth Century Anglo-American Travel Literature* (Cambridge: Cambridge Univ. Press, 1983).

34. James McIntosh, *Thoreau as Romantic Naturalist: His Shifting Stance toward Nature* (Ithaca, NY: Cornell Univ. Press, 1974).

35. A "nature essay," which is simply a musing exploration of any aspect of nature, may partake of natural history, or it may not. Sometimes nature essays are more akin to Wordsworthian poems than to natural history as I have defined it. The English counterpart to the American nature essay, as such, would probably be "rural" or "country" essays, such as those by William Cobbett, Richard Jefferies, Mary Webb, and Edward Thomas. See W. J. Keith, *The Rural Tradition: A Study of the Non-Fiction Prose Writers of the English Countryside* (Toronto: Univ. of Toronto Press, 1974).

36. Burroughs occupies a central position in the one study known to me that focuses on nature writing as a genre with discernible style, Philip Marshall Hicks's analysis of *The Development of the Natural History Essay in American Literature* (Diss. Univ. of Pennsylvania, 1924; privately published, Philadelphia, 1924.) See also, on the American nature essay genre, Robert Elman, *First in the Field: America's Pioneering Naturalists* (New York: Van Nostrand Reinhold Company, 1977), chapter 8, "John Burroughs and the Literary Publicists." The popularity in England of American nature writers, particularly Burroughs, is examined by Roger J. Harper in "The Literary Reputation of American Nature Writers in Nineteenth-Century British Periodicals (1865-1910)," (Diss. Green State Univ., 1976).

37. Scourse, p. 79.

38. Gilbert White, *The Natural History of Selborne*, ed. J. G. Wood (London: Routledge, Warne, and Routledge, 1864), p. 47n. Further citations to this edition are made within the text.

2

Cultural Manifestations

It now, therefore, remains for us to consider the impressions reflected by the external senses on the feelings, and on the poetic imagination of mankind. An inner world is here opened before us . . . the contemplation of natural objects as a means of exciting a pure love of nature. . . . The inducements which promote such contemplations of nature are, as I have already remarked, of three different kinds, namely, the aesthetic treatment of natural scenery by animated delineations of animal and vegetable forms, constituting a very recent branch of literature; landscape painting, especially where it has caught the characteristic features of the animal and vegetable world; and the more widely-diffused cultivation of tropical flora.[1]   ALEXANDER VON HUMBOLDT, *Cosmos*, 1863

When George Henry Lewes caught the fever of natural history, his symptoms could not have been more classic. Flushed with excitement, he began to see possibilities for wonder everywhere. Arming himself with an array of collecting tools, Lewes took long walks in search of natural curiosities. His attention concentrated, his vision quickened. He bought himself a microscope. More important, so great was his enjoyment that he could hardly wait to impart it to others: in breathless prose, he praised his new hobby, implored readers to walk with him, to join the ranks of natural history converts, almost as if it were a religion. Was the reader interested? Then "Where shall we begin? Anywhere will do." Natural history was everywhere, in the great and in the small. Setting out for a ramble across the heather of Wimbledon Common, Lewes thought it prudent to bring a net and wide-mouthed jar. The Common could only boast some humble ponds, but with the right equipment the naturalist could easily "ransack" them for "visible and invisible wonders."[2]

In his practice of natural history, Lewes exemplifies many of its most typical Victorian manifestations. He collects specimens, particularly at the beach or in freshwater. He makes use of such devices as the microscope, "a landing-net," "a wide-mouthed glass jar," "a quinine bottle," a "phial for worms and tiny animals," and a "pocket lens" (p. 48). No creature fails to interest him. A common frog? Fascinating—but better still, open it up to see the parasitic worms in its bladder: "Thus may our frog, besides its own marvels, afford us many 'authentic tidings of invisible things'" (p. 26). He becomes obsessed with objects, with identifying them, possessing them: "Make it a rule to pop every unknown object into your wide-mouthed phial" (p. 67). One must never squander a chance to acquire a novelty, which, although new, may yet be identified, classified, and minutely examined. Lewes lauds natural history as a hobby that anyone, anywhere, may enjoy. It is cheap, it is instructive, it is entertaining and pious; it offers healthful exercise while luring the naturalist on serendipitous rambles in search of surprises.

On the whole, Lewes was not really a naturalist at heart. His fondness for philosophical argument tended to pull him away from the concrete. And this very thing happens in *Studies in Animal Life*, which veers away from participatory natural history to become a hodge-podge of speculation, topical and philosophical. Its theme throughout is the broad abstract concept of "Life." That being the case, it is all the more remarkable that Lewes' book is positively riddled with the motifs and manifestations of the natural history craze.

Microscope and hand-lens, net and phial—these tools marked the activities of a naturalist, and they appear again and again in natural history texts. By endorsing them, Lewes revealed just how ingrained they had become. The urge to collect specimens with such devices dominated two of the most widespread manifestations of the natural history craze in Victorian Britain: botanizing and sea-side studies, which encompassed flower collecting, fern cultivation, gardening, beachcombing, and dredging. The features they had in common—collecting, particularity, exoticism—reveal many of the key tenets of Victorian natural history. But it had more subtle manifestations as well. Its mix of pleasure and didactic instruction meant that it harmonized with Victorian theories of education; consequently, natural history was prescribed by many writers as a suitably instructive activity for children. And if children could profit by it, so too could members of the working classes, who could learn directly from nature without benefit of schools.

Since Victorian Britain contained a large number of amateur naturalists, the tools for exploring the out-of-doors were familiar to a great many people. But even those members of Victorian society who never engaged in natural history themselves had not far to look to find its influence. The social and cultural manifestations of natural history were ubiquitous and enduring. For one thing, natural history gave a whole new impetus to the genteel avocation of gardening, which in turn supported the widespread taste for floral designs and patterns. Indeed, the interior of a Victorian middle-class home owed many of its design elements to natural history, from the objects it contained to the patterns on its walls. Flowers decorated book covers, cards, wallpaper, and fabrics; they were arranged in nosegays, assigned various moral qualities, and even served as signifiers in an elaborate romantic code: the Language of Flowers.[3] The love of flowers expressed itself in the form of botanizing— wherein collectors, often women, sallied forth in search of rare specimens for the purpose of collecting them, pressing them in pleasing arrangements, cultivating them in gardens, and identifying them with the help of the Linnaean system. In addition to bouquets and floral prints, other bits of nature were enshrined indoors and displayed as part of the bric-a-brac of cluttered Victorian homes. The more "knick-knacks" a room contained, the better. Along with china, paperweights, and wax fruit, "stuffed birds, reptiles, small animals, . . . flowers under glass domes" were very much in vogue in home decor.[4]

The English predilection for gardening had long been formidable; as P. H. Gosse declared, the "love of flowers, and the desire to have them about us, is preeminently English."[5] During the nineteenth century, gardening tastes turned away from the formal, closely groomed fashions of the eighteenth century toward more irregular, wilder, "romantic" ideals.[6] No longer was the face of nature most appealing when trimmed, regimented, and subdued to an Enlightenment ideal of harmony, balance, and proportion. The classicist's symmetrical garden now seemed too tame. At the same time, natural history was busily engaged in botanical exploration. In concert with the stylistic shift in garden tastes, overseas collecting of live plants introduced non-native, exotic species, such as orchids. Between 1750 and 1850, "an enormous upsurge of interest in the scientific and aesthetic value of plants" was responsible for the introduction of approximately five thousand foreign species into England.[7] The influx of foreign plants supported the growth of botanical showplaces such as Kew Gardens and Joseph Paxton's Great Conservatory (under construction from 1839 to 1841), which housed not only plants but also minerals, ores, tropical birds, and fish in heated pools.[8] The glass-house, or conservatory, achieved on a large scale what a terrarium did on a small scale; each gave year-round shelter to a dazzling bit of tropicana, obliterating England's dreary winter in the green fronds of an eternal summer.

Along with conservatories, moneyed Victorians constructed moss gardens and "rock-works," and the ambitious might attempt a saltwater seaweed garden.[9] Urbanization may have cut people off from the countryside, but the taste for nature, particularly objects from nature, never waned. Urged on by writers such as Shirley Hibberd, fashionable Victorians surrounded themselves with "rustic adornments." Hibberd recommended such earthy items as thatched beehives for the garden, promoting them along with touches of reeds, moss, and heather as suitable *Rustic Adornments for Homes of Taste, and Recreations for Town Folk in the Study and Imitation of Nature.*[10] The yearning for rustic cottages and simple nature, which enticed even Ruskin, meshed with a naturalist's interest in exotic curiosities. Traditional flowers and plants of the English countryside now competed for attention with introduced exotics.

One particularly interesting example of the popularity of exotic plants demonstrates how taste, botany, and art could intersect. The giant water lily, *Victoria amazonica* (originally named *Victoria regia*), was the object of intense fascination near mid-century. Discovered in British Guiana in 1837 and named in honor of the newly crowned queen, the lily was eventually grown from seed at Kew Gardens.[11] Philip Henry Gosse recounted the story of the plant's discovery in his book *The Romance of Natural History* as an instance of "The Memorable" in nature: upon rowing over to the unusual plant, its dazzled discoverer, Robert Schomburgk, exclaimed, "lo! a vegetable wonder!"[12]

This particular vegetable wonder had enormous floating leaves four feet wide, strong enough to support the weight of small children, who were frequently enticed into perching on them. Besides being gigantic, it was marvelously redolent of faraway jungles and exotic climes. In 1849, when the home-grown lily bloomed, *The Illustrated London News* trumpeted its success, and the "flowering caused the greatest excitement" among the public.[13] Fantastically strange and lovely, the flowers opened to a foot or more in diameter, while the strong ribbed undersides of the huge leaf-pads possessed more pragmatic beauty. Joseph Paxton, the gardener who succeeded in getting *Victoria* to bloom, noticed the efficient shape of the floating supports. Impressed, he shrewdly incorporated their ribbed design into his most famous creation, the curving, iron-ribbed Crystal Palace. Thus *Victoria amazonica* was both a naturalist's delight and an artist's inspiration, and even produced a vogue for lily designs in glassware.[14]

In addition to craving new discoveries in remote, exotic realms like the deep sea or the tropics, Britons combed their homeland looking for nature's novelties. As crowds of amateur naturalists swarmed over the countryside and succeeded in naming obvious forms, attention was increasingly focused on the obscure organisms, ones difficult to identify casually. As hand-lenses became easily available, cheap, and popular, whole classes of organisms, hitherto ignored, gained new importance. Their tiny features signaled a shift in natural history's scale—toward the microscopic. In the realm of botany and gardening, the plants most susceptible to minute scrutiny were ferns. Growing wild in out-of-the-way crannies, ferns represented romantic nature: fragile, lovely, and rare. But in addition, although not showy like flowers, ferns could boast some intricate features.

Ferns are perhaps the best example of how the microscope could elevate seemingly dull organisms to the pinnacle of beauty and interest. As David Elliston Allen has amply documented in his fascinating little study, *The Victorian Fern Craze*, throughout much of the nineteenth century ferns were the object of "widespread fascination."[15] They owed their popularity to two inventions. One was the inexpensive microscope, which first became available in the 1830s. Cheap, portable, and easy-to-use microscopes had, in fact, a great deal of influence on Victorian natural history as a whole (see Chapter 5), and such instruments opened up certain kinds of plants to intense visual curiosity. Microscopes divulged complex structures, previously invisible, found on ferns as well as on Cryptogams, such as mosses, lichens, algae, and fungi. Cryptogams, technically those plants that reproduce without flowers or seeds but rather with spores, frequently adorn Victorian natural history accounts (as do the Infusoria, or protozoans, also revealed by the new microscopes).

The second invention that promoted ferns specifically was the Wardian Case, a sealed glass case or bottle in which plants could grow. Ward was not the sole inventor of this early terrarium, but it was his personal cases that were seen in 1834 by J. C. Loudon, publisher of *Gardener's Magazine* and *Loudon's Magazine of Natural History*, and then enthusiastically promoted in these highly influential journals.[16] The British Association for the Advancement of Science subsequently studied the innovation, and Ward went on to describe it thoroughly in his *On the Growth of Plants in Closely Glazed Cases* (1842).[17] By then the Fern Craze was already a frenzy, and the search for the tiny individual structures of fern spores was on. As Allen points out, the Fern Craze is a most interesting offshoot of Victorian natural history because its rationale was more aesthetic than scientific,[18] although almost as a side effect it did advance the scientific understanding of ferns. To the average person, ferns were complex but classifiable, jigsaw-puzzle pieces that fit into a taxonomic scheme which already existed (thoroughly outlined by Edward Newman in his *A History of British Ferns*, published in 1839). But most of all, they were beautiful. The drawing-room collector sought them not for edification, but for display. And like so much of popular natural history, the Fern Craze, according to Allen, has been little studied because it falls between "the history of science" and "the history of taste."[19] Precisely. The Fern Craze, as an expression of natural history, merges science with appreciation; putting it into a realm I call aesthetic science.

Charles Kingsley, in his 1855 natural history book, *Glaucus; or, the Wonders of the Shore*, gives a nod to the ubiquity of fern collecting, especially among young ladies. He speaks to a reader who contemplates taking up the study of natural history:

> Your daughters, perhaps, have been seized with the prevailing "Pteridoma-nia," and are collecting and buying ferns, with Ward's cases wherein to keep them (for which you have to pay), and wrangling over unpronounce-able names of species (which seem to be different in each new Fern-book that they buy), till the Pteridomania seems to you somewhat of a bore: and yet you cannot deny that they find an enjoyment in it, and are more active, more cheerful, more self-forgetful over it, than they would have been over novels and gossip, crochet and Berlin-wool.[20]

Kingsley goes on to add, sardonically, that at the very least the "Venus's hair" and "Lady-ferns" ensconced in the drawing-room cases are more attractive than the inept knitting—"ghastly woolen caricatures"—pre-viously produced by the idle young ladies. Best of all, in true Victorian fashion, fern collecting keeps its practitioners usefully (educationally) employed and dutifully "self-forgetful." The Fern Craze, as an example of the many and various fads for collecting natural objects during the nineteenth century, highlights the centrality of acquisition to natural history.

Along with the Fern Craze, another manifestation of the popularity of natural history hit close to home. In 1853, Philip Henry Gosse published *A Naturalist's Rambles on the Devonshire Coast*, a description and study of shoreline animals and plants; it was "almost the first of such books."[21] The "most frequently reviewed of all" Gosse's many books, "praised without dissent," this volume had a remarkable effect on the public. Working in humble Devonshire, Gosse uncovered amazing life forms whose existence had previously been unnoticed. In effect, what Gosse's book did was make an Amazon basin of England's shores. Along with his companion volume, *The Aquarium*, published in 1854, it galvanized amateur naturalists into action and was largely responsible for a surge of interest in zoological beachcombing. One of Gosse's clearest messages was that the wonders he found seemed infinite. Eager to share in them, a wave of well-armed collectors attacked England's beaches. So prevalent did they become by 1857 that John Leech lampooned them in a cartoon in *Punch*, "Common Objects at the Seaside." In Leech's depiction, the beach is strewn with curious large limpet-shaped cones. On closer inspection these turn out to be ladies' skirts and petticoats, viewed from behind, with little legs sticking out. No heads or torsos are visible, because the ladies are bent clear over to the ground, picking at specimens.[22]

Edmund Gosse, son and biographer of Philip Henry, refers to this cartoon when he describes collecting groups he and his father encountered on the beach. In one of his descriptions, Philip himself leads a class in the "very novel and agreeable . . . amusement" of "shore-collecting":

> I recall a long desultory line of persons on a beach of shells—doubtless at Barricane. At the head of the procession, like Apollo conducting the Muses, my father strides ahead in an immense wide-awake, loose black coat and trousers, and fishermen's boots, with a collecting-basket in one hand, a staff or prod in the other. Then follow gentlemen of every age . . . and many ladies in the balloon costume of 1855, with shawls falling to a point from between their shoulders to the edge of their flounced petticoats, each wearing a mushroom hat with streamers.[23]

Ladies in similar balloon costumes were depicted by the painter William Dyce in his "Pegwell Bay, Kent—a Recollection of October 5th 1858." The painting shows a stretch of rocky beach beneath white chalk cliffs, where the low tide has exposed seaweed-covered hummocks. In the foreground, looking rather incongruous, three elaborately costumed women amble on the beach, swathed in voluminous skirts and shawls such as Edmund Gosse described. Each has a collecting basket, one of which can be seen to be full of seashells, which the women are stooping to gather. Dyce's painting is wonderfully detailed. He accurately represents natural features, such as the characteristic flint concretions on the beach, along with the colorful shells. Dyce even includes a carefully outlined mermaid's purse, which is the leathery egg-case of the sea skate. In his *Sea-Side Book* of 1849, W. H. Harvey described these purses as objects which "frequently attract us on the sands, as they are wafted to our feet by the wave, or left high and dry on shore from a previous tide."[24] They were, in other words, typical curiosities that mid-century collectors might find on the shore.

Drawn by shore-collecting classes and by Gosse's books, amateur naturalists in cumbrous costumes soon became difficult to avoid. Confident that nature's bounty was never ending (this was, after all, one of the

Victorian naturalist's most glowing promises), they grabbed whatever they found, with egregious abandon. To Philip Gosse's deep dismay, his acolytes in short order decimated tidepool populations of animals. Edmund and his father had to range farther and farther afield to locate unspoiled habitats:

> Our excursions were usually made to points a little beyond the reach of the amateur, but sometimes we crossed parties of collectors, in dainty costumes, such as Leech depicted, with pails or baskets, and we would smile and nudge each other on the reflection that they little suspected that the author of *The Aquarium* was so near them.[25]

If more adventurous, marine collectors could forsake the beach for deeper waters and try their hand at dredging. The dredge, or its freshwater analogue the dip-net, was a familiar motif. Gosse recommended it, as had W. H. Harvey in 1849, who said: "Among the amusements of the sea-shore there is, perhaps, none so capable of yielding a varied pleasure to a person whose taste for Natural History is awakened, as dredging."[26] Like the microscope, the dredge gave one the sense of entry into a hitherto hidden world. Harvey advised his readers to acquire a special "Naturalist's Dredge," made to order by a blacksmith, and gave detailed instructions on how to use it. He also provided a bucolic picture of the happy dredger at work:

> We will suppose the dredger afloat, on a fine day and in a favorable locality, furnished with his dredge, and with some collecting boxes and bottles, and a sieve to sort the smaller animals from the mud and silt. When the water is clear and not very deep, the aspect of the bottom, as the boat glides over it, often affords a charming submarine picture, as well as reveals the places where the dredge may most profitably be thrown down. The larger sea-weeds, [seem] like a forest waving in the clear water below you.[27]

In this scene, the well-equipped collector can gaze directly into the mysterious world beneath the surface. But even in deep water, where the bottom is not visible, the dredge, by scooping up samples of unseen inhabitants, permits the bottom to be revealed.

Dredging in very deep water, although technically beyond the means of most amateur naturalists, was nonetheless a source of fascination. During the latter half of the nineteenth century, Britain mounted several dredging expeditions, the most famous being the voyages of H.M.S. *Challenger* in 1873 and 1876. The surprises pulled up from the ocean depths appealed to the imagination of many amateurs, as they did to Charles Kingsley (see Chapter 9). One scientist, Edward Forbes, was even moved to celebrate the joys of dredging in a humorous poem entitled "The Song of the Dredge," of which this is a sample:

> Down in the deep, where the mermen sleep
> Our gallant dredge is sinking;
> Each finny shape in a precious scrape
> Will find itself in a twinkling!
> They may twirl and twist and writhe as they wist,
> And break themselves into sections,
> But up they all, at the dredges' call
> Must come to fill collections.[28]

In Forbes' estimation, the serious scientific dredger had the same essential motivation as did the casual dabbler in the art: collecting.

At one point in his zoological labors, P. H. Gosse enlisted the help of amateur naturalists in Britain. Needing a comprehensive collection of sea anemones and corals for his study *Actinologia Britannica*, Gosse advertised for specimens from the public. The response was tremendous, with the result that "the morning post commonly laid upon the breakfast-table at Sandhurst one, if not more, little box of a salt and oozy character, containing living anemones or corals carefully wrapped up in wet seaweed."[29] In the late 1850s, so many avid amateurs traded specimens with one another that one can imagine scores of these oozy little packages crisscrossing all England through the mails.

Collectors at this time acquired, displayed, and traded all kinds of specimens—be they corals, insects, shells, ferns, or flowers. How the objects were acquired had much to do with their charm. Healthful outdoor exercise with a definite object beckoned to amateur naturalists at a time when muscular exertion was just becoming fashionable. The pace of exercise for the naturalist, however, was leisurely. A walk along the downs or beach or through the glens might cover miles, but at a rambling pace. With eyes casting about for a glimpse of a rare fern or half-buried shell, it could hardly have been otherwise. In fact, it pleased naturalists to characterize themselves as "ramblers": meditatively meandering through nature, open to whatever sights might come their way, even across the most improbable terrain, such as water. One Cuthbert Collingwood thought of himself as rambling while sailing across the ocean, as evidenced by his title: *Rambles of a Naturalist on the Shores and Waters of the China Sea: Being Observations in Natural History During a Voyage to China, Formosa, Borneo, Singapore, Etc.*[30]

One reason the field of natural history teemed with amateurs had to do with England's educational system. Unlike subjects such as mathematics, natural history was not sanctioned as a formal university course of study, nor did it receive attention in public schools. As a result, there was really no such thing as a professional naturalist—no exams to take, no license to acquire, little money to be made. "Anyone could become a naturalist at any time, whatever his age or educational background," as Barber notes, and "the naturalist might be anyone from Darwin down to the lowliest Sunday bug-hunter."[31] Fortunately, for aspiring naturalists, the subject yielded itself to patient scrutiny and self-instruction. And while not a subject of formal schooling, the natural history method itself buttressed Victorian ideals of education. So natural history was frequently recommended as a means of improving one's mind, especially useful for children and the uneducated working class. The naturalist Frank Buckland catalogued the educational benefits of natural history in this way:

> I feel assured that the education of children, both in town and country, might be greatly forwarded if they were taught in the schools what and how to observe. Especially in the country should they be encouraged to make collections of common objects, animal, vegetable, and mineral. They should also be taught to recognize indigenous British birds and beasts, and to send in notes as to what they have observed of their habits. Such studies tend to sharpen the natural faculties, while they humanize the intellect.[32]

Dogged observation, collecting of specimens, and classification of animals according to their distinctions, all these activities hone the intellect and "humanize" it too, presumably because of the empathy with nature thereby developed.

Another advocate of natural history, Herbert Spencer, asserted in an 1861 essay on education that science is itself poetic. By this he meant, in part, that scientific understanding—such as a physicist has of the forces acting within a drop of water—increases one's awe of nature. But he also neatly summarized natural history activity of his own time while lauding its poetical—and tactile—benefits. These are Spencer's recommendations to all who would improve their minds:

> Think you that the rounded rock marked with parallel scratches, calls up as much poetry in an ignorant mind as in the mind of a geologist, who knows that over this rock a glacier slid a million years ago? The truth is, that those who have never entered upon scientific pursuits know not a tithe of the poetry by which they are surrounded. Whoever has not in youth collected plants and insects, knows not half the halo of interest which lanes and hedge-rows can assume. Whoever has not sought for fossils, has little idea of the poetical associations that surround the places where imbedded

treasures were found. Whoever at the sea-side has not had a microscope and aquarium, has yet to learn what the highest pleasures of the sea-side are.[33]

The hierarchical diction here says that some pleasures are "higher" than others, implying that some pleasures are "low" and thus base. Serious-minded Victorians, of course, aspired to the higher ideals, and natural history nicely dignified sensuous and tactile pleasures by giving them an intellectual and poetical component.

The opportunity for building up a store of useful facts while having fun made natural history a logical choice for children. Or rather, a logical choice for those who felt compelled to guide children, to instruct them in proper habits of mind. If natural history was important to the Victorians, one would expect to find it well represented in their children's books. And so it is. By its very nature, natural history as a topic lent itself especially well to tales for young people. It is visual, concrete, deals with things on a small scale, and enters other worlds—all attractive to children. In addition, a natural history book often features animals readily anthropomorphized or otherwise adaptable as characters. More important to its adult authors, natural history offers ample chances to teach lessons of piety, duty, and hard work.

Children's books can reveal much about their times. In them, because they are brief, simplified, and directive, even a culture's most problematic ethical precepts stand uncluttered and revealed. Overtly or not, children's books encapsulate the values that a society holds, the maxims it most wishes to bestow. And in Victorian times, when moralizing in literature was honorable, even indispensable, the lessons in children's stories were especially blunt and undisguised, often draped in the barest modicum of childish enchantment. But books for children, especially nineteenth-century ones, do more than preach; they mirror. Like a naturalist dredging the bottom of a bay, they are a drag-net pulled through cultural waters, capturing strange creatures unawares, culling representative samples among apparent debris.

Arabella Buckley (Sir Charles Lyell's secretary), Charlotte Yonge, Charles Kingsley, and Margaret Gatty are among those who tailored natural history to young readers. One story in Gatty's *Parables from Nature* (a series published between 1855 and 1871) illustrates how natural history could be used. The title of her book signals Gatty's intent to make natural incidents into occasions of virtue. Heavily laced with religious lessons, *Parables* prods children toward proper conduct. In "Knowledge Not the Limit of Belief," for instance, Gatty's message is clear: one must have faith in more than just material things. (This, by the way, is very similar to Kingsley's refrain in *The Water-Babies*; see Chapter 9.) But Gatty chooses a curious vehicle for this lesson. She imagines a dialogue between two naturalist's specimens:

> It was but the banging of the door, blown to by a current of wind from the open window, that made that great noise, and shook the room so much!
>
> The room was a Naturalist's library, and it was a pity that some folio books of specimens had been left so near the edge of the great table, for, when the door clapt to, they fell down; and a great many plants, seaweeds, etc., were scattered on the floor.
>
> And, "Do we meet again?" said a Zoophyte to a Seaweed (a Coralline) in whose company he had been thrown ashore—"Do we meet again? This is a real pleasure. What strange adventures we have gone through since the waves flung us on the sands together."[34]

Noteworthy first of all is the story's setting: a naturalist's library. Then, of course, there is the remarkable specificity of the two creatures who converse: a Zoophyte (a plant-like animal) and a Coralline Seaweed. Gatty clearly felt that these seemingly arcane classifications would be commonplace enough for children to recognize. The Zoophyte, the Seaweed, and a third character, a bookworm, discuss the naturalist, who to them represents a higher power. They cannot fully understand him but must believe in him anyway. The Seaweed, who has no eyes and thus cannot see, must learn to have faith in the naturalist's power of sight.

Yet while making her patently religious points, Gatty does give a very good description of what a Victorian naturalist does. The results of the naturalist's "seeing," the Bookworm says, are

> that he gets to know everything about you, and all the creatures, and plants, and stones he looks at; so that he knows your shape, and growth, and colour, and all about the cells of the little creatures that live in you— how many feelers these have, what they live upon, how they catch their food, how the eggs come out of the egg-cells, where you live, where you are to be found, what other Zoophytes are related to you, i.e., which are most like you—in short, the most minute particulars;—so that he puts you into his collections, not among strange creatures, but near to those you are most nearly connected with; and he describes you, and makes pictures of you, and gives you a name so that you are known for the same creature, wherever you are found, all over the world. And now, I'm quite out of breath with telling you all these wonderful results of seeing.[35]

What does the naturalist do? He looks closely, quantifies, classifies, collects, describes. He makes pictures, visual representations, and attaches individual names to them. He sees the world in terms of "minute particulars." The naturalist Gatty describes could hardly be more representative. Nor could any child fail to grasp the essence of natural history as Gatty presents it. The good naturalist must excel at observation, which is an important source of information. As the Zoophyte and Seaweed find out, however, there is another source: revelation. In Gatty's words, "Observation and Revelation are the sole means of acquiring knowledge." Many devout Victorians would have agreed; revelation, or revealed truth, constituted one channel through which God apportioned understanding. Reminiscent of the biblical book by that name, "Revelation" was a highly charged term. That being the case, it is interesting just how frequently it appears in natural history prose. In it, observation frequently *becomes* revelation ("revelations" of the microscope, for example), sight exalted to such a plane that what is seen becomes transcendent.

Obviously, Gatty trusted that children would be familiar with the naturalist as a type. In *The Water-Babies*, Kingsley also took this to be a safe assumption. And in fact much evidence exists that Victorian children often not only knew about natural history, but were enthusiastic participants—just as Buckland and Spencer had hoped. For example, Mary Ward (1827–1869), an amateur naturalist who wrote some very popular books on the microscope and telescope, learned natural history as a child. She and her two sisters collected specimens and kept them in cabinets; in their rooms, the walls "were covered with cases of insects, feathers, shells, rocks, and other natural objects."[36] Artistically inclined, Mary and her sisters also made careful sketches of their treasures, an approved method for learning to observe nature better.

Because natural history revolved around the idea of being taught to see, it offered great didactic possibilities for the ignorant members of the working class. At least, that was the model often tendered by better educated writers. Natural history was constructive and thoughtful, and drew one admirably toward higher pleasures. Workers had little of the leisure time allotted even to the middle class, yet many of them pursued nature studies with amazing assiduity. One of them, Hugh Miller, took up geology while he labored for long hours in a stone quarry, and later wrote a best-seller based on the experience, *The Old Red Sandstone* (see Chapter 10). Part of the working-class enthusiasm for natural history was achieved through middle-class propaganda; it was a pastime considered harmless or even healthy, and as such far better than "sinful" activities like drinking or gambling.[37]

For the Victorians, natural history was a pleasure that had all the virtues of work, since it required long hours, often physical discomfort, and precluded idleness. Given the serious Victorian temperament, such qualities were almost prerequisites to popularity. Naturalist writers themselves frequently harped on the moral, uplifting quality of their studies, and, indeed, in the first half of the nineteenth century, natural history was not only moral but also overtly religious. This religious substratum owed much to William Paley. In his influential book *Natural Theology* (1802), Paley crystallized an idea that had gained currency during the eighteenth century. Using the image of the watch that indubitably had a maker, Paley deepened the old argument from design: nature is so intricate that it, too, must have had a Maker. As one critic defines it, natural theology takes "the evidence of nature to prove God's existence and His goodness."[38]

Natural theology declared every object in nature to be the direct work of a benign God, assuming the world to be a static, single act of creation. Accordingly, the study of natural objects was tantamount to His contemplation. Deeply religious naturalists like P. H. Gosse joyously embraced this approach, as seen in this reaction to a dense flock of butterflies:

> To look then on the multitudes of beings assembled in so circumscribed a spot, all pursuing pleasure, and all doubtless attaining their end, each one with an individual perception and consciousness of enjoyment,—what a grand idea does it give of the tender mercy of God, as a God of Providence![39]

Natural theology provided a suitable moral skeleton for the vast body of natural history. In the footsteps of Paley, naturalists like Gosse found that "natural theology made the study of natural history not only respectable, but almost a pious duty," and as Barber points out, "there was nothing the Victorians liked so much as a duty."[40] Furthermore, as another critic makes clear, "it was the English who went furthest towards what has been called 'the divinisation of nature,'"[41] whereby a walk in the woods or a climb up a mountainside became a pilgrimage (which partly accounts for the British promotion of Alpine mountaineering).

By the turn of the nineteenth century, attitudes had shifted so that nature was widely felt to be not only aesthetically pleasing but also "morally healing" (as opposed to earlier attitudes that had viewed nature as hostile or ugly).[42] Nature could then be approached with an almost religious zeal and, in fact, natural history became a highly suitable avocation for clergymen. As J. C. Loudon noted in the *Magazine of Natural History*, in Victorian times, "compared even with a taste for classical studies, for drawing, for painting, or any other branch of the Fine Arts; or for amateur turning [lathe-work], or any other kind of mechanical employment; a taste for Natural History in a clergyman has great advantages." For in contrast to indoor hobbies, nature study finds the "naturalist abroad in the fields, investigating the habits and searching out the habitats of birds, insects, or plants, not only invigorating his health, but affording ample opportunity for frequent intercourse with his parishioners."[43] Gilbert White, whose *Natural History of Selborne* had such far-reaching influence, represents perhaps the quintessential clergy-man-naturalist, being both meticulous and pious. But devout naturalists like White proliferated in abundance, in reality and in literature, until Darwin's bombshell in 1859. After that, the relationship of natural history to religion became problematic, if not adversarial. At any rate, once the argument from design faltered, the attraction of nature studies for the clergy, as well as for pious laypersons, faded.

Until that occurred, natural history wooed the working class, with its promises of reverential and useful learning. G. H. Lewes described how it had won over one skeptical laborer. One day, while trying to capture sticklebacks, a fish remarkable for its habits but not for its flavor, Lewes was accosted by an "Irish labourer," who assumed he was fishing for salmon. After all, for what else did one fish? Lewes, of course, intended only to study his quarry. Knowing that the untutored man would find his true purpose ludicrous, Lewes feigned interest in salmon, all the while scooping up "invisible" things from the water. His onlooker was greatly puzzled at first. But gradually, "seeing at the same time how alive the water was with tiny animals," he "became curious, and asked many questions." Already a new world had opened for him. Lewes continued:

> I went on with my work; his interest and curiosity increased; his questions multiplied; he volunteered assistance; and remained beside me till I pre-pared to go away, when he said seriously: "Och! then, and it's a fine thing to be able to name all God's creatures." Contempt had given way to reverence; and so it would be with others, could they check the first rising of scorn at what they do not understand, and patiently learn what even a roadside pond has of Nature's wonders.[44]

In one pointed lesson, the lucky laborer realized how natural facts increase reverence for God. Lewes, meanwhile, felt all the smug satisfac-tion of an Evangelist who has just won a new convert. That tone was not at all unusual among natural history writers who proselytized in the name of their hobby. Its virtues were so obvious, they felt, that anyone would adopt them once the scales fell from their eyes.

Laborers and less privileged Victorians of all kinds did respond with surprising alacrity to the opportunity of doing yet more work in the service of natural history. In Victorian England's stratified class system, what appealed to one class might not necessarily attract another. But naturalists came from all stations, high and low. Indeed, one of the best gauges for measuring the pervasiveness of natural history is the degree of its influence on the unleisured "lower orders." While cultured aristocratic ladies had dabbled in natural history as early as the eighteenth century, in Victorian England the new middle classes and even ordinary and extremely overtaxed workers became caught up in the craze. Mrs. Gaskell includes in her "condition of England" novel of 1848, *Mary Barton*, the following description of natural history's popularity:

> In the neighborhood of Oldham there are weavers, common handloom weavers, who throw the shuttle with unceasing sound, though Newton's "Principia" lies open on the loom, to be snatched at in work hours, but revelled over in meal times, or at night. . . . It is perhaps less astonishing that the more popularly interesting branches of natural history have their warm and devoted followers among this class. There are botanists among them, equally familiar with either the Linnaean or the Natural system, who know the name and habitat of every plant within a day's walk from their dwellings; who steal the holiday of a day or two when any particular plant should be in flower, and tying up their simple food in their pocket handkerchiefs, set off with single purpose to fetch home the humble-looking weed. There are entomologists, who may be seen with a rude-looking net, ready to catch any winged insect, or a kind of dredge, with which they rake the green and slimy pools; practical, shrewd, hard-working men who pore over every new specimen with real scientific delight. (chapter V)

If Mrs. Gaskell's description seems to belong purely to the province of fiction, the life story of one working-class naturalist bears it out. Samuel Smiles, the apostle of Self-Help, wrote the biography of a totally self-made naturalist, the Scotsman Thomas Edward. Edward had such a passion for nature that by the age of six he had been expelled from three schools because of the snakes and other animals he kept smuggling into class. His education thus truncated, Edward never learned to read. This proved no hindrance to his becoming a naturalist; indeed, Smiles says, "his very absence of knowledge proved a source of inexhaustible pleasure to him. All that he learned of the form, habits, and characteristics of birds and animals had been obtained by his own personal observation."[45] Valuing direct, personal observation was one of the tenets of natural history, and Edward learned this lesson well. Of necessity, he also learned the shoemaking trade. He loathed this job, but stuck to it diligently to support himself and a family of eight, ultimately excelling from a sense of duty and pride. Since his trade occupied his days, Edward, incredibly, pursued his nature studies by night. Mrs. Edward must have possessed great forbearance, for her eccentric husband seldom spent the night at home. (Indeed, from Smiles' descriptions, it is difficult to imagine how Thomas Edward ever had the time or opportunity to produce his children.) Directly after work, he would set out on a ramble in search of specimens, staying out all night and snatching a bit of sleep in the wet fields.

Edward collected specimens in his pockets, in bottles and boxes, and in a special compartment built into his hat. He shot birds; he etherized insects; he climbed trees for birds' nests. In the dark, he learned to recognize animals by sound alone. With "unexampled assiduity and unwearied perseverance," he amassed a collection of two thousand specimens, which he housed in glazed cases he built himself. Unable to afford ready-made numbered labels, Edward toiled for hours cutting old almanacs apart to make his own. The long-suffering Mrs. Edward had to raise the family in a house "now filled with stuffed birds, quadrupeds, and such-like objects. Every room was packed with cases containing them" (p. 145). Of course, for Samuel Smiles the saga of the nocturnal naturalist served to illustrate the virtue of persistence in the face of "discouraging circumstances." In Smiles' version of events, Edward always showed saintly equanimity. Once he lost four years' work when 916 of his insect specimens were eaten right off their pins by mice. But Edward merely said, "Weal, it's an awful disappointment, but I think the best thing will be to set to work and fill them up again" (p. 143).

Even if the tenor of Smiles' biography is somewhat suspect, its basic facts are true: Thomas Edward toiled at a grinding trade but nonetheless made time for natural history. Like the weavers of Oldham, the Scotch naturalist found the rewards compelling. Chief among them were aesthetic pleasure, endless novelty, and a delight at delving facts directly from nature. Without much money, one could still own some facts, a little domain carved out from a familiar landscape by stubborn empiricism and sheer perseverance. Possession of something, even just of natural facts or a few grubby specimens, was no small reward for working people endowed with little to call their own. One could own specimens, in lieu of more traditional and costly material goods. In fact, judging by the regularity with which the word appears in their accounts, the urge to *possess* motivated naturalists on all social rungs.

Working-class naturalists were common enough that Smiles had little difficulty in finding a second subject who shared these traits. Like Thomas Edward, Robert Dick was Scottish, a self-taught naturalist, and a working man. Dick was fortunate in that, as a baker, he could work very early in the day and botanize and geologize when it was still light out. Dick also had the advantage of book-learning and even corresponded with some well-known naturalists (such as Hugh Miller, who had been a laborer also; see Chapter 10). But like Edward, Robert Dick worked hard at his hobby while working hard at a trade. The people of Dick's village

> did not quite understand the proceedings of their young baker. He made good bread, and his biscuits were the best in town. But he was sometimes seen coming back from the country bespattered with mud,—perhaps after a forty or fifty miles' journey on the moors in search of specimens.[46]

Smiles again lauds the good Victorian working man, who takes pride in his labors, arduous though they be. But if Dick seems a bit too perfect, still his pleasure in hands-on natural history is believable. Driven to possess nature for himself, Dick "was not satisfied with the observations of others. He must get at the actual facts. He must himself verify everything."

To Mrs. Gaskell's and Smiles' portraits of working-class naturalists can be added a splendid description by Philip Gosse of a Weymouth fisherman named Jonas. Gosse, who at the time was busily engaged in procuring specimens for the popular marine vivarium at the Zoological Gardens in Regent's Park, needed a boat for his dredging expeditions. Jonas quite happily hired his boat out to the naturalist and volunteered his hearty enthusiasm as well. Gosse found the incongruity of Jonas' language greatly amusing:

> He follows dredging with all the zest of a *savant*; and it really does one's heart good to hear how he pours you out the crack-jaw, the sesquipedalian nomenclature. "Now, sir, if you do want a *gastrochoena*, I can just put down your dredge upon a lot o' 'em; we'll bring up three or four on a 'stone.' I'm in hopes we shall have a good *cribella* or two off this bank, if we don't get choked up with them 'ere ophiocomas." He tells me in confidence that he has been sore puzzled to find a name for his boat, but he has at length determined to appellate her "*The Turritella*,"—"just to astonish the fishermen, you know, sir,"—with an accompanying wink and chuckle, and a patronizing nudge in my ribs.[47]

This is a telling, nearly Dickensian, portrait of a working-class naturalist whose diction swells all out of proportion to his accent.

However, Jonas' facility with Latin is by no means unusual. Pleasure in enunciating Latinate species names saturates Victorian natural history books. Jawbreaking nomenclature pleased because it gave the impression of precision, of particularity. After all, by saying the species' name one made a fine distinction between one specimen's tiny features and another's (for more about species identification, see Chapter 4). Tied to the latest classification schemes, Latin names seemed incontrovertibly scientific. Then, too, for a fisherman like Jonas, the Latin carried a fancy cachet. Latin species names were somehow "official," as opposed to "vulgar," a distinction that Philip Gosse makes in *Tenby* when he says that one "creature is called by the vulgar the Sea-Hare (by naturalists, *Aplysia punctata*)."[48] Soon so many people opted to eschew vulgar names that the Latin phrases no longer sounded remarkable in the least. The famous domestic anecdote from Edmund Gosse's *Father and Son* springs to mind. Edmund's mother looks up from her Bible at a fluttering moth to exclaim: "Oh! Henry, do you think that can be '*Boletobia*?'" But alas, as Philip Henry quickly discerns, it is only the common Vapourer, *Orgyia antiqua*.[49] Even Victorian children could spout Latin species names with aplomb. In consequence, writers for children often sprinkled Latin liberally throughout their books. For example, Paul du Chaillu, in his specially "narrated for young people" account of *Wild Life Under the Equator*, does not hesitate to say, "Now I must speak to you of another bird, a very curious one, the *Sycobius nigerrimus*."[50]

Latin terminology, with its patina of precision and its scientific gloss, became popular only because so many people thought of themselves as amateur naturalists. If one could gather specimens, one could name them, and for the Victorians the two processes—collection and denomination—were inextricably linked. Ultimately, the cultural manifestations of natural history shaped its language, for each activity had its linguistic analogue. Whether botanizing or dredging, collecting ferns or zoophytes or shells, amateur naturalists tended to describe their activity in language that reflected its essential qualities: novelty and surprise, curiosity, perceived abundance, awe, acquisitiveness. Cutting across class lines, the language of natural history struck a pose of didactic morality. Grounded in religion, it promised revelations. Glorifying empiricism, it delighted in concrete description. Like George Henry Lewes, armed with microscope, dip-net, and jars, legions of naturalists brandished the indispensable tools of this hobby. In turn, these materials became motifs and metaphors—for vision, discovery, and possession. As Lewes put it, naturalists ransacked the world for visible and invisible wonders. The next step was to put them into words.

Notes

1. Alexander Von Humboldt, *Cosmos: A Sketch of a Physical Description of the Universe*, trans. E. C. Otte (New York: Harper and Brothers, Publishers, 1863), II, 19–21.

2. George Henry Lewes, *Studies in Animal Life* (London: Smith, Elder and Co., 1862), pp. 8, 46. Further page citations are made within the text.

3. Nicolette Scourse, *The Victorians and Their Flowers* (London: Croom Helm; Portland, OR: Timber Press, 1983), p. 37. Scourse provides a wealth of information about every element of Victorian botany, gardens, and floral fads.

4. Elizabeth Burton, *The Early Victorians at Home: 1837–1861* (London: Longman, 1972), p. 95.

5. Philip Henry Gosse, *Tenby: A Sea-Side Holiday* (London: John Van Voorst, 1856), p. 219.

6. Enclosure and the hedgerowed plot controlled and regularized England's countryside to such an extent that the "wilder" gardens could, by contrast, appear desirable and beautiful. See Keith Thomas, *Man and the Natural World: A History of the Modern Sensibility* (New York: Pantheon Books, 1983), p. 263.

7. Burton, p. 275.

8. Burton, pp. 275–277.

9. Burton, see Chapter 7.

10. Scourse, pp. 39, 42.

11. Like museums, Kew Gardens flourished during the nineteenth century, under the direction of Sir William Hooker and later his son, the botanist Sir Joseph Dalton Hooker. From 1841 on, the gardens multiplied their facilities, museums, and greenhouses, forming in themselves another locus for the natural history craze. See W. B. Turrill, *Joseph Dalton Hooker: Botanist, Explorer, and Administrator* (London: Thomas Nelson and Sons Ltd., 1963).

12. P. H. Gosse, *The Romance of Natural History* (New York: A. L. Burt Company, Publishers, 1902), p. 183.

13. Burton, p. 288. Scourse also describes the lily affair in detail, pp. 109–112.

14. Scourse, p. 110.

15. David Elliston Allen, *The Victorian Fern Craze: A History of Pteridomania* (London: Hutchinson and Co., 1969), p. ix.

16. Allen, *Fern Craze*, pp. 8–15.

17. Allen, *Fern Craze*, pp. 17, 24.

18. Allen, *Fern Craze*, p. x.

19. Allen, *Fern Craze*, p. ix.

20. Charles Kingsley, *Glaucus; or, the Wonders of the Shore* (London: Macmillan and Co., Ltd., 1903), p. 4.

21. R. B. Freeman and Douglas Wertheimer, *Philip Henry Gosse: A Bibliography* (Folkestone, Kent: Dawson, 1980), p. 45.

22. This cartoon is reproduced in Lynn Barber, *The Heyday of Natural History: 1820–1870* (Garden City, NY: Doubleday and Company, Inc., 1980), p. 14.

23. Edmund Gosse, *The Life of Philip Henry Gosse, F.R.S.* (London: Kegan Paul, Trench, Trübner and Co., Ltd., 1890), p. 258.

24. W. H. Harvey, *The Sea-Side Book; Being an Introduction to the Natural History of the British Coasts* (London: John Van Voorst, 1849), p. 29.

25. Edmund Gosse, *Life*, p. 288.

26. Harvey, p. 116.

27. Harvey, pp. 118–119.

28. Quoted in Frank H. T. Rhodes and Richard O. Stone, eds., *Language of the Earth* (New York: Pergamon Press, 1981), p. 46. Unfortunately, I have been unable to procure a volume of Forbes' poetry, and Rhodes and Stone supply no bibliographic reference for this stanza.

29. Edmund Gosse, *Life*, p. 285.

30. Cuthbert Collingwood, *Rambles of a Naturalist on the Shores and Waters of the China Sea: Being Observations in Natural History During a Voyage to China, Formosa, Borneo, Singapore, Etc.* (London: John Murray, 1868).

31. Barber, pp. 28, 31.

32. From Buckland's introduction to an 1875 edition of Gilbert White's *Natural History of Selborne*, quoted in G. H. O. Burgess, *The Eccentric Ark: The Curious World of Frank Buckland* (New York: The Horizon Press, 1967), p. 139.

33. Herbert Spencer, "Education: Intellectual, Moral, and Physical," in *The Humboldt Library of Popular Science Literature*, Nos. 1–12 (New York: The Humboldt Publishing Co., n.d.), p. 271.

34. Margaret Gatty, *Parables from Nature* (London: G. Bell & Sons Ltd., 1914), p. 23.

35. Gatty, p. 28.

36. Harry G. Owen, "The Hon. Mrs Ward and 'A Windfall for the Microscope,' of 1856 and 1864," *Annals of Science*, 41 (1984), 472.

37. See Barber, pp. 31–37. In 1836, it was argued that opening the British Museum on Sundays would have the salutary effect of giving laborers "a taste for objects of natural history, rather than a taste for gin" at a public house. Richard D. Altick, *The Shows of London: A Panoramic History of Exhibitions, 1600–1862* (Cambridge, MA: Belknap-Harvard Univ. Press, 1978), p. 445.

38. Tess Cosslett, ed., *Science and Religion in the Nineteenth Century* (Cambridge: Cambridge Univ. Press, 1984), p. 2.

39. Philip Henry Gosse, *Letters from Alabama, Chiefly Relating to Natural History* (Mountain Brook, AL: Overbrook House, 1983), p. 149.

40. Barber, p. 23.

41. Thomas, p. 261.

42. Thomas, p. 260.

43. Quoted in David Elliston Allen, *The Naturalist in Britain: A Social History* (London: Allen Lane, 1976), p. 22. Allen does not identify the volume or year for this quotation.

44. Lewes, p. 72.

45. Samuel Smiles, *Life of a Scotch Naturalist: Thomas Edward, Associate of the Linnaean Society* (New York: Harper & Brothers, 1877), p. 96. Further page citations are made within the text.

46. Samuel Smiles, *Robert Dick, Baker, of Thurso: Geologist and Botanist* (New York: Harper & Brothers, 1879), p. 51.

47. Quoted in Edmund Gosse, *Life*, p. 247.

48. Philip Gosse, *Tenby*, p. 139.

49. Edmund Gosse, *Father and Son* (New York: W. W. Norton and Company, 1963), p. 32.

50. Paul du Chaillu, *Wild Life Under the Equator* (New York: Harper and Brothers, Publishers, 1869), p. 132.

3

Language and Discourse

Perhaps you will say I am somewhat extravagant in my admiration of these insects, but really I think that any words of description are insufficient to do justice to their surpassing beauty. Take a butterfly into your hand and examine it yourself for a moment superficially; for though the internal organization would be equally instructive, we will not enter into that at present. Look at the richness of the colours. What brilliant hues! Note the burnished metallic gloss and the changeable glow of many of them; the soft velvety downiness of all. Look at the distribution of the colours; into what elegant forms are they thrown—lines, and spots, and rings, and eyes; think that the whole surface is a mosaic, the most minute, the most elaborate, and the most perfect that can be conceived.[1]

PHILIP HENRY GOSSE, *Letters from Alabama*

The surpassing beauty of natural objects may indeed, as Gosse lamented, have exceeded the power of any description. But that did not stop naturalists from trying. The qualities that Gosse saw in his butterfly permeated the discourse of natural history, and marked it unmistakably. A butterfly was colorful, sensuous, visually complex, minutely detailed; the prose was also. The primary avenue of discovery for the butterfly catcher was visual; so its description exhorted the reader to "Look at it," and then look yet more closely. In describing a gorgeous specimen, a naturalist like Gosse could not help but respond to it emotionally, enthusing about its beauty, reacting to its intricacy with wonder. Underlying all the expressions of this prose was a new attitude: the apotheosis of singularity. Seeking out exotic natural objects and examining them closely reinforced that perception of each thing as unique. Like the butterfly's wing, the world was a mosaic, the most intricate that could be imagined, with no two of its features exactly alike. Realizing this, the naturalist experienced both the satisfying sense of solidity of holding a material object in the hand and the aching pang of knowing that such a

51

creation might never be again. Singularity—the motive engine of Victorian natural history—emphasizes possession and physicality, true. But its secret heart is temporal, awareness of the tenuousness, the impermanence, of details. Often preoccupied with loss and change, the Victorians were well disposed to embrace this quality. Like Victorian poetry, the discourse of natural history reflects both smug material solidity and evanescence.

Even a casual naturalist like George Henry Lewes could not help but absorb the tropes, the diction, and the motifs of this discourse. When Lewes discovered the joys of netting, collecting, and magnifying natural objects, he conveyed them in typical fashion. In *Studies in Animal Life*, Lewes becomes obsessed with vision: "Now look."[2] And then, "The ways are many; let us witness one" (p. 33). In fact, the thrill of vision utterly saturates his book. And equally typically, the vision he espouses ranges from wide views to narrow. It is dialectical, moving between the macroscopic—"what a fine sweep of horizon lies before us!" (p. 48)—and the microscopic—the unsuspected animals living in a drop of dew. The discourse of vision is a celebration of "jewelled light" (p. 5). Like so many naturalists, Lewes' appreciation of nature ranges from awe at its multiplicity, to scrutiny of its singularity. Natural history prose tends to be extremely conscious of its audience; indeed, it goes out of its way to include the audience. And that of Lewes is no exception. He adopts cozy first-person plural pronouns: "let us try a sweep with our net. We skim it along the surface" (p. 63). Or he adopts a second-person direct address—"watch that animalcule which you observe swimming about" (p. 9). Lewes chooses these pronouns because, like so many Victorian naturalists, he feels united with his readers in a community of wonder.

Natural history is participatory; so much so that Lewes issues commands to the reader, as if to a surgical assistant at his elbow. Together he and his readers perform the operations of discovery, while he narrates the progress of the procedure in the present tense, as though dictating into a microphone: "Give me the camel-hair brush. Gently the dab is removed and transferred to the vial" (pp. 67–68). Then he plunges into a rapt discourse of plenty, of nature's extravagance, of wonders never-ending. He cloaks his discoveries in the language of religious revelation: "Behold!" (p. 25). He serves up a generous portion of Latin names, delighting in differentiating one form from another. But although he writes about such scientific points of interest as the embryonic structures of *Monostomum mutabile*, Lewes' tone is emotional, awed, subjective. Deeply affected himself by the wonder of his subject, Lewes employs rhetorical strategies that will make his prose affecting to a reader.

What appealed to the legions of amateur naturalists—botanizers and shore collectors, children and laborers alike—was how natural history blended objective and subjective. Its mixed character accounts for many of the marked qualities of its discourse. Often dialectical, natural history prose swings between panorama and particularity, multiplicity and singularity, emotion and fact. It tries, on the one hand, to convey to its reader a sense of the variety and reality of true facts of nature. On the other hand, it imbues these facts with emotion, religious awe, drama, even in extreme cases sentimentality and moralistic precepts. Natural history texts are grounded in fact, but their tone is not scientific. They employ rhetorical strategies, like Lewes does in *Animal Life*, to generate wonder in the reader.

The hybrid pleasures of natural history—part scientific exactitude, part emotional pleasure—were encapsulated by J. L. Knapp in his 1825 book, *Country Rambles*. Inspired by White's *Natural History of Selborne*, Knapp was "led to the constant observance of the rural objects around" him.[3] His is a "journal of a traveller through the inexhaustible regions of nature" (p. vi) and, as Lynn Barber might predict,[4] it offers an eclectic amalgam of agricultural information (how wheat is harvested, for instance), bits of history (the Roman roads), and spurious anecdotes (the tale of a man whose feet were burned off in a lime kiln). But Knapp's journal also contains a fine summary of the lure of natural history:

> But the natural historian is required to attend to something more than the vagaries of butterflies and the spinning of caterpillars; his study, considered abstractedly from the various branches of science which it embraces, is one of the most delightful occupations that can employ the attention of reasoning beings: a beautiful landscape, grateful objects, pleasures received by the eye or the senses, become the common property of all who can enjoy them, being in some measure obvious to everyone; but the naturalist must reflect upon hidden things, investigate by comparison, and testify by experience. (p. 41)

Knapp goes on to "testify" that all nature is the "obvious design" of "the great Architect" (p. 61). An ardent believer in natural theology's immanent design, Knapp does impose his own bias onto his observations of nature. But his shrewd list of the pleasures of natural history can apply to any observer of nature: "a beautiful landscape, grateful objects, pleasures received by the eye or senses."

Beautiful landscapes, unusual objects, and sensory pleasures often seemed easiest to find in a foreign land. Like Knapp, the "traveller through the inexhaustible regions of nature" did not necessarily range far, but tropical pleasures seemed especially glamorous, especially to the novice. As a result, natural history writing, as a genre, became intimately entwined with the literature of travel. Britain's far-flung empire and vigorous Navy fed an appetite for travel and facilitated scientific expeditions, such as the voyage of Captain Sir James Clarke Ross from 1839 to 1843 on H.M.S. *Erebus* and *Terror*, which took him and his crew as far as Antarctica; aboard ship, they took botanist Joseph Dalton Hooker to serve as the ship's naturalist. The inclusion of a naturalist aboard surveying ships became quite routine—Huxley was aboard the *Rattlesnake* (technically as an assistant surgeon) and Darwin of course traveled with the *Beagle*.

In fact, so closely were naval expeditions and scientific observations tied together that in 1849 a military handbook appeared with the express purpose of aiding novice scientific travelers in their compilation of useful scientific notes. Published under the authority of the Lords Commissioners of the Admiralty, the book, entitled *A Manual for Scientific Inquiry; prepared for the use of Officers in Her Majesty's Navy, and Travellers in General*, was edited by none other than the esteemed astronomer and philosopher of science, John Herschel. It boasted chapters on various sciences written by experts in those fields—for example, George Airy on astronomy and Joseph Hooker on botany. Like much of natural history writing, this book aimed *not* to produce "very deep and abstruse research," but rather to give "directions . . . generally plain, so that men merely of good intelligence and fair acquirement may be able to act upon them," so as to know what "objects, and methods of observation and record, were important.[5] "Travellers in general" could advance natural history with a minimum of preparation, simply by training their powers of observation and staying alert.

Near mid-century, under Prince Albert's patronage, scientific expeditions flourished along with museums and exhibitions. Victorians ventured forth on travels in ever-greater numbers, drawn to the alpine vistas of the Continent by the recently developed Romantic appetite for craggy and awesome scenery; indeed, the nineteenth century saw the development of mountain climbing as a sport. Romantic tastes—for Burkean sublimes and neo-Gothic wastes[6]—prepared Britons to appreciate wilder scenes than could ever be found in long-domesticated, hedgerowed England. Perhaps relatively few Victorians could travel to the wilds of Africa, India, Malaysia, or the New World Tropics, but many could read about them, and did. Travel books like Alexander William Kinglake's *Eothen, or Traces of Travel brought Home from the East* (1844) or Isabella Bird's *Six Months in the Sandwich Islands* (1875)[7] sold in great numbers. So did African explorers' accounts—those of Livingstone, Speke, Petherick, Burton, du Chaillu, and Stanley—which were often sanctioned by the Royal Geographic Society.

Victorian natural history writing catered to the new taste for exotic climes. The traveling naturalist supremely personified the ideal naturalist: adventurous, open to new experiences, ever hopeful of uncovering natural novelties. Similarly, tropical nature offered all that a naturalist could hope for: color, variety, novelty, intricacy of form. As a result, travelers' reports often sported all the typical characteristics of natural history discourse in high relief. The language used to describe a Brazilian jungle applied equally well, although perhaps on a less grandiose scale, to a little pond on Wimbledon Common. Peering into either, the naturalist explored new territory, with all the excitement of the chase. To the sensitive imagination, the rewards were the same. Exploiting the language of natural history, books by peripatetic naturalists offered quantifiable scientific discoveries, emotional tone, curiosity, singularity, sensory detail in which vision predominated, a wealth of details, and rhetorically created drama.

Travelers or naturalists who ventured to tropical terrain enthralled readers with accounts of how different, how various, how *other* nature could be. The world's multitudinousness, as Arnold would say, was precisely what appealed. For instance, Henry Walter Bates, a naturalist now mostly remembered as the companion of Alfred Russel Wallace and as the discoverer of "Batesian mimicry" among dissimilar organisms, traveled to the Amazon River basin in Brazil and discovered incredible natural profusion. His account, *The Naturalist on the River Amazons*, makes this point most emphatically. On his first walk into the jungle, Bates encounters "sounds of multifarious life," "the teeming profusion of Nature," an "uproar of life," "a vast number and variety" of insects all around; in short, a "wealth of natural objects."[8] His overwhelming impression is of nature's seemingly inexhaustible plenitude.

Bates, who thinks of himself as a typical Victorian naturalist, a "forest rambler" (p. 447), finds the forest densely tangled with the "most diverse and ornamental foliage possible" (p. 139). The jungle "consisted of a most bewildering diversity of grand and beautiful trees, draped, festooned, corded, matted, and ribboned with climbing plants, woody and succulent, in endless variety" (p. 377). Far from temperate, domesticated England, the jungle in Brazil continually yields "treasures" (p. 447) to the naturalist, its "romantic" forests bejeweled with colorful creatures: "numbers of scarlet, green, and black tanagers and brightly coloured butterflies sport about" in the sun. In addition, Bates packs his narrative with irresistible tales of the most peculiar and dramatic animals of the jungle: monkeys, vampire bats, alligators, army ants, and toucans.

Visiting rather more civilized Alabama in 1838 (although the slavery he found there seemed thoroughly barbaric), Philip Henry Gosse used equally breathless prose to describe its natural variety. His language parallels that of Bates. Both reveled in nature's multitudinousness, variety, profusion, and abundance. Gosse hardly knew where to look first, since "so many charming things were every instant catching my attention, and enchaining my observation."[9] Butterflies were "abundant," while along the rail fences "there is always a dense and rank mass of vegetation," with flowers in "luxuriance." On a "woodland ramble," Gosse is enthralled by the "charm of absolute novelty" (p. 41) of everything he sees. No walk could be taken without "multitudes of objects to catch the eye and delight the mind of an observant naturalist" (p. 45). In one instance he stops to examine "several species of butterflies, revelling, with multitudes of bees, wasps, and other insects, on the thick beds of horehound (*Marrubium vulgare*), which abounds on each side of the road" (p. 51). To the naturalist, nature's profligacy was a dependable source of delight.

As the Admiralty's *Manual of Scientific Inquiry* noted, travelers could of course find many things to report on, "independently of matters of exact science"—for example, "Reports upon National Character and Customs, Religious Ceremonies, Agriculture and Mechanical Arts, Language, Navigation, Medicine, Tokens of value."[10] And works of natural history written as a result of travel or exploration often do include many of these subjects, especially notes on indigenous mores and customs.

Many travel accounts contained a good deal of anthropological detail. Customs, especially the scanty costumes of the "natives," titillated staid Victorian readers. Even such slightly naughty thrills were safer and more socially acceptable than those from idle novels. In her study of women travel writers, Catherine Barnes Stevenson makes the distinction between fiction, frowned upon by the evangelically pious, and nonfiction, exalted by the Victorian belief in true facts. She cites an advertisement by John Murray's, publishers of a series of travel books: "The aim of the publisher has been to produce a series of works as entertaining as romances, yet not frivolous, but abounding in useful information."[11] What *use* details of African geography would be to a London armchair reader is obscure at best. But any information was *potentially* useful, or at the very least, educational. (One immediately thinks of that wonderful Victorian institution, the Society for the Diffusion of Useful Knowledge, founded in 1827.) And to the Victorians, of course, terms like "useful" and "educational" were charged with positive moral electricity.

Allowing for the fact that travel books and natural history books both thrived on the mania for facts, both benefiting from new means of distribution (such as railway stands), a distinction should be made between them. As a category, the "travel book" or "travel essay" is of course rather nebulous. Really, any account of travel qualifies, whether its approach be introspective, cultural, scenic, or dramatic. The subject matter might or might not include nature. And if a Victorian travel book did describe nature, it would not necessarily take a naturalist's approach. Instead of seeing specimens, a travel book might notice only vague scenery, nature as a distant backdrop for other topics. Both the literature of travel and that of natural history thrived on the metaphorical implications of making a "voyage" into the unknown, of embarking on a quest. With their emotions heightened by novelty, both the general traveler and the naturalist were predisposed to make keen observations. But the impressions they recounted could be on very different subjects.

As a rule, Victorian travel books did include some natural history—detailed descriptions of natural objects, animals, plants, or incidents. After all, a subject so esteemed was difficult to ignore. Frequently, however, it was only a minor spice for an anthropological or cultural dish. While the rubric of natural history can, in its broadest sense, include anthropology (as the American magazine *Natural History* does today), for this discussion I must exclude it. Some notable works of travel did consist largely of natural history; Charles Waterton's *Wanderings in South America* (1825) is one. An idiosyncratic naturalist, like Frank Buckland, Waterton went to South America in search of strange animals (collecting and stuffing them whenever possible). Even his book, though, contains a generous helping of lore about the "primitive natives," which is to say, descriptive anthropology. Wallace and Bates, in their accounts, talk much about the natives, too.

An example of a travel book that does not contain much natural history is the *Narrative of the Voyage of H.M.S. Rattlesnake*, published in 1852 by John MacGillivray, naturalist to the expedition. (T. H. Huxley sailed on this trip also.) This account of the voyage concentrates on culture, with sections on "Native Ornaments," "Canoes of Coral Haven Described," "Natives and Catamarans," "An Aboriginal of Port Essington," "Natives Shew Thievish Propensities," "Slavery," and so on. The book dwells at length upon the history of previous exploring captains. When natural phenomena appear, as one might expect, the language quantifies or Latinizes: "To these succeeds a row of bushes of *Scaevola Koenigii*, and *Tournefortia argentea*, with an occasional *Guettarda speci-*

osa, or *Morinda citrifolia*, backed by thickets of *Paritium Tiliaceum*, and other shrubs supporting large *Convolvulaceae* . . ."[12]

Freighted with stories of the natives and unadorned lists of natural features, the *Rattlesnake* account is not, by my standards, natural history. MacGillivray has little flair for colorful description, nor much of an eye for affective beauty. Occasionally, however, perhaps almost by accident, he goes beyond dry ledgers of facts (which have, it is true, the interest of novelty) to give tantalizing glimpses of the power of natural history discourse. Such sections are of greater interest because in them MacGillivray mingles natural details with human responses, infusing them with life. One such passage describes a search for potable water for the ship's crew. MacGillivray accompanies a "party in two boats" that proceeds from the ship's anchorage a mile offshore to the mouth of a small creek. As the boats ascend the river, he writes first of the mangroves, "60 to 80 feet in height, with a circumference at the base of 6 to 8 feet" (all precisely quantified; p. 207).

Then, however, he describes other plants, not as something to be measured, but as a brooding background to the men's activities:

> To this succeeded during our upward progress a low bank of very large trees at intervals, and others arching over the stream, their branches nearly touching the water. Gigantic climbers hung down in long festoons passing from branch to branch, and the more aged trunks supported clumps of ferns and parasitical plants. Here and there an areca palm shot up its feathery stem surmounted by a cluster of pale-green feathery leaves, or the attention was arrested for a moment by a magnificent pandanus—its trunk raised high above the ground by the enormous supporting root-like shoots,—or some graceful tree-fern with dark widely-spreading foliage exceeding in delicacy the finest lace. (pp. 207–208)

As MacGillivray's attention is arrested, the reader's is, too. He is struck by the forms of the plants, not just by their species, and describes them in terms of their emotional effect on him; the tree that rivets his vision is "magnificent." Others are adjudged beautiful, as MacGillivray's comparative language reveals. The climbers are arranged in "festoons," like decorations at a ball or the roof of a gazebo. The tree-fern has the appearance of fine lace. And besides beauty, the plants have energy, autonomous life: the powerful roots of the pandanus hold its heavy trunk erect, while the palms "shoot up" out of the earth in their vigor.

Continuing upstream, MacGillivray reveals other vistas, giving the reader long shots of scenery. Even more important, he colors the scene with emotion, contrasting the natural with the human scale:

Meanwhile the creek had slightly narrowed, the dead trees in the water had become more frequent and troublesome, and the thickets on the banks encroached more and more upon the channel so as not to allow room for the oars to pass, obliging the men to use them as poles. At every turn in the windings of the stream (still too brackish to be fit to drink) some beautiful glimpse of jungle scenery presented itself as we passed upwards—long vistas and stray bursts of sunshine alternating with the gloomy shadows of the surrounding woods. A deep silence pervaded the banks of this water never before visited by civilized man, its monotony broken only by the occasional brief word of command, the splash of the oars, or the shrill notes of some passing flights of parrots. (p. 208)

The somewhat frightening sense of claustrophobia in the passage, with the narrow channel, the dead trees that impede progress and snatch at the oars, gives the description an emotional tone. Reinforcing this fright and awe are the "gloomy shadows," the "deep silence," and the encroachment into a virgin and unpredictable realm, "never before visited" (the natives, clearly, don't count). The open vistas of jungle, lit with sunlight, but unattainable, give glimpses of hope, and beauty. But the predominant impression is of a dangerous passage, on a deathly silent, Styx-like river; the voices of the men and the sound of their oars are reminders of human frailty and insignificance in the face of voluminous, patient nature. A simple search for drinking water becomes, fleetingly, a human encounter with nature's power. With a passage like this, MacGillivray does tap the potential of natural history discourse.

But to see the power of this genre, one should look at the most famous natural history book of the nineteenth century—Darwin's *Journal of Researches* (now generally called *Voyage of the Beagle*), published in 1839, memorable not only for its own innate charms, but also as an early work by the author of the momentous *On the Origin of Species*. Many readers search the *Journal* for clues to Darwin's germinating awareness of natural selection, systematized and published as the *Origin* twenty years later. Aside from these tantalizing hints, however, the book has other strengths. As its title indicates, Darwin's *Journal of Researches into the Geology and Natural History of the Various Countries visited by H.M.S. 'Beagle'* is a classic mixture of Victorian travel writing and natural history. Like MacGillivray, Darwin mixes quantification with emotion, nature with culture. Cultural curiosities often predominate: gauchos, bandits, Fuegans; ranches, revolutions, and religions. Far more frequently than MacGillivray, though, Darwin conveys to the reader his response to landscape. He lists and categorizes native animals, a perfect master of technical description, telling us that the sea-pen is a truncate zoophyte, with a vermiform fleshy appendage at one end (chapter V, "Bahia Blanca").[13] But he also shares his pleasure in discovery.

At one point, Darwin says he walked "some miles into the interior" of Patagonia, across a level plain of gravel and chalky soil:

> There was not a tree, and, excepting the guanaco, which stood on the hill-top a watchful sentinel over its herd, scarcely an animal or a bird. All was stillness and desolation. Yet in passing over these scenes, without one bright object near, an ill-defined but strong sense of pleasure is vividly excited. One asked how many ages the plain had thus lasted, and how many more it was doomed thus to continue. (chapter VIII, "Banda Oriental and Patagonia," p. 160)

Here, obviously, is a geologist musing about the form and duration of the landscape—but here also is a man who finds even a muted, unspectacular landscape evocative. Darwin goes on, in the best tradition of Victorian natural history, to give a quotation from "the Poets"—in this case Shelley on Mont Blanc.

Even more striking than Darwin's unabashed emotional response is his boundless curiosity. How often does he say "I was curious to observe" or a similar phrase! The diction corroborates his curiosity; to his alert and receptive intelligence everything stands out. Repeatedly, Darwin describes the specimens of South America as "singular": "A very singular little bird" (p. 89), or "a little toad . . . most singular from its color" (chapter V, p. 92). Or he pronounces them "remarkable," showing how keenly he perceives natural objects as highly individualistic specimens.

The word *singular*, in fact, occurs with great frequency in nineteenth-century natural history and science writing. It is a particularly felicitous word for natural history, since it suits the aims of the pursuit so well. *Singular* can have many gradations of meaning, as the *Oxford English Dictionary* amply attests, but for natural history the important denotations are first: unique, individual, one of a kind, *sui generis*; and second: remarkable, extraordinary, unusual, uncommon, rare, precious.

Natural history seeks out objects or phenomena that are both unique (that is, noteworthy for being so unlike anything else) and extraordinary (that is, exciting because so peculiar). A *singular* fact in this context is one that has not been noticed before or is very curious. Singular facts, then, partake of the mystique of the individuated object, the love of particularity. It is interesting that the *OED* cites many usage examples for all definitions of *singular*, but those pertaining to the first definition come from before the nineteenth century, while the significant examples given from the nineteenth century pertain to the second definition. One example is from Victorian science, under the meaning of "strange, odd, peculiar," from John Tyndall's *Glaciers of the Alps*: "I clambered up among these singular terraces." Tyndall's usage here, like Darwin's frequent use of the word, seems to imply that the terraces are unique and remarkable as well. Philip Henry Gosse peppers his observations with "singular" much as Darwin does, referring to, among other things, the "exceedingly singular" cry of a bird, fireflies "singularly beautiful," the brine shrimp "a singular creature," and the "beauty and singularity of the form" of a butterfly.[14] Similar examples can be found in almost every natural history text.

In addition to pouncing upon singularity, Darwin's *Journal* has a highly visual character. Darwin frames his revelations in a terminology of sight. The explorer sees, views, observes, beholds, watches. All around him are "extraordinary spectacles" (porpoises jumping, chapter III, p. 37), and scenery, wide views of "strange aspect" (Sierra de la Ventana, chapter VI, p. 102). He hears stories too bizarre to be believed, until he has "ocular proof" (chapter VI, p. 109). The primacy of sight for Darwin, especially when combined with frequent recourse to microscope and hand-lens, allies him to other naturalists of his day. As a group, Victorian naturalists revered vision, especially surreptitious sights—"Glimpses of Animal Life" (Arabella Buckley's subtitle for her book, *Life and Her Children*), or, as Philip Gosse so aptly put it, "peeps through Nature's keyhole at her recondite mysteries."[15]

Darwin's *Journal of Researches* is natural history at its best. It is precisely focused: "Moreover, if your view is limited to a small space, many objects possess beauty" (chapter III, p. 38). And it is unabashedly emotional, though not sentimental. Looking at a panorama of foliage, scanning from the treetops above to the undergrowth beneath, Darwin concludes: "It is easy to specify the individual objects of admiration in these grand scenes; but it is not possible to give an adequate idea of the higher feelings of wonder, astonishment, and devotion, which fill and elevate the mind" (chapter II, p. 24). Because of its quality, but mainly because of its author's reputation, the *Journal of Researches* is the most exhaustively analyzed work of natural history from Victorian times.

Of works that analyze Darwin's style, rather than his scientific substance, one of the more interesting, although controversial, is by Stanley Edgar Hyman.[16] He finds structures of drama, particularly tragedy, in *On the Origin of Species*, and I would agree with him that Darwin often uses dramatic narrative. In the *Journal* many of the most dramatic episodes are about the lives of insects (see, for example, the exciting odyssey of the "little aeronaut," the gossamer spider, in chapter VIII,

p. 152, or the saga of the attacking ants, in chapter II, p. 33). What Hyman finds in Darwin's style—a tendency to shape descriptions from nature into dramatic episodes—is in fact a common tactic in Victorian natural history prose.

Another relevant view of Darwin's style, James Paradis' "Darwin and Landscape," analyzes the prominent Romantic influences on Darwin's diction and thought. When these are reconciled or mingled with scientific attitudes of objectivity and theorizing, the result constitutes, as I see it, natural history. Paradis explains how Darwin hovers between two attractions, two compulsions—to see nature through two different lenses:

> In the text of the *Journal* Darwin consciously shifts from one descriptive mode to another, weaving his less formal aesthetic impressions with the more structured enumerations of specific landforms, fossils, and species. Two idealizations of the perceived landscape thus emerge in Darwin's voyage account, each a distillation of the common subject matter of visible nature, manifested in the separate but not entirely distinct vocabularies of personal meditation and systematic science.[17]

The changing frame of reference here is characteristic of natural history, though not so much of science. Confronted with a natural object, a naturalist like Darwin wants both to celebrate and specify its "singularity," its autonomy, *and* to marvel at it. "Wonder" and "astonishment"— these emotions can only be awakened in the soul of a human being, who cannot help but bring the meaning of his own life, and the context of the rest of nature, to bear on the singular object. Wonder mingles at times with problematic possession, the somewhat elegaic awareness of the singularity and thus irreplaceability of a given specimen. To a naturalist, natural objects and incidents evoke pleasant associations, with a power usually ascribed only to images in poetry. As Philip Gosse explained:

> How slight a thing will touch the chords of sympathy! The smallest object, the faintest note, will sometimes awaken association with some distant scene or bygone time, and conjure up in a moment, all unexpected, a magic circle, which unlocks all the secret springs of the soul, and excites emotions and affections that had slept for months, or perhaps years! The unlooked-for sight of a little bird lately had such an effect upon me. It was an unpretending little thing, a sort of sparrow, called the Snow-bird (*Fringilla nivalis*) . . .[18]

Bates, Darwin, and countless other traveling naturalists created records of natural wonders that mingled scientific with personal, even poetic, response. The potpourri of information found in Victorian travel books paralleled the catholic tastes of educated Victorians. Natural history books had the same sort of appeal, because of their breadth. Shaped by the curiosity of their writers, their structure is not logical, not goal-oriented, but eccentric, and thus tied to human concerns and human emotions in a way that science attempts to avoid. They are all-inclusive, interested in everything, precluding nothing, darting from one topic to another as the writer's attention does. The wide scope of natural history engenders a cheerful eclecticism—an open-minded optimism that treats every natural feature as potentially fascinating.

Each feature—an animal, a leaf, an object of any kind—has something to offer. Each could be evocative, especially if described by a skillful writer. Or, at the very least, each object could boast a wealth of intricate detail visible to the eye of the skillful observer. Accordingly, one of the most vivid traits of natural history discourse is its particularity: the tendency to seize on specific natural details (with the underlying assumption that these are more interesting and more valuable than general cases). The language of particularity thrived most of all on that *ne plus ultra* of the naturalist's vision—the microscope. Many natural history texts speak overtly about microscopes, microscopic details, or microscopic vision. Like vision itself, the microscope became a trope, a dominant motif for Victorian naturalists. (Because the instrument shaped natural history discourse so profoundly, I discuss microscopy at length in Chapter 5). The particularized language of naturalists reflects the energy they devoted to examining, collecting, and handling concrete objects, whether on a micro- or macroscopic scale. Preoccupied with collecting, naturalists thought of the world as a mosaic of discrete pieces, which formed, or could be arranged in, various pleasing patterns, like the mosaic on the wing of Gosse's butterfly.

Many factors combined to produce the Victorian obsession with details, with facts, with *things*. The invention of photography, the Pre-Raphaelite movement in painting, a technological obsession with material facts and a philosophical one with positivistic facts, and of course the widespread practice of natural history—all these played a part. For amateur naturalists, natural objects were palpable facts—colorful, intricate, pleasingly solid. It was easy to find them hypnotic, to become obsessed with materiality.

Literary critics often search for reasons for the Victorians' materialism. But they usually overlook natural history as a cause—not just the practice of natural history, but also its language and discourse, which are grounded in natural minutiae. In *The Finer Optic: The Aesthetic of Particularity in Victorian Poetry*, Carol T. Christ recognizes that *something* must have fostered the Victorian fascination with detail. For this Christ credits science, although not natural history as such. Like most critics, she simply seems unaware of natural history as distinct from science. Still, "science," or close study of the natural world, engendered an attitude that then permeated both literary and visual arts: "In much Victorian poetry and painting, detail becomes scientifically precise and minute, conspicuously particular."[19]

Christ goes on to speak of some of the applications of detail, noting that many Victorian writers and artists employed it. Tennyson especially was famous for his keen eye:

> The paintings of the Pre-Raphaelite Brotherhood, the writings of Ruskin, and even the poetry of Hopkins spring from a similar zeal for exact fidelity to natural detail. This fanatic concern for scientific accuracy, which made Tennyson keep charts of isothermals and isobars in his room to ensure the exactness of his scientific allusions and Holman Hunt go to the Dead Sea on the day of Atonement when painting The Scapegoat to make sure the light would be exactly as it had been on the day the goat was turned out of the temple, obviously results from the rising predominance of scientific views of truth in the Victorian period but the extraordinary sensitivity to minutiae that always accompanies such accuracy is less easy to explain.[20]

Natural history, I would suggest, offers just such an explanation. The widely disseminated writings of Victorian naturalists, and their exhortations to collect, to look closely, provided both a model and an impetus for an "extraordinary sensitivity to minutiae."

The pursuit of natural history encouraged people to look at nature carefully, sometimes microscopically, even myopically—numbering not only the streaks on Dr. Johnson's famous tulip, but the tiny stipples in the streaks as well. Johnson had made his remarks on the tulip (in *Rasselas*) in a discussion of the province of poetry, what poets ought to include, or exclude, from their descriptions. In the century that followed Johnson's, the ascendancy of natural history, by changing the way people looked at nature, also helped to change the way people looked at art and literature. In the eighteenth century, particularized natural history, Gilbert White notwithstanding, was at odds with the prevailing literary values; the tenets of literary taste predisposed people to snub details in favor of ideas. The Tulip had interest, as a type; particular tulips were less significant. Such an attitude mirrored the scientific approach, which did indeed see organisms as fixed, distinct types. Variation mattered less than essence, exceptions less than the rules. But continued close observation of nature helped convince people of the importance, and often the beauty, of detail. Fixed natural types began to crumble, and the variations they had obscured turned out to be more fascinating than anyone had thought. In a complex process, taste by the middle of the nineteenth century changed to incorporate, even demand, more detail—first in visual art and then in literary art. For the literary critic, natural history's contribution to this process is its single most important feature.

Cascades of detail, particularity, and microscopic metaphors overwhelm even the most casual reader of Victorian natural history texts. A good example of the language of particularity can be found in *Life and Her Children*, by Arabella Buckley. Like most Victorian naturalists, Buckley enjoys creating verbal analogues for unique physical objects, especially those in a magnified scene. In this passage, she is telling her young readers about some of the minute dwellers in the sea:

> Try for one moment to picture to yourself some quiet spot in the ocean-bed, where . . . every shell and seaweed carries some hundreds of tiny beings all stretching out their waving tentacles and flinging out their miniature lassos to strike their prey. You would see here and there among them the tall, graceful, animal trees, such as the sea-fir, which often grows up into a brown upright tree more than three feet high, with branches bearing as many as a hundred thousand cups, each with its pure white polypite stretching out, and looking wonderfully delicate against the dark stem; while side by side with it may be standing the tube-hydra, which has single yellow pipes, out of each of which a brilliant scarlet creature is waving its graceful tentacles. All this life is active and busy, and yet it all is made up of beings so insignificant to us that we have hardly any idea of their existence.[21]

Besides the specificity of the measurements (the hundred thousand cups on the three-foot-high tree), Buckley depicts the features and colors of each organism. (Footnotes carefully identify the sea-fir as *Sertularia cupressina*, and the tube-hydra as *Tubularia indivisa*.) Even in such a reduced area, there is always more detail to see: the "single yellow pipes" on the hydra or the "pure white polypite" extruding from each cup.

Buckley now attempts an even more difficult task. On the sertularia lives a smaller animal: the *Campanulina*, a type of coelenterate. Few people know this creature, and its appearance and life history are almost incredible. How can one describe it so the reader can visualize it? And, more difficult, how can one describe it so that the reader cares about it? Buckley uses the naturalist's descriptive technique: first analyze the animal, piece by piece, then compare each element to some homely, familiar thing. Use similes and concrete language, and combine these with emotive words. Of the *Campanulina*, Buckley says:

And while you were watching these thousands of tiny arms you might perhaps witness a strange sight if your eyes were sharp enough to see it. From an animal tree very like the sertularia, except that its horny cups are borne upon stalks, you might see escaping some little beings looking like green shining bubbles, and these, if seen under the microscope, turn out to be the most beautiful fairy jelly-bells, like pure crystal domes swimming gaily along on the water by driving in and out the jelly-veil spread across their rim.

Buckley expresses the arcane shapes of the animal by equating them to other, known objects; different parts resemble a "tree," "arms," a "cup," a "stalk." She uses explanatory similes, too: the "little beings" look like bubbles, and the bubbles in turn look like domes. Moreover, the various shapes have textures ("horny," "shining," "crystal") and color ("green"). Buckley gives action to the scene as well, as the little domes swim by rippling their jelly-veils. In addition to choosing concrete and sensory words, she engages the reader by using words that make or imply an aesthetic judgment ("beautiful," "fairy"), or words that impute feelings to the animals themselves ("swimming gaily").

The whole passage is a sensory paean to vision, color, and light. And in addition to being quite typically particularized and concrete, Buckley's ocean-floor vignette displays other traits of natural history discourse. Buckley speaks directly to the reader: "Try for one moment to picture to yourself . . ." Like Lewes, she sees her role as that of "witness," someone who may, if patient enough, be privy to one of the singular, "strange sights" of nature. She expects her readers, even children, to enjoy a word like "sertularia," which, after all, represents a very specific, identified object. And finally, Buckley's tone is unabashedly rapturous, her response aesthetic. These "most beautiful fairy jelly-bells"—what gorgeous objects they are!

If objective material fact stands at one end of the naturalist's spectrum of attention, then subjective emotional response stands at the other. Victorian naturalists respond to natural objects, reporting them as seen through the filter of their own personalities. As in the case of Arabella Buckley, one frequent personal reaction is a deep sense of religious awe. The tendency to approach nature from a moralistic or religious standpoint, trying to find in it evidence of God's design, sometimes results in an excessively moral tone in Victorian nature writing. Often combined with this is sentimentality, which hovers around the fringes of natural history prose because the genre admits emotion as a proper response to nature.

To be sure, injecting personal emotion into natural facts can lead to excesses. Mawkishness is an inherent danger. With objectivity removed as a counterweight, the reader is at the mercy of the writer's possibly cloying emotions. Buckley, I believe, succeeds in sounding enthusiastic and awed, without sounding too gushy. However, many rather regrettable works of natural history pepper the Victorian era, marred by just such faults. Subjectivity sometimes distorts too much: seeing nature not for itself, or as itself, but as a pathetic fallacy, a moral example, a series of set-pieces for human edification or quaint parables. Lynn Barber, in fact, sees this distortion as the primary feature of Victorian natural history. In it, she claims, animals are all too often shamelessly anthropomorphized and morally ranked according to their presumed characters.[22]

An example of moralizing and sentimentality gone overboard is *The Herb of the Field*, by Charlotte M. Yonge, which admonishes its readers to "see how in every plant God has set lessons of His Name and Nature for those who will look for them." How lucky for humankind that

> even with the smallest herb that grows; not only has their Maker created them so perfect and so lovely that we can hardly help recollecting how great, how kind, and how wise He is every time we look at them, but He has also set upon them His seal, so that we may trace out in them emblems of His Nature as revealed to us, which come to us as sweet lessons and helps, and might serve to support our faith, even if our other aids were far away.[23]

Admittedly, this book is aimed mainly at children, but its intrusive piety typifies one preachy Victorian style of natural history.

Yonge foists other heavy-handed manipulation of nature on her readers, too. She mixes scientific language with inexorable personification. Even worse, she is resolutely determined to see natural objects not as themselves but as raw material to be transmuted into something else (fairy tales or moral precepts). The sweet-pea, for instance, becomes here "a Sicilian lady, who has only come to live in England within the last two hundred years. She has but a weak, feeble climbing stem" (p. 37). In another case, Yonge believes that in the "pearly nautilus-like keel of the painted lady-pea," the king and queen of the fairies might sail (p. 39).

Standing at the zenith (or, some might argue, the nadir) of this category of sentimental works are those of the French historian, Jules Michelet. During the 1850s and 1860s he composed four nature books: *The Bird*, *The Insect*, *The Sea*, and *The Mountain*. Michelet is worth looking at (even though he is outside the British focus of my study) because he shows just how syrupy nineteenth-century natural history could be if its mawkishness was uncontrolled. About nature Michelet is optimistic, sentimentally rhapsodic, and relentlessly anthropomorphic. In *The Bird*, published in 1856 and translated in Great Britain in 1879, Michelet's avian creatures are like characters from Aesop's fables: brave or virtuous, cowardly or noble. And the moral worth of birds increases the closer they are to humans, in behavior or even in appearance. To Michelet, birds of prey are "sinister," "winged robbers," "murderers," and "vulgar assassins."[24] Of course, the exact diction here is that of the translator, but the tone is unmistakable. Michelet further asserts that the "flattened skull is the sign of these murderers" (p. 158). What is the basis for this phrenological judgment? Simply this: with their flattened skulls, such birds fail to look much like human beings—the standard of all worth. Michelet makes this quite clear:

> These birds of prey, with their small brains, offer a striking contrast to the numerous amiable and plainly intelligent species which we find among the smaller birds. The head of the former is only a beak; that of the latter has a face. What comparison can be made between these brute giants and the intelligent, all-human bird, the robin redbreast, which at this very moment hovers about me, perches on my shoulder or my paper, examines my writing, warms himself at the fire, or curiously peers through the window to see if the springtime will not soon return. (pp. 158–159)

Nasty creatures, birds of prey. Fortunately, Michelet finds most birds somehow "human" and thus quite admirable.

Swallows, for instance, qualify as noble birds, for "theirs is the hearth." The swallow "mansion" is passed down from generation to generation within the family (p. 194). Their "domestic life" is loving, faithful, and orderly. Better yet, they are the "friends" of man, happy to live near him and cheer him with song. To describe natural specimens such as these, only the most Romantic diction will do. Birds are beautiful, inspiring, sublime; they sing with "winged voices, voices of fire, angel voices, emanations of an intense life superior to ours." They have voices that sing to us of liberty, of freedom! (p. 236). Apostrophe and direct address are also irresistible for Michelet. Approaching the "Dreamer of the Marshes," the "meditative" heron, Michelet asks him about his mood:

> My fisher-friend, wouldst thou oblige me by explaining (without abandoning thy present position), why, always so melancholy, thou seemest doubly melancholy to-day? Hath thy prey failed thee? Have the too subtle fish deceived thine eyes? Does the mocking frog defy thee from the bottom of the waters? (p. 112)

Forewarned by Michelet's prose, one is not surprised to learn that the heron answers—nor to find that it has mastered a most eloquent style. Michelet has a great deal more to say about the bird, our "winged brother," but his strongly flavored prose turns sour on the modern palate.

Yonge and Michelet, with their unctuous sentimentality, are extreme in their subjective responses. At the opposite extreme, where language about nature claims strict objectivity, natural history shades into pure science, devoid of emotion. For example, to feed the popular mania for precise technical descriptions of wildlife, dozens of books appeared that were precursors of the "field guides" of today. These textbooks, often quite comprehensive, enumerated every detail of anatomy and habitat, distinctive species marks, and so forth; Philip Henry Gosse's *Actinologia Britannica: A History of British Sea-Anemones and Corals* (1860) is one such book. But such guides, although quite scientific in spirit—that is, concerned mainly with classification and technical description of species rather than with their charms—often shade into the subjective language characteristic of natural history. Even the driest of these textbooks tends to have a peculiarly Victorian flavor, that curious mix of technical and romantic diction produced by an aesthetic approach to the study of nature.

One interesting example of such a mixture is Edward Forbes' *A History of British Starfishes, and Other Animals of the Class Echinodermata* (1841). Forbes himself, oceanographer, geologist, and amateur poet, practiced natural history's dual methodology: precision and romance. His list of scientific papers (the "Report on the Distribution of Pulmoniferous Mollusca in the British Isles" or "On the Morphology of the Reproductive System of Sertularian Zoophytes, and its Analogy with that of the Flowering Plants") is quite daunting.[25] But Forbes often employs the language not of science but of natural history, as he does in his starfish book. Echinoderms, spiny-skinned marine animals including the starfish and sea urchin, would not seem a very evocative subject. Yet Forbes, although he provides a precise Latinate anatomical description for each type ("thirty-four pinnae on each side of each of the ten bifurcations of the arms"), cannot help but see them as objects of beauty. For him, stony fossilized echinoderms have the power to evoke poignant visions of departed worlds. Forbes' picture is much like Lyell's stunning vision of the sweeping vistas of ancient continents in *The Principles of Geology*. Lyell says of landscape:

> For as, by studying the external configuration of the existing land and its inhabitants, we may restore in imagination the appearance of the ancient continents which have passed away, so we may obtain from the deposits of ancient seas and lakes an insight into the nature of the subaqueous pro-

cesses now in operation, and of the many forms of organic life, which, though now existing, are veiled from sight. . . . Thus, although we are mere sojourners on the surface of the planet, chained to a mere point in space, enduring but for a moment of time, the human mind is not only enabled to number worlds beyond the unassisted ken of mortal eye, but to trace the events of indefinite ages before the creation of our race, and is not even withheld from penetrating into the dark secrets of the ocean, or the interior of the solid globe; free, like the spirit which the poet described as animating the universe. (From the Introduction, 1830)

Lyell makes a remarkable, almost cinematic progression here through space and time. Significantly, his mental journey results from an "insight," a vision greater than that possible for the eyes alone. But his account is couched in terms of seeing, of unveiling hidden sights. Stones and strata incite the imagination to grand visions "beyond the unassisted ken of mortal eye."

Forbes shares Lyell's sense of wonder at nature unveiled. For Forbes, fossilized crinoids, which look rather like many-armed starfishes mounted atop tall stems, appeal both as objects of meditation and of visual pleasure. Like a microscope, the fossils open up to us another world, full of intricate and foreign forms, a world lost in the past, one that can be seen only with one's imaginative eyes:

> For miles and miles we may walk over the stony fragments of the crino-deae; fragments which were once built up in animated forms, encased in living flesh, and obeying the will of creatures among the loveliest of the inhabitants of the ocean. Even in their present disjointed and petrified state, they excite the admiration not only of the naturalist but of the common gazer; and the name of Stone-lily popularly applied to them, indicates a popular appreciation of their beauty. To the philosopher they have long been subjects of contemplation as well as of admiration. In him they raise up a vision of an early world, a world the potentates of which were not men but animals—of seas on whose tranquil surfaces myriads of convoluted Nautili sported, and in whose depths millions of Lily-stars waved wilfully on their slender stems. Now the Lily-stars and the Nautili are almost gone; a few lovely stragglers of those once-abounding tribes remain to evidence the wondrous forms and structures of their comrades. Other beings, not less wonderful, and scarcely less graceful, have replaced them; while the seas in which they flourished have become lands, whereon man in his columned cathedrals and mazy palaces emulates the beauty and symmetry of their fluted stems and chambered shells.[26]

This is the language of natural history. It evinces an aesthetic apprecia-tion of "wondrous forms," "lovely stragglers," "the beauty and symmetry" of architectonic structures (chambers and fluted stems), and it makes a somewhat subjective assumption that the animals themselves experience pleasure (the Nautili "sport," rather than merely swim, and the Lily-stars wave "almost wilfully"). Forbes presents a grand, awed vision of another world whose inhabitants are not only technically complex, but "wonderful"; they create an emotional response in the viewer. And significantly, that viewer is not just the naturalist, but also the "common gazer." Here is beauty that anyone can enjoy. For natural history appeals to human beings as humans, whereas science often appeals only to specialists. Furthermore, by looking at natural objects closely, the common gazer in effect becomes an uncommon gazer. Visual acuity and aesthetic appreciation augment one another.

Forbes' description of the undersea echinoderm garden has much of the same precision and sense of otherworldliness as Tennyson's "Kraken" poem, with its "many a wondrous grot and secret cell/Unnumber'd and enormous polypi" (Forbes' undersea world is more positive, less threatening, than Tennyson's, however). Like the poem, Forbes' prose gives a glimpse into a secret world, a world that excites admiration and awe. *The History of British Starfishes* is a scientific textbook but, like much of Victorian "science," it blends the objective and the subjective. Even the engravings that frame the book's sections reflect this split in emphasis: those that precede sections are technical, anatomical drawings of specimens; while those that conclude sections are more humanistic (people studying books or lolling on a river's bank with specimen-net, romantic castles and ruins, fairies beneath toadstools, mermaids tossing starfish to each other, dramatic sea-cliffs and headlands, a woman reading with seashells on the table beside her, ships sailing off into sunrays streaking the sky).

Using the same term as Philip Gosse—romance—Forbes assures the reader that "in truth the history of the Feather-Star,—for so on account of its plumose appearance I would designate the starfish called by naturalists *Comatula*, —is one of the little romances in which natural history abounds."[27] *Comatula*, a scientific specimen, nevertheless lives in a romance, full of excitement, beauty, and emotion.

Naturalists are chroniclers of nature's romance. Inclined by temperament to take a subjective view of nature, they look for incidents and objects that will also engage a reader. Philip Henry Gosse once described the artistic effect of an Alabama night full of fireflies, saying that it was a scene "of romantic and high gratification."[28] Romantic and high gratification is exactly what the Victorian public hoped for from its natural history books. Victorian natural history discourse works by observing and then recreating scenes, putting a frame around an area of intense attention—so that the singular objects within it will glow like fireflies.

This is how Forbes treats the feathery Plumose *Comatula*. For Forbes, the starfish becomes far more than just a scientific category or an object of detached analysis. The terms and tone in which he describes it, the reverence with which he regards it, the fact that it lives in a romance—all mark his account as natural history. Forbes, Darwin in the *Beagle* account, Bates, and Lewes, all take the naturalist's approach. So do John Burroughs, Philip Henry Gosse, Charles Kingsley, and Hugh Miller (the subjects of later chapters). In this chapter, I have touched on some of the traits that mark their discourse: multiplicity and singularity, awareness of audience, concrete and sensory diction, preoccupation with vision, particularity, and the infusion of personal response into objective facts. The best natural history writers skirt the dangerous shoals of sentimentality, avoiding moralizing that has a palpable design upon the reader. But they also disdain language that is strictly referential, devoid of all design. Why should one write about *Comatula* or the Nautilus, or braving the gloom of the Amazon jungles? The Victorian naturalist has one reason—the thrill of it. The scientist has quite another.

Notes

1. Philip Henry Gosse, *Letters from Alabama, Chiefly Relating to Natural History* (Mountain Brook, AL: Overbrook House, 1983), pp. 79–80.

2. *Studies in Animal Life* (London: Smith, Elder and Co., 1862), p. 9. Further page citations are made within the text.

3. John Leonard Knapp, *Country Rambles in England; or, Journal of a Naturalist* (Buffalo, NY: Phinney and Co., 1853), p. v. Further page citations are made within the text.

4. Lynn Barber, *The Heyday of Natural History: 1820–1870* (Garden City, NY: Doubleday and Company, Inc., 1980). See her passage about the "light reading" potpourri found in Victorian natural history writing, p. 19.

5. Sir Robert S. Ball, ed., *A Manual for Scientific Inquiry; prepared for the use of Officers in her Majesty's Navy, and Travellers in General*, 5th ed. (London: Eyre and Spottiswoode, 1886). From the Memorandum Prefixed to the First Edition, p. iii in the 5th ed.

6. See Marjorie Hope Nicolson, *Mountain Gloom and Mountain Glory: The Development of the Aesthetics of the Infinite* (New York: W. W. Norton and Company, Inc., 1959).

7. Travel books by women became more numerous later in the century, from the 1870s on. My favorite title from among them is *To Lake Tanganyika in a*

Bath-Chair, by Annie Hore, 1886. See Dorothy Middleton, *Victorian Lady Travellers* (Chicago: Academy, 1982).

8. Henry Walter Bates, *The Naturalist on the River Amazons* (London: John Murray, 1864; rpt. Berkeley: Univ. of California Press, 1962), p. 5. Further page citations are made within the text.

9. Gosse, *Letters from Alabama*, p. 37. Further page citations are made within the text.

10. Ball, *Manual of Scientific Inquiry*, p. iii.

11. Catherine Barnes Stevenson, *Victorian Woman Travel Writers in Africa* (Boston: Twayne Publishers, 1982), p. 6.

12. John MacGillivray, F.R.G.S., *Narrative of the Voyage of H.M.S. Rattlesnake*, vol. I (London: T. and W. Boone, 1852), p. 88. Further page citations are made within the text.

13. Charles Darwin, *The Voyage of the Beagle*, intro. H. Graham Cannon (London: Dent/Everyman's Library, 1959), p. 94. For my short section on Darwin, I make use of this readily available edition, which contains Darwin's own additions. The standard edition of his original work is the *Journal of Researches into the Geology and Natural History of the Various Countries visited by H.M.S. Beagle, Under the Command of Captain Fitzroy, R.N., from 1832 to 1836* (London: Henry Colburn, 1839; rpt. New York: Hafner Publishing Company, 1952).

14. P. H. Gosse, *The Romance of Natural History* (New York: A. L. Burt Company, 1902), pp. 37, 41, 76, 169.

15. Gosse, *Letters from Alabama*, p. 134.

16. Stanley Edgar Hyman, *The Tangled Bank: Darwin, Marx, Frazer and Freud as Imaginative Writers* (New York: The Universal Library, Grosset and Dunlap, 1966).

17. James Paradis, "Darwin and Landscape," in *Victorian Science and Victorian Values: Literary Perspectives*, ed. James Paradis and Thomas Postlewait, Annals of the New York Academy of Sciences, vol. 360 (New York: The New York Academy of Sciences, 1981), p. 85. Literary critics also analyze Darwin's ideas; for example, see Walter F. Cannon, "Darwin's Vision in *On the Origin of Species*," and A. Dwight Culler, "The Darwinian Revolution and Literary Form," both in *The Art of Victorian Prose*, ed. George Levine and William Madden (New York: Oxford Univ. Press, 1968).

18. Gosse, *Letters from Alabama*, p. 294.

19. Carol T. Christ, *The Finer Optic: The Aesthetic of Particularity in Victorian Poetry* (New Haven: Yale Univ. Press, 1975), p. 14.

20. Christ, pp. 17–18.

21. Arabella B. Buckley, *Life and Her Children: Glimpses of Animal Life from the Amoeba to the Insects* (1880; rpt. London: Macmillan & Co. Ltd., 1957), p. 58.

22. Barber, pp. 18–19.

23. Charlotte M. Yonge, *The Herb of the Field* (London: Macmillan and Co., 1887), p. 44. Further page citations are made within the text.

24. Jules Michelet, *The Bird*, trans. W. H. Davenport Adams (Great Britain: Thomas Nelson and Sons, 1879; rpt. London: Wildwood House Limited, 1981), p. 157. Further page citations are made within the text.

25. For a study of Forbes' contributions to science and for an extensive bibliography, see Philip F. Rehbock, *The Philosophical Naturalists: Themes in Early Nineteenth-Century British Biology* (Madison: The Univ. of Wisconsin Press, 1983).

26. Edward Forbes, *A History of British Starfishes, and Other Animals of the Class Echinodermata* (London: John Van Voorst, 1841), p. 2.

27. Forbes, p. 6.

28. Gosse, *Letters from Alabama*, p. 29.

4

The Scientific Context and
the Two Cultures

During the last season I collected very largely, and put up and sent
away to various correspondents in Europe and America about 5000
specimens of about 600 species, reserving still for my own Herbarium
an abundant supply. This season I have not been less industrious . . .
C. W. SHORT, Letter of 1834

Permit me to advise you again not to load yourself with huge turtles,
fragments of the same, and fragments of the bones of the extremities of
animals, as they are comparatively worthless. Of mammals confine
your collections to skulls, teeth and fragments of the same, and only
under peculiar circumstances preserve other bones. Of reptiles all
vertebrate and articular fragments are of value, and of fishes the whole
body.[1]   JOSEPH LEIDY, Letter of 1859

During the nineteenth century, the study of the natural world came to
resemble the science of today. Victorian science saw the development of
specialized disciplines, pursued by paid professionals who were of necessity
minutely educated in their fields. Natural history, centuries old, fought
against the current. Adamantly it remained encyclopedic and amateur,
something that ordinary people could enjoy. Many of its salient qualities—
collecting, a subjective approach, classification, description—were spurned
by the sciences that supplanted it: geology and, especially, biology. But
natural history drew from these newer sciences, too, especially in its emphasis on the use of optical tools, and in its search for new species. It borrowed
large ideas as well, for instance, using the new concept of "Life"—that all
living things share the same processes and drives—to justify the detailed
examination of every creature, no matter how small. Like biology, natural
history thrived in the nineteenth-century intellectual climate that exalted
the scientific approach to the world and its exploration. Driven to under-

stand nature, science proceeded first by sampling, measuring, and dissecting it, unearthing in the process countless natural facts. Less dedicated to schema, natural history nonetheless shared with science the relentless quest for particularized pieces of information about the natural world. But once they were collected, science and natural history made different use of natural facts. Science strung them into theories. With its more aesthetic aims, natural history transmuted them into literary texts. Their differing attitudes placed them on opposite sides of a debate that has come to be called the Two Cultures. For all these reasons, Victorian natural history— as phenomenon and discourse—stands out more sharply when viewed in the context of science.

Historians of science often take pains to differentiate natural history from biology. Natural history is of course the older endeavor, a term used for centuries to describe the study of nature. From Pliny's *Natural History* in the first century A.D. to Comte Georges-Louis Buffon's massive *Histoire Naturelle, Générale et Particulière* (44 volumes), which began its publication in France in 1749, works of natural history abounded. Their subject, after all, was huge: everything on earth and in the heavens. The 1797 edition of the *Encyclopedia Britannica* began its article on natural history with a blunt definition of its scope: "Natural history, in its most extensive signification, denotes a knowledge and description of the whole universe." It dealt with "matters of fact respecting the heavens, meteors, the atmosphere, the earth, . . . all the phenomena, indeed, which occur in the world, and even . . . the external parts and actions of man himself."[2] The naturalist studied the "Terraqueous Globe in general, and its changes," as well as the "Fossil Kingdom" and Animal, Vegetable, and Mineral Kingdoms. Consequently, natural history had a "prodigious extent; so extensive is it, indeed, that the longest life is far from being sufficient to enable us to acquire a perfect knowledge of it" (p. 660).

At first merely enumerative, or a foundation for larger speculations on "the nature of things," natural history became by the eighteenth century a taxonomic enterprise. In France in this period particularly, natural history became nearly synonymous with classification. Following the lead of Linnaeus, the classification of organisms became a highly technical endeavor, one that increasingly depended on the close study of plant and animal anatomy and physiology. Many of the great naturalists of the eighteenth century, particularly those in France—for example, Jean Baptiste de Lamarck (1744–1829), Baron Georges Cuvier (1769–1832), and Buffon (1707–1788), the keeper of the Jardin du Roi in Paris—called their work "natural history," but had very different aims from those of the Victorian naturalists. The great French naturalists were concerned with plant or animal forms, their systematic relationships and development—in short, taxonomy. Thus Buffon's *Histoire Naturelle* is overwhelmingly concerned with finding the slight gradations between natural forms, so that they may be placed correctly in a universal system.

Gradually such specialized concerns split from the less systematic, more genially descriptive, old-fashioned natural history and were given a new name—biology. That term was first used in 1800 in "an obscure German medical publication" and was first popularized by the German Gottfried Treviranus and the Frenchman Lamarck.[3] Treviranus and Lamarck both defined biology as the science dealing with the structure, organization, processes, and movements of organisms. Neither included "traditional natural history" in the new field; that is, they excluded "general descriptive activity" whose practitioners had been called and would continue to be called naturalists.[4] In addition to systematics, biology would study respiration, gestation, digestion, embryonic development, growth, and movement: the "vital processes"[5] of animals and plants. These had not been concentrated on before, except, in the field of medicine, as they applied to humans.

The *Britannica* article of 1797 had hinted at the division that was to come between natural history and biology. While admitting that natural history's purview encompassed the whole universe, the article drew a distinction between natural effects—or visible manifestations—and causes. Effects, such as the "substances of which . . . the earth is composed," and the "organized bodies, whether vegetable or mineral which adorn its surface, which rise into the air, or live in the bottom of the waters," fell under the aegis of natural history. But the causes of these phenomena, and the "powers and properties of natural bodies, and their mutual actions on one another" (p. 670), these were the business of natural philosophy. Natural history studied appearances; natural philosophy investigated relationships. By comparing one appearance, one form to another, natural history excelled at description and classification of forms into groups. But natural philosophy sought to understand actions between forms. As applied to living organisms, the natural philosophy of the eighteenth century became the biology of the nineteenth. Biology studied actions, causes—the internal workings of life.

At the turn of the nineteenth century, these distinctions had not yet solidified. A naturalist could continue to investigate all the outward manifestations of the natural world, feeling no need to compartmentalize. One of the biggest appeals of late eighteenth-century and early nineteenth-century natural history was its breadth. Like the author of the *Britannica* article, Buffon effused about the scope of his subject: "Natural history

embraces all the objects the universe presents to us. This prodigious multitude of quadrupeds, birds, fish, insects, plants, minerals, etc., offers to the
curiosity of the human mind a vast spectacle, of which the whole is so great
that the details are inexhaustible."[6] The words he chooses are characteristic
of natural history: "curiosity," "prodigious multitude," "vast spectacle,"
"inexhaustible" details. Buffonian taxonomy contributed to the maturation
of biology; Buffonian breadth greatly influenced Victorian naturalists. In
attempting to embrace the "prodigious multitude" of life, natural history
was audacious, optimistic, unlimited—and powerfully attractive.

In 1800, science had not yet fragmented into various carefully delineated
specialties. In fact, students of the natural world resisted compartmentali-
zation, so that "many scientists of that time still had active professional
interests in two or more scientific fields, if not tendencies towards encyclopedic coverage of all sciences."[7] An encyclopedic, all-encompassing knowledge of nature still seemed possible. Perhaps influenced by the great
eighteenth-century interest in encyclopedias (Diderot's, of course, and the
Encyclopedia Britannica, which began in 1771, among others), a passion
that continued throughout the nineteenth century, scientists cherished the
goal of writing the essay in their field for one Cyclopedia or another, as
John Herschel, the astronomer, did for *Encyclopedia Britannica* or, for
that matter, as Carlyle did for the *Edinburgh Encyclopedia*. Even in the
1830s, science remained a broad pursuit, quite open to the amateur.

But science was changing. During the Victorian period, two developments irrevocably altered its character: professionalization and the growth
of specialized disciplines, such as physiology, embryology, and biochemistry, to replace the older natural history and even general biology. The old
dream of encyclopedic understanding faded in the glare of the world's ever-
increasing complexity. Many developments during the century point to the
growing seriousness of the practice of science.

In 1831, for example, the British Association for the Advancement of
Science (BAAS) was founded. It sponsored meetings, demonstrations, and
the presentation of papers on topics ranging from botany to chemistry,
optics to magnetism, and it wasn't long before membership in BAAS
became a prerequisite to scientific stature. As research in physics, chemistry, and physiology became more complex and expensive, and thus depen-
dent on laboratories, few hobbyists could afford to continue serious study.[8]
At Cambridge, members of the so-called Cambridge Network—including
John Herschel, William Babbage, George Peacock, George Airy, Adam
Sedgwick, and William Whewell—lobbied to establish the formal study of
science at the university.[9] (This reform stirred great debate, opposed by
those who favored classical and humanistic studies, and was not fully

achieved until quite late in the century.) Champions of science like T. H. Huxley pleaded both for increased professional status for scientists and for improved education in the sciences.[10] Elucidation of vital processes requires microscopic study, experimentation, chemical investigations, and quantitative measurements, which more and more in the nineteenth century became the province of experts. But while science specialized, gradually excluding the amateur, natural history remained broad. Because people from various backgrounds and social classes could practice it without special training or expensive equipment, "natural history . . . was the most widely pursued scientific activity in nineteenth-century America,"[11] and the same can be said of Britain.

In the early part of the nineteenth century, before the triumph of scientific specialization, natural history "still theoretically meant the study of the three kingdoms of Nature, animal, vegetable, and mineral."[12] Up until approximately 1860, a naturalist could think of himself as a sort of neo-Renaissance Man, knowledgeable and observant about all facets of nature. After that time, the sheer accumulation of known facts about nature became so overwhelming that the naturalist could no longer, to borrow Matthew Arnold's words, "see it whole." Nature then had to be apportioned, parceled out to specialists for understanding. The whole crazy-quilt of nature had never, of course, been comprehensible to a single observer, but that fond delusion had given the study of nature much of its power. In addition to hoping for intellectual cohesion, naturalists believed in their ability to juxtapose disparate details and make some sort of sense out of them, to take some pleasure in them, even if that sense or pleasure was primarily aesthetic. Natural history was aesthetic science, science pursued out of a personal sense of awe and beauty. During the nineteenth century, as newly minted sciences like physiology shone, natural history endured—a bit dusty, a bit antiquated, perhaps, but still tantalizing and wondrous to its adherents: the old curiosity shop of science.

Interest in natural history first deepened in the seventeenth century when, according to one historian, it became a "social activity"[13] and when cabinets of natural curios became the proud possessions of aristocrats. During the next century, natural history as a pastime gradually began to filter down from the aristocratic class and gentry to the common people. "Botanizing" became the popular genteel pursuit of cultured young ladies, given impetus by certain crucial inventions: the "vascula" or botanical specimen-collecting tin (1704) and the butterfly net (1711).[14] Nature books, written then for the first time in the vernacular, rather than Latin, began to sell widely.[15] And eventually, scientific jargon would become, as it were, a new form of Latin: a mysterious language known only to an educated few, which serves to exclude laypeople from the secrets of the scientific sect. Whether written in Latin or jargon, scientific prose speaks to the few. But from the eighteenth century to the present day, the language of natural history has been triumphantly vernacular: it speaks to the many. In a sense, then, natural history books fill a niche first created by the demise of scholarly Latin and later vacated by science in its rise to intellectual rigor.

By about 1750, natural history had already become "highly fashionable,"[16] with clubs and societies forming to bring enthusiasts together. Thomas Bewick was among the visual artists whose careful depiction of natural subjects helped fan the enthusiasm. Sumptuous volumes of color plates, particularly of plants or insects, graced the homes of wealthy aristocrats. By 1763 the fashion had spread among all the classes, inspiring the *Critical Review* to remark that "Natural History is now, by a kind of national establishment, become the favorite study of the time."[17] By the turn of the nineteenth century, the taste for natural history was well established, and in about 1820, according to Lynn Barber, the field practically exploded. Fads for one type of collecting or another had existed before, for example, the Great Shell Craze of the 1720s and 1740s in France, which produced a corresponding fashion for *rocaille*, or shell motifs, in fabrics and decoration.[18] But now they swept through England in successive waves: bugs, then mosses, then madrepores (corals), seaweeds, ferns, sea-anemones, sea-serpents, and Infusoria (protozoans), not to mention local fixations such as the "limpet fever" in Ireland in the 1820s.[19] After du Chaillu documented them in 1861, gorillas, though eminently uncollectible, were all the rage.

While the natural history of the preceding century had centered on the Continent (with some English contributors such as Thomas Pennant and, somewhat earlier, John Ray), the popular pastimes of botanizing and geologizing in vogue in the nineteenth century were very much English phenomena. There were parallels in the United States, but England was really the "mecca" for naturalists (as illustrated by the fact that, when Audubon published his *Birds of America* from 1826 to 1838, it was published in Great Britain, and ninety percent of its subscribers were British).[20]

Gradually throughout the nineteenth century a split developed and widened between two types of naturalists—those who collected and studied specimens outdoors, and those who were content to study specimens more carefully in the museum, as part of a comparative assemblage. These two groups were known as "field" and "closet" naturalists,[21] and serious differences of opinion arose between them as to which group had a more genuine understanding of nature. In England, the field naturalists as a type descended from the observant country pastor, Gilbert White. Field naturalists watched living organisms in their environment, precursors of the science that today goes by the name of ecology, often referred to in the nineteenth century as the "economy of nature."[22] Closet naturalists, on the other hand, tended to be comparative anatomists. The most dramatic among them were adept in identifying bones, especially fossil bones of dinosaurs and Megatheria (giant sloths)—those enormous creatures that created a sensation when their models were erected at the Crystal Palace gardens in 1853 under the direction of Richard Owen, the most famous Victorian anatomist of all.

The closet-field division is an important feature of nineteenth-century natural history. From a literary standpoint, however, this division is even more interesting, for it represents one expression of a major dialectic within nineteenth-century nature writing. What is important is not so much whether a given writer is a field or a closet observer, but the fact that a tension always exists between the broad view—natural ecology, the landscape as a whole, objects within their setting—and the narrow view—anatomical details, microscopic focus, the object as isolated. This dialectic figures importantly in various, seemingly unrelated, realms of nineteenth-century expression: Romantic poetry; Victorian poetry; Victorian painting, sketching, and photography; and natural history writing. The macroscopic-microscopic tension in natural history, previously unremarked on, influenced all the others. The dialectic of particularity and panorama infuses the practice of nineteenth-century popular microscopy (see Chapter 5), the art criticism of John Ruskin (see Chapter 6), and both natural history art and Victorian art in general (see Chapter 7). The debate between closet and field naturalists is, in fact, a very typical expression of a fundamental Victorian uncertainty about how best to confront nature: with a broad view? Or a narrow?

As a means of exploring and investigating the natural world, natural history was to some extent scientific. Its time-honored methodology could not have been more direct: take samples of natural objects, then describe them. As the accumulated mass of such descriptions grew, so did the impetus to interpret them, to understand the relationships between isolated phenomena. Of the developing scientific specialties in the nineteenth century, biology and geology matched the natural history method most closely, while chemistry, physics, and mathematics moved farthest away. Of the sciences, biology and geology are the most concrete. They theorize and generalize, but the objects of their attention are just that—tangible objects. Birds and flowers, minerals and rock outcroppings are far more "real" and have more palpable existence as objects than do chemical reactions, solutes, precipitates, heat, pressure, magnetism, or motion—the realm of chemistry and physics. Of course, during the nineteenth century some biological specialties, such as cell biology, did gradually relinquish the surface study of objects, substituting investigation of abstract processes and internal workings. But cells inhabit larger organisms, and so understanding them ultimately contributes to a fascination with the living objects themselves.

Because they all depend on natural objects to one degree or another, biology, geology, and natural history are most closely allied. Also, geology and biology tend to be evocative; certainly the Victorians found them so. And natural history, in its less scientific moods, cherishes evocation, the poetic effect that natural objects may have upon the meditative mind. Aldous Huxley has pinpointed biology, first cousin to natural history, as the science closest to ordinary human concerns:

> Biology, it is obvious, is more immediately relevant to human experience than are the exacter sciences of physics and chemistry. Hence, for all writers, its special importance. The sciences of life can confirm the intuitions of the artist, can deepen his insights and extend the range of his vision.[23]

Natural history, like biology, contemplates living forms, understandably of great interest to human beings, living forms themselves. Living (or once-living) objects, as fossils, also attract the geologist's attention. Significantly, the geological component of natural history most often takes the form of paleontology. Why? Because fossils have more evocative power than inorganic minerals; minerals have heft and color and shape, but fossils hint of lives lost and mysterious. Still both, as objects, have their fascinations.

Evocative objects: these were what the naturalist sought. One major reason for the Victorian and continuing popularity of natural history is the fact that it centers on collecting, the acquisition of natural objects that in themselves are colorful, intricate in form, pleasing to the eye, and gratifying to the touch. Such specimens were first collected for their own sakes, often arranged in intriguing juxtapositions in display cabinets (see Chapter 5). And much of the writing done in natural history consisted of describing the visual externals of these objects, whether bird skins, beetles, fossilized shells, or minerals. The ambitious natural historian might proceed from such description to the classification of items by type, paying particular attention to the naming of species, as determined by comparison of minute features between one specimen and the next. Fortunately, acquisition and description could still contribute to science, as well as to literature.

While much of biology, for example, became interpretive, theoretical, concerned with formulating laws to explain animal forms, growth, and life processes, some—the types that today would be called environmental biology or ecology—could still advance by simply collecting and comparing specimens. The distinction between the two strands of biology can be seen in modern university departments, where the two sometimes are split: environmental, organismic, botanical, and zoological biology (macroscopic) on the one hand; cellular, developmental, and molecular biology (microscopic) on the other. Biology in general was reluctant to give up the older, natural history elements of acquisition, because natural specimens themselves usually pleased the eye or hand. For, as David Elliston Allen remarks, "the very act of observing natural objects involves a strong aesthetic element which interpenetrates the scientific. It is this dual character, surely, which accounts for much of the subject's special fascination."[24]

Rooted in collecting, natural history advances knowledge in a manner fundamentally different from that of the "hard" physical sciences (mathematics, chemistry, and physics). Stephen Toulmin explains the difference in this way:

> Natural historians . . . look for regularities of given forms; but physicists seek the form of given regularities. In natural history, accordingly, the sheer accumulation of observations can have a value which in physics it could never have. This is one of the things which the sophisticated scientist holds against natural history: it is "mere bug-hunting"—a matter of collection, rather than insight.[25]

Such prejudice on the part of "sophisticated" scientists overlooks two crucial points. First, the methodology of natural history can achieve significant results, even though different from what physicists do. This was particularly true in the nineteenth century. P. H. Gosse, for instance, although not an "insightful" scientific theorist, by sheer accumulation of detail did considerably advance the science of marine biology. Second, naturalists, especially Victorian naturalists, may not even be wholly interested in pure science. The quarry they seek is as much subjective as objective. In the case of Gosse, his contributions to natural history literature and art far exceeded his scientific discoveries. His communicated delight in natural objects left a more lasting impression than his theories.

Acquisition or insight—this dichotomy of scientific methods developed during the nineteenth century. Like biology, geology was unsure which method to use, and unwilling to abandon the former for the latter. Impelled by a passion for hand specimens, empiricist British geologists often practiced a geology based mainly on collecting rather than on theorizing. Such, at any rate, was the criticism that the great German chemist Justus Leibig voiced in a letter of 1866 to Michael Faraday. About British geologists, Leibig complained: "in most of them, even the greatest, I found only an empiric knowledge of stones and rocks, of some petrifaction and a few plants, but no science. Without a thorough knowledge of physics and chemistry, even without mineralogy, a man may be a great geologist in England."[26] Leibig's comment is to some extent unfair; of course British geologists such as Hutton, Lyell, Sedgwick, De la Beche, and Murchison participated in major theoretical debates of the period about how mountains were formed (orogeny), how much time had elapsed in the geological past, how strata were related, whether catastrophism could best explain landforms, and how to account for volcanic heat.[27] Nevertheless, Leibig's remark does indicate the extent to which hands-on experience mattered in Britain. British science was highly empirical, buttressed by the English philosophical tradition of empiricism with its long string of proponents, including Bacon, Hobbes, Locke, Hume, and Mill. Isaac Newton fits into this tradition as well, as do the philosophers of science, Herschel and Whewell.[28] British politicians and educators worried a great deal about the superior science (and technology) of Leibig's Germany during the nineteenth century, but if British "empiric" geology, based on collecting, ranked as inferior science, it excelled as natural history.

Fossils, rocks, and minerals lend themselves especially well to amateur natural historians with a collecting bent. Heavy but portable, they can be easily trimmed to size for the cabinet with the help of a geologist's hammer, which had been invented before the eighteenth century.[29] As a science heavily grounded in collecting, geology made great strides in the nineteenth century. In the United States, paleontological collectors like Leidy, Marsh, and Cope unearthed fossil treasures from the arid formations of the West, including gigantic bones of those improbable creatures, the dinosaurs. Great Britain could not of course compete with America's geographical vastness, but in spite of its size, it happens to be geologically complex. As a result, field geology and paleontological collecting flourished also in Victorian Britain, particularly after railroad cuts and canal-building exposed formations that had few natural outcroppings.

A charming little book of popular geology, published in 1840, provides evidence for the popularity of both geological and botanical collecting. Couched in the congenial form of imaginary dialogues on geological topics, Granville Penn's *Conversations on Geology* opens with a discussion between "Mrs. R." and her children, Christina and Edward. Christina already enjoys botany, which she calls a "beautiful science," because "it invites us to the fields in the beautiful months of spring and summer, and makes us admire the beauty of the budding trees, the springing grass, and the opening blossoms: it enhances the pleasure of every walk."[30] Edward is just as eager to learn about geology; to begin his study, Mrs. R. proposes that he acquire "some knowledge of minerals."[31] Accordingly, she announces that she will find for him a cabinet of specimens:

> *Mrs. R.*: I shall, therefore, try to procure for you a little cabinet of the more important of these, and we shall begin our first lesson by examining a few of them.
>
> *Christina*: When will you get the cabinet, mother? I long to see it.
>
> *Mrs. R.*: Probably to-morrow; and, in the meantime, as the day is fine, we shall go a botanizing; so get your boxes in readiness.

Collecting specimens for natural history cabinets (see Chapter 5) was not necessarily a lonely or arduous vocation. On the contrary, the popularity of natural history often made its pursuit a most sociable endeavor. Meetings of natural history or science clubs frequently exhibited a light tone, with the emphasis on facts, true, but the attitude toward them far from ponderous. David Allen cites an agenda for one such meeting of the Oswestry and Welshpool Naturalist's Field Club & Archaeological Society. The gathering in December 1864 interspersed brief, fifteen-minute papers on such subjects as "A Quarter of an Hour in Old Oswestry Gravel Pit" with musical offerings ranging from violin and piano pieces to vocals by the Glee Club.[32] Nothing too intellectually strenuous here. Most of the papers presented had yet another entertaining advantage: copious illustrations.

A fine example of the convivial attractions of natural history is provided by Mrs. Hugh Miller, wife of the popular geologist. In dedicating her husband's last, posthumously published book to a Reverend Symonds, Lydia Miller praises the natural history club that he has fostered:

> The Malvern Club devotes stated periods—monthly, I think,—to rambles over twenty or thirty miles of country, when the naturalists of whom it is composed,—botanists, geologists, etc—carry on the researches of their various departments separately, or in little groups of two or three, as they may desire. They all dine afterwards together at an inn, or farm-house, as the case may be, where they relate the adventures of the day, discuss their favorite topics, and compare their newly-found treasures. As a consequence of this, the Malvern Museum is a perfect model of what a museum ought to be.[33]

The happy club members collect treasures for an educational museum and share their enthusiasm, as Lydia Miller puts it, in a "harmless" form of "recreation" that is fortuitously "invigorating to body and mind," as well as "beneficial in [its] results to science." In scouring the countryside for specimens, a good time is had by all—always safely within the Victorian limits of healthful, useful morality. Natural theology made even specimen collecting a pious pursuit.

Of all the treasures that an amateur naturalist might collect, none exceeded the value of a creature new to science. Discovering a new species gave pleasure twofold: one had the specimen, as always, but in addition one had the palpable proof of nature's variety. And—no small matter this—one might call the new creature by one's own mellifluous name. In England, from the turn of the nineteenth century to about 1850, quite a mania developed for naming new species. The Linnaean approach to plant classification especially spurred a zeal for nomenclature. Popular interest in the Swedish scientist was boosted by the British acquisition in 1784 of Linnaeus' own massive and precisely catalogued collection of natural objects and the subsequent founding of the Linnaean Society of London in 1788.[34] Linnaeus revolutionized botany, particularly as far as amateurs were concerned. In contrast to the abstruse systems used before, Linnaeus' system for classifying plants "simply involved counting first the male parts of the flower, the stamens, then the female parts, the carpels or stigma."[35] This accomplished, all that remained was to consult a reference work where the "numbers fitted the plant into a vegetable filing system." Although long since abandoned by botanists (binomial nomenclature, of course, remains), this method was neat, mechanical, and easy to understand. Applying it, even an amateur could have the satisfying sense of imposing order onto nature by labeling. The urge to attach labels to organisms increased even more when people realized how many humble British forms remained quite innocent of scientific names.

Attaching a species label seemed satisfyingly permanent. Once pinned down, a species was fixed forever, as stable as quartz. In thinking this, Victorian amateur naturalists clung to the traditional definition of a species. As the century advanced, the definition would change radically, as far as biologists were concerned, but naturalists would continue to prefer the older, more static idea. What constitutes a species? Today biologists see species as changeable, overlapping, fluid groups; one may shade into another, both over distance and over time. But before Darwin, species were seen as invariable, fixed units, much more capable of being pigeonholed. Paralleling this shift, the purpose of taxonomy and classification has changed. Victorian biologists were moving toward the modern definition of classification, which is "to give meaning by association."[36] In other words, knowing a species' name helps one understand its relationship to other similar organisms. To amateur Victorian naturalists, however, naming species fixed and individuated them. Such naturalists were relatively uninterested in associated information about the animal and its genus. What mattered was that the animal (or plant) had been named and thus made distinct from other specimens.

Clues to such distinctions, minute details that separated one form from the next assumed inordinate importance. A microscope was often requisite in the search; in fact, its role in discerning species-markers (in ferns, for example) was one reason for the instrument's popularity. Barber says this of the species-naming obsession:

> The facts that naturalists were most concerned with were those bearing on the description and classification of species. Finding new species was the highest goal to which they aspired; squabbling about names and priority was an occupational disease; describing, arranging and collecting ever more and more species was the business to which they devoted every minute of their working lives.[37]

When the push for species identification had succeeded in covering most British species, explorers sallied forth to other continents where fresh species awaited detection.

The entomologist Henry Walter Bates, in his account of *The Naturalist on the River Amazons*, vividly communicated his awe at the plethora of species to be found abroad in exotic locales. While traveling in Brazil for ten years (during which time he collected his incredible 14,712 species of animals), Bates discovered what a wealth of species inhabited the jungles:

> The neighborhood of Para is rich in insects. I do not speak of the number of individuals, which is probably less than one meets with, excepting ants and Termites, in summer days in temperate latitudes; but the variety, or in other words, the number of species is very great. It will convey some idea of the diversity of butterflies when I mention that about 700 species of that tribe are found within an hour's walk of the town; whilst the total number found within the British Islands does not exceed 66, and the whole of Europe supports only 321.[38]

Habitats far beyond the limited horizon of the British Isles teemed with novel species. These the traveling naturalist happily disclosed, pinning them down with names, as sharp as the pins that fixed them in boxes.

The scramble to identify new species had another motivation: self-aggrandizement. The appellation given a species would, with luck, stand as a monument to its discoverer. So many amateur naturalists hoped for eponymous fame that Charles Kingsley felt compelled to lecture his readers in *Glaucus* about the moral dangers of such pride. But if the dogged search for unnamed forms was selfish in Kingsley's sense, it was self-satisfying in a good way as well. Naturalists had a passion for the new—that is, a deep sense of astonishment at the variety and sheer number of nature's forms. By the nineteenth century, the taste for the peculiar or bizarre forms of nature coincided more and more with a demand for truth.

Weird animals have always been popular; even today hope persists for Bigfoot or the Loch Ness Monster. Victorian England had its share of zoological fakes salted into museum collections and sideshows. The naturalist Charles Waterton enjoyed foisting fakes on the gullible public, fakes such as the head of his "Nondescript." Even Philip Gosse argued earnestly for sea monsters as part of the old-fashioned Romance of natural history. But unlike the medieval yen for mythical and fabulous beasts—griffins and unicorns—the Victorian preference was for verifiable oddities. Delightful indeed if a baroque beast existed in fancy (Lewis Carroll's, perhaps, or Edward Lear's), but how much more wonderful if an intricate, improbable creature actually could be set swimming in an aquarium. An empirical age had no difficulty in reconciling true, objective facts with "wonder" and "curiosity"—two words that set the tone for Victorian natural history. A new species could not help but be amazing. Never seen before, it sprang into consciousness as if from some wild imagination. But it was real.

While borrowing the taxonomic category of "species" from biology, natural history also borrowed a related idea, one that also served superbly as a motivation for naturalists intending to collect. This was the concept of "Life." Life as an animating principle that all animals and plants have in common. Life as a characteristic of all cells. Protoplasm. Today this idea is a commonplace. No one thinks to doubt it; DNA is a great equalizer. Before the nineteenth century, however, prevailing schemes such as the Great Chain of Being and typological speciation emphasized distinctions between organisms, not connections. Some animals might resemble each other, but they were still separate types, with no overlap. Certainly human beings stood apart. Developments in cellular biology broke down the barriers by showing the fundamental similarities in the infinitesimal units making up all creatures. Also, of course, the evolutionary notion of "descent with modification" unmistakably implied connections. As a result, "this period saw the development of 'life' as an abstract concept, spawning considerable interest in the properties common to all living things."[39] Not only that—it suddenly lent glamour to living things hardly glanced at before. For if all organisms were related, then, many writers felt, we were all in this together. A look at pond scum became in a sense a social call on a distant branch of the family. (One in reduced circumstances, perhaps.)

The intellectual excitement of this new notion, Life, infuses Huxley's essay "On the Physical Basis of Life." It was also the jumping-off point for many natural history books. Perhaps because they seemed analogous to the watery protoplasm of the cell, watery habitats especially inspired naturalists to rhapsodies about Life. Frank Buckland, for instance, wrote an essay called "A Hunt in a Horse-Pond," in which he found inspiration in the murk: "Pray what is there to be found in a horse-pond except mud, dead dogs and cats, and duck-weed? the reader may ask. . . . The answer to such questions is, simply, 'Life'; Life in all diversity of form, beautifully and wonderfully arranged, each individual deriving benefit from the well-being of the mass."[40] The ubiquity of Life, its stubbornness, its tenacity in the midst of unsavory surroundings makes it all the more admirable, worth a closer look: "Well, let us have a look at the pond-world." Worlds within worlds: a common theme among the chroniclers of Life. George Henry Lewes, in his *Studies in Animal Life*, found "Life everywhere!"[41] but especially in ponds. He chided his readers for ignoring most animals, saying that "they are not alien, but akin." Like many naturalists, Lewes followed the trail of Life to its source in microscopic cells, amazed that "deep as the microscope can penetrate, it detects Life within Life, generation within generation, as if the very Universe itself were not vast enough for the energies of Life" (p. 27). If peering at cells meant that one gazed upon Life itself, who could resist the impulse to look into the microscope? Lewes explains that the Life of man "forms but one grand illustration of Biology—the science of Life. He forms but the apex of the animal world" (p. 2). And in a footnote Lewes explains that the "needful term Biology" is "now becoming generally adopted in England, as in Germany."

Arabella Buckley seizes upon Life as a familial metaphor. To Buckley, Life is not just an abstract concept, but the great Mother of all. All living things are her children. Befitting a Victorian naturalist, Buckley in her book *Life and Her Children* chooses as her first two words: "I wonder." She wonders "whether it ever occurs to most people to consider how brimful our world is of life?" Addressed to children, the charming prose in Buckley's book surveys the seven divisions of the animal world. (Plants, too, are children of Life, but regretfully Buckley must exclude them from this volume.) Buckley spends more than half her book on marine animals; the rest on insects. She divulges a great deal of technical information, all the while delighting in curious details, features of beauty and wonder. All the facts in her book, however, are marshaled in the service of Life:

> And now, since we live in the world with all these numerous companions, which lead, many of them, such curious lives, trying like ourselves to make the best of their short time here, is it not worth while to learn something about them? May we not gain some useful hints by watching their contrivances, sympathizing with their difficulties, and studying their history? And above all, shall we not have something more to love and care for when we have made acquaintance with some of Life's other children besides ourselves?[42]

Sharing kinship with Life gives the naturalist more than purely intellectual motivations for studying other creatures. Naturalists usually do admit emotion into their prose, but by overtly stressing sympathy, love, and care, Buckley goes further than most.

Inasmuch as Victorian naturalists so often glorify sight, it is not surprising that Buckland, Lewes, and Buckley do, too. But in the case of Lewes and Buckley it is interesting how the concept of Life provokes an identical image from each of them. In the scheme of Life, Lewes says, "we are all 'parts of one transcendent whole.' The scales fall from our eyes when we think of this" (p. 3). And Buckley says that, in search of the mysteries of Life, "let us, . . . rubbing the scales from off our eyes, peer into the hidden secrets of nature" (p. 14).

While natural history borrowed ideas from biology, biology in turn retained a tinge of natural history. For one thing, both are very visual. Philip C. Ritterbush, in his study of *The Art of Organic Forms*, points to the "prominence of visual and esthetic factors in biology."[43] Biological representations of organisms, whether whole or in part, macroscopic or microscopic, are usually visual—delineating shapes, outlines, organs, appendages. Illustration here serves as a crucial adjunct to understanding. In fact, Ritterbush discusses the close correspondence between nineteenth-century advances in embryology and cytology and the sketches made by biologists of cellular structures. Visual representation, with an eye to symmetry and beautiful forms, characterizes biological understanding; art and science here conjoin.

One noteworthy example of an artistic biologist is Ernst Haeckel (1834–1919), the notorious German promoter of social Darwinism. His *Kunstformen der Natur* (*Art Forms in Nature*) contains a famous display of the intricacies of natural objects, particularly the minute forms, such as Foraminifera and Radiolaria, with their elaborate whorls and spires.[44]

With his artistic outlook, Haeckel typified the biology of his day. Ritterbush quotes a microbiologist who experienced firsthand the "visual character of the genius" of nineteenth-century German biology:

> When I mention Bütschli's draftsmanship it comes to my mind how many of the old zoologists had this gift. I have already discussed Haeckel; I could add Carl Chun, the great marine zoologist, who adorned his house with frescoes; Boveri, who did oil paintings of merit; Doflein, the proto-zoologist, who was good at water colors; and many others. This ability can be understood as part of the sense of form which makes a good naturalist and morphologist, and even today, when scientific illustration has become less important, many examples of the gift of draftsmanship will be found among zoologists.[45]

Artistic talent among biologists was not limited to Germany. One thinks immediately of the Swiss-American Louis Agassiz (1807–1873), whose blackboard chalk sketches of animals were the highlight of his popular lectures. In a well-known photograph, Agassiz poses by the blackboard, a boldly sketched sea urchin behind him. He gained fame also for insisting on students' meticulous sketching of specimens: only through visual examination and rendition of details could students really know what form a fish, for example, had. Seeing and sketching formed the core of both his epistemology and his pedagogy.

Zoology students still practice their sketching as the best way to learn morphology: how else can one know what the parts of amphioxus or hydra look like, or how they fit together? Biology and natural history share the visual approach to nature. Like Haeckel and Agassiz, Victorian naturalists often painted or sketched, with Philip Henry Gosse a preeminent example. I explore the close connections between natural history and painting in Chapter 7. But it is important to recognize that biological illustration and natural history illustration do have different aims. Both produce a visual description (often to the complete exclusion of the other senses—What does a turtle smell like?); both may have an aesthetic effect. But biological depictions serve a didactic purpose. They generalize; they link forms to functions, development, and processes. Natural history depictions, as a rule, do not. They are aids not to understanding, but to appreciation. For them, beauty, or the display of intricate forms, is enough.

Species names, the idea of Life, and visual representations—these common concerns united Victorian natural history and biology. Collecting united natural history and geology. But the one thing that most tightly bound natural history to science was facts. For both, facts were the quarry, the treasure to be unearthed, the capital to be stored and hoarded. With this motivation, both science and natural history mirrored the materialistic spirit of the Victorian Age and, indeed, contributed to it as well. Science in general succeeded in gradually shifting attention from the human to natural objects, elevating the object, the fact, to new heights.

Patricia M. Ball, in her study of three writers who span the nineteenth century, from the Romantic period to the late Victorian, explains how science greatly augmented the Victorian preoccupation with objective reality and facts. In her view, the widespread dissemination of the idea of natural theology had the effect of diminishing Romantic views of nature. In the process, the meaning of nature shifted from being in the human mind to being actually in nature itself. In the 1830s, she explains, science began to take over the Romantic poets' function, "literally demonstrating heaven in wild flowers." But what kind of science was it that "adopted the revelatory role"? It was a science

> of classification and close description; its ambition was to read the object in all its detail and the passion for comprehending the character of each thing in itself was united with religious emotion. The universe to this view appears not as a vast symbolic utterance whose significance lies in its life within the mind, but as an inexhaustible granary of facts. The centre of interest, in sum, has shifted from subject to object.[46]

As a corollary, nature came to seem more autonomous. Natural objects were increasingly valued for themselves, not as reflections or projections of human needs. Natural history, interfused with the scientific spirit of objectivity, thus may well have augmented the decline of what Ruskin called the *pathetic fallacy*, a trend that began after the Romantic writers and has continued down to the present, as documented by Josephine Miles in her *Pathetic Fallacy in the Nineteenth-Century*.

With the shift from subject to object, an apotheosis of facts occurred. But given that both science and natural history contributed to this process, there were essential differences between the two. The crucial, watershed question is: What *use* do science and natural history make of facts? The first difference is that science collects facts for the purpose of discerning relationships between them, while natural history collects them simply because they are interesting in themselves. Indeed, with its emphasis on singularity, natural history often most enjoys the *distinction* between one fact, one object and another, as opposed to science which seeks to clarify the *relation* between them. Relations take the form of generalized laws; distinctions take the form of displays. The second difference, and the one most germane to the study of literature, is this: while its facts, relationships, and laws may be expressed in language, science does not primarily aim to transmute facts into texts. But for natural history, as for literature, texts (sheer collocations, descriptions, or arrangements of facts) are the point. Or, to put it another way, the discourse of science endeavors to be transparent, a clear glass through which the reader can see the ideas behind it. The discourse of natural history, however, is highly colored, meant to be beautiful and pleasing in itself, a gaudy mosaic.

The distinction between Victorian science and natural history shows up in high relief when one examines their texts. They cover a wide spectrum; inevitably, some overlap occurs, some blurring of the edges between categories. Textbooks, monographs, and science essays cluster toward one end, with natural history books toward the other. Between them lie some works of mixed aims, such as accounts by scientific travelers.

For pure scientists objectivity was the goal—to remove the observer's personality and responses from the natural scene in order to view it completely apart from human interference. This goal, or possibility of total objectivity, has been challenged more and more frequently by twentieth-century scientists, especially since the advent of the "new physics" and in the wake of Heisenbergian uncertainty, but it is still in one form or another pragmatically accepted in science that experiments or observations ought to be pared clean, insofar as possible, of human bias. Certainly the nineteenth-century conception of science assumed that it was both possible, and desirable, to separate the observer from the observed. With this aim, Victorian science produced texts that primarily conveyed information, either in the form of facts or theoretical explanations, or both.

The first harvest of objective observation might be sheer factual information. How many stamens in the flower of this species? What is the number and arrangement of teeth in that organism? Classificatory compendia concentrated on such details, often throughout the nineteenth century in the form of monographs like Gosse's *Actinologia Britannica*, which covered British sea anemones and corals. The purpose of such a text was to identify various species, and to this end it was packed with technical descriptions of their anatomy. Here was nature clinically displayed—the anemone flipped over for examination, every tentacle dissected, diagrammed, and accounted for. Such scientific information was of interest mostly to specialists in the field.

Another type of science text combined facts with overarching theoretical concepts in an effort to explain complex natural phenomena. In these books objective observation of nature yielded secrets in the form of laws.

Such books packaged the results of generalizing from particulars—that is, predictive statements, or laws, framed through the process of induction. With their ideas, these texts advanced knowledge. But style was of little concern. For example, one famous work of Victorian geology, Sir Roderick Murchison's *Siluria*, is a massive tome. Quite important in its day, *Siluria* detailed the stratigraphy, fossil content, and geographical distribution of certain Paleozoic rocks, representing what is now known as the Silurian Period. With its maps and charts, the book is exhaustive, thoroughly researched, and utterly dry. No ripple of wit disturbs its pages, no hint of Sir Roderick's estimable personality, no modicum of anecdote. Personality is irrelevant, indeed inimical, to its scientific intent.

A third type of science text paid more attention to style, because its rhetorical stance addressed a different audience: laypersons, not specialists. Some scientific essayists of the nineteenth century certainly wrote with conscious craftsmanship and with the intention of doing more than simply conveying information. In an age that celebrated prose, they wrote to inform, but also to delight a wide readership. T. H. Huxley and John Tyndall spring to mind as exemplars. Huxley, in an essay like "On a Piece of Chalk" or "On the Physical Basis of Life," wanted to convey information about the past worlds hinted at by fossils in the chalk or the protoplasm that all life holds in common. Huxley writes his essays to help readers understand scientific relationships (he has, in other words, a scientific intent), but he often does so in a lively metaphorical style. Since he was himself moved by the grandeur of scientific conceptions, his essays are moving as well. Although factual, they rise to the level of metaphor: the chalk becomes time; the protoplasm is the unity deep within the diversity of life. Scientific in their ground and didactic in their purpose, Huxley's essays have a literary effect. In the spectrum of Victorian nonfiction, they edge closer to the natural history end. And yet they remain science texts, not natural history, because of their ultimate purpose: to show relation, not distinction, between facts.

In the middle of this spectrum of books, one finds texts that combine scientific and affective aims. One example is the work of Alexander von Humboldt (1769–1859), whose *Personal Narrative* Darwin read avidly while aboard the *Beagle*. Humboldt exceeded even Buffon in breadth, for he included astronomy, geography, and physics in his studies, being particularly entranced with the earth's magnetism, earthquakes, weather, and tides. And he added an obsession of his own—precise measurement by instruments—to the armamentarium of science. But more important for naturalists, he exemplified a new type of traveler, by his own estimation: not an explorer, but a "scientific traveller."[47]

Humboldt himself traveled prodigiously, and his works showed just how an inquisitive observer might record nature's curiosities. Certainly the title of his central work, the five-volume *Kosmos*, which began publication in 1845 and had sold 80,000 copies by 1851,[48] shows that Humboldt's aims were far from modest. He managed to combine precise, detailed observation with exotic travel and to color it with his own personal reactions. As such, Humboldt helped forge the mold for Victorian naturalists. John Burroughs, the American nature-essayist (see Chapter 6), praised Alexander Humboldt's "poetic soul" and "love of beautiful forms," saying that in *Kosmos* he satisfied both the "understanding" and the "aesthetic sense."[49] Although one historian of science counts Humboldt's "physique de la terre" as a "major concern of professional science for some forty years or so,"[50] because Humboldt both observed and measured and theorized about laws or causes, it was such scientific aims combined with his "aesthetic sense" (what some writers have labeled his "romanticism")[51] that made Humboldt a naturalist and a model for naturalists.

Like Humboldt, a naturalist collected facts and then made something personal, something aesthetic, of them. For the nonspecialist, a strictly scientific, factual harvest might be dry and uninteresting. But naturalists could begin with facts, viewing nature as autonomous (of *it*self, not of *them*selves) and to that extent being objective, and still go on to color the facts of nature with their own personality and experience to help shape and hold together the particulars. And, most important of all, naturalists would add washes of color to the objective facts to make them more interesting *to a reader*. A natural history writer could thereby be as conscious an artist as any novelist or poet. In fact, this is what readers expected.

Barber quotes the editor of the *Entomologist's Annual*, who claimed that natural history was the best of both worlds, "as interesting as a novel, but gives the same employment to the higher faculties of the mind as are afforded by the abstruser studies of Political Economy and History." With such mixed aims, says Barber, natural history books were often motley in content and tone:

> What they actually retailed was fascinating facts, bizarre, curious and extraordinary anecdotes, sentimental interludes, long quotations from "the Poets" . . . personal reminiscence, pious homilies—in fact, all the usual ingredients of Victorian light reading. They invariably stressed the most strange and exotic aspects of their subject, as reflected in their titles—*Marvels* of Pond Life, *Wonders* of the Sea Shore, The *Romance* of Natural History—often at the expense of basic information, and although their purpose was ostensibly scientific, their style was that of the novel.[52]

Personal response to such marvels mattered a great deal in natural history. While serious science spurned emotion, natural history embraced it.

To sum up the differences, then, two main qualities differentiate Victorian science from natural history texts: tone (usually linked to style) and intent (or purpose). Generally, science is more detached, objective, and seeks to understand objects of nature in their relation to one another; its tone is neutral. Natural history is more personal, evocative, and seeks to enjoy the distinction between one natural object and any other; its tone is emotional. And natural history writing is often more suffused with the human responses of its author in order to entertain and move its reader.

The subject may be the same; but not the slant. For example, Victorian geology produced both Murchison's *Siluria*, a science text, and the natural history text *The Old Red Sandstone* by Hugh Miller. Miller's book, while chock-a-block with facts, and as much a conceptual catalyst as *Siluria*, is full of fancy. Miller's book parades its fossil fish before the reader as objects of beauty and tokens of wonder. No one can deny how valuable they are as aids to understanding the remote geological past, but how fantastic their shapes, how strange their implications! Murchison's science is instructive, but Miller's natural history is positively alluring (see Chapter 10).

Because it depends on facts, natural history writing is allied to science; because it deals with human response and emotion, it is allied to literature. As a result, the discourse of Victorian natural history falls squarely in the middle of a major argument about the respective qualities and aims of science and of the humanities. The Victorians, like the Romantics before them, reacted to the upstart sciences with extreme ambivalence, an uneasiness which persists today. In the twentieth century, the debate almost unavoidably makes reference to C. P. Snow's 1959 essay "The Two Cultures,"[53] in part because that phrase so neatly encapsulates Snow's thesis: science and the humanities are hostile, antithetical disciplines with fundamentally opposed aims. Snow deplored this situation, but saw little hope for reconciliation. As much as by anything, Snow's Two Cultures are divided by the attitude that they take toward objects, toward facts. Hence the special relevance of Snow's division for natural history. What good are natural objects or natural facts? Science makes one use of them, literature another. Which is better? Can their concerns overlap? Questions such as these about the "Two Cultures" have a great deal to do with why popular natural history was so attractive to the Victorians.

Although the phrase itself is modern, thoughtful Victorians were well aware of the "Two Cultures" debate. In Victorian prose, disputation about what literature and science do, should do, or ought not to do is nowhere more spirited than in discussions of education. The great champion of science, and science's "way of knowledge," is of course T. H. Huxley. In essays such as "A Liberal Education; and Where to Find It" (1868), "Technical Education" (1887), "On the Advisableness of Improving Natural Knowledge" (1866), and "On the Educational Value of the Natural History Sciences" (1854), Huxley vigorously maintained that understanding the "great and fundamental truths of Nature and . . . the Laws of her operation" (from "A Liberal Education") was as essential to a cultured man as familiarity with the great works of classical antiquity. The sciences should be studied partly because they could do so many useful things, but more importantly because they inculcated clear, rational habits of mind. And although Matthew Arnold, as a proponent of classical education as a prerequisite to ethical conduct and a love of beauty, reacted strongly against Huxley's view of education (specifically Huxley's 1880 essay, "Science and Culture"), Huxley was not so unfeeling a scientist that his study of nature made no allowances for beauty. Like many pure scientists, Huxley found the laws of nature inherently beautiful. But he also admitted that the objects of scientific inquiry (which he calls, in its broadest sense, natural history) could be aesthetically appealing in themselves:

> I do not pretend that natural-history knowledge, as such, can increase our sense of the beautiful in natural objects. I do not suppose that the dead soul of Peter Bell, of whom the great poet of nature says,—
>
> > A primrose by the river's brim,
> > A yellow primrose was to him,
> > And it was nothing more,—
>
> would have been a whit roused from its apathy by the information that the primrose is a Dicotyledonous Exogen, with a monopetalous corolla and central placentation. But I advocate natural-history knowledge from this point of view, because it would lead us to seek the beauties of natural objects, instead of trusting to chance to force them on our attention. To a person uninstructed in natural history, his country or a sea-side stroll is a walk through a gallery filled with wonderful works of art, nine-tenths of which have their faces turned to the wall. Teach him something of natural history, and you place in his hands a catalogue of those which are worth turning around.[54]

Natural history or science can lead a person to discover the obscurely beautiful objects of nature; for Huxley, this is one of its charms. Arnold might even consent to agree with him on this point, since he so values beauty. Clearly, however, Huxley also values the knowledge and classificatory precision inherent in the Dicotyledonous Exogen, though the term itself may not be evocative, and that sort of "fact" Matthew Arnold can do without.

Along with John Henry Newman, Arnold towers on the other side of the Victorian educational debate, representing the humanities. Both of these writers argue that science produces only sterile, disconnected facts, useful perhaps in a pragmatic technological application, but valueless to a human being as such. Scientific facts are not moral, nor aesthetic, and worse, they are dead dissected bits and pieces, connected to no overriding meaning. They do not help one to be a better person; they are not aids to conduct; and they do not uplift one. As a Catholic, Newman is not hostile to science per se, considering as he does that there is only one truth, indivisible, which may be reached either deductively through theology derived from Revelation or inductively through the natural sciences. To understand the methodology of science is important. But in *The Idea of a University*, Newman, because he is so committed to knowledge as a unified, whole vision for the "gentleman," opposes scientific or technical education if it consists, as it too often may, of mere accumulation of facts.

As I have suggested, for the Victorians, facts were frequently at the crux of the science-humanities debate. What good does the ever-mounting pile of facts do? If one learns too many facts, might one not, in the midst of their multitudes, lose sight of higher truths? Dickens' Mr. Gradgrind in *Hard Times* is the supreme literary example of the dangers of facts. Just as Mr. Gradgrind's (actually his pupil Bitzer's) gramnivorous quadruped definition completely misses the truth of what a horse is, Thomas Macaulay, in his 1828 essay on Dryden, insists that no description of a porcupine as class Mammalia, order glires, having two foreteeth, eight grinders, and quills can give one a "just idea" of what a porcupine is. The "vital principle eludes the finest instruments" and is far more than the sum of any number of facts.

This is precisely Arnold's objection to science. In reply to Huxley, Arnold (in "Literature and Science," from *Discourses in America*) maintains that science grinds out "pieces of knowledge" and "facts," which are, granted, "interesting"—but such facts can never appeal to one's need for beauty, emotion, and guides to conduct. Scientists are specialists, while humanists are generalists, and for Arnold, as for many of his fellow Victorians, general knowledge, "seeing it whole," is preferable to bits and pieces. Interestingly, with their drive toward encyclopedic knowledge, naturalists also wanted to see the world whole, in spite of their fascination with particular facts. Unlike Huxley, who can appreciate the knowledge encapsulated in a technical description of an animal or plant, even though the terminology itself is unlovely, Arnold views technical language with distaste, as Dickens and Macaulay do. Knowing that the human ancestor was a "hairy quadruped" and "probably arboreal in his habits" at best does one no good and at worst is degrading.

By the time Huxley, Newman, and Arnold entered into the fray, when the Cambridge-led campaign for more science in the universities was under way, the science-literature debate was already a hoary topic. In 1828, the Cambridge campaign begat University College, which expressly emphasized science. The Cambridge campaign also led to the reform of Oxford and Cambridge by Royal Commission in 1854 and 1856, stimulated the Department of Science and Art to be set up by the British government in 1853, and saw the arrival of Mechanics' Institutes, among other changes. The reforms had been a long time in the making.

Active in the eighteenth century,[55] the science-literature quarrel had been taken up with vehemence by the Romantic poets. Many Romantic works touch on the issue of science's effects on literature. For example, Keats' "Lamia" maintains that science "unweaves the rainbow." On the other hand, Peacock, in "The Four Ages of Poetry," says that science *should* be treated by poets, and Shelley, too, sees a "poetical element in science" when he makes his *Defence of Poetry*. The best philosophical consideration of the question occurs in Wordsworth's 1802 Preface to the *Lyrical Ballads*. Often quoted in "Two Cultures" essays, Wordsworth's passage is worth looking at here for it states succinctly the basic difference between literature and science that Victorians incorporated into their "Science = Mere Facts," "Literature = Human Significance" formulas.

Wordsworth believes that at some time in the future science might become part of the province of poetry (but then again, it might not): "The remotest discoveries of the Chemist, the Botanist, or Mineralogist, will be as proper objects of the Poet's art as any upon which it can be employed, if the time should ever come when these things shall be familiar to us, . . . shall be manifestly and palpably material to us as enjoying and suffering beings." Poetry, in other words, is greater than science, and greater because it is more human: "Poetry is the first and last of all knowledge— it is immortal as the heart of man," and the "Poet binds together by passion and knowledge the vast empire of human society." Poetry is emotional, of the human heart, while science is cold, objective, fundamentally concerned with things inhuman.

The knowledge of the poet, Wordsworth says, "cleaves to us as a necessary part of our existence," but the knowledge of the scientist "is a personal and individual acquisition, slow to come to us, and by no habitual and direct sympathy connecting us with our fellow-beings." Science is particular, and for Wordsworth, particularity is negative—meaning "limited," "not universal." According to Wordsworth, literature is far superior to science, because far larger in scope: "The Poet writes under one restriction only, namely that of the necessity of giving immediate pleasure to a human Being possessed of that information which may be expected from him, not as a lawyer, a physician, a mariner, an astronomer, or a natural philosopher, but as a Man."

Wordsworth neatly divides the categories along these lines: science = objective/inhuman; literature = subjective/human. With such value judgments hovering in the background, it is no wonder that so many Victorians feared science, or at least viewed it with suspicion. Of course, to some extent the Two Cultures debate creates a false dilemma, an either/or situation in which, depending on one's point of view, science is all good and literature all bad, or vice versa. One salient characteristic of Victorian natural history is that in general it refused to accept this dichotomy, seeing no reason why the best qualities of both pursuits might not overlap. Natural history texts could be both objective and subjective, concrete and human. But in the twentieth century the dichotomy has persisted.

Aldous Huxley, in his essay "Literature and Science," heightens differences by assigning distinct terminology to the two endeavors. Physical science, he says, is *nomothetic*, seeking general laws; however, literature is *idiographic*, concerned not with "regularities and explanatory laws, but descriptions of appearances and the discerned qualities of objects perceived as wholes, with judgments, comparisons, and discriminations."[56] Furthermore, he points out that the language of science values "systematic simplification," while literature prizes "novel arrangements" and "multiple meanings."[57] Or, as J. Bronowski puts it, science tries to resolve and minimize ambiguities, unlike literature which exploits and revels in them.[58]

Another critic, in an analytical study called *The Language of Science*, points out several interesting features of scientific diction, including the fact that by the nineteenth century new names for scientific phenomena and objects were gleaned almost exclusively from Greek and Latin roots.[59] Thus as new scientific words were being coined by the hundreds, scientific prose was further distanced from ordinary English. (However, as mentioned earlier, in the throes of the Victorian collecting mania, a large proportion of the English public could rattle off Latinate terminology with amazing facility.) But in addition to being Latinate and for that reason specialized, scientific prose has, according to Theodore M. Savory, another characteristic that sets it apart from literary or even other expository prose, and that is its "coldness." He explains that

> never, in ordinary circumstances, does it show a glimmer of feeling or of warmth; it expounds and explains without emotion, so that one can read, as one has read, many pages of scientific books with never a quickening of the pulse. Of course this is a consequence of the fact that the words of science, without the associations that everyday words acquire, can produce only informative, symbolic writing. A scientific paragraph says precisely what it means, and no more.[60]

No quickening of the pulse—an apt description of reading a Victorian science text such as Murchison's *Siluria*. And if pure scientific words, and their accumulated prose, have no associations, then one could say of them, as does Harold Cassidy, that they are strictly denotative. The language of literature, on the other hand, is connotative.[61] But much of Victorian natural history (and its modern forms, too) is couched in language that manages to be both, with an evocative warmth that heats the imagination of the nonscientist.

Science may have a kind of beauty—a mathematician may find a beauty of simplicity in an equation, or a chemist in an experiment, or a physicist in a theory—but beauty is not its purpose.[62] Knowledge is. In nineteenth-century scientific terms, any beauty found in science had to be the "property of the observer rather than a quality of natural things"; beauty was a subjective perception only, not an inherent quality of matter. And science's job was to study matter, not its human observer.[63] (With this precept twentieth-century science does not necessarily agree.)

Seen in those nineteenth-century terms, the aims of science and literature cannot help but diverge. If one is on the side of the scientists, literature seems "soft," muddle-headed, sentimental, impractical, useless, imprecise. If one sides with the poets, science seems cold, heartless, dissecting, inhuman, the enemy of beauty. In the Victorian context, what matters is not the debate itself,[64] or whether the Two Cultures will ever coalesce, or perhaps may have already, but the fact that for the Victorians the two streams did happily mingle in a hybrid discipline: natural history. Its special discourse displayed characteristics of both science and literature. No Wordsworth of natural history materialized, but poetic natural history texts certainly did, and literature gained a new genre, one which succeeded in making the "remotest discoveries" about nature "manifestly and palpably material to . . . enjoying and suffering beings."

The Two Cultures debate is of interest here not as an isolated episode in the history of ideas, but because it was the culture medium, the petri-dish agar in which popular natural history grew. With science playing an increasingly important role, more and more commandeering the realm of "truth," and with traditional solaces like literature and religion losing their grasp on the imagination, people were casting about for new sources of inspiration. One could not discount science. So pervasive did science become, so persuasive its approach to truth, that it attracted followers like converts to a religion, fervent believers in the worldview that has often been called scientism. The poet Swinburne, in 1872, bitterly pro-tested this turn of events:

> We live in an age when not to be scientific is to be nothing; the man untrained in science, though he should speak with the tongues of men and of angels, though he should know all that men may know of the his-tory of men and their works in times past, though he should have nourished on the study of their noblest examples in art and literature whatever he may have of natural intelligence, is but a pitiable and worthless pretender in the sight of professors to whom natural science is not a mean[s] but an end.[65]

Swinburne's plaint echoes a common fear. Scientists, he says, too often ignore the human implications of "bones and stones"; they care only for isolated facts, not overall meaning. "All study of details is precious," teaches science—but what is one to make of those details?

Mighty Victorian science garnered respect, but to many like Swin-burne could seem a bit cold. Literature embraced human thought and feeling and satisfied the aesthetic sense, but in this modern age of scien-tific discovery was it not a trifle unsophisticated, a throwback to more mythic, more naive times? Traditional literature was beginning to seem suspect; perhaps it would play no role at all in the scientific Arcadia to come. What a sensitive person needed was a way to scrutinize the intricacies of the world with a respectably scientific eye, and yet still be moved by them. In other words, how could one have one's facts and love them too? One solution, of course, was natural history.

Notes

1. Nathan Reingold, ed., *Science in Nineteenth-Century America: A Docu-mentary History* (London: Macmillan, 1966), pp. 47, 179.

2. *Encyclopedia Britannica*, third edition (1797), vol. 12, p. 651.

3. William Coleman, *Biology in the Nineteenth Century: Problems of Form, Function, and Transformation* (London: Cambridge Univ. Press, 1977), p. 1.

4. Coleman, p. 2.

5. Coleman, p. 3.

6. Quoted and translated in Alexander B. Adams, *Eternal Quest: The Story of the Great Naturalists* (New York: G. P. Putnam's Sons, 1969), p. 92.

7. Reingold, p. 48.

8. David Knight, *The Age of Science: The Scientific World-view in the Nineteenth Century* (New York: Basil Blackwell, 1986), p. 134.

9. For material on the professionalization and specialization of the Victorian sciences, see the Introduction to *Victorian Science: A Self-Portrait from the Presidential Addresses of the British Association for the Advancement of Science*, by George Basalla, William Coleman, and Robert H. Kargon (Garden City, NY: Anchor Press/Doubleday, 1970); and Susan Faye Cannon, *Science in Culture: The Early Victorian Period* (New York: Dawson and Science History Publications, 1978), especially chapters 5, 6, and 7.

10. These concerns permeate T. H. Huxley's work, but see in particular his famous essay "A Liberal Education; and Where to Find it," among others on the subject of education in his volume entitled *Science and Education: Essays* (New York: D. Appleton and Company, 1896).

11. Reingold, p. 162.

12. Lynn Barber, *The Heyday of Natural History: 1820–1870* (Garden City, NY: Doubleday and Company, Inc., 1980), p. 27.

13. David Elliston Allen, *The Naturalist in Britain: A Social History* (London: Allen Lane, 1976), p. 5.

14. Allen, *Naturalist*, p. 6.

15. Keith Thomas, *Man and the Natural World: A History of the Modern Sensibility* (New York: Pantheon Books, 1983), p. 282.

16. Thomas, p. 283.

17. Allen, *Naturalist*, p. 45. Thomas cites this same quotation, p. 283.

18. Allen, *Naturalist*, p. 30.

19. Barber, p. 13.

20. Thomas, p. 284.

21. See Barber, pp. 40–44, and Reingold, pp. 29–30.

22. See Donald Worster, *Nature's Economy: The Roots of Ecology* (Garden City, NY: Anchor Press/Doubleday, 1979).

23. Aldous Huxley, *Literature and Science* (New Haven, CT: Leete's Island Books, 1963), p. 79.

24. Allen, *Naturalist*, p. 2.

25. Stephen Toulmin, *The Philosophy of Science: An Introduction* (New York: Harper and Row, Publishers, 1960), pp. 53–54.

26. Quoted in W. H. G. Armytage, *A Social History of Engineering* (Cambridge, MA: The MIT Press, 1961), p. 230.

27. See Mott T. Greene, *Geology in the Nineteenth Century: Changing Views of a Changing World* (Ithaca: Cornell Univ. Press, 1982).

28. Wladyslaw Tatarkiewicz, *Nineteenth Century Philosophy*, trans. Chester A. Kisiel (Belmont, CA: Wadsworth Publishing Company, Inc., 1973), pp. 6–96.

29. David Elliston Allen finds the "first known mention" of a geologist's hammer in 1696; *Naturalist*, p. 6. Such hammers were common in the nineteenth century; Ruskin complains of the theologically annoying "clink" of them in a letter of 1851: "If only the Geologists would let me alone, I could do very well, but those dreadful Hammers! I hear the clink of them at the end of every cadence of the Bible verses." Edward T. Cook and Alexander Wedderburn, eds., *The Works of John Ruskin* (London: George Allen, 1903–1912), XXXVI, p. 115.

30. Granville Penn, *Conversations on Geology; Comprising a Familiar Explanation of the Huttonian and Wernerian Systems* (London: J. W. Southgate and Son, 1840), p. 6.

31. Penn, p. 15.

32. Allen, *Naturalist*, pp. 173–174.

33. From the Introductory Résumé of Hugh Miller's *Popular Geology: A Series of Lectures Read Before the Philosophical Institution of Edinburgh, with Descriptive Sketches from a Geologist's Portfolio* (Boston: Gould and Lincoln, 1859), p. iv.

34. Barber, p. 55.

35. Nicolette Scourse, *The Victorians and Their Flowers* (London: Croom Helm; Portland, OR: Timber Press, 1983), p. 70.

36. See Ernst Mayr, *Principles of Systematic Zoology* (New York: McGraw-Hill Book Company, 1969), p. 54. Mayr's chapter 4 usefully treats the history of biological classification and the "species problem."

37. Barber, p. 57.

38. Henry Walter Bates, *The Naturalist on the River Amazons* (London: John Murray, 1964; rpt. Berkeley, CA: Univ. of California Press, 1962), p. 62.

39. L. J. Jordanova, ed., *Languages of Nature: Critical Essays on Science and Literature* (New Brunswick, NJ: Rutgers Univ. Press, 1986), p. 40.

40. In L. R. Brightwell, ed. *Buckland's Curiosities of Natural History: A Selection* (London: The Batchworth Press, 1948), p. 1.

41. George Henry Lewes, *Studies in Animal Life* (London: Smith, Elder and Co., 1862), p. 3.

42. Arabella B. Buckley, *Life and Her Children: Glimpses of Animal Life from the Amoeba to the Insects* (London: Macmillan & Co. Ltd., 1957), p. 8.

43. Philip C. Ritterbush, *The Art of Organic Forms* (Washington, DC: Smithsonian Institution Press, 1968), p. 80. Agnes Arber also mentions the centrality of vision to biological studies in *The Mind and the Eye: A Study of the Biologist's Standpoint* (Cambridge: Cambridge Univ. Press, 1954), p. 115.

44. A readily available paperback collection of Ernst Haeckel's plates is *Art Forms in Nature* (New York: Dover Publications, Inc., 1974).

45. Ritterbush, *The Art of Organic Forms*, p. 69.

46. Patricia M. Ball, *The Science of Aspects: The Changing Role of Fact in the Work of Coleridge, Ruskin and Hopkins* (London: Univ. of London Athlone Press, 1971), p. 73.

47. Cannon, p. 75.

48. Adams, p. 234.

49. John Burroughs, "Science and Literature," in *Indoor Studies* (New York: Houghton Mifflin Company, 1889), p. 64.

50. Cannon, p. 77.

51. See Cannon, pp. 78–79.

52. Barber, p. 19.

53. C. P. Snow, *The Two Cultures: And a Second Look. An Expanded Version of the Two Cultures and the Scientific Revolution* (Cambridge: Cambridge Univ. Press, 1964).

54. "On the Educational Value of the Natural History Sciences," in Thomas Henry Huxley, *Science and Education: Essays* (New York: D. Appleton and Company, 1896), p. 63.

55. See Marjorie Hope Nicolson, *Newton Demands the Muse* (Princeton: Princeton Univ. Press, 1966).

56. Aldous Huxley, p. 8.

57. Aldous Huxley, p. 16.

58. J. Bronowski, *The Identity of Man*, rev. ed. (Garden City, NY: The Doubleday/Natural History Press, 1971), p. 54.

59. Theodore H. Savory, *The Language of Science* (London: Andre Deutsche, 1967), p. 60.

60. Savory, p. 133.

61. Harold Gomes Cassidy, *The Sciences and the Arts: A New Alliance* (New York: Harper and Brothers, 1962), p. 8.

62. See Judith Wechsler, ed., *On Aesthetics in Science* (Cambridge, MA: The MIT Press, 1978). Especially pertinent to Victorian studies is Howard E. Gruber's article, "Darwin's 'Tree of Nature' and Other Images of Wide Scope," pp. 121–140.

63. Robert M. Augros and George N. Stanciu, *The New Story of Science: Mind and the Universe* (Chicago: Gateway Editions, 1984), p. 37.

64. That the science-literature debate is an extremely compelling one is obvious from the number of books on the topic. The current consensus is that the dichotomy is stale, or altogether obsolete; yet the argument continues. In addition to those from which I have quoted, some other central works are: Harcourt Brown, ed., *Science and the Creative Spirit: Essays on Humanistic Aspects of Science* (Toronto: Univ. of Toronto Press, 1958); David K. Cornelius and Edwin St. Vincent, *Cultures in Conflict: Perspectives on the Snow-Leavis Controversy* (Chicago: Scott, Foresman and Company, 1964); Martin Green, *Science and the Shabby Curate of Poetry: Essays about the Two Cultures* (London: Longmans, 1964); W. T. Jones, *The Sciences and the Humanities: Conflict and Resolution* (Berkeley: Univ. of California Press, 1967); F. R. Leavis, "Two Cultures? The

Significance of Lord Snow," in *Nor Shall My Sword: Discourses on Pluralism, Compassion and Social Hope* (London: Chatto and Windus, 1972); Peter B. Medawar, "Science and Literature," in *The Hope of Progress: A Scientist Looks at Problems in Philosophy, Literature, and Science* (Garden City, NY: Anchor Press/Doubleday, 1973); and I. A. Richards, *Science and Poetry* (London: Kegan Paul, Trench, Trübner and Co., Ltd., 1926).

65. Algernon Charles Swinburne, *Under the Microscope* (London: D. White, 1872; rpt. New York: Garland Publishing, Inc., 1986), p. 1.

5

Museums and Microscopes: Particularity and Panorama

The eye is satisfied with seeing and strange thoughts are stirred as you see more surprizing objects than were known to exist; transparent lumps of amber with gnats and flies within; radiant spars and marbles; huge blocks of quartz; native gold in all its forms of crystallization and combination, gold in threads, in plates, in crystals, in dust; and silver taken from the earth molten as from fire. You are impressed with the inexhaustible gigantic riches of nature. The limits of the possible are enlarged, and the real is stranger than the imaginary. The universe is a more amazing puzzle than ever, as you look along this bewildering series of animated forms, the hazy butterflies, the carved shells, the birds, beasts, insects, snakes, fish . . .[1]

> RALPH WALDO EMERSON, on the Cabinet of
> Natural History in the Jardin des Plantes,
> from "The Uses of Natural History," 1833

A model existed in the nineteenth century for the aesthetic juxtaposition of fragments, bits collected from nature and then displayed, and that model was the cabinet. A cabinet was a small-scale museum, a collocation of curios, a personal archive. It might be a humble little box with drawers, or a beautifully crafted wood-and-glass display case. More informally, it might be merely an assortment of objects arranged on a parlor table. Whatever its shape, the cabinet was the physical analogue of the activity of collecting. It served as a repository for all manner of collected natural objects, which, stimulating to the mind and eye, lent themselves to contemplation and sheer aesthetic pleasure. Stocked with curious minerals or plants or shells, the cabinet invited careful scrutiny of its contents. As such, the natural history cabinet was firmly grounded not only in the collecting urge, but also in the ingrained belief that meticulous observation was important. The same belief fueled the popularity of the microscope. In essence, the cabinet and the microscope accomplished the same purpose, but on a different scale. Each glorified the specimen, whether of macroscopic size or microscopic; each encouraged the amateur naturalist to scour the countryside for material, and thus see nature with new eyes. In many a Victorian home both could be found, side by side, even sharing the same table. The cabinet and the microscope were so enticing, such a stimulus to the creative imagination, that they took on metaphorical overtones and frequently appeared as motifs in natural history prose.

Cabinets certainly existed well before the time of Victoria. Collectors since the Middle Ages had filled cabinets as an engaging hobby. But up until the late eighteenth century, cabinets had two peculiar qualities that set them apart from their Victorian descendants. First, they tended to be completely eclectic. A cabinet was a catchall for every sort of object: natural, cultural, antiquarian, mythological. A cabinet could contain almost anything—fossils, coins, carvings, statues, medals, stuffed birds, ivory, butterflies, deformed bones, antique bronzes, swords, pickled fish or fetuses, Egyptian mummies, even holy relics, or the putative feathers from the tail of a Phoenix. Little attempt was made to bring any kind of order to the miscellaneous hodge-podge on display. Second, earlier cabinets were by and large the province of aristocrats, virtuosi with money enough to buy expensive artifacts at their whim. Seldom did they themselves collect the objects in the field; instead, they viewed collectible rarities as commodities to be bought, hoarded, and sold.[2] By the nineteenth century, a cabinet usually denoted "cabinet of natural history" specifically. As museums would, cabinets became specialized. And rather than remaining a diversion for the idle rich, cabinets became a hobby for ordinary people. Anyone who cared to take a walk through the woods could pick up specimens for display; they need not be priceless rarities. Following the trend of natural history in general, Victorian cabinets and collecting became democratic.

The history of cabinets paralleled the growth and development of museums. Sometimes, in fact, the terms were interchangeable, although a cabinet was more likely to be private and small, a museum public and larger; this distinction sharpened as the nineteenth century approached. Museums began in the sixteenth and seventeenth centuries, with the botanical gardens kept for the purpose of studying *materia medica*, or medicinal herbs, and with the private cabinets of aristocrats that mirrored the Renaissance's eclecticism. Throughout the eighteenth century, for their own private enjoyment, many connoisseurs created small museums, some of them very fine. One such personal museum, that of Sir Hans Sloane, in 1759 became the nucleus of the British Museum. Many large private museums gained fame during this period, such as the Hunterian and Lever museums (the Hunterian had 13,682 specimens!).[3] These storehouses swelled with the vast accumulated debris of expeditions, such as those of Captain Cook or Captain Bligh. (Bligh's 1795 collection of tropical ferns from the West Indies, in fact, helped to spur the Fern Craze.)[4]

The Lever Museum had a direct influence on one prominent Victorian naturalist, Philip Henry Gosse. When he was sixteen, Gosse, already enthused about natural history and an avid reader of natural history books, attended Sir Ashton Lever's traveling exhibition. This touring collection from the Lever Museum contained a brilliantly colored South American butterfly, and it was seeing this specimen "which first awakened in Philip Gosse one of the master passions of his life, a love of exotic lepidoptera."[5] Like many collections of the time, the Lever show included some fabulous fakes of natural history, such as a "mermaid" fabricated from a conjoined monkey and salmon. Such sensationalistic exhibits attracted the crowds that then stayed to peruse more serious and educational specimens. But Gosse, even at sixteen, had the good sense to scorn the mermaid.

The nineteenth century saw the development of systematic museums. Gradually principles of display evolved: that like items should be grouped together, that some taxonomic order should control the chaos, that well-labeled specimens could advance the cause of knowledge. The museum's raison d'être became serious study rather than just entertainment. Struggling with these imperatives, the British Museum as the century advanced enlarged its collections, worked harder to educate the public, and finally took the logical step of separating the natural history collection from the antiquities by opening the Natural History Museum in South Kensington in 1881. Nevertheless, Victorian England fostered many odd museums, such as the small but popular collections of the Fish Museum begun in 1857 (as part of the separate, older South Kensington Museum) by Frank Buckland, one of the more eccentric naturalists of his day.[6] Buckland's museum, as "characteristic of Victorian museums generally," had the "tendency to accumulate the jetsam of imperial adventurers,"[7] serving as a repository for all kinds of bizarre curios, from a boa constrictor skin to a pickled mouse trapped in an oyster.[8] Advanced principles of museum science did not arrive all at once. Nor could they ever entirely displace the basic, visceral pleasure to be had in looking at freaks of nature, strange-but-true peculiarities (for example, stuffed whales or whale skeletons, baleen and all, the exhibition of which, according to Buckland, was "not uncommon").[9] Most serious museums, while attempting to educate their visitors and help closet naturalists do their work of classification, no doubt retained something of Buckland's personal motives: the unabashed love of objects and the pleasure at seeing them displayed.

Sheer pleasure alone would not have done as an excuse for visiting museums. Fortunately for serious-minded Victorians, however, museums easily could be construed as educational; in fact, visiting them could be nearly a devotional exercise. According to one critic, museums at the time functioned as "secular cathedrals,"[10] temples of nature's grandeur. A nineteenth-century visitor to a natural history museum expected, not the interactive displays and thematic groupings of today, but instead an aesthetic assemblage of unrelated objects conducive to lofty thoughts. This attitude was reflected in the Victorian museum's typical design: high ceilings, streaming natural light from above, spacious interiors (albeit often crammed with specimens), perpendicularity and vertical vaults, expansive galleries, and specimens in gorgeous cases as objects of veneration—much as the South East Mineral Gallery of the British Museum (Natural History) remains today, or the smaller Sedgwick Museum in Cambridge. Here one went to stand in awe, to feel uplifted, indeed almost to worship the God in nature.

Many museums and exhibitions of the time were, of course, technical or mercantile in nature, the Great Exhibition of 1851 being a prime example. Like natural history museums of the period, the Crystal Palace in which the Exhibition was housed was a cathedral of sorts. Its arching glass and iron architecture emphasized light, verticality, and spaciousness (and even glorified nature, since the building had been designed to accommodate several tall trees within it), and in this vast chamber, material objects of commerce were arrayed like objets d'art or sacred relics. The Palace represented that peculiarly Victorian conflation of sacred and profane, spiritual and material satisfaction. Technical or commercial museums, moreover, were marked by their love of gadgetry, of the concrete objects that were the devices of modern science or technology. A visitor to the Adelaide Gallery in the 1830s gave this description of its pedagogical science exhibits:

Clever professors were there, teaching elaborate science in lectures of twenty minutes each. Fearful engines revolved and hissed and quivered. Mice led gasping sub-aqueous lives in diving bells. Clockwork steamers ticked round and round a basin perpetually to prove the efficiency of invisible paddle wheels. There were artful snares laid for giving galvanic shocks to the unwary.[11]

Victorian science was very visible—unlike, say, the science of microchips and gene splicing today—and its visible paraphernalia delighted people. Hissing steam contraptions thrilled onlookers as incarnations of scientific knowledge and power. Massive iron flywheels, thrumming boilers, and surging pistons inspired feelings of awe. This was science, indeed! And power so impressive that it could seem nearly divine—although, granted, not everyone went as far as Kipling's engineer McAndrew, who found "Predestination in the stride o' yon connectin'-rod" (in "McAndrew's Hymn"). The flashy pageant of technological science had its detractors, of course, such as William Morris who yearned to "Forget six countries overhung with smoke/Forget the snorting steam and piston-stroke" (in "The Earthly Paradise"). But a ready audience clamored for explanations of the latest discoveries, keen to understand the basis for such scientific magic. Lectures, like those mentioned by the Adelaide visitor, were a popular form of science education, especially when accompanied, as they often were, by demonstrations or drawings. Naturalists as well as physical scientists exploited this form of promotion of natural facts: Louis Agassiz in America and Philip Henry Gosse in England held large audiences in thrall. With its demonstrations, the lecture could be a kind of museum in miniature.

The advance of scientific knowledge proceeded at a positively dizzying pace, but there was much that a single person could do to help. Sheer accumulation of valuable data was possible even if one could not claim the theoretical brilliance of a Richard Owen or Baron Cuvier. Contributing in their own way, industrious collectors amassed vast numbers of specimens, in the name of science, or beauty, or more often both. So rapid was the growth of the science of geology, for instance, that an indefatigable collector of fossils could contribute to geological knowledge almost by default. So much was unknown that nearly every specimen, it seemed, revealed something new. One thinks of Mary Anning and her ichthyosaurs from Lyme Regis. Or consider the zeal of another dedicated amateur, William Willoughby Cole, Earl of Enniskillen in Ireland.[12] His fossil collection was remarkable in that it consisted almost entirely of fish. A superb aggregation of specimens, it eventually found a deserved place in the British Museum (Natural History), and Louis Agassiz found it an invaluable adjunct to his massive study of fossil fish. While Cole's collection exceeded many in size—consisting of nearly 10,000 pieces—it was otherwise not atypical. He collected for the sheer love of it, and part of his enjoyment came from the construction of a private museum on his estate, complete with vaulted glass ceiling, wood-and-glass display cases, and a centerpiece skeleton of a massive extinct Irish elk.

In the nineteenth century, the figure of the museum-collector assumed heroic dimensions. One of the best examples of such a hero can be found in the French science-fiction (that is, science-adventure) novel by Jules Verne, *Twenty Thousand Leagues Under the Sea*. Verne's 1869 adventure mirrors Victorian obsessions with science in many ways. It is fascinated by technology: Atlantic cables, diving suits, electric propulsion, and the like. Geographical exploration is a major theme, exploration of the Antarctic, the Mediterranean, Sargasso Sea, echoing the true adventures of the times. Like much of natural history and scientific accounts by explorers such as Humboldt, Verne's novel exhibits a passion for quantification. Statistics abound: exact figures for latitude, longitude, ocean temperatures, dates, distances, lengths of objects, land volumes.

But most important, *Twenty Thousand Leagues Under the Sea* features two scientist-heroes. One is the familiar mad scientist, with an Ahab-like propensity for vengeance: Captain Nemo. The other hero is a quintessential nineteenth-century scientist-collector, off on expeditions to find specimens to collect, categorize, and send back for exhibit: Aronnax, Professor of the Paris Museum, and author of that authoritative work, *Mysteries of the Great Ocean Depths*.

The assistant to Professor Aronnax, his servant Conseil, is a walking compendium of taxonomy, always ready and able to categorize any sea creature by order, family, genus, and species, in a post-Linnaean frenzy: "Some zoophytes had been dragged up by the chain of the nets. For the most part they were beautiful phyctallines, belonging to the actinidian family, and among other species, the *Phyctalis protexta. . . .*" The inclusion of so many lists of organisms in a novel of adventure, in the underwater saga of the Nautilus, strikes the modern reader as odd or even tedious, detracting from narrative intensity. But as Conseil says after one lengthy list, it is "somewhat dry, perhaps, but very exact."[13] And such exactitude mattered very much to the nineteenth-century reader, especially if he had been conditioned, as was very likely, by the reading of nonfictional accounts of travel and natural history. To such a reader, Professor Aronnax, well-traveled collector, is a noble, exciting, and enviable character, for one simple reason: collecting is a wonderful pursuit.

But why collect? Collecting—that is, plucking individual natural objects out of their environment and context, so that they may be admired and accumulated—is not an innate human urge. It is a learned activity, peculiar to a certain time and culture. To consider collecting important, one must already subscribe to assumptions about the validity of close visual scrutiny—that it is a means to finding beauty—and about the value of novelty in nature. Collectors are obsessed with pushing the limits of novelty even farther. A basic type is not enough for them: they know what a land snail is, for example, but aren't satisfied until they see how many variations or permutations of form it may exhibit. Variety, novelty, and intricacy of form are paramount to the collector.

An anecdote from *The Malay Archipelago*, by Alfred Russel Wallace, highlights the peculiarity of collecting. Wallace was an avowed and formidable collector, who by his own estimation amassed 125,000 specimens of animals (not to mention plant specimens) during twelve years in the tropics. He collected partly for scientific reasons, to investigate the geographical distribution of animals in Malaysia. And his conclusions on that matter closely paralleled Darwin's about the evolution of animals to fit certain niches. But he also collected for the sheer love of it, to fill the "cabinets of Europe." He was assisted in his collecting by the people of the islands he visited. Although helpful, the island people were mystified by this weird pursuit. They accused Wallace of lying to them about the dead animals; surely, they thought, he really wanted them for some sort of sorcery:

> They then attacked me on another point—what all the animals and birds and insects and shells were preserved so carefully for. They had often asked me this before, and I had tried to explain to them that they would be stuffed, and made to look as if alive, and people in my country would go to look at them. But this was not satisfying; in my country there must be many better things to look at, and they could not believe I would take so much trouble with their birds and beasts just for people to look at. They did not want to look at them; and we, who made calico and glass and knives, and all sorts of wonderful things, could not want things from Aru to look at.[14]

The people of Aru, as outsiders to nineteenth-century European culture, provide a different perspective on collecting. They are amazed at how much trouble Victorian naturalists, and their public, went to—*just to look at things*. The Aru inhabitants had their own ideas about the purpose of Wallace's gigantic collection. One queried him about the specimens:

> "What becomes of them when you go on the sea?" "Why, they are all packed up in boxes," said I. "What did you think became of them?" "They all come to life again, don't they?" said he; and though I tried to joke it off, and said if they did we should have plenty to eat at sea, he stuck to his opinion, and kept repeating, with an air of deep conviction, "Yes, they all come to life again, that's what they do—they all come to life again."[15]

And in a sense, they do. In England the specimens *would* come to life again as evocative, aesthetic objects—a different kind of life, surely, than they had in the jungles, but vibrant nonetheless. To the museum visitor in England, the stuffed Bird of Paradise was more alive, with beauty and with connotation, than it was to the Aru natives, perhaps, who did not really see it. In Aru the birds were not seen, partly because they were familiar, but also because no social convention existed for the intent scrutiny of isolated, variegated natural objects.

To an Englishman well steeped in that convention, like Wallace, the excitement of collecting was tremendous. His account abounds with breathless captures of rare treasures, described with heightened emotion. Such emotional captures, full of the thrill of novelty and possession, are recounted by nearly every naturalist of the nineteenth century, from Darwin in his *Autobiography* to P. H. Gosse in his letters and books. Even the paraphernalia needed for collecting is a source of pleasure, consisting, again, of various concrete objects: "boxes . . . books, pen-knives, scissors, pliers, and pins, with insect and bird labels"[16] or, for Gosse, phials, glass jars, baskets, and cabinets with intriguing little draw-ers. But joy in the specimen reigned supreme, as Wallace says of one butterfly he netted:

> The beauty and brilliancy of this insect are indescribable, and none but a naturalist can understand the intense excitement I experienced when I at length captured it. On taking it out of my net and opening the glorious wings, my heart began to beat violently, the blood rushed to my head, and I felt much more like fainting than I have done when in apprehension of immediate death. I had a headache the rest of the day, so great was the excitement produced by what will appear to most people a very inadequate cause.[17]

Here both the possession of the insect and its beauty at close range combine to produce nearly an orgasmic pleasure in the naturalist. The butterfly-as-object is gorgeous and, in addition, representative of the perceived inexhaustible richness of nature's forms that await discovery and capture. Furthermore, it would make a stunning exhibit for some-one's cabinet.

A museum scaled down to the grasp of an ordinary person remained a "cabinet." In America, and in England as well,

> leading natural historians strived to form a network of relations . . . which would yield a steady supply of specimens of plants, rocks, animals, as well as aboriginal artifacts. These were accumulated in "cabinets," often in conjunction with "philosophical apparatus" [scales, flasks, retorts, and the like] from the physical sciences. The development of the cabinets, the study of their contents, the use of the contents in classrooms and in popular

lectures was the life of science for many Americans for well into the century.[18]

References to cabinets of curiosities appear so frequently in works of Victorian natural history, in fact, that they become in essence a metaphor for the Victorian attitude toward nature.

The cabinet collects minutiae, disparate items, often inherently beautiful or well formed, and by juxtaposing them becomes in itself an artistic creation, a work of composition pleasing in color, form, and symmetry. The critic Susan Stewart treats such a collection as a product of "longing," of desire. From her semiotic point of view, such a juxtaposition of objects "is a form of play, a form involving the reframing of objects within a world of attention and manipulation of context."[19] Individual items within the cabinet are frequently a source of intense sensuous pleasure, such as the "indescribable" beauty of Wallace's butterfly. Arranging them also can be pleasurable, as indicated by the care taken to place each precious object in its new "home," the miniature world within the cabinet, a domicile ruled by its benevolent collector. In a sense, the naturalist plays with the cabinet much as a child might play with a dollhouse; Frank Buckland distinctly creates this impression when he talks of how specimens "meet" in the cabinet, "in their snug beds of cotton wool, and bedsteads of cardboard, canopied over by a gorgeous mansion of mahogany."[20]

The cabinet is a little kingdom; the naturalist is its king. The element of control contributes to the cabinet's attraction, much as the element of possession does to collecting. As Stewart says, a collection makes a "gesture of standing for the world" in two ways: "first, the metonymic displacement of part for whole, item for context; and second, the invention of a classification scheme which will define space and time in such a way that the world is accounted for by the elements of the collection."[21] And most especially, a "museum of natural history allows nature to exist 'all at once,' in a way in which it could not otherwise exist." By merely juxtaposing objects the cabinet implies an order, a connection, a correspondence, a whole, which, even if it cannot be articulated, still can be perceived. Or which, if need be, the naturalist can simply create.

In this context a journal entry of Ralph Waldo Emerson is most interesting. Emerson found that a cabinet had the effect of enlarging the "limits of the possible," using juxtaposition as a method to show nature's extravagance. Traveling from America to some of the centers of natural history on the Continent, he wrote in Paris on July 13, 1833:

I carried my ticket . . . to the Cabinet of Natural History in the Garden of Plants. How much finer things are in composition than alone. 'Tis wise in man to make Cabinets. When I was come into the Ornithological Chambers, I wished I had come only there. The fancy-coloured vests of these elegant beings make me as pensive as the hues and forms of a cabinet of shells, formerly. It is a beautiful collection and makes the visitor as calm and genial as a bridegroom. The limits of the possible are enlarged, and the real is stranger than the imaginary. . . . Ah said I this is philanthropy, wisdom, taste—to form a Cabinet of natural history. . . . Here we are impressed with the inexhaustible riches of nature. The Universe is a more amazing puzzle than ever as you glance along this bewildering series of animated forms—the hazy butterflies, the carved shells, the birds, beasts, fishes, insects, snakes . . . I am moved by strange sympathies, I say continually "I will be a naturalist."[22]

Clearly, Emerson fully appreciated the splendors of the Jardin des Plantes, one of the best and most active of nineteenth-century museums.

Several things are noteworthy about Emerson's response. Perhaps most important is his recognition of the aesthetic principle involved in the cabinet: things are "finer in composition than alone." Juxtaposition is evocative, creative. Second, of course, there is his enthusiasm for the cabinet as a microcosm of nature, where one can experience nature's variety in concentrated doses. And third, Emerson's delight in the halls of the Jardin des Plantes shows just how influential nineteenth-century natural history was. Although British Victorians were perhaps its most avid adherents, its practice and characteristic motifs charmed Americans and Europeans, too. So it was not unusual to find an American writer enthralled with the idea of natural history collecting and to see him undertake a trip to France to visit a center for natural history study.

In spite of his declaration, though, Emerson never did become a naturalist. In truth, his whole approach to the world was not that of a naturalist at all. His pivotal essay *Nature* (1836) revealed that Emerson was really very little interested in the things of nature per se. Ultimately, for him, they were only valuable as emblems of moral or spiritual truths. (See especially the sections "Language" and "Idealism and Spirit" in *Nature*: "Nature is the symbol of spirit.") Yet even such a dedicated idealist as Emerson could not help but be swept up in the tide of natural history.

The cabinet, then, is one dominant metaphor for the aesthetic science of natural history. As a metaphor, or motif, it surfaces frequently as representative of an order created from disorder. If eclectic, the cabinet's display retains some of the Romantic love for the evocative fragment; if highly organized, some of the Victorian taste for a systematic and objective compilation of facts. In particular, fossils arrayed within cabinets acquired a special potency in the nineteenth century, because they represented a hitherto unsuspected past. After all, dinosaurs had been unknown before the 1820s, and biblical notions of time had truncated the prehistorical scale. But paleontological discoveries and Darwinian suggestions made people aware that eons of time and multitudes of creatures had passed away, leaving few but tantalizing traces.[23] (Like the public today, the Victorian public was quite captivated by dinosaurs—witness the excitement caused in 1854 by the dinosaur models exhibited at Sydenham.) As a result, fossils, in addition to displaying unmistakable physical charms, possessed considerable imaginative power—all the more intoxicating because the worlds they embodied had lain hidden for so long. An iguanodon tooth within a cabinet was a talisman capable of evoking a mysterious, unimaginably ancient past. And, in part, the Victorian fascination with objects in cabinets derived from a need to intuit the whole of nature from the contemplation of its parts.

To collect things is to look at them closely. Not surprisingly, then, optical metaphors or motifs pervade Victorian natural history writing. Vision, sights, spectacles—the importance of "ocular proof"—occur again and again. Perhaps the most ubiquitous optical motifs are provided by the microscope (or by its counterpart, the telescope), and by the techniques of microscopy, because during the nineteenth century the microscope came into its own. Magnifying instruments had been available for two centuries, of course, but became widely available and relatively cheap only after 1830. Soon they were in the hands of countless natural history hobbyists, who spent long enjoyable hours scrutinizing pond water and feathers, insect legs and blood cells.

In the seventeenth century, the early era of microscopy, discovery was constrained by equipment: simple instruments with rather crude lenses, which had limited powers and inherent distortions. Compound microscopes were more versatile than those with a single lens (such as Leeuwenhoek had used), but until the early nineteenth century these remained delicate and cumbersome; they were rarely used and imperfectly understood. Nevertheless, during the eighteenth century optical theory advanced tremendously. Nascent in the Middle Ages, optics accelerated with the publication of Sir Isaac Newton's *Opticks* in 1704. And far from being an obscure discipline, this science captured the popular imagination. Marjorie Hope Nicolson has amply demonstrated the effects of Newtonian optics on poetry of the eighteenth century. With Newton's explanation of spectral colors, Nicolson notes, poets began an "obsession" with "Light itself"[24] and "labored to understand the physics of light, and still more the physics of sight, becoming acutely aware of the structure and function of the human eye, that mysterious liaison between the world 'out there' and the mind 'in here.'" More important, as a prelude to optical obsessions among Victorians in general and naturalists in particular, during the eighteenth century "sight was exalted as the greatest of the senses."[25]

Eighteenth-century poetry primed readers to think in terms of optics, and in this seedbed the hobby of microscopy easily took root. Public awareness of microscopes was increased by news of their accomplishments, which in turn depended on technical improvements in design and manufacture, and an accompanying fall in price. A major barrier to the microscope's usefulness had been the color fringes that surrounded the image produced by early lenses. By the 1820s, the technical problems of chromatic distortion had been solved, and microscopes could produce much sharper images. In 1831 Robert Brown used a microscope to discover the cell nucleus, and "the enormous interest aroused by this led to rapid improvements in microscope design. In the next ten years, prices fell fivefold."[26] Soon an instrument powerful enough to examine the intricacies of cell architecture could be had for about three guineas. J. G. Wood, author of *Common Objects of the Microscope*, recommended a bargain model to his readers as being "a compound microscope . . . a really admirable instrument . . . quite achromatic,"[27] ideally suited to hobbyists who could hardly afford the "fabulous" professional models which could cost forty or fifty pounds or more.

No aspiring microscopist need despair, even if the three-guinea price was too dear. Penury was no excuse, for, as Wood chided his readers, "there are few instances where a person so minded may not possess himself of a microscope that will do a considerable amount of sound work and at an inappreciable cost" (p. 5). For a "few pence," anyone could buy at least a magnifying glass, and in a pinch, Wood claimed, "a very respectable microscope may be extemporized out of a strip of card, wood, or metal, and a little water" (p. 6), with the drop of water serving as the lens. Wood boasted that he himself had once created a perfectly adequate dissecting microscope "out of an old retort-stand, a piece of cane, and six inches of elder branch," which "did its work as effectually" as any "shining-lackered [*sic*] brass instrument." And while a wide variety of microscope accessories could be purchased ready-made from an optician, Wood promised his readers that many of these, too, could be fabricated at very little cost. Following his detailed instructions, even a beginner could bend needles and affix them to wooden handles to make probes, for example, or heat glass tubing over a flame to create tapered pipettes. And if one had the advantage of some ready cash, a whole host of fancy aids was easily obtainable, such as a "Live-Box or Animalcule cage" (p. 31) for holding a miniature menagerie of specimens under the lens. Thus equipped, many a Victorian parlor afforded amateur micro-scopists hours of amusement and amazement.

Even for those people who did not have one at home, the microscope was a familiar sight. Routinely "hawked about the streets" of London, Wood said, were "penny microscopes, composed of a pill-box and a drop of Canada balsam." And the far more powerful oxy-hydrogen micro-scope was very "popular at exhibitions" (p. 160). This instrument gave particularly impressive views because through combustion of oxygen-hydrogen gas it could shine bright light on the material to be examined, often water crawling with micro-organisms. Such a startling look at the denizens of ordinary water served to "discompose the public mind" and pull the microscopic world into public consciousness. Tennyson and Arthur Hallam were among the enthralled spectators at an oxy-hydrogen microscope exhibition in 1833.[28]

Aside from its entertainment value, the microscope proved invaluable for scientists like Theodore Schwann on the Continent, and serious amateurs too saw its potential for discovery. In 1839, the same year that Schwann published the results of his animal-cell investigations, enthusi-asts in England formed the Microscopical Society of London (later the Royal Microscopical Society) to further research. Its founders included such disparate scientists as Joseph Lister and Nathaniel Ward,[29] inventor of the Wardian (fern) case. P. H. Gosse became a devoted member in 1849. As new microscope models appeared, the circle of microscopists widened. For example, in 1865 the popular "Universal" instrument was being widely promoted. This model appealed to natural history amateurs as well as to scientists, and, although it cost nine pounds, the Universal was a very sophisticated instrument for the price.[30] With it, even an amateur could pursue quite serious investigations into microscopic phe-nomena.

By 1865, a contemporary observer noted that "the use of the micro-scope has spread widely among the educated section of the public."[31] When Wood wrote his book to guide hobbyists in the techniques of microscopy, at about the same time, he felt that his choice of subject matter needed no justification:

With the last few years the microscope has become so firmly rooted among us, that little need be said in its praise. The time has long passed away when it was held in no higher estimation than an ingenious toy; but it is now acknowledged, that no one can attain even a moderate knowledge of any physical science without a considerable acquaintance with the microscope and the marvellous phenomena which it reveals.[32]

Wood goes on to say that, "even to those who aspire to no scientific eminence, the microscope is more than an amusing companion, revealing many of the hidden secrets of nature, and unveiling endless beauties which were heretofore enveloped in the impenetrable obscurity of their own minuteness." Wood's perceptions were typical: that the microscope served as a means of access to whole other worlds, and that it could elevate even the most common of objects to the status of objets d'art. Not everyone who peered through a microscope had the reaction of Philip Gosse, who after buying his first microscope in 1849 found that "this purchase revolutionized his whole life"[33] But the microscope worked a powerful magic, and its devotees were legion. Microscopy guidebooks like Wood's, or those of Mrs. (Mary) Ward, which were displayed at the International Exhibition at the Crystal Palace, Sydenham, in 1862,[34] kept the marvels of the instrument before the public.

The microscope was one of several nineteenth-century devices that "unveiled hidden beauties" in the natural world. It was by far the best known, especially by the public. But others, like the telescope, gave much of the same heady sense of limitless possibilities for human sight, revealing new worlds through the power of optics. In the field of medicine, especially, innovations permitted physicians to see inside a previously opaque natural object: the living human body. For example, in 1850 the invention of the ophthalmoscope allowed doctors for the first time to peer into the dark pupil of the eye and see the retina. The visual metaphor was so compelling that, oddly enough, the stethoscope was frequently characterized as "an instrument for 'seeing' into the chest."[35] And the microscope played its part, both for serious researchers, who investigated physiology and disease processes, as well as for the amateur naturalist, who could include his or her own blood cells in the pantheon of marvels revealed by the lens.

A volume of *Chambers's Miscellany of Instructive & Entertaining Tracts* attests to the microscope's sway over the popular imagination. Alongside articles on Peter the Great, Heroism in Humble Life, Ballads, A Visit to Edinburgh, Christmas, and the Life of Columbus rests an essay on "Wonders of the Microscope." The volume is not dated, but from internal evidence it appears to be from the 1880s, and it introduces the microscope by saying:

> The microscope, of late years, has claimed so much attention from almost
> all observers of natural history, and has added so much to our knowledge
> of the various changes and processes going on in the organic kingdoms,
> that a slight glance at the wonderful phenomena revealed by its aid, may
> not be unacceptable to the general reader.[36]

The information provided by the microscope is described here, quite
typically, in quasi-religious terms, as "Revelations" of nature's "Wonders." Heavily technical, the tract is crammed with arcane details of
optics, zoology, and microscopical techniques. Obviously, however, such
details were not thought too esoteric for popular consumption and were
meant to be taken as practical tips, to be "instrumental" if only "in
causing one person to examine closely into the wonders which surround
him in nature, and thereby enable him to while away a few hours which
otherwise might have passed uselessly or heavily."[37] Heaven forbid an
idle hour!

By the latter half of the century the terminology of microscopy had
entered the mainstream of language. If one meant to examine a subject
closely, one put it "under the microscope." Swinburne employed this trope
in a scathing essay of the same name, lambasting literary critics, whom the
poet considered to be parasites. To expose them to his scorn, Swinburne
proposes to "bring [them] under our microscope, as it were."[38] Critics are a
species of unattractive insect, vastly inferior to creative writers and so
insignificant that "they would be imperceptible from above but for the
microscopic lens which science enables us . . . to apply to themselves and
their appliances." The microscope here has become metaphor.

Today, one is apt to be rather blasé about microscopes and lenses.
Most people are quite used to them, and science after all has advanced
microscopy beyond optics with the electron microscope. To recapture
some of the excitement that nineteenth-century amateur naturalists felt
when they looked through their lenses, consider an extra-European perspective. Recall the Malay Archipelago inhabitants that Alfred Wallace
met, who reacted with such amazement to his activities. Not only his
collecting, but his technological tools amazed them. Looking through a
hand-lens created a sensation:

> One afternoon when I was arranging my insects, and surrounded by a
> crowd of wondering spectators, I showed one of them how to look at a
> small insect with a hand-lens, which caused such evident wonder that all
> the rest wanted to see it too. I therefore fixed the glass firmly to a piece of
> soft wood at the proper focus, and put under it a little spiny beetle of the
> genus Hispa, and then passed it round for examination. The excitement

was immense. Some declared it was a yard long; others were frightened and instantly dropped it, and all were as much astonished, and made as much shouting and gesticulation as children at a pantomime, or at a Christmas exhibition of the oxyhydrogen microscope. And all this excitement was produced by a little pocket-lens, an inch and a half focus, and therefore magnifying only four or five times, but which to their unaccustomed eyes appeared to enlarge a hundredfold.[39]

Wallace implicitly compares the islanders' reactions to the hand-lens with the English public's reaction to the more complex microscope. The degree of magnification is different, but the response is the same. An ordinary natural object, a common beetle, if changed in scale becomes a source of wonder and astonishment. For the island people, who have no means or convention for seeing nature out of scale, the result is a comic pandemonium. The English no doubt were a trifle more sedate, controlling their gesticulation—but they were undeniably excited when tiny objects loomed large through the lens.

Aside from being an enjoyable pastime, microscopy sent some resounding reverberations through the Victorian imagination. For one thing, the widespread use of lenses and microscopes among amateur naturalists, and even the general public, surely led to a new concentration on details. As Allen says,

This general use of the microscope had the wider effect of bringing before people's vision an unsuspected realm of delicate forms and brilliant colourings. What had seemed drab and insignificant objects now revealed their splendour and held their beholders enthralled. . . . Years of peering closely trained the eye in the admiring of minutiae, the intricate details, the lowly magnificence of Creation. With their microscopes, the Victorians found a means of penetrating to nature's furthermost recesses, of laying bare new aspects of the elemental.[40]

Tiny objects looming large—if that is what one often looks at, it means that details of all kinds tend to become more important. The microscope did more than enlarge the subject matter available for description; it also brought with it a whole new approach. Through the microscope, the world becomes a vast collection of microscopic details, a mosaic (as Gosse described the butterfly's wing) of infinitely tiny pieces. In this sense, cabinets, collecting, and microscopes all foster a kind of reductionism—reducing complex processes and forms to bits which might, by themselves, make no more sense than does one individual piece of a picture puzzle. For the naturalist, the details are beautiful in themselves, so much so that overall coherence is not a major issue.

However, when the microscopic method is transferred from natural history discourse to literature, the concentration on details can produce a disoriented sense of fragmentation, of a loss of unity. This sometimes occurs in the poems of Tennyson, Browning, or the Pre-Raphaelite poets. One thinks, for example, of the reductionism in Rossetti's "The Woodspurge," where the mind of the speaker, numbed by grief, is unable to extract any meaning from the experience except the extraneous and dissected detail that "the woodspurge has a cup of three" (referring to the structure of the flower). Or, to give an example even more famous, the insane speaker in Tennyson's "Maud" finds that, when he is overwrought, sensory details are heightened for him:

> Strange, that the mind, when fraught
> With a passion so intense
> One would think that it well
> Might drown all life in the eye,—
> That it should, by being so overwrought,
> Suddenly strike on a sharper sense
> For a shell, or a flower, little things
> Which else would have been past by!
> (section II, stanza VIII)

If grief or passion can heighten the "life in the eye," then perhaps, the Victorians worried, the reverse might be true. Spending time peering too closely at the details of a shell[41] or flower might in itself induce an undesirable emotional state. For if one lost sight of the whole—the moral order, as it were—that way did madness lie. Thus, seductive though detailed concentration might be, it posed a danger.

Carol T. Christ studies the literary implications of the "microscopic eye" in her book *The Finer Optic: The Aesthetic of Particularity in Victorian Poetry.*[42] As a chapter heading, she links "particularity" with "morbidity," finding that, in Tennyson especially, excessive concentration on details often indicates that the persona in a poem is depressed, morbid, or insane, as in "Mariana." Too many details signal a failure of meaning, a collapse of unity, the death of hope. For Browning, Christ finds that particularity is linked with "Atomism and the Grotesque" (chapter 2 in Christ), as seen, for example, in the limited vision, moral or otherwise, of "Caliban Upon Setebos." Only in Hopkins (or occasionally in Browning) does she find in particularity the symptoms of something good, what she calls the "good moment," or the fleeting recognition of the transcendent in the concrete (chapter 3 in Christ).

Christ's theory is suggestive and often well substantiated. In light of her association of particular details with morbidity and madness, it is interesting to consider the case of John Ruskin. Throughout his life, Ruskin sketched and drew from nature, but in his later years, as he slipped toward insanity, he became obsessed with objective, detail-drawings of isolated objects. Unable to grasp wholes, devoid of optimism, lacking a perception of the spiritual or moral energy in nature, Ruskin compulsively sketched single feathers, or shells, or stones. Earlier in his life, such studies would have been done in the "unifying context of a landscape sketch."[43] Now they were broken little pieces; acutely observed, but without meaning.

That is the dark side of the Victorians' obsession with microscopic vision. Just as often, however, and especially in the writings of naturalists, microscopic examination of details is breathlessly, exuberantly endorsed, and related with a wondrous sense of being privy to a whole new miniature world. Frequently, enthusiastic proponents of the minuscule recommend it to all who would truly see the world—especially artists. In Ruskin's case, for example, his fervor for "slaty crystallines" gave him many more years of joy than sorrow, degenerating from reverence into despair only at the very end of his life, and for complex reasons, most of them having nothing to do with natural history. For much of his life, natural history inspired him.

In fact, Ruskin based many of his artistic principles on close examination of nature's minutiae (see Chapter 6). Similarly, another Victorian writer on art, James K. Colling, pens very Ruskinian passages brimming with a similar ebullient advocacy of a microscopic outlook on nature. In a now-obscure volume called *Art Foliage*, Colling pleaded for a revival of carved plant forms as decoration for buildings, as had been so prevalent in Gothic architecture. Twenty years of nature study had convinced Colling of nature's primacy as the foundation for art. Colling's work demonstrates both the Victorian enthusiasm for microscopic nature and the relationship between close nature studies and Victorian art. First he tells his readers how to look at nature:

> The infinity and beauty of nature in small things are most wonderful—they go far beyond our natural powers of observation. Even with the aid of the microscope we can form no conception of the extent or termination of the minute world of beauty—a vast world, shut out from all ordinary observation. Look, for instance, at the elegant and very suggestive forms of pollen grains, when viewed under the microscope (See the *Elements of Botany*, by John Lindley, M.D.). Who would have supposed that in the golden dust, which we see borne away by the industrious bee, were to be found such

perfect geometrically divided globes? In the star-like crystals of snow, again, is another familiar instance of the beauty of the minute world.[44]

Looking at nature with an intent, and then magnified, eye, one beholds successive waves or ranges of beauty. The pollen, already beautiful to the ordinary viewer as "golden dust" (and having something transcendent about it, as it is "borne away" into another realm by the bee), becomes even more stunning when magnified. The grains become complex, intricate, little marvels of minute architecture, as snowflakes are. The "minute world of beauty" is a "vast world," another realm opened up to wondering eyes.

Even without the aid of a microscope, though, ordinary nature gains in significance when scrutinized carefully: "However, without calling in the aid of the microscope for the purpose of our studies, there is an astonishing appropriateness and singular beauty in some of the smallest and most humble plants, which at once point out their fitness for the purpose of the artist" (p. 3). Colling takes note of the popularity of "fine gardens and magnificent green-houses," where people like to go to see the blatant beauties of "rare exotics" (p. 4). Certainly they excite the imagination, but Colling urges an equally rapt approach to the common plants; if inspected lovingly, they too will dazzle. "Often the lowliest objects and the commonest weeds contain beauties that we little dream of, until we examine them minutely and diligently, and with the eye of an artist" (p. 3). The artist can learn the most from common objects. This notion, of course, pervades Victorian natural history: that the naturalist, by seeing, can transform the common into the fabulous, elevate the ordinary to an extraordinary plane. Colling's diction echoes the Reverend J. G. Wood's approach in his best-selling book *Common Objects of the Country*, as well as Wood's other books, *Common Objects of the Sea-side* and *Common Objects of the Microscope*. Common objects challenge the artist because they are inherently complex yet overlooked, but mostly because they force the artist to train his eye. One must *learn* to see. One must make seeing active, not passive:

> But the copyist may say he can see no beauty in thistles, and docks, and buttercups. Yes; but how do you look at them? They must be studied attentively and assiduously, and then, I will ask, "Can you see no vigour of form in these lowly outcasts—the very power of which you are in search, to give life to your own works: no beauty in the thistle with its sturdy stem, its ever-varying form, in its energetically spiked leaves, its great variety of light and shade? Look again at its flower; set like an amethyst among its green ray of spines: and the common creeping crowfoot, too, that pest to the

farmer, that insinuates its roots unseen beneath the ground to throw up its elegantly formed leaves in every vacant space, to teach a simple lesson of beauty." But all this is lost upon us! We see not the elegance in these homely things, because we look upon them as if we were blind! (p. 4)

In his own scrutiny and delineation of nature's forms, Colling shows a marked predilection for the common, made new again by magnification. He is particularly fond of tiny buds, which seem to him "emblems of purity and innocence," and urges his readers to diligence in sketching them, "two or three times their natural size, or in many cases much larger, as when seen under a powerful magnifying glass" (p. 112). In reference to his illustrations of newly opened ferns, Colling cautions: "It must be clearly remembered, that nearly all of these examples are very much magnified, so that a person searching for them in nature, may easily overlook them if he is not extremely careful. A score of the little buds, before they are much developed, may be put into an ordinary sized pill-box" (p. 116). But the cunning contours of the ferns reward the search. They give both visual pleasure and artistic inspiration.

Colling's art manual represents a triumph of the microscopic perspective. And his tone of awe about the miniature world is by no means unusual in Victorian nature writing. David Allen cites a similar, typical expression by J. E. Bowman: "I am absolutely filled with wonder and in an ecstasy of delight at the structure and contrivance of some of the extremely minute specimens. . . . How many beautiful and interesting productions we tread daily underfoot and pass by unnoticed!"[45]

But if microscopes narrowed and focused human vision, by encouraging close attention to minute details, so also, in another sense, they widened it. The experience of looking through the lens became dialectical. Closet and field naturalists can be said to represent a dialectic between two views of nature: close, focused, and static versus sweeping, contextual, and shifting. So too did the microscope foster a dual perspective on the natural world. Close-focused vision might involve peering at single-celled Infusoria, or fern spores, but it also involved looking at whole new worlds. With a microscope or hand-lens, one could peer down into an entirely unsuspected realm, a miniature landscape, a small but multitudinous universe.

The giddy sense that resulted was one of "opening up" a new dimension. Over and over again Victorian accounts of the microscope speak in terms of crossing over into a magical world. The microscope functions much like Keats' magic casement or Alice's looking glass. With it, one crosses a threshold, a window into another reality; one is transformed.

This sense of "opening up" a new realm resulted, too, when looking through a telescope, or the more curious device known as a "water telescope."

Frank Buckland, ever the advocate of fish and their beauty, recommended that those "who spend their time at the seaside and are fond of observing living fish and other forms of subaqueous animal life in their wild state" should try the water telescope as an aid to observation. Essentially a glass-bottomed bucket or metal cylinder, the water telescope would, he felt, prove "invaluable" to the naturalist.

What is most interesting about Buckland's device is the descriptive language it inspires: the diction of vistas. If the water telescope is used,

> the beauties and luxurious growth of the submarine forests of sea plants will also to many be a most novel and interesting spectacle. To water parties who picnic on rivers or near lakes the water telescope will be found a great adjunct to the day's enjoyment, as by means of it subaqueous scenery may, possibly for the first time, be brought into view, and many a beautiful panorama opened up to the human eye.[46]

Here the employment of an unusual lens displays, perhaps for the first time, a whole new world of "subaqueous scenery." What the human eye thus can see is not necessarily small details, but a whole new landscape in sweeping breadth: a "panorama."[47] What image of a naturalist does Buckland present? The naturalist is a person whose pleasure comes from searching out ever-new "spectacles," in this case whole underwater realms—not a plant or two but "submarine forests" that stretch out before the eye like pine forests swaddling Alps. The long view is what matters here, and just as the Alps by this time could engender awe, gazing upon the underwater landscape inspires a sense of beauty and wonder. With characteristic gusto, Buckland promises that the panorama beneath the waves will be "opened up" to the eye—and thence to the imagination.

Another example of a lens giving the long view can be found, not in a work of natural history, but in an early science-fiction story from 1858: Fitz-James O'Brien's "The Diamond Lens." With the aid of a fifteen-dollar mail-order microscope, its protagonist becomes entranced with miniature universes discovered in a drop of rainwater, a "universe of beings animated with all the passions common to physical life, and convulsing their minute sphere with struggles as fierce and protracted as those of men."[48] Common mildew becomes "enchanted gardens, filled with dells and avenues of the densest foliage and most astonishing verdure, while from the fantastic boughs of these microscopic forests hung strange fruits glittering with green, silver, and gold" (p. 329).

Eager to see more, the microscopist, by underhanded means, acquires a much superior "diamond" lens with greater magnifying power. The views become even more breathtaking. Through the diamond lens he sees, like Buckland, not detail as such, but "a vast space" (p. 344), a "dazzling expanse" (p. 344), "gaseous forests" that stretch "far away into the illimitable distance" (p. 345). In this "newly discovered world" (p. 345) dwell, not protozoa, but beautiful female forms. Utterly bedazzled, the by now somewhat crazed explorer falls in love with one of them.

Here the adventures of microscopy are taken, of course, to a completely impossible extreme. Yet "The Diamond Lens," which one critic calls the first "fictional plunge" that "opened up" (that term again) a microscopic world (p. 322), nonetheless vividly expresses the rapture that many Victorians felt when using their hand-lenses or telescopes, or reading books of natural history. The story's very exaggeration, in fact, underscores the microscope's imaginative potency. It is the same rapture that motivated Philip Henry Gosse to pen his *Evenings at the Microscope* (1859). As O'Brien's protagonist puts it: "It was no scientific thirst that at this time filled my mind. It was the pure enjoyment of a poet to whom a world of wonders has been disclosed" (p. 329). The microscopist, or natural historian, spends his time "poring over marvels" (p. 329), his eyes alert not only to minute particularities, but also to a whole new kind of landscape.

From 1830 on, then, the microscope reinforced a dialectic of vision, one that pervades natural history as well as literature and visual art. Gerhard Joseph's article, "Tennyson's Optics: The Eagle's Gaze," finds that Tennyson's poetry is based on a "way of seeing" that is dialectical or even contradictory in precisely this way. Tennyson was notoriously nearsighted, a fact frequently remarked upon by people who met him. Because he suffered such drastic myopia, Joseph says, Tennyson had to bring objects close to his eyes for examination, thus learning "an extreme fidelity of detail, especially of botanical detail," which he transferred to his poetry. Having to work hard at seeing seemed to teach him to pay close attention and to appreciate details all the more. As one acquaintance of his recollected, "his sight though very short was most extraordinarily keen for small objects, and for microscopically tiny details which would escape the notice of men with apparently four times his power of vision."[49] Obsessed with close vision, Joseph maintains, Tennyson would even "bring a naturalist's care" to details he could only imagine, like the kraken under the sea.[50] Joseph equates such detailed vision with a naturalist's, and quite rightly so.

Tennyson is widely acknowledged as one of the writers of Victorian literature most influenced by science, which he followed avidly. However, many of the details in his poetry seem more akin to a naturalist's observations than to a scientist's. This may reflect the fact that while Tennyson studied science, he was an amateur naturalist in his own right. His grandson recalled: "He was a tremendous walker. . . . As he walked, he ceaselessly observed—he was a great naturalist and a keen student of geology, astronomy and the various forms of natural science."[51] Tennyson's observation swung dialectically between two poles. On the one hand, to use Carol T. Christ's words, Tennyson adhered to an "aesthetics of particularity" (which could have negative effects: details could frighteningly overwhelm the observer, or stand in isolation apart from any meaning, or even presage madness). On the other hand, Tennyson insisted on the opposite visual extreme (or "optical bias"): a "compensatory movement toward distanced perspectives and vagueness."[52]

Such a phrase cannot help but call to mind Ruskin, who with his own talent for careful sketching advocated concentration on "the pure fact" (*Modern Painters III*, part IV, chapter 12), while insisting that, as Turner so supremely demonstrated, one must also allow a broader vision. The broader view leaves an "essential mystery" to be seen in the haze of distance. Of Ruskin I have much to say in Chapter 6. His opinions on vision, in the context of his art criticism, were highly influential. And his careful sight provides a paradigm for the kind of approach to nature that a naturalist ought to have.

In light of what I have said about the influence of one aspect of the natural history craze—the microscope—on Victorian perception, Gerhard Joseph's summary of the "bifocal dialectic" of Victorian poets is worth noting. The Romantic willingness to move from neoclassical general truths to seeing the truth, or world, in a particular thing, a grain of sand, can lead to

> a lyric solipsism, to a hypnotic containment within the object, or to a sense of atomistic discontinuity of all objects. The Victorian poet's recognition of such dangers led to a vacillation between concreteness and diaphaneity, between specific and vaguely generalized landscape, between microscopic verisimilitude and distanced syntheses, between central emphases and circumferential sweeps, between focal-point concentration and vantage-point panorama.[53]

Like Christ, Joseph points out the dangers of "atomism" that Victorian writers feared. But in response, he maintains, they instinctively gravitated to the other extreme of vision, "sweeps." Here is the same split vision that one finds in the amateur naturalists: particularity and panorama.

Just as for the poets an excessive concentration on minute details might be seen as dangerous, for some writers the microscope itself was an enemy. Goethe, Emerson, and Burroughs all scorned it, and Ruskin especially denounced the device. (They would have felt no need to be so vehement, of course, had the microscope not captured the public imagination as it did.) Although he himself was highly "eye"-oriented, Ruskin felt that the microscope perverted sight, perhaps even causing natural sight to atrophy, and worst of all tempted one to dissect natural details out of their context, rendering them useless:

> Flowers, like everything else that is lovely in the visible world, are only to be seen rightly with the eyes which the God who made them gave us; and neither with microscope nor spectacles. . . . The use of instruments for exaggerating the powers of sight necessarily deprives us of the best pleasures of sight. A flower is to be watched as it grows, in its association with the earth, the air, and the dew; its leaves are to be seen as they expand in sunshine; its colours, as they embroider the field, or illumine the forest. Dissect or magnify them, all you discover or learn at last will be that oaks, roses, and daisies, are all made of fibres and bubbles; and these again, of charcoal and water; but, for all their peeping and probing, nobody knows how.[54]

Anyone who wears glasses might wince at Ruskin's insistence upon looking at the world totally without any artificial aids. But Ruskin has philosophical points to drive home.

Having trained his own vision to be keen, Ruskin advocates, first of all, a trained, intently conscious sight, really a microscopic eye without the microscope. Second, Ruskin here mirrors the closet-field split within natural history; clearly, he belongs in the "field" camp. A flower can only be rightly seen, in its true essence as a flower, when in context. As an ecologist would understand the flower only within its web of living relationships, so would Ruskin see it. Third, Ruskin here betrays traces of vitalism, a nineteenth-century belief that life itself, with its mysterious vitality, can never be reduced to, or explained by, mechanism. A living creature is more than the sum of its elements, a flower more than the combination of carbon and water. So what is the point of reducing the whole to its parts? Just, at the very least, to see that the parts may themselves be beautiful.

In his comments on vision, however, Ruskin seems as "bifocal" as Tennyson. He desires both the panorama—the flower in its field, artistically "embroidering" the fabric of a meadow—and the close particularity given by a careful eye. For Ruskin, though, particularity can be carried too far. Looking at fibers and bubbles, one cannot see the daisy. Beyond a fear of mechanism, Ruskin clearly feels trepidation over how much to trespass into realms that humans were never meant to see. Like others of his time, Ruskin distrusts close vision, which might become myopic. And myopia may miss the larger truths.

Ocular scrutiny, trained and careful looking at nature (or architecture, or painting) obviously mattered greatly to Ruskin. So much so, that some critics find vision to be central to his whole credo. For example, Elizabeth K. Helsinger, in *Ruskin and the Art of the Beholder*, studies Ruskin's way of seeing and how it was influenced by landscape traditions in art, by Romantic ideas of perception, and by the tradition of the eighteenth-century genial traveler. Helsinger says Ruskin develops a visual "language":

> To read Ruskin is to see with a new intensity—to look at both natural and painted landscapes in a different way. The claim could easily be reversed, however: to see intensely with Ruskin is to learn to "read" what we see—to consider landscape, natural or painted, as art, and visual art as a language requiring interpretation to yield its various kinds of meaning.[55]

Among travel books that influenced Ruskin, Helsinger includes those of the "roving natural scientist,"[56] which makes perfect sense when one realizes that such scientists took a naturalist's view of the world.

Robert Hewison also sees vision as central to Ruskin's credo, as the title of his study hints. In *John Ruskin: The Argument of the Eye*, Hewison ferrets out a most provocative fact about Ruskin's education. Noting the fascination that mineral collecting held for Ruskin, Hewison proposes an interesting corollary to his mineralogical studies: Ruskin's "principle of direct observation" is one based on "an attitude to nature that rests upon externals."[57] Ruskin may have been encouraged to value externals so highly by one of the books he studied in youth: Jameson's *System of Mineralogy*. Jameson describes his system as "founded on what are popularly called the External Characters of Minerals," which are "totally independent of any aid from Chemistry. This . . . may be termed the Natural History Method."

In other words, a Jamesonian geologist would classify minerals solely on the basis of their color, crystal shapes, and luster—their appearance—ignoring all chemical groupings such as sulfates, carbonates, and so on. This Jameson calls the Natural History Method, as opposed to the Scientific Method. Why? Because it depends on relationships apparent to the eye and hand, not those open only to rational examination. Treasuring nature's externals alone is contrary to a truly scientific examination of them, which delves and probes and picks apart. So Ruskin loves the face of nature, yet recoils from science. For him the distinction between natural history and science is palpable. His approach to nature is essentially a naturalist's: a preoccupation with vision and also with collecting. Both emphasize nature's pleasing externals, color and form. If the perception of externals is primary, then aesthetics shoulders its way past rational understanding.

By concentrating on externals, the cabinet and the microscope both created new metaphors for looking at nature. Both made nature into an exhibit, a display for the eye to linger on. Certainly the objects in a cabinet and the objects seen through the microscope's eye-piece emphasized particularity. They were, indisputably, particular things. But particularity in itself would have had less attraction for Victorian amateur naturalists had it not also suggested panorama. In the case of the cabinet, the panorama consisted of the meaning created by the objects' juxtaposition. By choosing specimens for a cabinet and then arranging them within the frame of wood and glass, the naturalist created a little world, a world which reverberated with possibilities of the larger world. In the case of the microscope, the panorama also was inherent, paradoxically, within the little world revealed, opened up, by the lens. To look into the microscope, naturalists said again and again, was to enter another world.

One of the most pleasurable sensations experienced by the Victorian naturalist was that of falling through a seemingly opaque and solid reality, to arrive on a new plane crowded with previously unsuspected forms. For the microscopist, especially, the natural world became an infinite series of Chinese boxes, endlessly amusing. Open one, and there is another, smaller one, within. Open that—there is another, and another still. As the magnification increases, the naturalist discovers worlds within worlds. Rapturously wielding his microscope, George Henry Lewes described the process like this:

> Take the tiny insect (*Aphis*) which, with its companions, crowds your rose-tree; open it, in a solution of sugar-water, under your microscope, and you will find inside it a young insect nearly formed; open that young insect with care, and you will find in it, also, another young one, less advanced in its development, but perfectly recognizable to the experienced eye; and beside this embryo you will find many eggs, which would in time become insects!

This is the panorama within the particular. The microscope and cabinet confer potent imaginative and transformational abilities: to enlarge, as Emerson would say, the limits of the possible. "In your astonishment," says Lewes, "you will ask, Where is this to end?" But it will not end, not for the Victorian naturalist. The naturalist perceives nature simultaneously as infinitely broad and infinitely small, with imbricating layers of detail that have no limit. As Lewes describes nature,

> She fills the illimitable heavens with planetary and starry grandeurs, and she makes the tiny atoms moving over the crust of earth the homes of the infinitely little. Far as the mightiest telescope can reach, it detects worlds in clusters, like pebbles on the shores of Infinitude; deep as the microscope can penetrate, it detects Life within Life, generation within generation, as if the very Universe itself were not vast enough for the energies of Life.[58]

But not too vast for the probing eye of the naturalist, moving with ease through the apertures of scale, resolving the world into its particular atoms, magnifying and arranging pebbles into panoramic worlds.

Notes

1. Stephen E. Whicher and Robert E. Spiller, eds., *The Early Lectures of Ralph Waldo Emerson: Volume I, 1833–1836* (Cambridge, MA: Harvard Univ. Press, 1959), pp. 9–10.

2. Richard D. Altick, *The Shows of London: A Panoramic History of Exhibitions, 1600–1862* (Cambridge, MA: Belknap-Harvard Univ. Press, 1978), chapters 1 and 2. For a detailed list of the contents of a well-stocked eighteenth-century cabinet, see the article on "Nature History" in *Encyclopedia Britannica*, third edition (1797), vol. 12, pp. 668–669.

3. Altick, *Shows*, p. 28.

4. David Elliston Allen, *The Victorian Fern Craze: A History of Pteridomania* (London: Hutchinson and Co., Ltd., 1969), p. 2.

5. Edmund Gosse, *The Life of Philip Henry Gosse F.R.S.* (London: Kegan Paul, Trench, Trübner and Co., Ltd., 1890), p. 27.

6. Buckland seemed to feel that one of the best ways to appreciate nature was to eat it—just as his father before him, Dean William Buckland, the geologist of *Bridgewater Treatise* fame, had relished cooked hedgehog, ostrich, or echinoderm. But then Darwin also ate his way with gusto through South America, as reported at length in *Journal of Researches*. And from Philip Gosse there is this report of a "gastronomical test" of boiled sea-anemone:

> I must confess that the first bit I essayed caused a sort of lumpy feeling in my throat, as if a sentinel there guarded the way, and said, "It shan't come here." This sensation, however, I felt to be unworthy of a philosopher, for there was nothing really repugnant in the taste. As soon as I had got one that seemed well cooked, I invited Mrs. Gosse to share the feast; she courageously attacked the morsel, but I am compelled to confess that it could not pass the vestibule; the sentinel was too many for her.

In Edmund Gosse, *Life*, pp. 241–242.

7. G. H. O. Burgess, *The Eccentric Ark: The Curious World of Frank Buckland* (New York: The Horizon Press, 1967), p. 118.

8. Burgess, p. 125.

9. From the essay "London Whales," in L. R. Brightwell, ed. *Buckland's Curiosities of Natural History: A Selection* (London: The Batchworth Press, 1948), p. 85.

10. Mark Girouard, *Alfred Waterhouse and the Natural History Museum* (London: British Museum [Natural History], 1981), p. 27.

11. W. H. G. Armytage, *A Social History of Engineering* (Cambridge, MA: The MIT Press, 1961), p. 146. Compare Tennyson's description of a Mechanic's Institute in the Prologue to "The Princess":

> and here were telescopes
> For azure views; and there a group of girls
> In circle waited, whom the electric shock
> Dislinked with shrieks and laughter: round the lake
> A little clock-work steamer paddling plied
> And shook the lilies: perched about the knolls
> A dozen angry models jetted steam:
> A petty railway ran: a fire-balloon
> Rose gem-like up before the dusky groves
> And dropt a fairy parachute and past:
> And there through twenty posts of telegraph
> They flashed a saucy message to and fro
> Between the mimic stations; so that Sport
> Went hand in hand with Science . . .

12. See Kenneth W. James, "'Damned Nonsense!'—The Geological Career of the Third Earl of Enniskillen" (Ulster: The Ulster Museum, 1986).

13. Jules Verne, *Twenty Thousand Leagues Under the Sea*, trans. Walter James Miller (New York: Pocket Books, 1966), p. 327.

14. Alfred Russel Wallace, *The Malay Archipelago: The Land of the Orang-utan and The Bird of Paradise, A Narrative of Travel with Studies of Man and Nature* (London: Macmillan and Company, 1869; rpt. New York: Dover Publications, Inc., 1962), p. 351.

15. Wallace, pp. 351–352.

16. Wallace, p. 297.

17. Wallace, pp. 257–258.

18. Nathan Reingold, ed., *Science in Nineteenth-Century America* (London: Macmillan, 1966), p. 30.

19. Susan Stewart, *On Longing: Narratives of the Miniature, the Gigantic, the Souvenir, the Collection* (Baltimore: The Johns Hopkins Univ. Press, 1984), p. 151.

20. From "A Geological Auction," in L. R. Brightwell, ed. *Buckland's Curiosities of Natural History: A Selection* (London: The Batchworth Press, 1948), p. 61.

21. Stewart, p. 162.

22. Joel Porte, ed., *Emerson in His Journals* (Cambridge, MA: Belknap Press-Harvard Univ. Press, 1982), pp. 110–111.

23. Gillian Beer sees geological time as implicated in the Victorians' fascination with "traces" and "decipherment" in science, history, and fiction. See her provocative article, "Origins and Oblivion in Victorian Narrative," in *Sex, Politics, and Science in the Nineteenth-Century Novel*, ed. Ruth Bernard Yeazell, Selected Papers from the English Institute, 1983–1984, New Series, No. 10 (Baltimore: The Johns Hopkins Univ. Press, 1986).

24. Marjorie Hope Nicolson, *Newton Demands the Muse: Newton's Opticks and the Eighteenth Century Poets* (Princeton: Princeton Univ. Press, 1946), p. 36.

25. Nicolson, p. 4.

26. David Elliston Allen, *The Naturalist in Britain: A Social History* (London: Allen Lane, 1976), p. 128.

27. J. G. Wood, *Common Objects of the Microscope* (London: George Routledge and Sons, n.d.), p. 26.

28. Mentioned in Altick, *Shows*, p. 370. Altick discusses the oxy-hydrogen microscope as one of many Victorian public spectacles.

29. S. Bradbury, *The Microscope: Past and Present* (Oxford: Pergamon Press, 1968), p. 148.

30. Bradbury, p. 161.

31. Bradbury, p. 161.

32. Wood, p. 2.

33. Edmund Gosse, *Life*, p. 222.

34. Harry G. Owen, "The Hon. Mrs Ward and 'A Windfall for the Microscope,' of 1856 and 1864," *Annals of Science*, 41 (1984), 471.

35. Stanley Joel Reiser, *Medicine and the Reign of Technology* (Cambridge: Cambridge Univ. Press, 1978), p. 45. Michel Foucault assigns this same visual quality to medicine, exploring how in the latter part of the eighteenth century the previously hidden interior of the body became accessible to the medical "gaze"; see *The Birth of the Clinic: An Archaeology of Medical Perception* (New York: Vintage Books, 1975).

36. *Chambers's Miscellany of Instructive & Entertaining Tracts*, rev. ed. (London and Edinburgh: W. and R. Chambers, n.d.), Tract 83, p. 1.

37. *Chambers's Miscellany*, p. 32.

38. Algernon Charles Swinburne, *Under the Microscope* (London: D. White, 1872; rpt. New York: Garland Publishing, Inc., 1986), p. 13.

39. Wallace, pp. 263–264.

40. Allen, *Naturalist*, p. 129.

41. Tennyson begins section II of his poem with three stanzas describing a tiny seashell. The persona says that the shell is empty, "forlorn," and wonders what its inhabitant looked like when alive: "Did he stand at the diamond door/Of his house in a rainbow frill?/Did he push when he was uncurl'd/A golden foot or a

fairy horn/Thro his dim water-world?" (stanza III). The "rainbow frill" detail here suggests an interest and familiarity on Tennyson's part with the elaborate forms of real marine invertebrates.

42. Carol T. Christ, *The Finer Optic: The Aesthetic of Particularity in Victorian Poetry* (New Haven: Yale Univ. Press, 1975).

43. Paul H. Walton, *The Drawings of John Ruskin* (Oxford: Clarendon Press, 1972), p. 99.

44. James K. Colling, *Art Foliage, For Sculpture and Decoration; with an Analysis of Geometric Form, and Studies from Nature, of Buds, Leaves, Flowers, and Fruit* (London: Published by the Author, 1865), p. 3. Further page citations are made within the text.

45. Allen, *Naturalist*, p. 129.

46. Frank Buckland, *Natural History of British Fishes; Their Structure, Economic Uses, and Capture by Net and Rod* (London: Society for Promoting Christian Knowledge, n.d.), pp. 379–381. This book was originally published as *Familiar History of British Fishes* in 1873, and revised and published with this new title in 1881.

47. Panoramas appealed to the Victorians, both as a word and in various concrete manifestations. A panorama was usually a 360-degree (or nearly so) view from a tall vantage point, rendered in sketches or photographs, and displayed, preferably, in the round. The fad seems to have begun in 1821, with Thomas Horner's 2,000 sketches of London from the spire of St. Paul's Cathedral, made, interestingly enough, with the aid of a telescope. The diorama, or painted scenery lighted for three-dimensional effect, fit in with the craving for sweeping views, and was also quite popular. See Richard D. Altick, *The Shows of London* (Cambridge, MA: Belknap Press-Harvard Univ. Press, 1978), chapters 11, 12, and 13, and, for photographic panoramas, see Beaumont Newhall, *A History of Photography* (New York: The Museum of Modern Art, 1964), p. 14. That Daguerre, pioneer of photography, was first a painter of dioramas is intriguing.

48. In H. Bruce Franklin, *Future Perfect: American Science Fiction of the Nineteenth Century,* rev. ed. (New York: Oxford Univ. Press, 1978), p. 329. Further page citations are made within the text.

49. Norman Page, ed. *Tennyson: Interviews and Recollections.* Totowa, NJ: Barnes & Noble Books, 1983), p. 128.

50. Gerhard Joseph, "Tennyson's Optics: The Eagle's Gaze," *PMLA*, 92, No. 3 (1977), 420.

51. Page, p. 166

52. Joseph, p. 421.

53. Joseph, p. 426.

54. From *Praeterita*, II, section 200. E. T. Cook and Alexander Wedderburn, eds., *The Works of John Ruskin* (London: George Allen, 1903–1912), vol. XXXV, p. 430.

55. Elizabeth K. Helsinger, *Ruskin and the Art of the Beholder* (Cambridge, MA: Harvard Univ. Press, 1982), p. 167.

56. Helsinger, p. 67.

57. Robert Hewison, *John Ruskin: The Argument of the Eye* (London: Thames and Hudson, 1976), p. 21.

58. George Henry Lewes, *Studies in Animal Life* (London: Smith, Elder and Co., 1862), p. 26.

Collecting natural curiosities along England's rocky shore: "Pegwell Bay,
Kent—a Recollection of October 5th 1858." (Oil painting [1859-60] by William
Dyce. Reproduced with permission from the Tate Gallery, London.)

"It matters little where we go—we are surrounded with Life": plants, insects, mollusks, and amphibians. (From Lewes' *Studies in Animal Life*, 1862; frontispiece, hand-colored lithograph.)

Nature's multitudinous profusion: "Brazilian Forest Scene." (From Gosse's *The Romance of Natural History*, 1886; engraving by Whymper from a drawing by Wolf.)

Vegetable wonders of the jungle: "A Group of Tree-Ferns." (From Gosse's *The Romance of Natural History*, 1886; engraving by Whymper from a drawing by Gosse.)

Using the "naturalist's dredge" to collect specimens from the ocean floor. (From Harvey's *The Sea-Side Book*, 1849; engraving.)

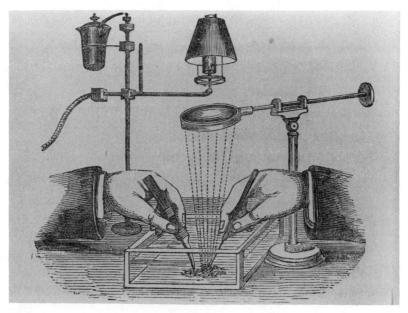

Preparing specimens for examination with a lens, under strong light: "Dissecting Under Water." (From Wood's *Common Objects of the Microscope*; engraving.)

Fig. 2.

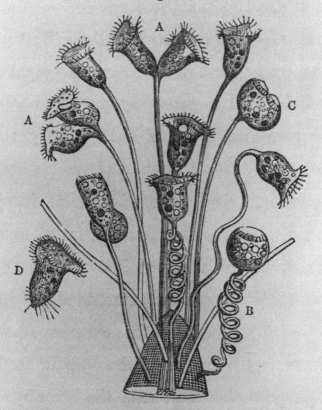

GROUP OF VORTICELLA NEBULIFERA, on a Stem of Weed, Magnified.

A One undergoing spontaneous division.
B Another spirally retracted on its stalk.
C One with cilia retracted.
D A bud detached and swimming free.

Infusoria (ciliated protozoans): "Group of *Vorticella nebulifera*, on a Stem of Weed, Magnified." (From Lewes' *Studies in Animal Life*, 1862; engraving.)

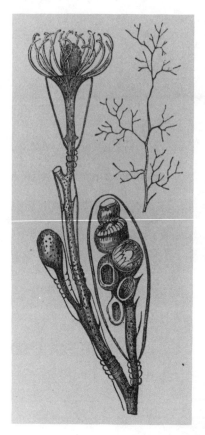

Zoophyte (invertebrate animals that resemble plants), Hydroid type; a single vase-like polype: "Campanularia, Magnified, and Natural Size." (From Lewes' *Studies in Animal Life*, 1862; engraving.)

Nothing is too extravagant for nature: "The Hercules Beetle." (From an edition of Wood's *Illustrated Natural History*; wood engraving.)

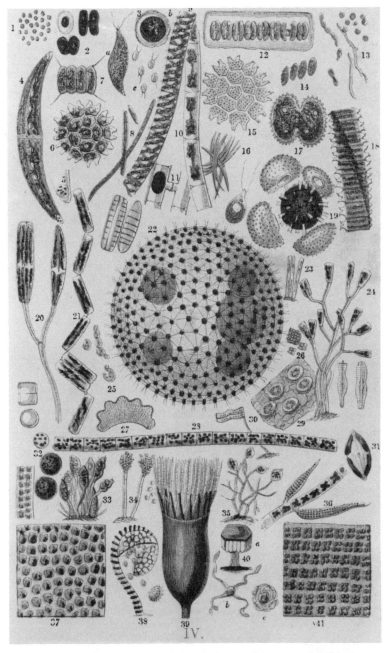

Microscopic details of plants and fungi (mold, mildew, yeast), with the flagellate colony *Volvox globator* at center. (From Wood's *Common Objects of the Microscope*; chromo-lithograph.)

Particularity and panorama: sea anemones in the foreground, human life in the background. (From Gosse's *Tenby*, 1856; frontispiece, hand-colored lithograph by Gosse.)

Luminous transparency under the microscope: "The Bowerbankia." (From Gosse's *Tenby*, 1856; hand-colored lithograph by Gosse.)

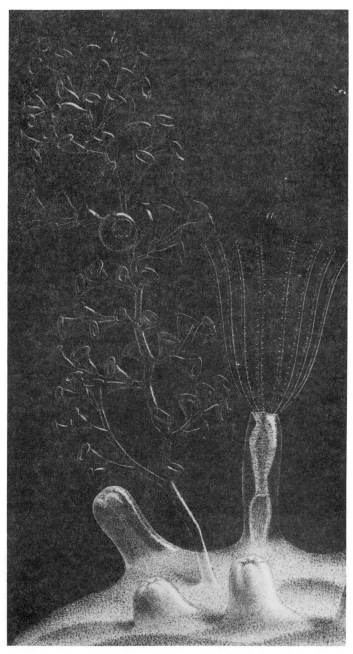

"A very curious and interesting spectacle": "The Stag's-horn Polype." (From Gosse's *Tenby*, 1856; hand-colored lithograph by
Gosse.)

The wonders of the shore: Sea anemones, *Actinia mesembryanthemum*, *Bunodes crassicornis*, and *Carophyllea smithii*. (From Kingsley's *Glaucus*, 1903; frontispiece, chromo-lithograph.)

Marine bottom-dwellers, including Tube-worms (second from left), Sea-slug (second from left, foreground), Nudibranch (lower right), and various Mollusks. (From Kingsley's *Glaucus*, 1903; chromo-lithograph.)

A monster from the geological past: "The armored fish, *Coccosteus cuspidatus*." (From Miller's *The Old Red Sandstone*; engraving.)

6

Burroughs and Ruskin—
"The More and Fresher Facts
the Better"

On fine days, when the grass was dry, I used to lie down on it and
draw the blades as they grew, with the ground herbage of buttercup
or hawkweed mixed among them, until every square foot of
meadow, or mossy bank, became an infinite picture and possession
to me, and the grace and adjustment to each other of growing leaves,
a subject of more curious interest to me than the composition of any
painter's masterpiece.[1]   JOHN RUSKIN, *Praeterita*

The plea for science—scientific accumulation and investigation of facts—
to have human significance, the power to move, uplift, and amaze ordinary human beings, is often best expressed by writers and artists. Two of
the most eloquent nineteenth-century voices in support of humanistic or
aesthetic science were those of the American nature writer John Burroughs and the English art critic John Ruskin. They express similar
concerns with the beautiful aspects of natural facts—the concerns, as I
have shown, not of hard science, but of natural history. Each of them
articulates a paradigm for the artistic study of natural details. Each
makes a plea for an approach to nature that bridges, in an absorbing and
pleasurable way, the gap between the curious artifacts of the natural
world and the responsive human being who plucks, captures, or chisels
them out, according to taste. Each emphasizes the dialectical play between isolated fact and overall meaning. In so doing, Burroughs and
Ruskin establish themselves as eloquent natural history theorists. Their
writings led the chorus clamoring for evocative facts.

   John Burroughs' attitudes are the more straightforward and ultimately
less complex. The "leading American nature essayist of the late nine-

teenth century,"[2] Burroughs (1837–1921) produced volumes of essays. Late in the twentieth century, his fame has dimmed somewhat, overshadowed by the reverence accorded his American contemporary, the less prolific but more politically active conservationist, John Muir. Not by temperament a scientist, Burroughs made no great contribution to biology, although he spent his life devotedly observing the habits of animals, especially birds. He considered himself foremost a writer: "By his own definition he was not a 'scientific naturalist'—one who enlarges the body of known facts by indefatigable researches into minutiae; instead, and at times almost apologetically, he described himself as a 'nature essayist' whose interest (and appeal to his readers) was primarily aesthetic, artistic."[3] So well did he succeed that Burroughs is generally considered the "father of the nature essay." Branching from the more meditative trail blazed by Thoreau, he focused his own essays more singlemindedly upon observations of nature. As a result, he inaugurated a new literary genre[4] and became, in the view of one critic, a "literary publicist" for nature.[5]

Compared to most Victorian naturalists, Burroughs is somewhat anomalous in that he dislikes cabinets; consequently, the language of capture and juxtaposition, the syntax of the museum, is not found in his writings. He also speaks more harshly of science than do many naturalists. But he is an insistent spokesman for principles of keen observation, praising the rewards of looking at nature on a small scale, with focused microscopic vision. He finds the variety and profusion of nature endlessly fascinating. Even more important, though, he is deeply concerned with a key naturalist's problem: how to make rhetorical use of natural facts, that is, how to create meaning with them, in a literary context. Like Darwin in the *Beagle* account, or Forbes or Gosse or any other writing naturalist, Burroughs worries about how best to present natural facts to a reader.

Precise description—of birds, mammals, flowers, seasons—is the meat of Burroughs' essays, but always spiced with emotion. A shrewd and careful observer, Burroughs certainly knew nature intimately. But mere objectivity, or scientific detachment, did not interest him. His tastes mirrored the natural history of his times and, in turn, influenced the kind of nature writing he produced. According to Philip Hicks, Burroughs influenced the development of the natural history essay in four important ways: he united disparate influences in the field, popularized the study of nature, wrote a vast number of nature essays, and established definite standards for the natural history essay.[6] For students of literature, the last is by far the most important. Burroughs' stated standards for fitting natural history into a proper literary form are scattered throughout his many essays, yet remain remarkably consistent.

What is the first prerequisite for a good natural history essay? Accurate facts: "The literary naturalist does not take liberties with facts; facts are the flora upon which he lives. The more and fresher the facts the better."[7] Accurate reporting of minute particulars is fundamental. But why must the writer master these details? To transmute them, change them into something more cohesive, more valuable. As Burroughs goes on to say: "I can do nothing without them, but I must give them my own flavor. I must impart to them a quality which heightens and intensifies them." As Hicks points out, Burroughs here reveals the second and third standards for the natural history essay: appeal to the imagination and appeal to aesthetic or intellectual values.

For the process of nature writing, Burroughs proposes a natural analogy. Facts are gathered by the writer as nectar by the bee. But flower nectar, sweet though it is, can still be improved, into honey. To effect the change, the bee must add something of itself to the raw material: in this case, formic acid from its own body. The resulting honey "always reflects her environment, and it reflects something her environment knows not of."[8] In similar fashion, the literary naturalist gleans facts from nature and later expresses them "tinged with the colors of the spirit." Like Ruskin, like so many nineteenth-century naturalists, Burroughs emphasizes factual accuracy, but just as insistently emphasizes that mere facts, in and of themselves, are not enough. If they are to nourish the spirit, they must be given a coloring, or placed into a framework, of human or aesthetic significance.

Skillful nature writing, Burroughs concludes, exploits the dialectic between objective nature and subjective human response. With this contention, he plants himself firmly in the camp of nineteenth-century natural history. It is not too surprising, then, to find that he also shares the microscopic outlook typical of Victorian naturalists. Burroughs continually insists on a fruitful tension between small and large: tiny, seemingly insignificant facts of nature, and their broader implications. One vehement opinion of Burroughs', however, does set him apart from other naturalists of his day: he intensely disliked cabinets and collecting. He compared cabinet specimens to corpses and found the viewing of them "funereal."[9] He was a field naturalist by inclination, not a closet naturalist, preferring to see animals not only alive but within their proper ecological sphere, fully connected to their environments. To Burroughs, as is generally true of Ruskin, nothing should be viewed in isolation.

On the subject of looking at nature on a small scale, Burroughs wrote a typically enthusiastic essay entitled "Nature in Little." In it, he asserts that "mere size does not count for much with Nature; she is all there, in the least as in the greatest. A drop of dew reveals the rainbow tints as well as the myriad drops of the summer shower."[10] This being true, it is not only more practical, but more interesting, to study nature in miniature, to look, if not actually through a microscope, then with an acutely focused microscopic eye. For, as Burroughs points out, nature is

> as much in evidence in the minute as in the gigantic, in the herb as in the oak, in the gnat as in the elephant, in the pond as in the sea. In the clay-bank washed by rains you may perceive the same sculpturing and modeling that you see in vast mountain-chains. In California I have seen, in a small mound of clay by the roadside that has been exposed to the weather for a few years, a reproduction in miniature of the range of mountains that towered about it, the Sierra Madre.[11]

Burroughs' miniature Sierra Madre is somewhat reminiscent of Thoreau's famous image of the slumping railroad bank in *Walden* ("Spring"), which Burroughs undoubtedly had read. For Burroughs, the mound of clay mimics mountain-carving processes; for Thoreau, the thawing sand in the bank mimics not only the channeling of rivers and the elongation of cave stalactites but also the swelling growth of vegetation and flesh: "Thus it seemed that this one hillside illustrated the principle of all the operations of Nature." Like Thoreau, Burroughs shows a marked preference for zeroing in on the small forms of nature. At the same time, in typical dialectical fashion, minute details find analogues in larger forms, processes, or truths. For as Burroughs says elsewhere, "exact knowledge is good, but vital knowledge is better; details are indispensable to the specialist, but a knowledge of relations and of wholes satisfies me more."[12]

The notion of miniaturized landforms was oddly compelling—so much so that there is a passage in Ruskin that bears a striking similarity to Burroughs' image of the sculptured clay-bank. Ruskin speaks (in *Modern Painters IV*, part V, chapter XVIII) not of clay but of stones:

> For a stone, when it is examined, will be found a mountain in miniature. The fineness of Nature's work is so great, that into a single block, a foot or two in diameter, she can compress as many changes of form and structure, on a small scale, as she needs for her mountains on a large one; taking moss for forests, and grains of crystal for crags, the surface of a stone . . . is more interesting than the surface of an ordinary hill; more fantastic in form and incomparably rich in colour.[13]

The similarity of diction between the two passages is striking, as is the concept itself: the clay bank sculpted into a miniature Sierra Madre, the mossy, crystalline stone emulating a forested, craggy mountain. Both passages maintain that the "reproduction in miniature," the "mountain in miniature," are as worthy of attention as mountains themselves. In these passages as in so many writings of the nineteenth-century naturalists, the microcosm is more spellbinding than the macrocosm. Moss and crystals, peered at from close range, or picked up and handled, have an intrinsic beauty and fascination. True, placing the minute forms in a larger context enhances their meaning. But often, looking metaphorically through the "diamond lens," one can see forms and colors more fantastic than those found in the larger landscape.

Whether peering at herb or gnat or clay-bank, Burroughs stresses observation, consciously focused sight. Coupled with nature as subject matter, this, as critic Hicks sees it, qualifies him as a natural history essayist. And such a writer, or by extension any writer who expresses the particulars of natural history, must have two talents. First, according to Hicks, "an accurate and curious eye." And, second, "an equally active inward eye, to see the fact in relation to other facts, to man and life, and to touch it with emotion."[14] Fundamental in Hicks' formulation, as in most nineteenth-century natural history writing, is the primacy of vision: the accurate, curious, and yet inward eye. In this context, Emerson's famous "transparent eyeball" metaphor comes to mind.[15]

In other ways, too, John Burroughs forges a standard for the practice of natural history. Besides advocating sharp vision, he actively explores two dialectics: one between natural facts and human applications, and the other between small details and large contexts. Likewise, he wrestles with the dialectic, or area of intersection, between science and literature, especially since one seems to deal with objective facts exclusively and the other often seems to renounce them. In an important essay, "Science and Literature," Burroughs struggles with the apparently discrete domains of the two disciplines, trying, like so many Victorians, to forge a bond between them. Taking elements from both, he essentially creates an intermediate pursuit, a pursuit I would call natural history. Burroughs' 1889 essay contains one of his most concentrated formulations of the "two cultures" debate, one that reprises many of the main positions on either side (the Huxley-Arnold argument, for instance).

"Interested as I am in all branches of natural science, and great as is my debt to these things," Burroughs begins, "yet I suppose my interest in nature is not strictly a scientific one."[16] Science has great practical value, Burroughs admits, and many of its discoveries are inherently interesting. What then is wrong with science? Following in the tradition of the Romantics, many of whom he quotes (Goethe and Wordsworth, for example), Burroughs attacks the natural sciences for investigating "dead dissected nature" (p. 49). Note the echo of Wordsworth's damning phrase: "we murder to dissect." Part of the problem is that the sciences study the dead organism in the laboratory rather than the living animal in the web of its environment. Here again Burroughs displays his distaste for "closet" studies, his predilection for life in the open fields.

But just as studying a dead stuffed specimen is a sterile occupation, accumulating "increased stores of exact knowledge" (p. 51) also can become mechanistic and meaningless. Unlike poems or "other works of the imagination," the sere facts of science "fail" to give one "joy of the spirit" (p. 50; note how Burroughs excludes science from the realm of imaginative creation, which few modern scientists would do). With a nod to the long-running battle between classical education and scientific or technical education, Burroughs declares that without this joy of the spirit, science will never usurp the place of literature in education. The sciences do have the capability of "becoming instruments of pure culture, instruments to refine and spiritualize the whole moral and intellectual nature [of man]" (p. 53). But they can fulfill this promise only if they can appeal to the human spirit's need for sentiment.

"Funereal" science can look heartlessly at nature and wield a piercing, killing vision; Burroughs dismisses it as mere "peeping and prying into nature" (p. 60). And while Burroughs' diction implies an illicit gaze that cruelly exposes nature's most private secrets,[17] this sharp sight is also the source of "what we owe to science." Namely, its "tending to foster a disinterested love of truth, as tending to clarify the mental vision or sharpen curiosity, or cultivating the spirit of fearless inquiry, or stimulating the desire to see and know things as they really are" (p. 73). All science need add to this alertness is "that kind of knowledge which the heart gathers" (p. 57): love, human responses to the world, holistic wisdom. Burroughs insists this is an ancient and universal interest that people have in the natural world:

> an interest as old as the race itself, and which all men, learned and unlearned alike, feel in some degree,—an interest born of our relations to these things, of our associations with them. It is the human sentiments they awaken and foster in us, the emotion of love or admiration, or awe or fear, they call up; and is in fact the interest of literature as distinguished from that of science. The admiration one feels for a flower, for a person, for a fine view, for a noble deed, the pleasure one takes in a spring morning, in a stroll upon the beach, is the admiration and the pleasure literature feels and art feels. (p. 61)

To take a literary, aesthetic interest in nature—that is the promise of natural history. To dissect without murdering. To scrutinize with love. To transform nature into text.

In "Science and Literature," it might almost be Matthew Arnold speaking of the human need for beauty and emotion. But Arnold was adamant; science could never fulfill these needs. Burroughs is much more optimistic, more so even than Wordsworth, who thought that science *might* one day become the province of literature. Burroughs believes that sometimes science *does* rise to the level of literature; a mixture of the two otherwise contrary forms can occur. Their aims are different: "demonstrable fact" for one, and "sentiment" for the other. But in the hands of certain literary scientists or naturalists—Burroughs particularly praises Alexander Humboldt and Charles Darwin—they can blend:

> Until science is mixed with emotion, and appeals to the heart and imagination, it is like dead inorganic matter; and when it becomes so mixed and transformed, *it is literature*. (My italics; p. 53)

As an enthusiast, Burroughs writes and champions what I would define as natural history: science mixed with emotion and appreciation of beauty, "science fired with faith and enthusiasm, the fascination of the power and mystery of nature" (p. 62). When expressed in language, and shaped so as to move a reader, such science approaches literature. Natural history prose becomes a literary genre, with a characteristic style of its own.

One of the characteristics that marks Burroughs' style, a quality that shows his mixed aims, is his tendency to speak of human situations in terms of natural or scientific metaphors. For example, in "Science and Literature," at one point Burroughs pens a panegyric to literature, all about how literature opens the mind, fills it with noble sentiments, allows uplifting empathy with other great souls, builds moral character. To express this supremely humanistic sentiment, however, Burroughs chooses a rather surprising metaphor from nature—a metaphor, moreover, that describes not external natural beauty, but internal process, a process that he understands in a scientific way. Literature, Burroughs decides, fertilizes the mind, adding necessary nutrients: "The great literatures of the world add something to the mind that is like leaf-mould to the soil, like the contribution from animal and vegetable life and from the rains and the dews" (p. 53).

Burroughs' characteristic mingling of scientific or natural terminology with human sentiments marks him as a natural history essayist. Science fascinates him, but not for scientific reasons. The facts revealed by science are "leaf-mould" for his essentially literary imagination. And he feels most akin to scientists or naturalists who share this slant. For example, ignoring the vast implications of Darwin's theories and concentrating instead on the pleasure to be gained from reading Darwin's books, Burroughs decided that "Darwin's interest in nature is strongly scientific, but our interest in him is largely literary" (p. 63). Few modern biologists would agree, but the point remains that Darwin's works of natural history (particularly his *Journal of Researches*) can indeed be profitably read as literature. So can many works of Victorian science, if they do what Burroughs said they ought—if they in fact retain the tinge of natural history. As he said in "The Pleasures of Science":

> All the facts of natural science that throw light upon the methods and the spirit of nature, are doubly welcome. I can assimilate them. I can appreciate their ideal values. I can link them up with my intellectual and emotional experiences. They make me feel more at home in the world because they so enlarge my field of interest. (p. 176)

Yes, Burroughs can assimilate natural facts and link them to his intellectual and emotional life; those are the qualities that give his essays enduring value. Readers share his aesthetic pleasure and emotional responses to particular facts as he rambles among the infinite curiosities of natural history and tells what he sees. Particularity, emotion, vision, description—the paramount concerns of the wanderer in natural history.

A scrupulous thinker, Burroughs conscientiously grappled with a key nineteenth-century problem. In such enlightened, scientific times, what relationship ought one to have with nature? Science revealed hundreds of new natural facts almost daily but simultaneously threatened to strip them of meaning. In response, Burroughs formulated a heartfelt natural history doctrine. In his scheme, natural facts resonate with emotional overtones—beauty and metaphor—and thus retain their human significance. Because he continually examined his own relationship to nature, and experimented with the forms it might take in language, Burroughs is a major theorist of natural history.

Burroughs has a somewhat surprising English counterpart: the art critic John Ruskin (1819–1900). Ruskin, of course, is not usually thought of as a naturalist, yet, albeit in a different context from Burroughs, he comes to many similar conclusions about the uses of natural history and its particular facts. Although Ruskin writes primarily about art, art must often draw from nature. Consequently, exacting descriptions of nature abound in *Modern Painters*, as do discussions about their importance. Moreover, Ruskin has special relevance to a study of Victorian natural history and its influences on perception, for several reasons.

In the first place, not only was Ruskin well apprised of the achievements of Victorian science, but he was an ardent student of natural history. So strong were these influences that Ruskin based his whole aesthetic—his standards for beauty and for great painting and architecture—upon them.[18] In Ruskin's view of art, these things reigned supreme: Nature, and truth to Nature achieved through careful observation. A friend at Oxford of Dr. William Buckland, the catastrophist-school geologist, Ruskin early acquired a taste for geology. Geology, in fact, permeates the volumes of *Modern Painters* (especially volume IV). He loved stones, and kept a mineral collection throughout his life. As a young man, his first published works were essays of scientific explanation (for Loudon's *Magazine of Natural History*), and on his travels he carried scientific instruments with him, often using them to supplement his drawings (precisely measuring the blue of the sky, for example, or experimenting with the *camera lucida* as an aid to his sketching). In 1840, at the age of 21, Ruskin was elected a Fellow in the Geological Society. He later became interested in Lyellian geology, which is based on gradual transformation (as opposed to periodic catastrophes), and incorporated images of shifting landforms and changing landscapes into his writings.

So Ruskin in his own life personified the magnetism of Victorian science and natural history. And yet he made a name for himself, not in science, but in art. The second reason for his centrality to a study of natural history is the tremendous influence that his aesthetics had. Observing, collecting—the activities of natural history—moved Ruskin to insist on truth of details and precision of facts, tenets that would soon change Victorian artistic perceptions. His defense of Turner and of the Pre-Raphaelite Brotherhood helped turn the tide against traditional, Royal Academy notions of painting. Ruskin's advocacy of facts was the most eloquent and sustained expression of a new cultural mania for objectivity. And objectivity, at least in the sense of a fascination with objects, went hand in hand with the rise of natural history.

Third, Ruskin not only realized the dangers of sterile, detached observations, which so many Victorians, from Tennyson to Dickens, feared, but he concocted an antidote. Like Burroughs, Ruskin demanded that facts be linked to some larger meaning—Truth—spiritual, moral, or holistic. And finally, Ruskin celebrated the joy of natural facts in highly colored passages of descriptive prose. Penned in the service of art criticism or instruction, these nevertheless were quite similar in spirit to passages of descriptive prose in works of natural history. The love of intricacy, of color, of form, of concreteness, of relatedness in both was the same. Savoring rocks and clouds, Ruskin could describe them with all the precision, and all the sensory fervor, of a Philip Gosse or Hugh Miller.

Unlike Burroughs, who was aware of the nineteenth-century fervor for museums but disliked them, Ruskin was profoundly affected by the idea of museum as metaphor. As I have said, the cabinet of curiosities could function not only as a repository for an otherwise unwieldly collection of objects, but as a work of art in itself. By juxtaposition, disparate objects could come together in a new order, an order that might be seen either as unique and fortuitous, or as an emblem of an immanent order in the world—the unity one too easily overlooks when dazzled by multiplicity. Ruskin saw the cabinet (or museum) as a simultaneous expression of both the glories of individual objects and of the order that connects them.

One Ruskin biographer, John Dixon Hunt, finds that all during his life, Ruskin's mind functioned as both collector and curator, busily stocking the displays of a vast metaphorical museum. As a child, Ruskin was taken for a visit to Crosthwaite's Museum in Keswick, an eclectic Victorian collection mingling nature and culture, fact and fancy. Old manuscripts, "musical stones," the ribs of giants—all these fascinated the young Ruskin. As Hunt says,

> Faced with this indiscriminate profusion of objects collected and lovingly displayed by one man, it is difficult to talk of incoherence or irrelevance. The same dedication to a seemingly inchoate mass of items, ideas and pursuits, which apparently delighted John in 1830, never ceased to enthrall him. . . . Such a cabinet of curiosities . . . is the apt emblem of a mind for which "digression" is virtually a meaningless term.[19]

The favorable impression of Crosthwaite's Museum was later intensified when, at Oxford, Ruskin fell under the sway of William Buckland, the geologist. Like his eccentric son Frank, the curator of the Fish Museum, the elder Buckland had a museum mentality. Dr. Buckland's private study was, as Hunt describes it, an "extraordinary chaos" which was "richly anarchic—another virtuoso's cabinet, a more scholarly Crosthwaite's Museum," Ruskin enthusiastically wrote home about the weird collection of "frogs cut out of serpentine—broken models of fallen temples, torn papers—old manuscripts, stuffed reptiles."[20] Ruskin's imagination seized upon such collections as metaphors for the world; to him, "the world was simply a grander, indeed infinite, cabinet of curiosities, wherein a flower, an aspen, a piece of ivy, a rock, a picture, red light on a mountain, a newspaper, or travelling from Geneva to Chamonix, all had equal status."[21] While young, Ruskin once referred to nature itself as a gigantic museum, saying that he had found a large crystal of rose fluor (fluorite) "at the Cabinet of Natural History on this mountain."[22] Toward the end of his life, Ruskin obsessively planned museums, designing display cabinets and at one time actually contributing materials and plans for a collection at Walkley.[23] As a result, a museum at Coniston now forms, according to Hunt, "the most authentic memory" of Ruskin.[24]

Another of Ruskin's biographers, his friend W. G. Collingwood, draws attention to the centrality of geology in Ruskin's life. Here again the importance lies not so much in the theories as in the specimens of the earth:

> Of less interest to the general reader, though too important a part of Mr. Ruskin's life and work to be passed over without mention, are his studies in Mineralogy. We have heard of his early interest in spars and ores; of his juvenile dictionary in forgotten hieroglyphics; and of his studies in the field and at the British Museum. He had made a splendid collection, and knew the various museums of Europe as familiarly as he knew the picture-galleries. In the "Ethics of the Dust" he had chosen Crystallography as the subject in which to exemplify his method of education; and in 1867, after finishing the letters to Thomas Dixon, he took refuge, as before, among the stones, from the stress of more agitating problems.[25]

Especially significant here is the equal weight given to natural history museums (which would contain mineral collections) and to picture-galleries.

Frequently people think of Ruskin as having had an educated Victorian gentleman's interest in science, among other intellectual trends of the day, but few realize the extent of his enthusiasm for natural history. Busy as he was with architecture, art history, Continental travel, his own sketching, and the defense and worship of Turner, Ruskin remained profoundly inspired by his delight in natural history. From a letter written by Thackeray's daughter after Ruskin had given her a tour of his house at Brantwood in 1876, Hunt provides another wonderful image of Ruskin swept up in a fervor for natural objects. Here one sees, not Ruskin the art critic, but Ruskin the naturalist, Ruskin the museum curator. Enjoying his role as guide, he led visitors through his private museum. Miss Thackeray recounted what a magical experience it was, as Ruskin

> meanwhile illustrat[ed] each delightful, fanciful, dictatorial sentence with pictures by the way—things, facts, objects interwoven, bookcases opening wide, sliding drawers unlocked with his own marvellous keys—and lo! . . . We are perhaps down in the centre of the earth, far below Brantwood and its surrounding hills, among specimens, minerals, and precious stones, Ruskin still going ahead, and crying "Sesame" and "Sesame," and revealing

each secret recess of his king's treasury in turn, pointing to each tiny point
of light and rainbow veiled in marble, gold and opal, crystal and emerald.[26]

This is a fabulous imaginative journey to the depths of the earth, a bit like
a fairy tale—Alice's fall down the rabbit hole, or Tom the Sweep's voyage
to the land of the Water-Babies (see Chapter 9). Ruskin was equally
adept at journeying through time, making connections between the world
of nature and the history of art. But the image of the man enthralled by
his own collection of natural specimens helps balance the standard picture of Ruskin, the lover of Venice and Gothic cathedrals. The aesthetic
of eclectic juxtaposition, so prominent among natural history writers in
the nineteenth-century, affected Ruskin too.

Ruskin's writings are so monumental in scope that it is impossible to
do them justice here. Nevertheless some fairly consistent patterns may be
discerned. In the five volumes of *Modern Painters* especially, but also in
his manual of instruction for beginning amateur artists, *The Elements of
Drawing*, and in his memoir, *Praeterita*, Ruskin repeatedly wrestles with
the role of natural facts and details—in art and in the proper perception
of any alert human being. Like Burroughs, Ruskin insists on two, seemingly contradictory, points: first, the primacy of the individual autonomous object, clearly and painstakingly seen in its own right, and second,
the harmony of all objects in a unified scheme. Ruskinian vision seeks to
be precise without being prosaic. As George Levine maintains, "Typically, Ruskin's astonishingly precise vision is never quite literal; the
power of the moment depended on what was not visible, on the fact that
'those very springing flowers and ever flowing streams had been dyed by
the deep colours of human endurance, valour and virtue.'"[27] Once, for
instance, Ruskin tried to imagine a mountain scene and did so with great
pleasure—until he thought of the same scene "in some aboriginal forest,"
totally devoid of human presence; then all pleasure in the picture vanished for him. By itself, nature lacked charm. Instead, like the stones in
The Stones of Venice, which Ruskin hoped would be both themselves
and also touchstones, or *prima materia*—alchemical philosopher's stones
that could transform consciousness—natural objects should serve two
functions. They should be autonomous, but also inspire the imagination.

Objective observation of facts exercised a powerful attraction for
Ruskin, partly, as I have shown, because of his interest in science and
natural history collections. Patricia M. Ball in her important study of
Ruskin, *The Science of Aspects: The Changing Role of Fact in the Work
of Coleridge, Ruskin and Hopkins*, credits science with shaping Ruskin's
perceptions. All three of these writers, according to Ball, exhibit "inter-

esting conjunctions of scientific and poetic awareness,"[28] but Ruskin is especially caught up in the scientific spirit of his time. The "concentration on the features of the earth, involving both a curiosity about appearance and structure and an aesthetic admiration for objects of nature," which Ruskin displayed at an early age, "was not peculiar to Ruskin in this period of the nineteenth century." Indeed, "the trend of the time roughly from 1820 to 1850," says Ball, "was in general sympathy with his devotion to facts."[29] (Notice how closely Ball's dates correspond to Lynn Barber's dates for the "heyday of natural history": 1820–1870. Ball characterizes this segment of the nineteenth century as rather a heyday for "the enthusiasm for fact.") To Ball, the energies of science,

> especially during the 1830s were largely devoted to the collection, classification and close scrutiny of phenomena. . . . It was a science concerned with detail—animal, mineral and vegetable—and Ruskin's taste for descriptive analysis was fostered by it.

Natural theology, which provided a chance, indeed even a duty, to see God's handiwork in nature, buttressed some of this scientific enthusiasm. But it was not a pure passion for God or for the cool theoretical atmosphere of scientific investigation that attracted most people to nature studies. For the hordes of natural history hobbyists, the point was nearer to hand. As Ball puts it, it was the "passion for fact, for the thing seen and handled."

Yet while Ruskin falls in love with facts, his attitudes about science remain ambivalent. He often voices suspicions about the technical advances of science and sometimes rails against its very purpose. Just as Burroughs dislikes museums, finding them devoid of the beauty and energy nature possesses in the field, Ruskin excoriates microscopes. For one thing, they unfairly aid vision; Ruskin contends that people should train their eyes to see precisely, not augment their power artificially. In the second place, Ruskin is something of a vitalist and, like Burroughs, something of an aesthetic ecologist. Nature is beautiful, and truly itself, only when it is whole. Dissect little bits and pieces out of context, mount them on a glass slide, and all the life and beauty goes out of them:

> It is of no use, to determine, by microscope or retort, that cinnamon is made of cells with so many walls, or grape-juice of molecules with so many sides;—we are just as far as ever from understanding why these particular interstices should be aromatic, and these special parallelopipeds exhilarating as we were in the savagely unscientific days when we could see only with our eyes, and smell with our noses.[30]

Ruskin's writings on science, published late in his life, especially *Proserpina* on botany and *Deucalion* on geology, are often considered something of an embarrassment. They rankle the modern temperament because they are so adamantly subjective—that is, unscientific. But, as Frederick Kirchhoff explains, for Ruskin pure objectivity in science was an evil, not a good. People should neither be dominant over, nor be dominated by, nature, if both humanity and nature are to retain their autonomy and dignity. It sounds strange to modern ears, but Ruskin wants a science of respect and love for nature.[31] Science should represent "a virtuous relation between equals," and among equals, one party does not dissect the other. Besides disdaining objectivity, Ruskin is unscientific in another way. As Kirchhoff puts it, he does not care so much about the *essences* of things—what makes them tick—as he does about their *aspects*,[32] what they look like on the surface. Ruskin loves the facts of nature, and his interest in them is highly concrete—but in an aesthetic way. As George Levine says, he is precise, not literal.

One of the clearest statements Ruskin makes about the proper relationship between humanity and the natural world comes in the middle of the "pathetic fallacy" discussion in *Modern Painters III* (part IV, chapter 12). Here, speaking of poets, Ruskin defines three ways in which a person can relate to nature. The categories vary from pure objectivity, to pure subjectivity, to a mixture of the two—and it is the last he values most highly. The familiar dialectic that asserts itself in Burroughs and in most natural history writers is present in Ruskin also: truth to nature, and response to nature. In fact, his oft-quoted passage might serve as a definition of a natural history writer as well as of a poet:

> So, then, we have three ranks: the man who perceives rightly, because he does not feel, and to whom the primrose is very accurately the primrose, because he does not love it. Then, secondly, the man who perceives wrongly, because he feels, and to whom the primrose is anything else than a primrose: a star, a sun, or a fairy's shield, or a forsaken maiden. And then, lastly, there is the man who perceives rightly in spite of his feelings, and to whom the primrose is forever nothing else than itself—a little flower apprehended in the very plain and leafy fact of it, whatever and how many soever the associations and passions may be that crowd around it.[33]

The first of these types is no poet at all. He is the objective scientist, who perceives nature only rationally (excluding for the moment any debate about whether emotion has a place in scientific observation). The second type, excessively emotional, represents the inferior poet. And the last, which mixes true observation (the flower is itself, clearly seen, autonomous) and emotion (nevertheless I may love it), is the type of the true poet.

What could be more appropriate than applying this Ruskinian definition to a poet like Tennyson? Wilfrid Ward, who knew Tennyson well, did exactly that in a reminiscence. Ward quotes Ruskin's primrose passage, with its three levels of perception, and then states emphatically that "Tennyson's imagination was eminently of the third kind. The vividness it gave was not a halo which may blur or obscure the true features it surrounds, but a strong limelight which shows the minutest details accurately."[34] As a poet ought, Tennyson could keep sight of the plain and leafy fact, while simultaneously transforming it with his imagination. To Ward, Tennyson's "habitual accuracy of memory and perception, and knowledge of detail, instead of being confused when his imagination became most vivid, came out all the more clearly." Though they seem contradictory, accurate perception and vivid imagination happily coexisted in Tennyson's verse.

For Ruskin, this mixture of true observation and human response is paramount: it is the germ of poetry. Verbal descriptions of nature, in other words, require this dialectic in order to interest a reader. (Ball makes clear how Ruskin struggled to achieve just this balance in his own descriptive writing.[35]) Of the two elements, though, Ruskin is usually inclined to emphasize true observation. As he says in a later passage, one of the signs of a great writer is his ability to eschew the pathetic fallacy and "to keep his eyes fixed firmly on the *pure fact*, out of which if any feeling comes to him or his reader, he knows it must be a true one."

A pure fact from nature gives Ruskin the greatest happiness. He confers the dignity of emotional response upon it; he respects it. If contemplating the whole of nature, not to mention its human implications, is too overwhelming, then cling to one pure pleasurable fact. The small specimens of nature are what the mind craves for its refreshment. In *Modern Painters III* (part IV, chapter X), Ruskin tells of a day when he took a Sunday walk through a valley below Mont Blanc. Although glorious scenery surrounded him, he was unable to take any pleasure in it. His imagination, he discovers, is numbed by grandeur. In his words,

[I] could not for a long while make out what was the matter with me, until at last I discovered that if I confined myself to one thing,—and that a little thing,—a tuft of moss, or a single crag at the top of the Varens, or a wreath or two of foam at the bottom of the Nant d' Arpenaz, I began to enjoy it directly, because then I had mind enough to put into the thing, and the enjoyment arose from the quantity of the imaginative energy I could bring to bear upon it; but when I looked at or thought of all together, moss,

stones, Varens, Nant d'Arpenaz, and Mont Blanc, I had not mind enough
to give to all, and none were of any value.[36]

Small details always have the power to please him. Just as he said of the
stone, which with its little forests of moss and little crags of crystal may
be more beautiful than the mountain, a small wreath of foam may be
more interesting to the mind than a whole river.

In fact, the human mind and eye seem better suited to details than to
vistas. Recognizing this, Ruskin feels "great contentment; thinking how
well it was ordered that . . . the human mind, on the whole, should enjoy
itself most surely, in an antlike manner, and be happy and busy with the
bits of sticks and grains of crystal that fall in its way to be handled, in
daily duty."[37] Nothing demeaning, no shame in encountering the world in
an antlike way: it is direct and tactile and honest. Here, choosing the ant
as a metaphor for the workings of the human mind, Ruskin honors the
sense of touch as well as sight. In a world strewn with sticks and crystals,
begging to be picked up and handled, people quite naturally play the role
of antlike inspectors, even hoarders, collectors. And with little bits of
their surroundings humans may be happiest, eyeing and fingering the
individual specimens of nature's cabinet of curiosities.

Ruskin's curator/collector impulses carry over into his art criticism
and into his own art. Truth to facts, whether natural or architectural, is
the foundation on which he builds his aesthetics. And like many nineteenth-century gentlemen and ladies, Ruskin studied drawing, under
various masters. He always considered himself an amateur, but by modern standards his sketching was both ambitious and assiduous. Kenneth
Clark says, "Ruskin drew almost every day of his life. He drew, as he
said, from sheer love and appetite. He also drew to teach himself the laws
of nature: every morning after breakfast he followed in a fine pen outline
the mode of growth of a leaf or a handful of grasses."[38] Ruskin's love of
sketching small details did much to shape his ideas about art. For an
artist like himself, the details mattered most. It took a sublime painter, a
great artist like Turner, to succeed in a higher realm: capturing large,
energetic overall impressions in addition to details.

The distinction—that amateurs should focus on fundamentals of detail—was clearly drawn in Ruskin's own manual for artists, *The Elements
of Drawing* (1857). Its purpose was to train people to have "innocence of
eye," that is, to train the eye to make factual records, and thereby be
more alert to beauty. Ruskin's techniques were "all ways of making direct
studies from nature, not methods of composing pictures."[39] What Ruskin
wanted amateurs to achieve through sketching was much the same as

what popular naturalists wanted amateur collectors to achieve through nature study: a keener eye and heightened powers of observation and appreciation. As Frank Buckland said, such studies tend to "sharpen the natural faculties." Two seemingly disparate methods of nature study: sketching and collecting. Yet their aims correspond remarkably well.

At one point in his art education (*Modern Painters I*, part II, section I, chapter VII) Ruskin compared his sketches to those of his teacher, Harding, and felt that his own were poor in comparison:

> Harding does such pretty things . . . and yet I am sure I am on a road that leads higher than his. . . . His sketches are always pretty because he balances their parts together and considers them as pictures; mine are always ugly, for I consider my sketch only as a written note of certain *facts* and those I put down in the rudest and clearest way, as many as possible. Harding's are all for impression; mine all for information.[40]

Prominent here is Ruskin's judgment that information, the clear and careful recording of facts, represents a higher road than the mere creation of a compositional whole. A complete composition like Harding's may be pretty—balanced, symmetrical, and polished—while little recorded facts may be ugly, rude, and fragmentary. But the isolated little bits, true to facts they record, are more important. Why? Because facts, concrete objects that actually exist in the world, have their own vibrant, autonomous life, more real and significant than any human construct. Ruskin's clearest pronouncement about this primacy of natural facts comes in *Praeterita* (volume II, section 77), when he describes his epiphany of the aspen tree. "Languidly, but not idly," he says, he began to draw the tree, and discovered that

> As I drew, the languor passed away: the beautiful lines insisted on being traced,—without weariness. More and more beautiful they became, as each rose out of the rest, and took its place in the air. With wonder increasing every instant, I saw that they "composed" themselves, by finer laws than any known of men.[41]

Natural objects have their own vibrant being, beauty, and harmony. Since this is so, a simple factual record of an object—whether in a sketch or a hand-held specimen—suffices for human satisfaction.

The emphasis on facts trickles down from Ruskin's own drawing to saturate his aesthetics. In *Modern Painters I*, Ruskin proclaims that the "representation of facts . . . is the foundation of all art; like real foundations, it may be little thought of when a brilliant fabric is raised on it; but it must be there" (part II, section I, chapter I).[42] In *Modern Painters III*, defending Turner, Ruskin reiterates this point:

> There is not the slightest inconsistency in the mode in which, throughout this work, I have desired the relative merits of painters to be judged. I have always said, he who is closest to Nature is best. All rules are useless, all genius is useless, all labour is useless, if you do not give facts; the more facts you give, the greater you are; and there is no fact so unimportant as to be prudently despised. (part IV, chapter X)[43]

When it comes to poetry, there as well no fact can prudently be despised. As in painting so in poetry, the more facts the better. In speaking of the "grand style" in art in *Modern Painters III* (part IV, chapter I), Ruskin propounds one of his most cherished rules—that the greatest art is that which contains the greatest ideas. This would seem to augur an idealized, generalized poetry, such as perhaps Dr. Johnson would approve, which exalts Tulips but not any particular tulip, let alone its idiosyncratic streaks. Poetry, Ruskin says, should suggest to the imagination noble emotions, along with ideas. But how should it do this? Through wealth of details.

Comparing a Byron poem to a historical account of the same events, Ruskin finds that the poem is, somewhat surprisingly, more specific. The poem contains more facts:

> This is a curious result. Instead of finding, as we expected, the poetry distinguished from the history by the omission of details, we find it consists entirely in the addition of details; and instead of being characterised by regard only of the invariable, we find its whole power to consist in the clear expression of what is singular and particular![44]

Such particular poetry succeeds because its facts, as images, have tremendous power to "excite the feelings." The reader will respond to carefully chosen facts with his own feelings. Singularity again reigns supreme.

Nevertheless, one could have too much of a good thing. Ruskin, for all his love of the concrete, the tufts of moss and little clumps of grasses, did not believe that photographic realism is necessarily the most truthful, whether in poetic images or in paintings. Thus the paradox of positive particularity: truth depends on facts, but simultaneously transcends them. Ruskin's reaction to daguerreotypes is characteristic, showing him to be of two minds about facts. According to Paul Walton, Ruskin was charmed by early photographs, saying that having one of a favorite building was nearly the same as carrying off the stones themselves, stains and chips and all, [45] and he occasionally used such photographs as an aid to his sketching. But daguerreotypes, like *camera lucida* tracings, lacked something. Or rather, they were too full of something. They lacked a "truth of impression" (the rallying cry of *Modern Painters IV*), any perception of mystery, any spirituality. And at the same time they were too cluttered with details. No selecting eye had chosen those of greatest singularity, as Ruskin said everyone should learn to do: paint with our eyes by picking out details (in *Modern Painters V*). For Ruskin, photographs—as bad paintings or poems could be—were too democratic. Facts were supremely important, true, but they should be *selected* facts. There is no virtue in fussy, compulsive detail, what Ruskin would call excessive finish. Painters must

> beware of finishing, for the sake of finish, all over their picture. The ground is not to be all over daisies, nor is every daisy to have its star-shaped shadow; there is as much finish in the right concealment of things as in the right exhibition of them. (*Modern Painters I*, part II, section I, chapter VII)[46]

If one recalls Ruskin's three ranks of poets, then his dual attitude toward facts becomes clearer. The true poet, remember, sees the true, autonomous nature of the flower as a plain, leafy fact; while at the same time he feels, responds to the flower. Part of that response involves selection: not every pure fact is chosen for scrutiny, but each one chosen is scrutinized with the greatest concentration, in the hope of apprehending its unique truth. Governed by this dialectical approach, Ruskin paints with his eyes, then sketches, and writes. To each leafy fact Ruskin pays tribute. And the "proper tribute in Ruskin's view is not possible if the observer is more concerned with his reacting self, his emotional response, or with any other centre which seems to deprive the object of the full attention it merits in its independent existence."[47] But such objects, although autonomous, ought not to be the focus of scientific inquiry. Uniquely and properly themselves, still they play upon the human imagination, which is transfixed with their beauty.

Keenly interested in science and art, at a time when "the criterion of accurate visual perception was paramount, encouraged in art and science alike,"[48] Ruskin, like Burroughs, forged a field of inquiry and enjoyment that straddled both science and art. Just as Burroughs pleaded for careful science that could yet touch the human heart, an aesthetic and evocative natural history, Ruskin sought a representation of natural objects that would be objectively, scientifically true to them, and yet allow response to their beauty. Landscape, he said in *Modern Painters V*, has "an essential connection" with "human emotion." If one fails to realize this, one runs the danger of becoming a mere "scientific mechanist."[49]

With sentiments like these, Ruskin closely allies himself to naturalists, whose brand of science even in the nineteenth century was seen as somewhat reactionary because it quaintly insisted on taking delight in nature. Ruskin's view of science, in fact, is distinctly old-fashioned. He persists in valuing, against the tide of modernism, a rambling, loving relationship with the natural world. With his love and awe of the plain leafy facts of the world, Ruskin is far more akin to Victorian natural history writers than might be apparent from his reputation as an art critic. Unintentionally, perhaps, Ruskin promoted natural history while he advocated art.

In choosing the topic of science, Ruskin might seem to be mining the same vein as writers such as Huxley and Tyndall. But their concerns were overwhelmingly theoretical and functional. Their essays speak of natural objects, but only in order to explain how they work, how they came about, how they are related: the protoplasm that is the physical basis of life. Such concerns are inherently scientific. Ruskin makes no such claims. He perceives energy and unity in natural objects but does not analyze them. Like a naturalist, he appreciates them. And one of his main concerns, like a true naturalist's, is to re-present objects, either visually or verbally, for the pleasure of others.

Frequent passages of highly detailed nature description sparkle like crystals in the matrix of Ruskin's works. These passages, Patricia Ball contends, constitute one of Ruskin's greatest achievements. With them, he elevated descriptive prose to the status of art, when before it had been considered peripheral or preliminary (the nature descriptions in Coleridge's journals, for example, serving only as material to be reworked into the true art, his poems). Ruskin does this, she says, by transforming standard tour or guidebook descriptions into art.[50] The increased prestige Ruskin lent to nature description dovetails nicely with the explosion of travel—and natural history—writing in the middle of the nineteenth century. In his verbal descriptions, Ruskin tried to combine a painter's color with a scientist's accuracy, to produce a poet's effects. As Ball puts it:

> Ruskin sees boldly and subtly and his language, in its controlled profusion, its concreteness, its richness and its vigour, embodies his vision. He establishes the poetry of description as a verbal art of prestige and authentic imaginative value, showing that to seize the object "in its very core of reality and meaning" is not an inferior exercise, but one to be respected as a legitimate enterprise, for the poet as for the painter.[51]

The descriptions of water, clouds, and rocks in *Modern Painters* are deservedly famous. Unrecognized, though, is how closely they resemble outright natural history prose.

For example, in *Modern Painters IV*, Ruskin describes rocks of a "slaty crystalline" character. He analyzes the rock types so that artists will understand how they contribute to landforms, and thus to scenery, which can then be accurately rendered in paint. To do this, Ruskin employs a hypothetical traveler who encounters the rocks:

> But, as he advances yet farther into the hill district he finds the rocks around him assuming a gloomier and more majestic condition. Their tint darkens; their outlines become wild and irregular; and whereas before they had only appeared at the roadside in narrow ledges among the turf, or glanced out from among the thickets above the brooks in white walls and fantastic towers, they now rear themselves up in solemn and shattered masses far and near; softened, indeed, with strange harmonies of clouded colours, but possessing the whole scene with their iron spirit. . . . And when the traveler proceeds to observe closely the materials of which these noble ranges are composed, he finds also a complete change in their internal structure. . . . They are now formed of several distinct substances, visibly unlike each other; and not pressed but crystallized into one mass . . . without the least mingling of their several natures with each other. Such a rock, freshly broken, has a spotty, granulated, and, in almost all instances, sparkling, appearance. (chapter VIII, sections 3, 4)[52]

Ruskin's description here is both precise and emotional, both clinical and grand. Near the end, when the "traveler proceeds to observe closely" the rock itself, Ruskin provides a concrete visual description of the hand specimen that any student of geology would recognize as igneous or metamorphic rock. "Spotty," "granulated," and "sparkling" are terms for luster and grain size that a field guide might include for the purposes of identification. At the same time, particularly in the context of what precedes their inclusion, the terms give a clear layperson's impression of texture; Ruskin's previous remarks about the integrity of each individual crystal make this texture seem both beautiful and admirably independent. The landscape description that opens the selection also mingles objective and subjective: the forms of the rock are individuated, clearly identifiable ("irregular," "towers," "shattered masses")—but Ruskin also imparts evocative and emotional qualities to them. Like Darwin in his *Journal of Researches*, Ruskin here sees—and, in words, paints—landscape in Romantic terms. The landforms are "gloomy," "majestic," "wild," "fantastic," "solemn," with almost mystical and mysterious "strange harmonies of clouded colours."

Compare Ruskin's passage with this one from the naturalist Philip Henry Gosse. Gosse here recounts a hypothetical journey through Siberia, where the landscape catches his attention:

It is a region where . . . the framework of the solid earth itself stands revealed in unrivalled gorgeousness. The cliffs here are of crimson or purple porphyry, as brilliant as the dyed products of the loom, there of dark-red granite seamed with thick veins of pure rose-coloured quartz, transparent as glass. Here a vast, uncouth column of black basalt rears its fused cylinders from the midst of a narrow ravine; and here a vast precipice appears of white marble . . . while, above all, the rich and splendid jasper rises in enormous masses, as if it were the vilest rock, yet glittering in gorgeous beauty,—mountains of gems.[53]

Gosse's landscape is precisely described; rock types are identified and named, and their landforms noted ("fused cylinders," "narrow ravine," "column," "precipice"). But Gosse's landscape, like Ruskin's, is evocative, mysterious, even pulsing and twisting with its own life. Just as the basalt towers here "rear" up and the earth "stands revealed," in Ruskin's passage the rocks "glance" out or "rear themselves up."

Both passages are natural history: scientific accuracy for poetic effect. And if Gosse is a hybrid creature—part zoologist, part evocative naturalist—so too is Ruskin a hybrid of scientist and artist. Ruskin's landscapes, the clouds, rocks, and leaves, are scrutinized with painstaking care, and *Modern Painters* is shot through with coolly dissected details: "You will observe that each shoot is furrowed, and that the ridges between the furrows rise in slightly spiral lines, terminating in the armlets under the buds which bore last year's leaves" (*Modern Painters V*, chapter VI, section 5).[54] But the details (which one might *not* have observed without Ruskin as a guide) are the skeleton for the larger endeavor: judgment (some landforms are "noble," some not), feeling, and aesthetic appreciation.

In much of his work, then, Ruskin proves himself a highly percipient and persuasive naturalist. Like more recognized Victorian naturalists, Ruskin seeks, and praises, the singular. Observing nature with a keen eye, he promotes a responsive visual aesthetic based on the collection of details. Ruskin's aim was, as John Burroughs said of art's, "the beautiful, not *over* but *through* the true." In Ruskin's descriptions, as in those of a naturalist, "the facts are not falsified; they are transmuted. . . . You shall find the exact facts in his pages, and you shall find them possessed of some of the allurement and suggestiveness that they had in the fields and woods."[55] Fretting about a contradiction—science's dissecting sterility, yet the potent allure of natural facts it revealed—Ruskin and Burroughs both arrived at a happy resolution. Transmute the facts, but see them true. That was the bedrock, the ethical and aesthetic foundation, for an honest and pleasurable relation with nature. Burroughs the essayist and Ruskin the artist embraced this aesthetic for different reasons. But theirs was the naturalist's solution.

Notes

1. *Praeterita*, volume II, section 199, in E. T. Cook and Alexander Wedderburn, eds., *The Works of John Ruskin* (London: George Allen, 1903-1912), vol. XXXV, p. 429.

2. Donald Worster, *Nature's Economy: The Roots of Ecology* (Garden City, NY: Anchor Press/Doubleday, 1979), p. 15.

3. Robert Elman, *First in the Field: America's Pioneering Naturalists* (New York: Van Nostrand Reinhold Company, 1977), p. 200.

4. Elman, p. 202.

5. See Elman, chapter 8.

6. Philip Marshall Hicks, *The Development of the Natural History Essay in American Literature*, Thesis, Univ. of Pennsylvania (Philadelphia: privately published, 1924), p. 124. Burroughs' standards are summarized on p. 139.

7. John Burroughs, *Wake-Robin*, in *The Complete Nature Writings of John Burroughs* (New York: Wm. H. Wise and Company, 1871; rpt. 1913), p. xv.

8. Burroughs, *Wake-Robin*, p. xv.

9. John Burroughs, "Science and Literature," in *Indoor Studies* (New York: Houghton Mifflin Company, 1889), p. 49.

10. John Burroughs, "Nature in Little," in *Field and Study*, in *The Complete Nature Writings of John Burroughs* (New York: Wm. H. Wise and Company, 1919), p. 113.

11. Burroughs, "Nature in Little," p. 112.

12. John Burroughs, "The Pleasures of Science," in *Field and Study*, in *The Complete Nature Writings of John Burroughs* (New York: Wm. H. Wise and Company, 1919), pp. 175-176.

13. Cook and Wedderburn, vol. VI, p. 170

14. Hicks, p. 32.

15. An interesting study of Emerson's visual metaphors is Sherman Paul, *Emerson's Angle of Vision* (Cambridge, MA: Harvard Univ. Press, 1952).

16. Burroughs, "Science and Literature," p. 49. Further page citations are made within the text.

17. Note the remarkable similarity of Burroughs' lament about science "peeping and prying into nature" to Ruskin's (cited in Chapter 5) about microscopes "peeping and probing." For many naturalists, however, "peeping" had positive connotations, as in Gosse's enthusiastic comment (cited in Chapter 3) about taking "peeps through nature's keyhole."

18. Carl Dawson mentions Ruskin as an example of an "aesthetic norm" based on nature, in *Victorian Noon: English Literature in 1850* (Baltimore: The Johns Hopkins Univ. Press, 1979), p. 32.

19. John Dixon Hunt, *The Wider Sea: A Life of John Ruskin* (New York: The Viking Press, 1982), p. 46.

20. Hunt, p. 86.

21. Hunt, p. 131.

22. Hunt, p. 68.

23. Hunt, p. 360.

24. Hunt, p. 46.

25. W. G. Collingwood, *The Life of John Ruskin* (London: Methuen and Co., 1905), p. 246.

26. Hunt, p. 360.

27. George Levine, "High and Low: Ruskin and the Novelists," in *Nature and the Victorian Imagination*, ed. U. C. Knoepflmacher and G. B. Tennyson (Berkeley: Univ. of California Press, 1977), p. 140.

28. Patricia M. Ball, *The Science of Aspects: The Changing Role of Fact in the Work of Coleridge, Ruskin and Hopkins* (London: The Univ. of London Athlone Press, 1971), p. 2.

29. Ball, p. 53.

30. Quoted in Frederick Kirchhoff, "A Science Against Sciences: Ruskin's Floral Mythology," in *Nature and the Victorian Imagination*, ed. U. C. Knoepflmacher and G. B. Tennyson (Berkeley: Univ. of California Press, 1977), p. 251.

31. Kirchhoff, p. 247.

32. Kirchhoff, p. 250. Ruskin uses this term in *Modern Painters III*.

33. Cook and Wedderburn, vol. V, p. 209.

34. Norman Page, ed., *Tennyson: Interviews and Recollections*. (Totowa, NJ: Barnes & Noble Books, 1983), pp. 105–106.

35. Ball, p. 85.

36. Cook and Wedderburn, vol. V, pp. 183–184.

37. Cook and Wedderburn, vol. V, p. 184.

38. Kenneth Clark, *Ruskin Today* (New York: Penguin Books, 1982), p. 353.

39. Paul H. Walton, *The Drawings of John Ruskin* (Oxford: Clarendon Press, 1972), p. 95.

40. Cook and Wedderburn, vol. III, pp. 200–201, note.

41. Cook and Wedderburn, vol. XXXV, p. 314.

42. Cook and Wedderburn, vol. III, pp. 136–137.

43. Cook and Wedderburn, vol. V, p. 173.

44. Cook and Wedderburn, vol. V, pp. 26–27.

45. Walton, p. 70.

46. Cook and Wedderburn, vol. III, p. 178.

47. Ball, p. 55.

48. Ball, p. 60.

49. Ball, p. 70.

50. Ball, p. 80.

51. Ball, pp. 99–100.

52. Cook and Wedderburn, vol. VI, pp. 129–130.

53. P. H. Gosse, *The Romance of Natural History* (New York: A. L. Burt Company, Publishers, 1902), p. 49.

54. Cook and Wedderburn, vol. VII, p. 61.

55. John Burroughs, "The Literary Treatment of Nature," in *Ways of Nature, The Writings of John Burroughs*, vol. XII (Boston: Houghton Mifflin Company, 1905), p. 208.

7

Natural History Art and Pre-Raphaelitism

Let me state, in the first place, that I have no acquaintance with any of these [Pre-Raphaelite] artists, and very imperfect sympathy with them. No one who has met with any of my writings will suspect me of desiring to encourage them in their Romanist and Tractarian tendencies. . . . But I happen to have a special acquaintance with the water plant *Alisma Plantago*, among which the said gold fish are swimming; and as I never saw it so thoroughly or so well drawn, I must take leave to remonstrate with you, when you say sweepingly that these men "sacrifice *truth* as well as feeling to eccentricity." For as a mere botanical study of the water-lily and *Alisma*, as well as of the common lily and several other garden flowers, this picture would be invaluable to me, and I heartily wish it were mine.[1]

JOHN RUSKIN, Letter to *The Times*, 1851

Primacy of vision, potency of response—for John Ruskin, these tenets guided his relationship to nature. Keenly observed natural facts, Ruskin maintained, lend themselves to two kinds of creative expression. One sort of expression is verbal: painstaking description in words of tree stems, or mists, or compact crystallines. The other is pictorial: drawings in pencil or ink of the same phenomena. As Patricia Ball implies, Ruskin's "science of aspects" often involves finding equivalences between the two techniques, in word paintings or graphic descriptions. Ruskin glorifies these precisionist renderings of natural objects, and it does not matter whether the medium is the mind alone, or prose, or a sketch. Before one can describe, before one can paint, one must *see*. The details garnered by the observant eye become a hoard that memory, the writer, or the artist can plunder with equal delight. To Ruskin, the interfusing of visual and verbal art is both natural and essential.

163

But Ruskin was by no means the only Victorian who exploited the connection between sharp, even microscopic vision and pictorial art. Countless journeyman artists, busily documenting the hoard of newly discovered material facts, developed a style consistent with the prevailing climate of particularity. As an adjunct to science, illustrative technical art captured the material details of discovery, whether of bridge trusses or living cells. Advances in the technology of reproducing art in books enhanced scientific illustration, making possible more detail and sharper color in biological plates, for example. Such improvements clearly benefited serious wildlife artists such as John James Audubon and John Gould. Equally important, however, they greatly increased the likelihood that low-priced, popular books of natural history would contain pictures as well as text. So prevalent was scientific and natural history illustration that, as a style, it spilled over into "fine art"—art whose purpose was not at all scientific. Much Victorian art had aims other than particular description; but a great deal of Victorian art, especially that of the Pre-Raphaelites, indulged in it heavily.

Like natural history writing, the Victorian art of this genre suffers from being classified as "low" art. Often in the form of book illustrations, intended as a record of facts, it could be dryly objective. But like the prose, the art of natural history could also be vivid, lively, infused with color, and emotional. It similarly bridged the "two cultures" gap between a purely scientific response and a humanistic one, producing such scientific artists as Marianne North who invested botanical records with vibrant emotion. As a testament to the magnetic pull of concrete, particularized objects, the art of natural history attracted artists interested in capturing nature's singularity. And because it achieved in paint what natural history prose did in words—precise delineation—many Victorian naturalists were attracted to both media. Philip Henry Gosse is perhaps the outstanding example. Talented with both brush and pen, Gosse illustrated his own books. Edward Lear, bird illustrator and nonsense writer, is another Victorian who combined science and art.

When people think of artists of the nineteenth century, North, Gosse, and Lear do not exactly spring to mind. Although important as a type of natural history discourse, their brand of art may seem limited in the larger artistic context. Yet their techniques and vision did have a counterpart among better known artists. The distinct outlines, vivid colors, specificity of details, and biological accuracy in the art of natural history are also found in the paintings executed by the loose confederation of "serious" artists known as the Pre-Raphaelites (established as a Brotherhood in 1848). Such techniques, anathema at first to Royal Academy hegemony, gradually changed the "look" of English landscape painting. Dark, moody chiaroscuro and a limited palette gave way to the bright greens of individuated leaves, the iridescent recognizable swallows flitting through the cattails in a painting like Waterhouse's *Lady of Shalott* (1883). Paintings in the Pre-Raphaelite style are famous for their particularity, exhibiting a perfect mania for detail. Where did it acquire this predilection? Critics often, albeit somewhat hesitantly, posit the influence of science. I would maintain that Pre-Raphaelite particularity falls within the discourse of natural history. In addition, since some of the Pre-Raphaelite painters were poets as well, their work demonstrates a neat chain of precisionist perception, from science or natural history to visual and then verbal art.

Like cabinets and collecting, natural history illustration certainly predated the nineteenth century. All, in fact, flourished in the preceding century. But like eighteenth-century cabinets, nature illustration in the eighteenth century catered to the aristocracy (even, in the case of France, to royalty). Many sumptuous nature books with colored plates were produced just to grace the private libraries of the wealthy, who alone could afford them. Frequently, fine illustrated books could be had by subscription only; if not enough patrons could be found, then publication could not take place. Ordinary persons were seldom patrons. The quality of the nature art was often very high, but it had a limited distribution and hence little popular influence. Buffon's *Histoire Naturelle*, for instance, was copiously illustrated, but was such a massive undertaking, comprising numerous expensive volumes, that only a few could acquire the series. Such a work had scant opportunity to influence popular taste because it was just too expensive: engraving and hand coloring came dear.

From the early eighteenth century on, nature illustrations matured in technique and sophistication. At one extreme, the figures for Buffon's series were highly Neoclassical, with animals posed incongruously in front of Doric columns. But much work done in the eighteenth century was far more scientifically accurate, giving its subjects their due. Both British and Continental artists concentrated on illustrating such creatures as insects, shelled mollusks, armored urchins, and fish. The engraving technique used at the time produced precise renderings, if sometimes a bit rigid. The somewhat stiff plates by Mark Catesby (1683–1749), with their black outlines and scratchy textures overlain with color, represent one use of the medium. Maria Sybilla Merian (1647–1717), on the other hand, displays the technique at its most powerful. Her carefully striated drawings portray the interrelationship between insects and plants, showing pupae, caterpillars, butterflies or moths, and the flowers and plants on which they feed—including holes chewed in the leaves, which some might not find beautiful. Engravings such as Merian's were frequently collaborative: the artist made paintings or drawings, and an engraver worked from the originals to make a reproducible plate.

Some excellent nature art never found a wide audience in its day because it was not reproduced at all. Many paintings were made simply as records, to be studied by naturalists in museums but not publicly displayed. Royal patronage in France encouraged this archival work,[2] as practiced by such masters as Pierre-Joseph Redouté (1759–1840). His paintings of bunched blossoms and butterflies—pansies and roses and carnations—have a sensitivity of line, shading, and color that can only be described as superb. They are very pretty, lush and sensuous, appealing more perhaps to gardeners than naturalists. Adhering to picturesque tenets of beauty, Redouté was much less inclined than Catesby or Merian to include caterpillars or grubs or flies among his choice flowers. But like those of the other artists, Redouté's plates are meticulously accurate, right down to the drops of dew on the leaves, thorns on the rose stems, or the swollen tips of the butterflies' antennae.

Natural history illustration could reach a wide audience and help fan the flames of enthusiasm for natural history only after what one art historian has called "The Lithographic Revolution."[3] For a lithograph, the nature artist could execute his own drawings on stone, eliminating the need for a stable of skilled engravers, thus cutting costs and increasing the artist's control over the work. Lithographs also lent themselves especially well to depictions of the most popular animals (those with fur and feathers as opposed to insects, mollusks, and so forth) because, while the engraver's burin cuts crisp, short lines, the lithographer's grease pencil suggests soft textures and fluid curves. Lithography also made color plates easier to produce. Discovered late in the eighteenth century, this technical innovation produced a veritable explosion in the number of illustrated nature books available to the average person. Older expensive classics, like Buffon's, came out in cheap illustrated editions. Readers began to equate text with pictures as never before, to expect visual equivalents for verbal descriptions. As one result, children's books boasted copious illustrations. As another, nature illustrators like P. H. Gosse became famous.

With demand so great for pictures of nature, several techniques coexisted with lithography throughout the century.[4] For expensive projects, copper or steel engravings were still used to produce full-page plates, which were then hand-colored to the artist's specifications. Audubon exploited this technique with great success. If black and white pictures would do, wood engraving was the method of choice (the woodcut, incised along the grain rather than across it, was a much older, coarser technique). In fact wood engravings produce the typical "look" one associates with nineteenth-century illustrated books and periodicals; assiduous engravers captured current events and fictional plot-twists until photography supplanted their craft. Wood engravings of natural history subjects trace their lineage to the endearing bird prints of Thomas Bewick (1753–1828). Subsequent engravings varied a great deal in quality. At one extreme were exquisite renderings printed on deckled vellum, such as anatomical diagrams in marine biology guidebooks; at the other were journeyman, even maladroit, animal pictures in cheap editions, printed darkly in thick ink on coarse paper. From 1850 on, illustrated encyclopedias of nature captivated buyers.[5] Usually such works featured small wood engravings scattered throughout the text—from gorillas to beetles, giraffes to crows. The ubiquitous *Illustrated Natural History* of J. G. Wood, available in several different editions throughout the century, is a good example.

Accuracy in Victorian natural history illustrations was not always achieved, with exigencies of publication sometimes fostering hasty or incompetent work, but it was highly valued. Verisimilitude—getting the facts right about an animal's appearance—counted heavily, for only if the animal or plant was correctly drawn could one experience appropriate wonder at its form. Often the background to the specimen was slighted, with only the foreground objects precise, because of a sort of atomism of attention enjoyed by the viewer. The creature itself, the object in the front, however, should be clear and correct in outward appearance and color. Such a demand for accuracy seems quite natural from a late twentieth-century viewpoint, but it represented a considerable change from previous pleasing pictures of animals. In medieval bestiary pictures, for example, the *idea* of an animal mattered more than its actual *appearance*; thus an originally inaccurate sketch of an animal would be copied again and again without apparent concern for its lack of similarity to the animal itself.

By the nineteenth century, the demand for accuracy had grown so strident that naturalist-artists tried, whenever possible, to draw live animals, rather than dead ones. (Not, of course, that the demand for positively dead, and thus eminently identifiable and collectible, specimens abated much in natural history circles; such enlightened restraint was a twentieth-century development.) Such on-the-spot efforts sprang less from a desire to capture the animal in its ecological setting than from a realization that some anatomical details could only be accurately rendered when vivified or set in motion: how feathers arched on a bird's wing, for example, or what expression lit its eyes. Audubon's efforts to capture birds in more lifelike poses spring to mind, although ironically he often resorted to shooting his hapless subjects to achieve that end. Another avian artist, Edward Lear, also painted from life. He had an advantage over Audubon in that, instead of having to thrash through swamps and thickets in search of his prey, he could watch exotic species comfortably and at close range—at the zoo. Like many Victorian naturalists and artists, Lear profited from the increasing popularity of public zoos, menageries, and aquariums where live animals could be closely observed.

Lear is a good example of a man remembered today for his literary achievements—his nonsense poems—whose interest in natural history is often overlooked.[6] But Lear began his career in search of precision in nature paintings and only later switched to looser, caricature drawings and poetry. He crossed the boundary between natural history and art, just as did another Victorian, Marianne North (1830–1890), a widely traveled botanical artist. Among family friends from many walks of life, especially the sciences, North grew up knowledgeable about science and comfortable about pursuing her own talents for art. As one biographer characterizes North: "like all Victorians who cared for the things of the mind, Marianne was uninhibited by that tedious modern invention, the two cultures."[7] Her paintings, now housed in a special gallery at Kew Gardens, serve as scientific records of plant species but also have about them a vivid energy and marked personal style. The brilliant colors and otherworldly, rococo forms of the plants in her tropical paintings pulsate with garish ominousness: they are so *other*, they are almost frightening. Botanical records, grounded in fact and precise observation, they nonetheless spark emotional fires.

Victorian natural history art could have considerable visual and emotional impact. As a result, many natural history books became popular successes because of their illustrations. For example, sales of Charles Kingsley's *Glaucus* (which I discuss in Chapter 9) were greatly increased when excellent illustrations were added to the book after its first edition. The plates, executed by the honored firm of G. B. Sowerby, formed an *Illustrated Companion* to the descriptions. Kingsley's prose was certainly animated enough to stand on its own, but the subjects of his work—curious natural creatures—became more eye-catching in pictures. This is but one instance in which, as one critic claims, "the plates sold the books in those days, as they still do."[8]

Of the many natural history illustrators who toiled in the service of representing novel natural objects, one of the most popular was Philip Henry Gosse. Gosse was not the most skillful illustrator, nor the most daring, nor the most rigorous. Gosse's degree of influence can be attributed to one simple fact: his drawings appeared in his own best-selling books. A great many people saw his art, and this, coupled with the fact that it was accompanied by his lively prose, made it extremely influential. (In Chapter 8, I devote considerable attention to Gosse's natural history writing). Indeed, in some ways his art, or rather his way of seeing the world through artist's eyes, was more important than his prose. Peter Dance, in fact, claims that "it was undoubtedly his brush rather than his pen which made him a best-selling author."[9]

And Gosse's style did more than affect natural history illustration; it became clearly visible in the mainstream of Victorian art. Isolation of objects, bright colors, hard-edged outlines, lack of perspective or background, and careful rendering of details mark Gosse's drawing. As his son Edmund pointed out, the fact that Philip's father had been a professional painter of miniatures predisposed Philip himself to a certain painterly style:

> Philip Gosse as a draughtsman was trained in the school of the miniature painters. When a child he had been accustomed to see his father inscribe the outline of a portrait on the tiny area of the ivory, and then fill it in with stipplings of pure body-color. He possessed to the last the limitations of the miniaturist. He had no distance, no breadth of tone, no perspective; but a miraculous exactitude in rendering shades of colour and minute particularities of form and marking.[10]

His later method of composition, Edmund goes on to explain, was to draw each item, whether sea anemone or coral, separately and then to arrange them on one plate, washing in a vague sandy background later. This technique emphasized their isolation as objects. Its methodology was simple: capture and juxtaposition. Gosse's paintings were the two-dimensional equivalents of the naturalist's cabinet, and the method by which each created meaning was the same.

The plates that Gosse created for one of his seaside books, *Tenby: A Sea-Side Holiday*, exemplify his style. The frontispiece shows a group of sea anemones. The point of view Gosse has chosen is unusual: the viewer's eye is level with the anemones which cling to the rocks, as if the viewer were partially submerged in a tidepool. (Actually, for Gosse the viewpoint was totally realistic, since he spent a great deal of time at

Tenby mucking about in sea pools and cliffside caves.) The broken, bedded rocks of the foreground have been rendered in soft grease pencil and printed in shades of gray. Also traced in black and white is the Romantic background scene, which shows a tranquil bay bordered by rocky cliffs on the left and an abrupt, truncated island on the right. The background includes a couple of faint human touches: a magnificently spired though somewhat generic church on the cliff, a rude hut on the island. But they are remote and tenuous, clearly peripheral to Gosse's main purpose. The weirdly tentacled anemones in the foreground dominate this world. These curious creatures are larger and more detailed than anything else in the picture; in fact, one bulbous animal dwarfs, indeed almost engulfs, the building behind it. And the anemones alone are in color—rust-orange, olive-green, an exquisite yellow, and, on the middle species, a shocking pink. The color washed onto each animal serves to isolate it from its monochromatic surroundings, so that each becomes a specimen.

Most of Gosse's lithographs in *Tenby* renounce entirely any attempt at scenery or panorama. Each focuses on a single, isolated organism, often an unusual or unexpected ocean dweller. No pretty birds or cuddly mammals here—Gosse chooses polyps, young barnacles, crab larvae, Infusoria. The single most remarkable feature of Gosse's Tenby drawings is that most of them have a black background rather than white. Fascinated as he is by the luminescence of many sea creatures, Gosse portrays them as they would look at night. Their transparent bodies are outlined in white, their luminous organs touched with spots of red, streaks of orange, washes of dazzling chartreuse. The effect is quite stunning. The gauzy animals float against a rich dark background, velvety with nearly a mezzotint's tactile black. Delicate white stippling defines their sheer surfaces, delineates each waving flagellum. Centered in a dark halo, each gorgeous creature is *sui generis*—remarkable and distinct.

Ultimately, P. H. Gosse turned the "limitations of the miniaturist" to his advantage. That a miniaturist's techniques might be especially conducive to natural history illustration has been suggested by one art critic. Referring to the achievements of eighteenth-century French natural history artists, Peter Dance maintains that the "clear superiority of French artists in the period immediately before use of lithography became widespread seems to be connected, to a certain extent, with the art of miniature painting, an art to which the French had long been devoted and at which they excelled."[11] "Miraculous exactitude," bright color, exquisitely reproduced particularities—these were the characteristics of nature as Gosse saw it with his miniaturist's eye. Given the popularity of his books, the widespread acquaintance with his sharply focused versions of natural objects, it is not too far-fetched to suggest that Gosse's style influenced other painters—and writers—who were not themselves naturalists.

The colors he saw in marine life had not been widely noted before, and his illustrations of tidepool creatures, published in his volume *A Naturalist's Rambles on the Devonshire Coast* (1853), confounded the public. As Edmund Gosse explains, the plates

> were at that time a revelation. So little did people know of the variety and loveliness of the denizens of the seashore, that, although these plates fell far short of the splendid hues of the originals, and moreover depicted forms that should not have been unfamiliar, several of the reviewers refused altogether to believe in them, classing them with travellers' tales about hills of sugar and rivers of rum.[12]

Once readers got over their initial discomfiture at the novelty of the colors and realized that such tints were not only stunning but true to fact, they acclaimed Gosse's illustrations. According to Edmund Gosse, a later volume, *The Aquarium* (1854), not only instigated the aquarium craze but "made a positive sensation, and marked an epoch in the annals of book publishing." Gosse's colorfully rendered specimens of nature inculcated new methods of observation and modes of artistic representation.

New modes of representation figured prominently in the work of other artists as well—artists less narrowly specialized than the natural history illustrators. An obsession with facts, with precisely observed details, was one of the touchstones of the painters known as the Pre-Raphaelites. They preached what one critic called "observant literalism."[13] To achieve this, they raised the ambiguous banner of "Truth to Nature." As William Michael Rossetti said in his description of the original Pre-Raphaelite Brotherhood, "Nature was to be their one or their paramount storehouse of materials for objects to be represented; the study of her was to be deep, and the representation (at any rate in the earlier stages of self-discipline and work) in the highest degree exact."[14] As the parenthetical remark implies, Pre-Raphaelite representation might rise above pure literalism, for other ends, but it began with exact details. As F. G. Stephens put it in *The Germ*, the dedicated Victorian painter should evince a "determination to represent the thing and the whole of the thing, by training himself to the deepest observation of its fact and detail, enabling himself to reproduce, as far as is possible, nature herself."[15]

Some of the painters (and poets) of the loosely defined Pre-Raphaelite school were seized by a passion for detail that would rival any naturalist's. Indeed, it was just this passion that Ruskin joyfully recognized in their paintings. As Robert Peters expresses it:

> The poets' vivid, often exaggerated word painting, and the artists' finicky accounting in brush, pen, and language for the infinite hues and shapes of grass blades, flower structures, cloud formations, mottlings of insects, and fabrics of clothing, revealed an enthusiasm which they shared with geologists and evolutionists and which they attempted to make spiritually significant.[16]

I would venture to substitute "naturalists" for Peters' "geologists and evolutionists"—but in any case the fount for passionate detail is the same. In his *Germ* article, Stephens proposed a parallel between scientific truth and artistic truth, saying that empiricism and strict adherence to fact advance them both:

> The sciences have become almost exact within the present century. Geology and chemistry are almost re-instituted. . . . And how has this been done but by bringing greater knowledge to bear upon a wider range of experiment; by being precise in the search after truth? If this adherence to fact, to experiment and not theory,—to begin at the beginning and not fly to the end,—has added so much to the knowledge of man in science; why may it not greatly assist the moral purpose of the Arts?[17]

Stephens voices the deeply felt belief, so ingrained in the nineteenth century, that truth somehow lives in details, just as life inhabits the cells. The aim of the artist, he says, should be "truth in every particular"; that is, every detail of truth, and truth in every detail. There is goodness in every "fact of truth, though it be only in the character of a single leaf earnestly studied."[18]

A belief in "truth in every particular" underlies the nineteenth-century veer toward artistic realism. Just as realism constitutes one major preoccupation in the Victorian novel, so does it also in Victorian painting. Within that "realism," admittedly a problematic quality, there are two contrasting tendencies: emphasis on story, and emphasis on setting. A painting of the first type, sanctioned by the Royal Academy, presents a complex, multilayered vignette. In the two-dimensional painting lurk numerous clues about the narrative flux through time that the picture has temporarily arrested. *Misfortune*, in the *Past and Present* triptych (1858) by Augustus Egg, for example, contains a tableau of domestic life and a moral, all at once. The slumping husband has just learned of his wife's betrayal; the viewer notes the clues such as his posture, the letter crumpled in his hand, her prostrate form, the cozy symbols of hearth and home in the well-upholstered room, the children behind them innocently at play, their symbolic house of cards collapsing. It is a painting, but also a narration: time compressed. The narrative impulse also manifests itself to some extent in the painting of the Pre-Raphaelites. In Millais' *Ophelia* (1851–1852), for instance, Ophelia is caught at one moment in her mad drift toward death; her whole story and Shakespeare's play hover as narrative context behind her.

But at the same time a painting like *Ophelia* displays an increased emphasis, not on narration (time), but on setting (place). Egg's painting is quite detailed, but in Millais' work the details jump out from the background to overpower the central figure of the floating woman. Details here take precedence over the story and, furthermore, the details are natural objects. Each blade of grass, each flower is painted exactly— almost, one might say, myopically, as if each were being examined not from normal standing height and distance, but from a bending crouch.

Ophelia is perhaps the supreme example of the "observant literalism" of the Pre-Raphaelites, but they executed dozens of paintings in which sharply observed, carefully differentiated details of nature stand out. For example, in William Holman Hunt's *Our English Coasts* (*Strayed Sheep*) (1852), each leaf of the foreground vegetation is distinct, with orange, black, and white butterflies clinging to pink flowers. It is not surprising that natural details dominate a painting like Arthur Hughes' *The Woodsman's Child* (1860), because the subject is country life. While the father cuts firewood and the mother collects sticks in the background, the contented child lies asleep on a blanket, surrounded by the objects of the forest: a squirrel, bluebells, a robin perched on a branch, white asters, carefully drawn leaves, bark, and moss. But even in paintings ostensibly not about nature, it often crowds into the picture, as for example in John Everett Millais' *James Watt and His Granddaughter* (1849). Here the subject of the painting sits in a cluttered interior, on a red chair. But there are flowers on the table near him, and behind him a window looks out onto the foliage in the garden, giving the effect of a conservatory.

One critic, W. F. Axton, applies to Pre-Raphaelite painting—and much of the rest of Victorian art as well—the terminology of microscopic optics that I have been tracking down in Victorian natural history. He mentions that Hunt acquired the nickname of "Bird's Nest" because he did so many studies of natural specimens, "patient, careful watercolors of natural minutiae seen up close."[19] His *Primroses and Bird's Nest* renders ivy, flowers, pale green-blue eggs, moss, and lichen of a nest with meticulous care. That Hunt did so many small studies of natural details brings to mind Ruskin's daily sketching. It also signals a rise in the prestige of the humble sketch or study. Axton, however, sees Hunt's style of painting as part of a trend that damaged Victorian painting: "more and more demands for literal attention to microscopic detail drew all painting, but especially landscape, into the straitjacket of literally minute finish."[20] Ruskin warned, also, of the dangers of too-great finish, but more important for the purpose here is Axton's terminology. The Pre-Raphaelites, especially, he judges, employed an "all-over myopia of vision and microscopy of depiction"[21]—the very same terms that Gerhard Joseph applies to Tennyson.

In a painting like *Ophelia*, Axton ventures, the natural details are meticulously assembled, each one drawn with so much exactitude that its reality fights for attention with every other one. Any unity of impression is thus lost. The aesthetic success or failure of such a style (it may tend toward fragmentation, as do the details of "Mariana," and "The Woodspurge")[22] is not as important here as its genesis. In light of the Victorian natural history vogue, one would suspect a link between the legions of British bug-hunters and the painterly style of the Pre-Raphaelites. And, in fact, Axton seizes on just such a connection. "Natural detail observed under conditions of contracted sight" in painting was "perhaps a product of a native English empirical habit of mind, certainly the artists' equivalent of the naturalist's method of recording his observations, which had reached a pinnacle of prestige by the time of Victoria."[23] Just as Gerhard Joseph suspects a relationship between Tennyson's close eyesight and his detailed literary style, Axton relates the myopic or "contracted" observations of naturalists to the Pre-Raphaelites' artistic technique. Far from being myopic, the naturalist Philip Gosse had just the opposite kind of eyesight, "exceedingly powerful"[24]; yet he was in the habit, nevertheless, of supplementing it with a hand-lens for close work. His son, Edmund, associates his father's obsessive eyesight with his detailed painting style.

Along with the microscopic eye—a potent trope of natural history—another trope of the naturalists surfaces in the Pre-Raphaelite style of painting: the cabinet or museum. In *Ophelia*, Millais painstakingly assembles hundreds of individual specimens of plants and flowers. The banks of Ophelia's stream bristle with differentiated blades of grass. They are a collection of thin oily representations, it is true, not actual leaves—but they are a collection just the same. Millais has, in effect, painted the contents of a cabinet—a common Pre-Raphaelite tactic. Geoffrey Hemstedt, in a survey of Victorian painting, sees a comparison between "Tennyson's sense of nature on a small scale (the Romantic turned botanist)" and the "sharply detailed, and pointedly chosen, flora in the work of Arthur Hughes," among other painters. But his interpretation of

Ophelia bears even greater significance. The painting looks to him like a museum diorama or display:

> In his *Ophelia*, landscape has become a bowering enclosure of greenery, an effect emphasized by the curving top of the frame. It is curiously like looking into one of those glassed recesses in natural history museums which recreate the "natural setting" for the stuffed coyote or dabchick.[25]

It is as though nature, looked at with the probing, raptorial eye of the intent naturalist, cannot help but become a specimen. Millais' fussy care over each blade of grass does have the effect of fixing them in a permanent display, the way a dabchick might be wired or stuffed for eternity, or a starfish dipped into glycerine for permanent preservation.

Indeed, stories about the Pre-Raphaelite painters' contrivances for ensuring absolute accuracy of detail—Millais' insisting that the model for *Ophelia* lie immersed day after day in a tub of water, for example—sound very much like naturalists' tales of collecting specimens. Through a great deal of manipulation of details, it is hoped, the overall effect will be a lifelike specimen for display. The eccentric naturalist Charles Waterton sets the tone in an 1825 essay "On Preserving Birds for Cabinets of Natural History":

> In dissecting, three things are necessary to ensure success; viz. a penknife, a hand not coarse or clumsy, and practice. The first will furnish you with the means; the second will enable you to dissect; and third cause you to dissect well. These may be called the mere mechanical requisites.
>
> In stuffing, you require cotton, a needle and thread, a little stick, the size of a common knitting-needle, glass eyes, a solution of corrosive sublimate, and any kind of a common temporary box to hold the specimen. . . .
>
> But, if you wish to excel in the art, if you wish to be in ornithology, what Angelo was in sculpture, you must apply to profound study, and your own genius to assist you. And these may be called the scientific requisites.
>
> You must have a complete knowledge of ornithological anatomy. You must pay close attention to the form and attitude of the bird, and know exactly the proportion each curve, or extension, or contraction, or expansion of any particular part bears to the rest of the body. In a word, you must possess Promethean boldness, and bring down fire, and animation as it were, into your preserved specimen.[26]

Did the Pre-Raphaelites possess, in Waterton's terms, only the mere mechanical requisites? Did they merely place little specimens into the common temporary box of the picture's frame? Or did they succeed in breathing animation into their specimens? Whether, as art, their method of thread and needle, glass eyes and little sticks succeeds, critics do not agree. Certainly they began, like the naturalist intent on filling a cabinet, with the study of nature's little parts. And like a collector, they juxtaposed these objects within a frame, a delimiter of attention—the sides of a cabinet or the edges of a painting. The framing of such disparate objects had a focusing intent. An object within a cabinet, within a picture's frame, within the field of view of a microscope, or within a camera's viewfinder, assumes sudden, magnified significance.

The novelty of being able to frame a scene mechanically, with a camera, as well as being able to capture details with unprecedented accuracy, definitely influenced the Pre-Raphaelite painting style. William Bell Scott, who visited Rossetti's studio and knew many of the P.R.B. (Pre-Raphaelite Brotherhood) painters, surmised in his *Autobiographical Notes* that "the seed of the flower of Pre-Raphaelitism was photography," particularly its "perfection of the impression on the eye."[27] Its subject might be "history, genre, mediaevalism, . . . but the execution was to be like the binocular representations of leaves that the stereoscope was then beginning to show."

Influences on the Pre-Raphaelite style were, of course, complex. One factor certainly consistent with the taste for natural history is the rise of *plein air* painting. In their doctrine, the Pre-Raphaelites rejected dark-palette studio work, preferring instead, in the words of Holman Hunt, that the "windows of the edifice" of art should be "opened to the purity of the azure sky, the prismatic sweetness of the distant hills, the gaiety of hue in the spreading landscape, and the infinite richness of vegetation," so that "nothing should henceforth be hidden from the enfranchised eye."[28] Through an open casement, the artist finds a freedom of sight, the ability to look directly at nature, unfettered by old artistic conventions. Such directness of gaze was encouraged by Romanticism and abetted in all likelihood by natural history. Hunt's curious term for the appearance of distant hills, "prismatic," also hints of the influence of Victorian recreational optics—the widespread enthusiasm for microscopes, telescopes, kaleidoscopes, cameras, and prisms, all devices for exploiting light and its constituent colors.

Plein air painting went hand in hand with the nineteenth-century emphasis on landscape art. Even more interesting in the context of natural history is another artistic change that accompanied the new passion for landscapes—namely, the elevation of the sketch to the level of high art. Peter Galassi, in a fascinating study of artistic conventions that directly preceded the invention of photography, discusses the change in status of the sketch. As Galassi notes, two types of sketches had been recognized by painters since the Renaissance: the *ébauche* (a compositional study for a whole painting) and the *étude* (a study for a little detail of nature). Both were mere preliminaries to the true art: a finished, carefully composed painting on a grand scale. But at the end of the eighteenth century, the lowly *étude*, "meant as a record of observation,"[29] began to gain importance. The Neoclassical tide was ebbing, and the Romantic fascination with fragments was ascendant. By 1820, making candid oil sketches, for their own sake, was a widespread artistic practice in both England and Europe.

Such sketches were symptomatic, Galassi contends, of a change in the "convention of representation." "Devoted to the problem of transcribing the appearance of nature,"[30] oil sketches attempted to capture the precise details of a little swatch of turf or tangle of shrubs. Much like Ruskin's sketches, or the *Bird's Nest* painting of Hunt, the on-the-spot sketches of the major painters, particularly Constable, demonstrated a "heretical concern for the visual aspect of the most humble things."[31] The sketch painstakingly recorded a little patch of complex nature simply for itself rather than as a contribution to a larger, more formal work. And, as Galassi points out, the sketch works as a kind of snapshot, having much the same scope and complexity as a photograph of nature. Both are predicated upon a new "syntax" or arrangement of forms. In Galassi's words the sketch contains

> a new and fundamentally modern pictorial syntax of immediate, synoptic perceptions and discontinuous, unexpected forms. It is the syntax of an art devoted to the singular and contingent rather than the universal and stable. It is also the syntax of photography.[32]

Moreover, I would add, it is the syntax of the cabinet of curiosities, or of a microscopic field of vision, which necessarily focuses on a somewhat arbitrary section of a much bigger whole, showing fascinating and complex but "discontinuous, unexpected forms." Galassi's new "syntax" fits natural history very well, which is not, after all, the science of a biologist looking for a unified theory, but the aggregations of an admirer fascinated by aesthetic fragments. Darwin certainly was a scientist, but in his work of natural history, *The Journal of Researches*, he was pursuing the "art devoted to the singular and contingent" (that is, that which is accidentally present), as his repeated use of the word "singular" suggests. Like the sketch, like the snapshot, a book of popular natural history displays whatever pleasing forms have been snagged in the net. Arbitrariness of the collection is not an issue, because the singularity of the specimens matters most. Interestingly, those Victorians offended by Pre-Raphaelite art attacked it precisely because it emphasized the singular, feeling that what art should do is represent norms, not exceptions. A hostile review of an 1850 Pre-Raphaelite exhibition sniffed that "abruptness, singularity, uncouthness, are the counters by which they play for game."[33] Here singularity becomes pejorative, in complete contrast to the laudatory sense in which Victorian naturalists regarded the term. The degree to which singularity is valued depends on the weight given to novelty versus that assigned to patterns.

The ascendancy of the previously humble *étude*, the exhortations of Ruskin about the importance of careful sketching, the invention of photography, the Pre-Raphaelite love affair with details, and the scrutinizing concerns of natural history—all interpenetrate. All show a preoccupation with nature's smallest details to the extent that, by 1850, "natural" usually meant "what is delineated most fully, is most complete in detail."[34] The language used by the practitioners of each of these arts often reveals remarkably similar aims. Daguerreotypes influenced Pre-Raphaelite paintings; conversely, the English co-inventor of photography, William Fox Talbot, spoke of his invention in terms of painting. In *The Pencil of Nature* (1844), Talbot said that photographs captured humble details well and used painting to justify this approach:

> A painter's eye will often be arrested where ordinary people see nothing remarkable. A casual gleam of sunshine, or a shadow thrown across his path, a time-withered oak, or a moss-covered stone may awaken a train of thoughts and feelings, and picturesque imaginings.[35]

A naturalist's eye also fixes on the seemingly unimportant detail, and for him, too, a train of associations and emotions is triggered. John Burroughs, for example, proclaims that details in nature can arrest (using the same word as Talbot) the eye, if the mind is intent upon them as well:

> The book of nature is always open winter and summer and is always within reach, and the print is legible if we have eyes to read it. But most persons are too preoccupied to have their attention arrested by it. Think of the amazing number of natural things and incidents that must have come under the observations of the farmer, the miner, the hunter, that do not interest him, because they are aside from his main purpose.[36]

As Talbot thought a detail could arrest a photographer's or a painter's eye, so Burroughs thought nature's detail could arrest the naturalist's. But in each case the eye must be aimed—figuratively, through purposeful attention, or literally, through a camera lens and viewfinder. Burroughs, in his essay, "Sharp Eyes," employs almost the terminology of photography to describe how the eyes focus. He does not speak of a camera, but rather of aiming a gun, which is rather a similar action:

> Nevertheless the habit of observation is the habit of clear and decisive gazing: not by a first casual glance, but by a steady, deliberate aim of the eye, are the rare and characteristic things discovered. You must look intently, and hold your eye firmly to the spot, to see more than do the rank and file of mankind. The sharpshooter picks out his man, and knows him with a fatal certainty from a stump, or a rock, or a cap on a pole.[37]

If the eye, steady and aimed like a gun, concentrates on a little bit of nature, it will discover "individuality—that which separates, discriminates, and sees in every object its essential character." And, adds Burroughs, "this is just as necessary to the naturalist as to the artist or the poet. The sharp eye notes specific points and differences,—it seizes upon and preserves the individuality of the thing."[38]

The sharp eye, which Burroughs calls essential to both artist and naturalist, is indispensible most of all to the man or woman who is both. The naturalist who wishes to render what he sees in paint needs a sharper, more steadily aimed, more patient eye than a landscape artist requires. The painter-naturalist may not have, or need, a large comprehensive vision—the scope of a Constable or a Turner—because he works piecemeal on isolated specimens. Like Gosse's, many natural history illustrations require little in the way of background. They rely instead on a dazzling foreground of floating shells, or insects, or starfish. Paramount in these illustrations is the precision evident in the delineation of each object: every dot of color, every line of tentacle or antenna. When one looks at a painting by Turner, one drinks in the whole scene, experiences its swirling energy, grandeur, and human scope. When one looks at a natural history illustration, on the other hand, the response is "Look at that! This one has green stripes, and golden eyes. And here is one with an oddly fluted shell." Natural history paintings, or engravings, or sketches, show *this one*. They are concerned with Darwin's singularity, with Burroughs' individuality. They are, in that sense, like photographs, or like *études*; they render palpable the reality of a snippet of nature.

Natural history illustration, then, like the new medium of photography, or like the new direction taken in fine art by the hitherto insignificant sketch, is one source of the mid-Victorian insistence on details. The demand for "graphic accuracy" and a "widespread interest in verisimilitude," as Carl Dawson notes,[39] spills over from one medium to another. From photography to Pre-Raphaelite painting, from the realism of the novel[40] to the painstaking compilation of facts in the service of history or lexicography or biography—the tracks all intersect. The visual acuity of the eye could be captured perhaps more easily in paint or on film than in words. But the very precision of paintings or photographs motivated attempts to find verbal equivalents, equally precise descriptions. In natural history descriptions and Pre-Raphaelite poetry, language rearranged itself according to the new syntax of photography, the syntax needed to "read" the "book" of nature pictorially. Such a sketch of nature would be less a composition, more a capture of elements, but such would be the intrinsic fascination of those elements that their capture could still be affective.

The syntax of capture and juxtaposition, in other words, could create meaning. In the case of photography, as Talbot said, a captured detail could trigger a train of associations or emotions. Just as in a cabinet of natural history, these emotions might be simply wonder that such a strange creature even exists, or aesthetic appreciation of its beauty, or the poignancy of realizing that such a one might never exist again. (True, Victorian naturalists were slow to realize that nature's abundance could be depleted, but in the case of any given specimen, possession implied possible loss; perhaps one might never repeat the glory of a particular capture.) Just as Ruskin and Burroughs insisted on such a mix of accuracy and evocation, British landscape photographers from the 1850s to the 1880s did also. In an essay to accompany a series of Victorian photographs, Charles Millard points out this English amalgam of approaches. English photographers combined the French approach, essentially pictorial, and the American approach, highly scientific, to blend "emotional evocation" and "objective assertion of sheer physical fact" in their work.[41]

Similarly, the Pre-Raphaelite tendency to value natural objects as specimens and then to elevate them into evocative subjects for painting is striking. Obviously, Pre-Raphaelitism involves more than fidelity to nature. It teems with elements not related to minute natural depiction—emblematic or iconographic symbolism like Rossetti's lilies and stars in *The Blessed Damozel*, for example, or picturesque medievalism. Yet surprising parallels can be discerned between natural history and paintings on entirely different subjects. For instance, Ford Madox Brown's famous painting *Work* would seem devoid of natural elements, since it is an elaborate allegory on social and moral themes. But in his own description of the painting, Brown justifies the inclusion of certain human elements by likening them to natural specimens:

> I would beg to call your attention to my group of small, exceedingly ragged, dirty children in the foreground of my picture, where you are about to pass. I would, if permitted, observe that, though at first they may appear

just such a group of ragged dirty brats as anywhere get in the way and make a noise, yet, being considered attentively, they, like insects, molluscs, miniature plants, &c., develop qualities to form a most interesting study, and occupy the mind at times when all else might fail to attract.[42]

This seems to me a most remarkable instance of natural specimens being considered *more* valuable than human beings. Rather than counting his human subjects as primary, Brown somewhat surprisingly considers non-human objects to be central. It is the mollusks who have automatic, intrinsic interest; the ragged children who must measure up to them.

Looming behind Brown's statement, most likely the result of the popularity of natural history and its inclusion as an acceptable subject by painters like Millais, are an aesthetic and a value judgment. Brown takes for granted the worth, and beauty, of natural objects—even those that to a modern reader might not seem particularly appealing: insects and, even more odd, mollusks. If one were unaware of the extent of the natural history boom, if one did not know that it included fads for collecting seashells, and even for keeping their tenants—mollusks—alive in aquariums, Brown's choice of comparison might seem a puzzle. If, however, one takes into account the fervor of British bug-hunters who, like Darwin in his famous anecdote (from his *Autobiography*), were perfectly willing to pop a rare beetle into their mouths to carry it home if their hands were full of others, and if one knows of the tidepool invasion launched by works like Gosse's *The Aquarium*, Lewes' *Sea-Side Studies*, and Kingsley's *Glaucus*—that is, if one knows the background of Victorian natural history—Brown's statement makes sense. In *Ophelia*, natural history is part of the painting; in *Work*, it is not. But beneath the surface of both lies the same confident assumption. Objects of natural history are the touchstones of a new aesthetics. Brown assumes that everyone would recognize the artful collection of insects or plants—the cabinet—and tacitly affirm its worth.

Thus, the popularity of natural history had an influence on the style of the Pre-Raphaelite painters. Their Brotherhood coalesced during the heyday (to use Lynn Barber's term) of natural history, a time when the close scrutiny of natural objects was valued and came to be taken for granted. In such a climate, naturally a Pre-Raphaelite painter would, if he depicted a butterfly in a painting, make it a particular, recognizable kind; in Millais' *The Blind Girl*, as one critic points out, "the butterfly on the blind girl's shawl is unmistakably a Red Admiral."[43] The point is not that the Pre-Raphaelite painters necessarily traipsed about collecting shells and drying fronds for herbariums,[44] but rather that, as artists, they set themselves in the same relation to nature as did the naturalists. Although they were concerned with how to represent natural objects, not so much with how to collect them, their vantage point, their use of sight, their use of natural detail, stemmed from the same root: belief in the intrinsic value of singularity. The idiosyncratic streaks on Johnson's tulip now became the exact locus of its value. *This* tulip, the exact like of which one will never see again.

The fervor for natural details and the new syntax of capture and juxtaposition entranced not only the Pre-Raphaelite painters but the poets as well. Along with medievalism, sensuousness, Beautiful Lady themes, precise detail, and even quantification (the use of numbers) are characteristics of Pre-Raphaelite poetry. Nearly every critic of the school mentions its concentration on details, sometimes approvingly, sometimes not. W. W. Robson, for example, comments on the use of numbers, three lilies or five swans, which often seem foisted on the reader as extraneous details, along with "the particularity of sensory detail, of which again the thematic relevance is not obvious."[45] But perhaps its importance is not thematic. The particularity in the poetry is simply there for its own sake, an end in itself. Why? For the same reason that a specimen in a cabinet is there—for its intrinsic beauty. The quantification goes along with the natural historian's tendency to count and measure, as seen in MacGillivray's and Darwin's narratives. Behind Pre-Raphaelite depictions, both in paint and in poetry, lurks the cult of the natural object.

Critics of Pre-Raphaelite poetry so frequently highlight particularity of detail that it seems automatically taken for granted as a stylistic mark of the group. Rossetti, author of "The Woodspurge," frequently gets singled out as a poet with the "gift of realistic observation" or an "intense sensitivity to detail."[46] Pre-Raphaelite poetry seems more difficult to generalize about than is the painting, but in large part it seems to share the standard of "fidelity to nature," meaning "the visible world," that Cecil Y. Lang summarized for the painting. The Pre-Raphaelites, according to Lang, make

> a self-conscious effort to render faithfully what their eyes saw—color, shape, and number, leaves on a tree, blades of grass, threads in a carpet, words on the spine of a book or on a sheet of music or in a newspaper. The traditional admonition to a young student learning to draw a cross-section under the microscope—"Don't draw every cell you see, but see every cell you draw"—could have been their motto.[47]

Once again, what is the Pre-Raphaelite painters' crusade? See the world sharp, and paint it true. Lang's comparison of their technique to microscopy is altogether fitting. Such comparisons are commonly made for their poetry, too; for example, Derek Sanford speaks of "the almost microscopic employment of detail that constitutes a *poetry of particulars*" [his italics].[48]

The "poetry of particulars," of course, is not the exclusive property of the Pre-Raphaelite poets. Some of them, like Christina Rossetti, are not especially concrete or visual, while other poets outside the movement are very much so. Many critics, in fact, ignore the boundaries of the Brotherhood altogether and simply concentrate on stylistic similarities. Carol T. Christ, for example, links the poetic practice of Rossetti, Tennyson, and Browning. "Pre-Raphaelite" detail, yoked, as Robert L. Peters points out, to the "literalist and scientific impulse of the day," infused many disparate works, from "the detailed journals and notebooks of Sidney Dobell, of William Holman Hunt, and of Gerard Manley Hopkins," to

> Ruskin's elaborate descriptions of clouds, mountains, and vegetable forms; Browning's eft-things, pompion-plants, oak-worts, gourd-fruits, honeycombs, and finches; Tennyson's splendorous Arthurian detail; Dobell's Spasmodic work, . . . George Meredith's nature passages, . . . Rossetti's mannered sonnets, . . . Swinburne's own beautifully detailed vignettes.[49]

Under such a broad umbrella of Pre-Raphaelite poetic sensibility, one often finds included such poems as Tennyson's "Mariana," or "The Lady of Shalott" (with its natural details of the "bearded barley," "starry clusters," "margin, willow-veil'd," and "bearded meteor, trailing light"), or Browning's "The Englishman in Italy" ("great butterflies fighting, / Some five for one cup" of each yellow "sprig of bold hardy rockflower").[50] Meredith, a peripheral Pre-Raphaelite, often glories in precise natural detail, as in this passage from "Love in the Valley":

> Yellow with birdfoot trefoil are the grass-glades;
>   Yellow with cinquefoil of the dew-grey leaf;
> Yellow with stonecrop; the moss-mounds are yellow;
>   Blue-necked the wheat sways, yellowing to the sheaf.
>   (ll. 113–116)

Here Meredith's detail includes mentioning specific names of plants as well as visual details of color, especially the way the color of wheat changes along its length.

Rossetti's most famous use of detail occurs in "My Sister's Sleep," where the details are not only visual but auditory and tactile: the "cold moon" with its "hollow halo . . . like an icy crystal cup," the "subtle sound / Of flame" by the fireside, the mother's knitting needles that make a sound when "met lightly" together, and the noise when her "silken gown settled." A good example of Pre-Raphaelite visual and natural detail, however, occurs in a sonnet from Rossetti's *The House of Life* sequence. Sonnet XIX, "Silent Noon," demonstrates how the poet can make even silence into a visual image, wrought of carefully noted details:

> Your hands lie open in the long fresh grass,—
>> The finger-points look through like rosy beams:
>> Your eyes smile peace. The pasture gleams and glooms
> 'Neath billowing skies that scatter and amass.
> All round our nest, far as the eye can pass,
>> Are golden kingcup-fields with silver edge
>> Where the cow-parsley skirts the hawthorn-hedge.
> 'Tis visible silence, still as the hour-glass.

Here indeed is "visible silence," a frozen diorama of details, with the lovers surrounded, like Ophelia, by individuated plants. The pasture with its "gleams" of light and the "billowing skies" are somewhat generalized, but the woman is described in terms of specifics—not just hands, but the points of fingers. And, as in Meredith's "Love in the Valley" passage, the flowers are catalogued in a roll-call of specific names and colors. And in the next few lines of the poem, Rossetti describes an insect, too, a dragon-fly among the plants that "hangs like a blue thread loosened from the sky."

Like the cabinet-specimen approach of Pre-Raphaelite painting, then, Pre-Raphaelite poetry (and its cousins among other Victorian poetry) often depends heavily on natural detail. Botany and entomology—their specimens widely available and easily plucked—seem to predominate: willow, rock-flower, birdfoot-trefoil, stonecrop, cinquefoil, kingcup, cow-parsley, hawthorne, butterflies, and dragonflies. Or, from Browning's "Two in the Campagna," the "yellowing fennel" is coupled with the flower's "one small orange cup" that "amassed/Five beetles—blind and green." The specimens are vibrant, individuated, sensuous, and it is for these reasons that they catch the poet's or painter's eye.

For the painter or writer, the challenge was to represent the vibrancy of reality, reality in its new sense of singular parts that make up the whole. In natural history illustration, especially, artists might find their technique inadequate to the task. But so gorgeous was the subject, so varied, so startling the natural forms that the artist's motivation was extremely strong. For example, when in the 1860s J. G. Wood published his how-to book of microscopy, *Common Objects of the Microscope*, he found that illustrations of "upwards of four hundred objects" were required in order to begin to give the reader a sense of their intricacies. And yet, Wood cautioned, his reader must not expect "that any drawings can fully render the lovely structures which are revealed by the microscope." The microscopic objects are so extraordinary that, although "their form can be given faithfully enough, and their colour can be indicated," they cannot truly be captured:

> No pen, pencil, or brush, however skilfully wielded, can reproduce the soft, glowing radiance, the delicate pearly translucency, or the flashing effulgence of living and ever-changing light with which God wills to imbue even the smallest of his creatures, whose very existence has been hidden for countless ages from the inquisitive research of man, and whose wondrous beauty astonishes and delights the eye, and fills the heart with awe and adoration.[51]

Wood here sums up the dilemma: natural forms are too beautiful to truly represent, but too beautiful not to try to render. Their smallest details delight the eye (in fact the more microscopic the better), and if the artist can render but a portion of their reality, they can stir the heart. Every natural object trails luminous wonder behind it, like a comet's tail. Thus the challenge for art: capture the tangible and, paradoxically, suggest the wonderful.

Nearly always present in Victorian particularity is the attempt to make the details mean or suggest something. When this fails, the result is disquieting. Natural history, like Pre-Raphaelite painting or poetry, or like photography, attempts to juggle both balls at once: objective facts and personal response. Painting objects from nature, simply as records of their existence, tends to emphasize uniqueness, autonomy, oddity, and singularity—as does a cabinet collection. Like a cabinet, such a painting also accentuates what is most astonishing, most wondrous, about the objects. During the nineteenth century, the growth of natural history illustration mirrored the popularity of cabinets, because their aims and methods are complementary. Both rely on isolation and juxtaposition as artistic principles. Both encourage a view of nature as a collection of individuated, inexhaustible, mysterious objects.

In valuing singular facts and exact representation, Victorian natural history illustration and Pre-Raphaelite art propose a similar method for the visual rendition of natural facts. The parallels between the two types of art were immediately apparent to Edmund Gosse when he was taken, as a child, to visit a Pre-Raphaelite exhibition. Other visitors, steeped in the murky monochromality of the European tradition and the Royal Academy, recoiled from the garish colors on display. Accustomed to looking at Philip Gosse's meticulous drawings of starfish and anemones, Edmund found nothing shocking in the bright, sharp Pre-Raphaelite tints. He noticed at once their similarities to his father's familiar technique, the naturalist's method:

> Some of the other visitors, as I recollect, expressed astonishment and dislike of what they called the "Preraphaelite" treatment, but we were not affected by that. Indeed, if anything, the exact, minute and hard execution of Mr Hunt was in sympathy with the methods we ourselves were in the habit of using when we painted butterflies and seaweeds, placing perfectly pure pigments side by side, without any nonsense about chiaroscuro. This large, bright, comprehensive picture made a very deep impression on me, not exactly as a work of art, but as a brilliant natural specimen.[52]

Notes

1. A response to an article critical of a Pre-Raphaelite exhibition, quoted in Linda Nochlin, *Realism and Tradition in Art: 1848–1900*, Sources and Documents in the History of Art Series, ed. H. W. Janson (Englewood Cliffs, NJ: Prentice-Hall, Inc., 1966), pp. 118–119.

2. S. Peter Dance, *The Art of Natural History: Animal Illustrators and Their Work* (Woodstock, NY: The Overlook Press, 1978), p. 90.

3. Dance, p. 111.

4. See "Discourse in Pictures," chapter 7 in David Knight, *The Age of Science: The Scientific World-view in the Nineteenth Century* (New York: Basil Blackwell, 1986).

5. Dance, p. 191.

6. On Edward Lear the naturalist, consult Susan Hyman, *Edward Lear's Birds* (New York: William Morrow and Company, Inc., 1980), and Joseph Kastner, "The Runcible Life and Works of the Remarkable Edward Lear," *Smithsonian*, 12, No. 6 (1981), 107–116.

7. Dorothy Middleton, *Victorian Lady Travellers* (Chicago: Academy, 1982), p. 55. See also, for North's paintings, Anthony Huxley, J. P. M. Brenan, and Brenda E. Moon, eds., *A Vision of Eden: The Life and Work of Marianne North* (Exeter, Eng.: Webb and Bower, 1980).

8. Dance, p. 200.

9. Dance, p. 198. Dance makes rather disparaging remarks about Gosse's prose, and Victorian prose in general, with which of course I cannot agree.

10. Edmund Gosse, *The Life of Philip Henry Gosse, F.R.S.* (London: Kegan Paul, Trench, Trübner and Co., Ltd., 1890), p. 341.

11. Dance, pp. 89–90.

12. Edmund Gosse, *Life*, p. 340.

13. Robert L. Peters, ed., *Victorians on Literature and Art* (New York: Appleton-Century-Crofts, Inc., 1961), p. 1.

14. In Derek Sanford, ed., *Pre-Raphaelite Writing: An Anthology* (London: Dent, 1973), p. 16.

15. Sanford, p. 70.

16. Peters, *Victorians*, p. 1.

17. Sanford, p. 73.

18. Sanford, p. 76.

19. W. F. Axton, "Victorian Landscape Painting: A Change in Outlook," in *Nature and the Victorian Imagination*, ed. U. C. Knoepflmacher and G. B. Tennyson (Berkeley: Univ. of California Press, 1977), p. 288.

20. Axton, p. 291.

21. Axton, p. 302.

22. In light of the connections between excessive detail and madness, such as I have hinted at in some poetry of Tennyson, Browning, and other poets, the example of the painter Richard Dadd is most interesting. Dadd stabbed his father to death and, consequently, spent the remaining years of his life in asylums, haunted by psychotic visions. During his incarceration, Dadd did a great deal of painting and sketching. From 1854 to 1858, he completed the incredibly detailed painting, *Contradiction: Oberon and Titania*. The art critic Robert Hughes notes that it combines "teeming fantasy" with "minute observation." Like another of his most laborious paintings, *The Fairy Feller's Master-Stroke*, the portrayal of the inhabitants of Titania's kingdom is disturbing and Bosch-like. And in it, says Hughes, the "details of leaves, grasses, butterflies and flowers are done with a molecular precision that exceeds even the English Pre-Raphaelites." ("From the Dark Garden of the Mind," *Time*, July 8, 1974, p. 64.)

23. Axton, p. 291. David Elliston Allen is far more tentative when he says, after a discussion of the microscope's popularity: "Is it too far-fetched to see in the 'microscopic Romanticism' that resulted a major contributory cause of that over-concern with details that so fatally injured Victorian art?" *The Naturalist in Britain: A Social History* (London: Allen Lane, 1976), p. 129.

24. Edmund Gosse, *Life*, p. 339.

25. Geoffrey Hemstedt, "Painting and Illustration," in *The Victorians*, ed. Laurence Lerner, The Context of English Literature Series (New York: Holmes and Meier Publishers, Inc., 1978), p. 144.

26. Charles Waterton, *Wanderings in South America* (London: Oxford Univ. Press, 1973), pp. 180–181.

27. Sanford, p. 181.

28. W. Holman Hunt, *Pre-Raphaelitism and the Pre-Raphaelite Brotherhood*, quoted in D. S. R. Welland, *The Pre-Raphaelites in Literature and Art* (Freeport, NY: Books for Libraries Press, 1969), p. 71.

29. Peter Galassi, *Before Photography: Painting and the Invention of Photography* (New York: The Museum of Modern Art, 1981), p. 20.

30. Galassi, p. 18.

31. Galassi, p. 21.

32. Galassi, p. 25.

33. Sanford, p. 30.

34. Carl Dawson, *Victorian Noon: English Literature in 1850* (Baltimore: The Johns Hopkins Univ. Press, 1979), p. 33.

35. Quoted in Beaumont Newhall, *The History of Photography*, 4th ed. (New York: The Museum of Modern Art, 1964), p. 34.

36. John Burroughs, "Nature in Little," in *Field and Study*, in *The Complete Nature Writings of John Burroughs* (New York: Wm. H. Wise and Company, 1919), p. 121.

37. John Burroughs, "Sharp Eyes," in *Locusts and Wild Honey*, in *The Writings of John Burroughs*, vol. IV (Boston: Houghton Mifflin Company, 1879), pp. 49–50.

38. Burroughs, "Sharp Eyes," p. 50.

39. Dawson, p. 168.

40. There are many arguments, of course, about what, if anything, constitutes realism in the novel. But the piling-on of material details certainly is part of it. A neat summary of the nineteenth-century practice of fiction can be found in Robert Louis Stevenson's complaint, late in the century, about it: "How to get over, how to escape from the besotting particularity of fiction. 'Roland approached the house, it had green doors and window blinds; and there was a scraper on the upper step.' To hell with Roland and the scraper!" Quoted in Patrick Parrinder, *Science Fiction: Its Criticism and Teaching* (New York: Methuen, 1980), p. 8.

41. Charles Millard, "Images of Nature: A Photo-Essay," in *Nature and the Victorian Imagination*, ed. U. C. Knoepflmacher and G. B. Tennyson (Berkeley: Univ. of California Press, 1977), p. 24.

42. From Brown's Exhibition Catalogue, 1865, quoted in Nochlin, p. 97.

43. Welland, p. 34.

44. Rossetti, at least, had no demonstrated interest in natural history practice per se, if one believes William Allingham, who reported that Rossetti "cares nothing about natural history, or science in any form or degree," by way of emphasizing his preference for "pungent, mordant" sensations and "spasmodic passion." Quoted in Sanford, p. 177.

45. W. W. Robson, "Pre-Raphaelite Poetry," in *From Dickens to Hardy*, vol. 6 of The New Pelican Guide to English Literature, ed. Boris Ford (New York: Penguin Books, 1982), p. 356.

46. Lionel Stevenson, *The Pre-Raphaelite Poets* (New York: W. W. Norton and Company, Inc., 1974), p. 32; Carol T. Christ, *The Finer Optic: The Aesthetic of Particularity in Victorian Poetry* (New Haven, CT: Yale Univ. Press, 1975), p. 38.

47. Cecil Y. Lang, ed., *The Pre-Raphaelites and Their Circle* (Boston: Houghton Mifflin Company, 1968), p. xiii.

48. Sanford, p. xviii.

49. Robert L. Peters, "Algernon Charles Swinburne and the Use of Integral Detail," in James Sambrook, ed., *Pre-Raphaelitism: A Collection of Critical Essays* (Chicago: Univ. of Chicago Press, 1974), p. 207. Along the same lines, see especially the essay in the same volume by Jerome J. McGann, "Rossetti's Significant Details."

50. Carol T. Christ does a good job of analyzing Tennyson's and Browning's details.

51. J. G. Wood, *Common Objects of the Microscope* (London: George Routledge and Sons, n.d.), p. iv.

52. Edmund Gosse, *Father and Son: A Study of Two Temperaments* (New York: W. W. Norton and Company, 1963), p. 184.

8

Philip Henry Gosse:
"Feasting of the Eager Eyes"

The eye is so fitted to the face of nature or the face of nature to the
eye that the perception of beauty is continually awakened in all
places and under the most ordinary of circumstances. The beauty of
the world is a perpetual invitation to the study of the world. Sunrise
and sunset; fire; flowers; shells; the sea—in all its shades, from indigo
to green and gray, by the light of day, and phosphorescent under the
ship's keel at night; the airy inaccessible mountain; the sparry cavern;
the glaring colours of the soil of the volcano; the forms of vegetables;
and all the elegant and majestic figures of the creatures that fly,
climb, or creep upon the earth—all, by their beauty, work upon our
curiosity and court our attention. The earth is a museum.[1]

RALPH WALDO EMERSON, "The Uses of Natural History"

Of Philip Henry Gosse (1810–1888), two legacies remain—both of them
unfortunate. Philip Gosse the entomologist, marine biologist, naturalist,
nature illustrator, and popularizer of the wonders of nature through the
written word is forgotten. If anyone thinks of Gosse at all, it is as the
stern, unyielding, grimly pious parent of Edmund Gosse, so vividly
portrayed in *Father and Son*. Or, in the context of religion, P. H. Gosse
might be remembered as the hapless fighter of a rearguard action against
theories of evolution, in his infamous work, *Omphalos: An Attempt to
Untie the Geological Knot*. Both portraits of Gosse are true, as far as they
go, but by singling out the dogmatic side of him, they are unjust. Gosse
was preeminently a naturalist, instrumental in imparting his own closely
focused views of nature to thousands of Victorians who eagerly read his
many books.

By sweeping aside the pathetic, unappealing monuments to P. H.
Gosse, the zestful naturalist beneath may be excavated again. Edmund
Gosse grew to manhood fully aware of his father's reputation as an

190

author and naturalist. Seeing how his father was valued, Edmund felt compelled to document his father's life in an official biography: *The Life of Philip Henry Gosse*. He also, however, felt compelled to divulge the unpleasant side of his upbringing with such a father, and the result was *Father and Son*, the wonderful memoir still widely read today. The biography concentrates on his father's accomplishments in an objective way and, as such, proves very valuable in any study of P. H. Gosse, as illustrator, author, or naturalist. The memoir, on the other hand, is highly subjective, concerned with the limitations of his father's personality, especially those that made life for his child emotionally claustrophobic.

In *Father and Son*, which was published at first anonymously, Edmund Gosse speaks of how his childhood was restricted by his father's religious dogmatism. Philip belonged to the Plymouth Brethren, a sect of scriptural literalists who forbade the reading of novels and most other activities that a young boy would consider fun. So devout was Philip Gosse that early in his life he felt called to the ministry. Even after he became a naturalist he continued to preach. The conflict between Scripture and biological science was never resolved for him; faced with a choice between the Bible and natural selection, he chose the Bible.

P. H. Gosse was born in 1810 and did not marry until 1848. His wife was, if anything, even more devout than her husband, and so Edmund Gosse was born, in 1849, into a highly pious household. On her deathbed a few years later, Emily Gosse begged her husband to see that their son dedicated himself to God, and the repressive noose began to tighten around little Edmund's neck. Philip Gosse became fanatical in his probing interest in his son's thoughts and conduct. This is the picture one recalls from *Father and Son*:

> With the advance of years, the characteristics of this figure became more severely outlined, more rigorously confined within settled limits. In relation to the Son—who presently departed, at a very immature age, for the new life in London—the attitude of the Father continued to be one of extreme solicitude, deepening by degrees into disappointment and disenchantment. He abated no jot or tittle of his demands upon human frailty. He kept the spiritual cord drawn tight; the Biblical bearing-rein was incessantly busy, jerking into position the head of the dejected neophyte.[2]

In very witty but nonetheless painful prose, Edmund Gosse describes the torment of enduring his father's "postal inquisition," relentless inquiries into the state of his young soul. Almost pathetic in his grasping faith and a grimly rigid disciplinarian, Philip Henry Gosse becomes, for the reader of *Father and Son*, something of a monster. As described by the son, the father seems singularly joyless. There is little hint of Philip's paradoxical materialism, of the boundless zest for nature's beauties that colors his natural history books.

A classic Victorian patriarch, an autocrat of the breakfast table Gosse certainly was, looming over little Edmund as Leslie Stephen did over Virginia Woolf. And if Philip Gosse failed as a father, so too did he fail ultimately as a biologist. He was a brilliant naturalist—in the traditional sense of collector, scrutinizer, describer. But he could not come to terms with explanatory theories that unified the disparate phenomena of his beloved world of nature. He could not stomach the most important biological concept of all: evolution. Even before Darwin's book about the origin of species appeared in 1859, Gosse knew of Darwin's ideas through their correspondence. He could sense the dangerous shift in biological currents, and vainly he tried to channel them back into the old pattern again. Living organisms Gosse could deal with very well, but fossils disturbed him. How could such different and, it would seem, completely eradicated forms have figured in God's scheme of creation? Cuvier had suggested that there had been several creations, with God destroying one set of creatures catastrophically, then starting anew. Others began to hint that past creatures had simply died out. Worse yet were intimations of ancestry, of gradual change from one form to the next.

Unyielding in his belief in the literal text of the Bible, P. H. Gosse felt compelled to make a statement. As a result, in 1857, Gosse published *Omphalos: An Attempt to Untie the Geological Knot*, which featured as its main contention the idea that God had created the earth and its creatures all at once—fossils and all. The rings in the tree trunks in Eden, Adam's bellybutton, and fossils were *prochronic* remnants; they indicated God's *ideas* about pre-creation events, not actual events themselves. Adam's navel (or *omphalos*, from the Greek) did not indicate that he had been born of a womb—which clearly, from Genesis, he had not—but only that God had already thought about the birth process and knew that the mark of the umbilicus would accompany it in the future.

Gosse's complicated, one might say tortuous, theories sound absurd today. As one historian says, "rather than untying the knot, Gosse succeeded only in tying himself in knots."[3] Creationists might still applaud him, but biologists certainly do not.[4] Unfortunately for Philip Gosse, *Omphalos* severely damaged his reputation, both in his own time and thereafter. Even his upstanding religious friend, Charles Kingsley, rejected the *Omphalos* idea completely, saying that Gosse's theory made

God into a liar, a joker who tried to fool mankind, and that was intolerable.[5] Gosse had ranked as the premier British zoologist, but with his ill-advised foray into geology, "Christians and naturalists alike scorned this book of a heretofore popular writer."[6]

Philip Gosse's desperate mistake in *Omphalos* indelibly stained his career. So the case remains today that if one thinks of Gosse at all, it is as Edmund's father, the religious fanatic, the laughable creationist. But, as even Edmund points out, the elder Gosse had great strengths to go along with his weaknesses. The two qualities were, in fact, related. Untroubled by theoretical ramifications, Philip Gosse was free to concentrate on the externals, the details of nature. His mind was "acute" but "narrow," Edmund says; as such, he was unfit to be a biologist, but perfectly well suited to be a naturalist. Of his father in the 1850s, Edmund says: "As a collector of facts and marshaller of observations, he had not a rival in that age; his very absence of imagination aided him in that work."[7]

In fact, Philip Gosse demonstrates all the pleasures, as well as the limitations, of the microscopic eye, the naturalist's eye: "He saw everything through a lens, nothing in the immensity of nature."[8] But peering through that lens, and then writing and painting about what he saw, Gosse helped establish a standard of vision—the microscopic standard of vision that so pervades the nineteenth century. As one writer says of Gosse, he "was a fine observer, a faithful and exact recorder and gifted with high artistic powers; his paintings of shore life have rarely been equalled." And because of the beautiful precision of his work, "to the Mid-Victorians his name was a household word as the author of a unique series of books on shore life."[9] This is the forgotten side of Philip Gosse: the observant naturalist that coexisted with the religious autocrat. The stern religious piety of Gosse influenced his son, and the tortuous biological thinking of Gosse influenced scientists—both in a bad way. But his microscopic attention to and vivid rendering of nature in prose and paint had a widespread positive influence on Victorian culture. And this is the P. H. Gosse that I wish to bring to light once more.

Gosse is the epitome of a Victorian naturalist. His interest in nature is visual, acquisitive, descriptive. Gosse made contributions to science, but they were descriptive and classificatory, not theoretical. He tirelessly collected daunting numbers of specimens, particularly corals, sea anemones, and microscopic marine animals; and because he savored their intricate forms and had a keen eye and a steady hand for recording them, he catalogued the minute differences among species. As his son summarizes Philip's scientific strengths, he notes that his father used, very modestly, to describe himself as "a hewer of wood and a drawer of water" in the house of science, but no biologist will on that account underrate what he has done. His extreme care in diagnosis, the clearness of his eye, the marvellous exactitude of his memory, his recognition of what was salient in the characteristics of each species, his unsurpassed skill in defining those characteristics by word and pencil, his great activity and pertinacity, all these combined to make Philip Gosse a technical observer of unusually high rank.[10]

A naturalist at heart, Gosse was happiest when surrounded by the paraphernalia of that pursuit. Whether with gun, net, hammer, tongs, or dredge, he sallied forth to augment his collections. He was adept at "fixing" specimens, pinning insects, or keeping marine life alive in jars, pans, and aquariums—which were after all his own invention. His home was crammed with fish tanks, plant-houses, bottles, cabinets for insects, a telescope for looking at the stars, and a microscope for peering at animals. He was, in short, for all his spirituality, a man who loved the concrete world. One of his most valued possessions followed him through his early travels and his later settled life: an insect-cabinet of his own design. This was crafted to his specifications in Hamburg and shipped to him in Newfoundland. A rather rickety affair, this cabinet nevertheless contained a wealth of little compartments that Gosse spent much time "enriching" with pinned insects, and by ship or coach he kept it with him.

As befits a naturalist, Gosse's earliest fervor for natural objects—for entomologizing—was stimulated by the reading of a book on the microscope. As a young man, Gosse had been apprenticed to a merchant's firm in Newfoundland, where he stayed for several years. There, says Edmund, "in 1832 Philip Gosse, suddenly and consciously, became a naturalist" (*Life*, p. 70). Gosse had shown talents for keen observation before, but had not known where to apply them. In 1832, Philip says, he bought at auction,

Kaumacher's edition of Adams's *Essays on the Microscope*, a quarto which I still possess. The plan of this work had led the author to treat largely of insects, and to give minute instructions for their collection and preservation. I was delighted with my prize; it just condensed and focussed the wandering rays of science that were kindling in my mind, and I enthusiastically resolved forthwith to collect insects. (*Life*, p. 70).

In light of the emphasis I have placed on the predominance of visual metaphors in natural history, it is intriguing that Gosse chose the metaphor he did: the microscope focused the "wandering rays of science" for him; the instrument immediately proved congenial to a man with such keen powers of attention and sharp sight. In his later years, especially when working on his compendium on the Rotifera (microscopic organisms fringed with cilia), he would quite contentedly spend "eight or nine hours in uninterrupted work at the microscope" (*Life*, p. 320), day after day—all the more remarkable since he was in his late seventies at the time. In his popular writing, Gosse is frequently at his best when immersed in the microscopic world of darting, spinning, dazzling creatures.

For some of his life, Gosse fit the mold of the traveler-naturalist, living successively in Newfoundland, then other parts of Canada, Alabama, and Jamaica. He thus experienced a wide range of climates and habitats, which figured in some of his books. His most valuable experience, because it had been the most intense, was, however, the thirty years he spent on the coasts of England, where he "emerged from his years waist-high in the rock-pools irremediably dazzled."[11] His intimate contact with tidal life led him to invent the aquarium and to write the books that launched the shore-collecting fad in England. It also made him famous.

The Aquarium (1854), the book explaining and promoting the creation of glass-enclosed "mimic seas" ("The Mimic Sea" had been the working title of the manuscript), sold, as Edmund Gosse recalls, "like wildfire" (*Life*, p. 252), being "the most successful of all my father's literary endeavors." And Philip Gosse's literary endeavors were indeed numerous and diversified.[12] He wrote everything from technical monographs, with titles like "On the Structure, Functions, and Homologies of the Manducatory Organs in the Class Rotifera," to popularized "pot-boilers" (to use Edmund's term for them) on scientific or historical subjects. One fitting the category of pot-boiler was a little Christmas volume entitled *Glimpses of the Wonderful*. Several of his books were essentially textbooks, written under the auspices of the Society for the Promotion of Christian Knowledge. Chief among these were his five volumes on zoology, one each on Mammalia, Birds, Reptiles, Fishes, and Mollusca. Other textbooks would include *Popular British Ornithology* (1849), *Text-book of Zoology for Schools* (1851), *Introduction to Zoology* (1844), and *Handbook to the Marine Aquarium* (1855). Occasionally Gosse strayed into nonbiological areas, writing about the monuments of Egypt, sacred streams of the Bible, Assyria, or the history of the Jews.

But by far the bulk of his writing features biology or natural history. Of his biological works I have previously mentioned two: the classificatory compendium on corals and sea anemones, *Actinologia Britannica* (1857–1860), and the ill-fated *Omphalos*. Gosse described and classified organisms with tremendous care and patience, his scientific work being "exclusively concerned with the habits, or the forms, or the structure of animals, not observed in the service of any theory or philosophical principle, but for their own sake" (*Life*, p. 336). And in this vein Gosse made important contributions with the *Actinologia*, *The Birds of Jamaica* (1847), and *The Rotifera* (as co-author, 1886).

It was natural history, however, that inspired him. Through sheer accumulation of facts, Gosse advanced science. But he did not amass those facts *for* science; instead, they were the by-product of his own fascination with objects. "His interest in natural objects," comments Edmund, "was mainly aesthetic and poetical, depending on the beauty and ingenuity of their forms" (*Life*, p. 349). Somewhat to his own surprise, the reclusive and shy Gosse discovered that he had two talents—skill with the brush and the pen—which enabled him to communicate to others his own sense of awe and wonder at the intricate beauties of nature. His first book of natural history, *The Canadian Naturalist* (1840), had a somewhat clumsy structure, but was nonetheless received well by the English public, who liked the "unacademic freshness" (*Life*, p. 160) of Gosse's mind and style. He was not stuffy. Furthermore, he firmly advocated not closet studies, but field work—not ponderous disputation but adventure, a chase through sunlit fields and glistening pools with net in hand. According to Edmund Gosse, as a writer Philip was most closely akin to England's beloved Gilbert White, the Darwin of the *Beagle* journal, and the Thoreau of the Concord and Merrimac rivers account (*Life*, p. 161). There were few writers who could match him for his "picturesque enthusiasm, the scrupulous attention to detail, the quick eye and the responsive brain, the happy gift in direct description" (*Life*, p. 161).

Gosse put these attributes to use in a string of popular natural history books written during twenty prolific years. In the estimation of Edmund (a literary critic of some discernment) there are "eight or nine volumes, which are books in the literary sense, which are not liable to extinction from the nature of their subject, and which constitute [Philip's] claim to an enduring memory as a writer" (*Life*, p. 344). Relaxed in tone and aesthetic in approach, the volumes might include *The Ocean* (1845), *A Naturalist's Sojourn in Jamaica* (1851), *A Naturalist's Rambles on the Devonshire Coast* (1853), *The Aquarium* (1854), *Tenby: A Sea-side Holiday* (1859), *Evenings at the Microscope* (1859), *The Romance of Natural History* (1860), and *A Year at the Shore* (1865).

Even in the titles of these works one can easily detect Gosse's affable, diverting approach to natural history. The naturalist takes sojourns or meditative rambles through nature, perhaps even a holiday, all in search of pleasure. He spends long congenial hours at the microscope, exploring the minute realm as if he were rambling through it. The naturalist's lot is not arduous, but rather resembles a pleasant walk through the great cabinet of nature, like Wordsworth strolling through the Lake Country in search of scenes.

Of all these books—seldom available in the United States and scarce even in England—two written at the height of Philip Gosse's powers will serve to demonstrate the characteristic tenor of his discourse. The more important one is *The Romance of Natural History*, originally titled *The Poetry of Natural History*. Edmund recalls that his father gave "unusual care" to the "composition" of this book, "and it remains, perhaps, the nearest approach to an English classic of any of Philip Gosse's writings" (*Life*, p. 291). With its appealing emphasis on a subjective response to nature, *Romance* went through numerous editions. The public applauded its style, which was the "most picturesque, easy and graceful of all his writings" (*Father and Son*, p. 177). The second text, *Evenings at the Microscope*, is somewhat drier, more didactic and classificatory, but nonetheless fits solidly within the tradition of Victorian microscopic natural history. Though the book is instructional, guiding readers in the scrutiny of unfamiliar territory, Gosse's excitement about nature never glows more brightly than when he enters the microscopic world. (Microscopic Rotifera were his most abiding passion, after all; he planned a popular book about them, to be titled "The Pond Raker," but concluded reluctantly that the infinite varieties of Rotifera were a bit too arcane for best-selling status). Although the subject of *Evenings* may seem weighty, Freeman and Wertheimer point out that it was "one of the most successful of Gosse's books," and the last to go out of print, in 1905.[13]

In *The Romance of Natural History*, Gosse plainly proclaims his intentions in the Preface: "this book is an attempt to present natural history in its aesthetic fashion."[14] Sounding remarkably like John Burroughs, Gosse rails against closet naturalists and advises eschewing dry facts in favor of "the poet's way" of responding to nature:

There are more ways than one of studying natural history. There is Dr. Dryasdust's way; which consists of mere accuracy of definition and differentiation; statistics as harsh and dry as the skins and bones in the museums where it is studied. There is the field-observer's way; the careful and conscientious accumulation and record of facts bearing on the life-history of the creatures; statistics as fresh and bright as the forest or meadow where they are gathered in the dewy morning. And there is the poet's way; who looks at nature through a glass peculiarly his own; the aesthetic aspect, which deals, not with statistics, but with the emotions of the human mind,—surprise, wonder, terror, revulsion, admiration, love, desire, and so forth,—which are made energetic by the contemplation of the creatures around him. (p. iii)

Always, Gosse says, he has had "a poet's heart" for nature, quoting Wordsworth to underscore his meaning. In that spirit, he intends to present "a series of pictures, the reflections of scenes and aspects in nature, which in my own mind awaken poetic interest" (pp. iii–iv).

Toward this end, Gosse has carefully managed his material, adopting not a chronological order, such as is frequently found in books by traveling naturalists (Darwin's *Journal of Researches*, for example, or Bates' *The Naturalist on the River Amazons*) where natural wonders are described as they are stumbled upon, but a thematic order, where natural facts are grouped according to their connotations or what they represent. Consequently, in *Romance* one finds chapters on "Times and Seasons," "Harmonies," "Discrepancies," "The Vast," "The Minute," "The Memorable," "The Wild," and so forth. By using these categories, Gosse can elicit greater emotional response from his readers. The last chapter concerns "The Great Unknown." It is prefaced by sections urging "Scepticism," "Necessity of Caution," and "Liability to Error," but posits nonetheless the existence of some sort of sea-serpent, related, Gosse thinks, to a fossil form of marine reptile, the *Enaliosauria*. This conjecture created a sensation among Gosse's Victorian public and increased the book's sales, probably because genuine marine fossils, such as Mary Anning's ichthyosaurs, had already primed the public imagination.[15]

Whether the sea-serpent proposition is tenable or preposterous, Gosse's interest in it is quite in line with his approach to natural history— and his public's as well. Having seen many incredible and improbable natural curiosities in different lands (and in *Romance* Gosse draws upon a very wide geographical range of examples), Gosse remains open to even more amazing forms. To the Victorian naturalist, nature was, through exploration and study, constantly unveiling, unfolding, revealing new forms—that was the heady adventure of it. And if new rococo animalcules could be revealed almost daily on the microscopic level, why could not bizarre discoveries lurk in the macroscopic world, at the large end of the scale as well?

At any rate, Gosse hopes that his readers will see the creature's possibility through his "spectacles" (p. iv), and spectacles, or sights, are exactly what Gosse provides. In *Romance* one looks variously at nature: sometimes as a panorama (a sweeping view of landscape and its inhabitants), sometimes as a single scene (from one point of view one watches an action unfold, such as a dawn in the jungle), and sometimes as a close-up (of a single animal or detail).

Gosse is at his best when he recalls scenes from his own natural history work; in such cases he is most inclined to describe them visually, often adding dramatic narration for spice. Frequently, in *The Romance of Natural History*, however, he relies on quoted accounts from travelers who have visited regions that he has not. These borrowed passages are, as Edmund finds them, sometimes in a style "a little otiose" (*Life*, p. 291). The writers that Gosse chooses to cite, though, make an interesting list of natural historians of the time, especially since he tends to pick those who do practice some form of aesthetic science, as I have defined it. In addition to offering literary quotations from Melville, Bryant, Cowper, and Words-worth, Gosse includes anecdotes from Henry Walter Bates, Frank Buck-land, Hooker, Wallace, and Humboldt. He likes the African stories of Livingstone. And, in spite of his disapproval of natural selection, he quotes Darwin's *Beagle* account more frequently than any other book.

As an example of a Gosse passage based on his own experience, an insect chase stands out. Drawing on his own early years of fervent entomologizing, Gosse produces a little narration full of energy and zest. For the narration, Gosse creates a hypothetical character to stand in his stead, an English schoolboy "just infected with the entomological mania." This boy prepares for his captures by daubing tree trunks with beer and treacle, returning again to the site as the sun is going down, "armed with insect-net, pill-boxes, and a bull's-eye lantern." To express the excitement of the chase, Gosse employs the present tense, short clauses, vivid verbs, and copious exclamations:

> Watchfully now he holds the net; there is one whose hue betokens a prize. Dash!—yes! it is in the muslin bag. . . . Yonder is a white form dancing backward and forward with a regular oscillation in the space of a yard, close over the herbage. That must be the "ghost-moth," surely!—the very same; and this is secured. Presently there comes rushing down the lane, with headlong speed, one far larger than the common set, and visible from afar by its whiteness. Prepare! Now strike! (*Romance*, p. 32)

Nature, in ever more gorgeous forms, is streaming forth into the lantern light and also into the reader's vision. Gosse's emotional diction here is reminiscent of Alfred Russel Wallace's charged description of how the blood rushed to his head after an entomological capture.

And the dizzying excitement of capture increases in Gosse's narration as even more beautiful moths arrive. A switch from third-person to second-person pronouns announces the heightened pitch:

And now comes a dazzling thing, the "burnished brass," its wings gleaming with metallic refulgence in the lamp-light; but (*O infortunate puer!*) a nimble bat is beforehand with you, and snaps up the glittering prize before your eyes, dropping the brilliant wings on the ground for your especial tantalisation. Well, never mind! the bat is an entomologist, too, and he is out mothing as well as you. . . . But what is this moth of commanding size and splendid beauty, its hind wings of the most glowing crimson, like a fiery coal, bordered with black? Ha! the lovely "bride!" If you can net her, you have a beauty. A steady hand! a sure eye! Yes!—fairly bagged! (p. 33)

Noteworthy here, in addition to the skillfully managed narration, is the emphasis on a primarily visual aesthetics. The moths have lovely, beautiful colors which directly strike the eye by being "dazzling," "gleaming," "glittering," "glowing," "brilliant." The boy goes home at the close of the anecdote "inhaling the perfume of the thorn and clematis," and "listening to the melody of the wakeful nightingales." But the incident is mainly visual, especially since Gosse sets the scene with the houselights, so to speak, going down while the spotlights on the boy come up. In the distance, the dusk fades, stars come out, while in the circle of the lamplight the moths glow like tiny suns. Also one notes here the naturalist's two indispensable requirements: "A steady hand! a sure eye!" Hands for collecting and sharp eyes for appreciating, seeing intensely.

Gosse excels at using his own imaginative eye like a movie camera, panning or zooming in through successive stages of a natural scene. A particularly striking example of this occurs in a fragment of description that Gosse originally intended to use in *The Ocean*, but which saw publication only in his biography. This visual scan imaginatively reveals the ocean depths:

Waiving our privilege of breathing the thin and elastic air, let us descend in imagination to the depths of ocean, and explore the gorgeous treasures that adorn the world of the mermaids. We will choose for our descent one of those lovely little groups which speckle the Pacific, the wondrous labour of an insignificant polyp. The sun is no longer visible through the depth of the incumbent sea; but a subdued greenish light, soft and uniform, sufficiently reveals the wonders of the scene. We find ourselves at the foot of a vast perpendicular cliff, the base of a coral island, entirely composed, to all appearances, of glistening madrepore, of snowy whiteness. (*Life*, pp. 173–174)

Gosse moves from an airborne sort of view of the island amid the Pacific Ocean to a close-up view that drops downward through the layers of water along the coral shore. That vantage point would not be surprising for a modern scuba diver, but it is an astonishing creation for Gosse, who could see it only with his mind's eye. In the moth-capturing story, Gosse used dramatic narration to involve the reader; here he chooses the device of sweeping the reader along with him on his fantastic journey, with a cozy first-person plural narration.

One cannot help but note in this passage, again, Gosse's fascination with visually exciting objects, particularly those having beautiful colors, and with the play of light over them. Even the coral islands "speckle" the ocean, forming a visual pattern, and in the "greenish light" beneath the waves the "snowy whiteness" of the coral is "glistening." Continuing down into the depths, Gosse catalogues the colors—crimson, gray, black, yellow—and the "grotesque," "fantastic," or "singular" shapes, like mushrooms, or trees, "vases, or tables, or horns, or tubes, or globes, or many-fingered hands." After a long description of the animals of the sea—especially the fish in their "gemmed and glittering mail"—the narrator culminates the journey with a tour de force of visual description:

> It is night. Yet darkness has not fallen upon the scene, for the whole mass of the sea is become imbued with light. A milky whiteness pervades every part, slightly varying in intensity, arising from inconceivably numerous animalcules, so small as to be separately undistinguishable, but in their aggregation illuminating the boundless deep. Among them are numerous swimming creatures, of perceptible size and greater luminousness, which glitter like little brilliant sparks; and when a fish swims along, its path becomes a bed of living light, and we may trace it many fathoms by its luminous wake. Some of the larger creatures also are vividly illuminated; the medusae, which by day appear like circular masses of transparent jelly, now assume the appearance of cannon-balls, heated to whiteness; and yonder sun-fish seems like a great globe of living fire. (*Life*, pp. 176–177)

The play of light and luminosity seem almost to belong to some transcendent other world. In this fantastic—but nonetheless true—realm, things are as weirdly beautiful and as compelling as they are in the completely nonrealistic world of O'Brien's "The Diamond Lens." In each case the reader has been permitted to look into a world normally closed to human perception, a natural habitation full of darting, glittering, living sparks. When Gosse in fact looks through his "diamond lens," or microscope, his description retains much of this same character.

In *The Romance of Natural History*, under the heading of "Harmonies," Gosse swoops down with the reader into "the gorgeous gloom of a Brazilian forest." Light and color continue to fascinate him, while, in addition, the profusion and variety of natural forms hold him rapt. Here, the butterflies are not "the small and pale or sombre-hued species" of Britain, but show the "most splendid colors," some iridescent, one so "intensely lustrous that the eye cannot gaze upon it in the sun without pain" (p. 63). (This is almost the experience of a man who has seen heaven on earth, or looked upon the face of God.) The numbers of insects are "prodigious; their variety bewildering." And the vegetation is equally ornate:

> Solemn are those primeval labyrinths of giant trees, tangled with ten thousand creepers, and roofed with lofty arches of light foliage, diversified with masses of glorious blossom of all rich hues; while from the borders of the igaripes, or narrow canals that permeate the lower levels, spring most elegant ferns, lowly sensitive mimosas, great and fantastic herbaceous plants, marbled and spotted arums, closely compacted fan-palms with spreading crowns, and multitudes of other strange forms of vegetation in an almost inconceivable profusion. (p. 64)

As in MacGillivray's description of the jungle (from the *Rattlesnake* account; see Chapter 3), the plants acquire tremendous energy in Gosse's prose. They spring up, spread, creep, tangle, and form looming arches; they are sensitive, seem almost sentient, watching and surrounding the traveler. The permutating forms are delightful, although also perhaps overwhelming. Again Gosse is arrested by the visual patterns or textures created by the plants' overlapping: how they are spotted or marbled or, in a later section, "interlaced and entangled," like twisted poles or rings, or "myriads of lianes" hanging to the ground or suspended in the canopy above (p. 65). Colorful flowers create their own pattern against the "deep shades" of green in the "solemn and mournful" jungle.

In these passages, it is clear that Gosse does take the poet's approach to nature, usually choosing natural scenes and objects that are aesthetic or that call forth emotions. Obviously he evokes emotion not only by his choice of scenes, but also by his choice of words. Like Darwin in his *Beagle* record, Gosse manifests a highly Romantic diction. He is ever alert to the picturesque. And he never hesitates to pronounce an event "solemn," "gloomy," "wonderful," or "fantastic." In addition, he sometimes employs a slightly archaic diction or syntax to add gravity to his scenes, saying to the moth-hunting boy, for example, "But, stay!" rather than the more colloquial "Wait!" Edmund revealed in his *Life* of Gosse that his father was fondest of eighteenth-century prose, and that his letters sometimes read like selections from *The Rambler*, which may account for some of his peculiarities of style.

In *The Romance of Natural History*, whose very title betrays his bent, Gosse tells of the experience that led him to "woo fair nature in many lands." From initial indifference, he came to think of nature with a lover's unbounded enthusiasm. Conveniently thinking of himself as a suitor in relation to "female" nature, he expected to be continually moved and amazed by her complexity, and never found himself disappointed. (As in the case of Wallace's near-orgasmic butterfly capture, the sexual sublimations and expressions involved in Victorian natural history could fill the pages of another book.)

Gosse was first attracted to the study of nature when he was "pursuing with much ardor an acquaintance with the insects of Newfoundland" (*Romance*, p. 22). Across the boggy Newfoundland terrain, he would set out on entomologizing excursions, looking for lakes fringed by water-lilies. These watery bowers swarmed with hidden creatures. To spy on them, Gosse had to stretch himself full-length on the bank, and carefully "peer in between the lily leaves." Looking down through a lens of lake water as if it were a microscope, he could enter the aquatic world. His description of what he finds there demonstrates his extraordinary talent for imbuing minute nature with zestful autonomy:

> The merry little boatflies are frisking about, backs downwards, using their oar-like hind feet as paddles; the triple-tailed larvae of dayflies creep in and out of their holes in the bank, the finny appendages at their sides maintaining a constant waving motion; now and then a little water-beetle peeps out cautiously from the cresses, and scuttles across to a neighbouring weed; the unwieldy caddis-worms are lazily dragging about their curiously-built houses over the sogged leaves at the bottom, watching for some unlucky gnat-grub to swim within reach of their jaws; but lo! one of them has just fallen a victim to the formidable calliper-compasses wherewith that beetle-larva seizes his prey, and is yielding his own life blood to the ferocious slayer. (*Romance*, pp. 23–24)

Many devices contribute to the vitality and power of Gosse's lake description. The fact that the entire passage takes the form of one long compound sentence creates the illusion of continuous, multilayered action in the pond, since no period interrupts to chop the action into discrete segments. Also efficacious is the dramatic character of the action. Gosse crowds his stage with players (in this context it is interesting that the viewing platform for a microscope is called a stage) and gives them dramatic roles to play. Victims or villains, the waterbugs take on human characteristics: the boatflies are "merry," the water-beetles tread "cautiously," the beetle-larvae are "ferocious." Vivid verbs pack the passage with action and energy, particularly verbs such as "frisking about" and "scuttles." So precise is the description that one can almost feel how pleasurable it must be to move through the water by paddling with oar-like back feet, or finny appendages, and one likewise feels the dangerous suspense of a world where "ferocious slayers" lurk.

Here the dramatic quality of the natural history prose is particularly interesting since this tendency to dramatize nature has been remarked upon by critics of Darwin and Huxley. Stanley Edgar Hyman[16] finds *On the Origin of Species* to be structured like a drama (specifically a tragedy). Although Hyman's view is controversial, the organisms in Darwin's grand sweep of action do seem to be actors in dramatic scenes, and the life symbolized in Darwin's culminating "tangled bank" image is akin to Gosse's description in energy and complexity. In addition, James G. Paradis has pointed out that T. H. Huxley, when explaining abstract scientific ideas, has "a strong tendency to dramatize" them in "concrete images."[17] (Carlyle shares this trait according to Paradis.) Others have found the chessboard metaphor in "A Liberal Education" to be an example of Huxley's personification of ideas; Paradis sees it as one example of "dramatic representation" used to illuminate a concept of nature. Nineteenth-century scientific prose, then, often dramatizes ideas to give them energy and force; Gosse's natural history prose dramatizes nature.

That Gosse sees animals as animals—vibrant with their own life—and not as specimens—dead and disjointed—is evident even in his more technical work, *Evenings at the Microscope*. For the purpose of examining blood circulation in the vessels of a frog's foot, Gosse explains how to secure the animal to the "frog plate" of the microscope. He describes the operation with a sense of humor: "This is to be Froggy's bed during the operation"; but he also shows sympathy for the frog: "for we must make him as comfortable as circumstances will permit."[18] Never does the frog become just an object. He remains a creature with feelings, albeit an anthropomorphized one:

> Well, then, we take this strip of linen, damp it, and proceed to wrap up our unconscious subject. When we have passed two or three folds round him, we pass a tape round the whole, with just sufficient tightness to keep him from struggling. One hind-leg must project from the linen, and we now pass a needle of thread twice or thrice through the drapery and round the small of this free leg, so as to prevent him from retracting it. Here then he lies, swathed like a mummy, with one little cold foot protruded. (*Evenings*, pp. 43–44)

The little frog-mummy looks comical, but he has been most gently treated. Gosse and the reader are now rewarded with a look at the miniature world within the web: "What a striking spectacle is now presented to us!" Typically, Gosse treats this view like a landscape, full of exciting textures ("delicate angular lines" of the "tessellated epithelium" tissue), "fantastic forms" (pigment cells), and vistas ("Wide rivers, with tortuous course, roll across the area, with many smaller streams meandering among them"—these, of course, being the blood vessels).

I have said that *Evenings at the Microscope* is a technical work, and in one sense that is true: Gosse intends the book to be not only an account of what he has found beneath his lens, but also a lab-manual to guide the reader's researches. So the chapters of *Evenings* successively unfold the anatomy of blood, feathers, mollusks, crabs, barnacles, worms, jellyfish, Infusoria, and so forth. Six entire chapters are devoted to insects, because of the intricacy of their eyes, wings, feet, stings, mouths, and breathing tubes. Realizing that such a text could easily become ponderous and dry, Gosse chooses to cast it in the form of "imaginary *conversaziones*, or microscopical *soirées*, in which the author is supposed to act as the provider of scientific entertainment and instruction to a circle of friends" (p. 5). A delightfully Victorian notion—the microscopical *soirée*! With Gosse as genial host, microscopic study becomes a garden party, held in an exotic garden indeed.

Evenings promises to help the reader acquire "the power to observe and to discriminate what he has under his eye" (p. 5)—that is, to sharpen his sight. But there are more details in the minute world than even 468 pages of *Evenings* can catalogue, so Gosse admits that he has been forced to sweep "rapidly across the vast field of marvels, snatching up a gem here and there, and culling one and another of the brilliant blossoms of this flowery region, to weave a specimen chaplet, a sample coronal" (p. 3). The opening paragraph of his Preface establishes the tone for the book:

> To open the path to the myriad wonders of creation, which, altogether unseen by the unassisted eye, are made cognizable to sight by the aid of the Microscope, is the aim and scope of this volume. Great and gorgeous as is the display of Divine power and wisdom in the things that are seen of all, it may safely be affirmed that a far more extensive prospect of these glories lay unheeded and unknown till the optician's art revealed it. Like the work of some mighty genie of Oriental fable, the brazen tube is the key that unlocks a world of wonder and beauty before invisible, which one who has once gazed upon it can never forget, and never cease to admire. (p. 3)

The optician's art here is almost a magician's art. The passage is full of the sorts of responses to the microscope that I have already noted: the sense of opening up another world, one with a "prospect" like a landscape, the sense of wonder and amazement at microscopic "glories." The microscope, an extended eye, is a "brazen tube"—brass, of course, but also brash, bold as it pokes into a "world of wonder and beauty before invisible."

Microscopic creatures fascinate Philip Gosse for many reasons. In *The Romance of Natural History*, in fact, in the chapter called "The Minute," he lists eight reasons for their "strong hold on our imagination," including their numbers, their part in the economy of life, the variety of their forms, their beauty, their movements, and their minuteness itself (pp. 152–153). But two of these reasons seem paramount: the intricacy of their shapes and the autonomy of their lives. In the course of his studies, Gosse must sometimes kill and dissect living creatures, but, as with the frog, he always treats them with respect. He is awed by the vibrancy of their lives, which he mirrors in the active verbs that he chooses for their description. And, as in the case of so much Victorian science, some of Gosse's pleåsure in studying nature is meditative:

> It is a startling thought that there exists a world of animated beings densely peopling the elements around us, of which our senses are altogether uncognisant. For six thousand years generation after generation of *Rotifera* and *Entomostraca*, *Infusoria* and *Protozoa* have been living and dying, under the very eyes and in the very hands of man; and, until this last century or so, he has no more suspected their existence than if "the scene of their sorrow" had been the ring of Saturn. (*Romance*, p. 149)

Tiny animalcules lead Gosse to ponder time, mortality, and the value of life, much in the way that the tiny fossils in a piece of chalk inspired Huxley to meditate about time and change. In addition, the animated motes have for Gosse an autonomous existence, indeed almost human lives (they "people" the world), to a degree remarkable in such a devout Christian.

Gosse's descriptions of microscopic life are the most direct and energetic sections of his works, and like his other descriptions they tend to divide themselves into three rhetorical categories: passages of approach, of aesthetics, and of animation. Passages of approach begin with the larger view, the overall setting, and then narrow down to the creatures or objects to be investigated (the descent along the coral reef already quoted uses this technique also: from panorama to particular). Approach passages often include dramatic narration of a specimen's capture (as the butterfly hunt passage did). After the approach has elicited objects for study, Gosse includes passages of aesthetics, which celebrate the form, intricacy, and beauty of the animalcules. Finally, Gosse often shifts to passages of animation that energize the creatures (as did the description of waterbugs in the Newfoundland lake) showing them as moving, darting, zesty, and autonomously alive.

An approach passage opens the "Jelly-Fishes" chapter of *Evenings at the Microscope.* "As this afternoon was delightfully calm and warm—the very model of an autumnal day," Gosse begins, "I took my muslin ringnet and walked down to the rocks at the margin of the quiet sea." Beginning with this account of his moving along a scenic shore, Gosse first narrows the visual focus to a particular pool of water, and then down to its native inhabitants:

> Nor was I disappointed; for the still water, scarcely disturbed by an undulation, and clear as crystal, was alive with those brilliant little globes of animated jelly, the Ciliograde and Naked-eyed Medusae, apparently little more substantial than the clear water itself. (*Evenings*, p. 348)

The jellyfish live serenely undisturbed in their own element. As mere bits of jelly they might seem insignificant, but in Gosse's prose they take on independent life. So active are they that they seem imbued with emotions as well:

> Multitudes of them were floating on the surface, and others were discerned by the practiced eye, at various depths, shooting hither and thither, now ascending, now descending, now hanging lightly on their oars, and now, as if to make up for sloth, darting along obliquely with quickly-repeated strokes, or rolling and revolving along, in the very wantonness of humble happiness. (*Evenings*, p. 348)

Obviously Gosse offers a naturalist's perspective, not purely a scientist's, for objective biology would deny, or at least be highly skeptical of, happiness in the activities of the jellyfish. Gosse vivifies, and to some extent personifies, the jellyfish in order to make them come alive for a reader. His own pleasure and amazement over them influence the language he chooses, and why should they not? Because he is a naturalist, no scruples about strict objectivity constrain his rhetoric. Gosse continues, "After gazing a while with admiration at the undisturbed jollity of the hosts, I made a dip with my net." When he lifts it up, the net is "lined with sparkling balls of translucent jelly." These beautiful objects he culls and separates, finally narrowing the field to one specimen to be looked at in detail. The scenic narration has culminated in a smaller focus—the terrain of the jellyfish's body.

Another cinematic zoom from wide field of view to narrow opens the chapter on "Zoophytes." Again the collecting zone is the seashore, where "it is pleasant to go down" at lowest tide to the exposed "wilderness of rugged rocks draped with black and red weed" (*Evenings*, p. 368). Gosse helps the reader make the tortuous journey:

> On cautious foot round some frowning point whose base is usually beaten by the billows; to travel among the slippery bowlders [*sic*], now leaping from one to another, now winding between them, now creeping under their beetling roofs: to penetrate where we have never ventured before, and to explore with a feeling of undefined awe the wild solitudes where the hollow sea growls, and the gray gull wails. (p. 368)

The mysterious quest through a foreign landscape finally reaches caves beneath limestone arches, of which Gosse says, "What microcosms are these rugged basins!" The reader drops now from a world of human scale to one of minute dimensions: from the macrocosm of landscape and human habitation to the microcosm of the zoophytes, which, although tiny, teems with life:

> What arts, and wiles, and stratagems are being practiced there! what struggles for mastery, for food, for life! what pursuits and flights! what pleasant gambols! what conjugal and parental affections! what varied enjoyments! what births! what deaths! are every hour going on in these unruffled wells, beneath the brown shadow of the umbrageous Oarweed, or over the waving slopes of the bright green *Ulva* or among the feathery branches of the crimson *Ceramium*! (pp. 368–369)

Gosse's readers have left the beach and boulders to enter a different "wilderness," one where the seaweeds loom large as trees in the landscape of the little zoophytes. Again Gosse ascribes emotions to the inhabitants of the microcosm, but not sentimentally so. His ability to enter into the world of living animalcules reminds me, not of Charlotte Yonge's fairy flowers or Michelet's nuptially happy birds, but of Keats, projecting himself outward into the lives of the sparrows, and picking and scratching with them amid the gravel. Gosse seems able to leave his own frame of reference, to squeeze through the aperture of scale, and enter into other animal lives.

After masterfully describing the approach to the microcosm, Gosse often shifts, as I have said, to aesthetic passages, which concentrate on the complexity of form and color displayed beneath the lens of the "wonder-working instrument" (*Evenings*, p. 42). Diatoms, for example, display shells of glassy flint, yellow or brown, having a "determinate form, which often assumes extraordinary elegance, and is usually marked with series of specks, which are either knobs or pits, arranged in the most varied and exquisite patterns" (*Romance*, pp 96–97). *Eudorina* "comes rolling by, with majestic slowness, a globe of glass, with sixteen emeralds imbedded in its substance, symmetrically arranged, each emerald carrying a tiny ruby at one end; a most charming group" (*Romance*, p. 154). Organisms assume the form of pears, trumpets, poplar leaves, irregular balls, disks, fans, chains, vases, bells, and springs; they sport bristles, tubes, wreaths of cilia, teeth, specks, globules, and ruby spots as adornments. The shapes seem inexhaustible and beautifully symmetrical, and Gosse labors to impress his readers with the ways they catch the light, or pass through it in their "ruby-like translucent brilliancy" (*Romance*, p. 162).

The aesthetic passages often shade into passages of animation, for even in the minute world beneath the 'scope "the amount of life is at first bewildering; motion is in every part of the field; hundreds and thousands of pellucid bodies are darting across, making a mazy confusion of lines" (*Romance*, p. 154). The energy is simply astonishing, especially since it is packed into such a small space. "Truly," he says,

> this world in a globule of water—this world of rollicking, joyous, boisterous fellows, that a pin's point would take up, is even more wonderful than the shoals of whales that wallow in Baffin's Bay, or the herds of elephants that shake the earth in the forests of Ceylon. (*Romance*, p. 165)

Gosse chooses vigorous words that are charged with the vitality and, one might almost say, the personality of these infinitesimal animals, the "rollicking, joyous, boisterous fellows," or the "giddy little monads . . . whirling heedlessly along" (*Romance*, p. 159), or "a restless little rogue . . . grubbing among the decaying vegetable matter" (*Romance*, p. 159).

So thoroughly is the reader enmeshed in the microscopic jungle that to leave it is a shock. But Gosse, at the end of his "Minute" chapter, reverses the journey of scale that began it. Gosse left the vast beach behind and entered the microcosm; now he snaps back into his normal surroundings. When one has been absorbed in peering through the brazen tube, he says, "scarcely anything more strikes the mind with wonder" than to "suddenly remove the eye from the instrument" and look at the slide with the naked eye:

> Is this what we have been looking at? This quarter-inch of specks, is this the field of busy life? are here the scores of active creatures feeding, watching, preying, escaping, swimming, creeping, dancing, revolving, breeding? Are they here? Where? Here is nothing, absolutely nothing, but two or three

minutest dots which the straining sight but just catches now and then in one particular light. (*Romance*, p. 165)

It is as if a magical spell were suddenly broken. And only reluctantly does one relinquish the view afforded by the "diamond lens."

That lens has enabled Gosse's audience to explore a "miniature archipelago," to use an Edmund Gosse term (*Life*, p. 286). And it is easy to understand why the microscope became the "dominant passion of Philip Gosse's life" (*Life*, p. 223). With the light microscope, one discovers a whole world of light—where complicated structures glitter and shimmer and glow, studded with the purest colors. In the presence of luminosity, Gosse always feels rapturous. Whether composed of sparkling jellyfish or glistening madrepore, nature for Gosse is a radiant realm of light, which is the very emblem of its goodness and beauty. It is not too far-fetched to propose that in luminous nature Gosse found the concrete counterpart of God's heaven. Even the death of Infusoria can become a miniature transfiguration. These creatures, Gosse notes, "not only die but *vanish*" before his eyes. This puzzles him until he sees that, at the very instant of death, each bursts and dissolves (a process biochemists now call "lysis"). First the "skin" dissolves, then "the interior parts seem to escape," in the form of "vesicles of a pearly appearance . . . and then the whole became evanescent" (*Evenings*, p. 462).

Repeatedly, Gosse's descriptions concentrate on stunning images of natural objects whose beauty is so striking that it seems almost holy. Sometimes an absence of color or a clarity becomes an emblem of purity, of perfection, as in the case of *Melicerta*. This "tiny atom" is characterized by an "apparatus exquisitely beautiful"; a "broad transparent disk," which is both "pellucid" and "colourless" (*Romance*, p. 146). Its vitreous luster is breathtaking. At other times, a flash of intense color stands out against a darker background, suggestive of a beauty that transcends ordinary life. Such startlingly chromatic objects intrude upon a larger scene with a hard-edged clarity reminiscent of a Pre-Raphaelite image. *The Romance of Natural History* abounds with examples, such as the yellow and black butterfly, *Heliconia charitonia*, that Gosse sees in Jamaica. Within the "gorgeous glooms of South American scenery," he comes upon the insect "fluttering, slowly and fearlessly, over a great thicket of *Opuntia* in full flower, itself a memorable object to behold." But the butterfly, with its "beauty and singularity of the form," its "very remarkable shape of the wings," and particularly its "brilliant contrasts of colour" utterly dazzles Gosse, taking, he says, a "strong hold on my imagination" (*Romance*, p. 169).

Such moments of incandescent particularity—one might call them natural epiphanies—are the naturalist's reward. Gosse cherishes them and passes these "memorabilia" on to his readers in the form of imagistic vignettes. He explains the impact of these moments and how they can impress the naturalist whose mind is "poetic in temperament":

> Every naturalist can recall certain incidents in his communion with nature, which have impressed themselves upon his imagination with a vividness that the lapse of time in no wise effaces, and which he feels never will be effaced. They came upon him with a power which at the moment burnt-in the image of each in his remembrance; and they remain, and must remain while memory endures, ever and anon starting up with a palpable clearness that is all the more observable from the ever increasing dimness and vagueness into which the contemporary impressions are fading. They form the great landmarks of his life: they stand out like the promontories of some long line of coast, bold and clear, though the intervening shore is lost to view. (*Romance*, p. 166)

Typically, Gosse thinks of these incidents in terms of images burning bright in his consciousness, standing out clearly from the dimness of memory. Again, light dominates his thinking: he says later on that his "remembrance" of such incidents "invests" a "particular object" with a "halo."

Religious diction permeates Gosse's prose. His descriptions of nature are full of light, transfigurations, evanescence, transcendent moments; he writes of communion with nature, of the naturalist's "halo of hope" (*Romance*, p. 256). And obviously, for Gosse himself, the investigation of nature was a religious experience. In his *Life* of his father, Edmund mentions that "awe, an element almost eliminated from the modern mind, was strongly developed in Philip Gosse's character" (p. 336). He felt awe when he surveyed the endlessly varied objects in nature, not only because of their intrinsic beauty, but also because he regarded them as manifestations of God. As his wife Eliza pointed out, for Gosse "wandering among the rocks and pools" was equivalent to "mingling all his thoughts and sympathies with the God who formed these wonderful varieties of creation" (*Life*, p. 365).

Gosse believed that there were two ways to know God: through His works (nature), and through His words (the Bible). Assiduous in his reading of nature, Gosse was equally exacting in his reading of the Scriptures. His wife approvingly recalled that "he manifested the same eager and enthusiastic spirit in his study of Divine things, as in his scientific pursuits. He studied the Bible as he would study a science. . . . He was microscopic in his readings, and in his interpretations of the

Word of God, for he most implicitly believed every word of the original languages to be Divine" (*Life*, pp. 355–356). Interestingly, Edmund Gosse also characterizes his father as a sort of Scriptural microscopist, saying that he would take a passage of Scripture, and "dissect it, as if under the microscope, word by word, particle by particle" (*Life*, p. 329).

As long as what Gosse saw in nature, and what he discerned in the Bible, coincided, he was happy. But if a conflict arose, without hesitation he believed the Book. Edmund is emphatic about this point:

> No question is more often put to me regarding my father than this—How did he reconcile his religious to his scientific views? . . . The word "reconcile" is scarcely the right one, because the idea of reconciliation was hardly entertained by my father. He had no notion of striking a happy mean between his impressions of nature and his convictions of religion. If the former offered any opposition to the latter, they were swept away. The rising tide is "reconciled" in the same fashion to a child's battlements of sand along the shore." (*Life*, pp. 335–336)

A conflict did arise, of course, in the case of evolution—so Gosse swept the offending theory away. Not every Victorian naturalist with strong religious convictions reacted like this, because not all took the Bible literally. For example, Charles Kingsley (the subject of the next chapter) did reconcile his science and his religion. In fact, he quite happily embraced evolution as a religious concept, as an idea that demonstrated God's creativity. Gosse was a special case—a fossilized remnant, Edmund suggested, of seventeenth-century morality. When it came to interpreting the word of God, Gosse was absolutely unyielding. So rigid, so strict of conscience was he that, sadly, sooner or later he alienated most of his friends, as well as his own son. In the end he estranged even Kingsley, who was one of his closest companions for several years.

Philip Gosse was a man baffled by his own century, unable to countenance its modern ideas. But in his library and laboratory, in his books and his five thousand drawings of nature, he created a world for himself—a world of wonders. Edmund described his infinite capacity for taking pleasure in details: "never lonely, never bored, he was contented with small excitements and his butterflies, happy from morning till night" (*Life*, pp. 334–335). Fortunately for Gosse, his own temperament was mostly drawn to concrete objects, not theory. Taking nature as he found it, without worrying about how it worked (that, he felt, was God's province, not his), he concentrated on the transcendental, magical qualities of individual animals. Like other Victorian naturalists, Gosse amused himself endlessly by opening nature's nested boxes. And he succeeded in conveying to his readers his own sense of perpetual surprise and delight at what he found there.

In a typical passage of unfolding discovery, Gosse narrates the acquisition of an orchid from high in a tree. Writing energetically in the present tense, the literary naturalist conveys "the palpitation of hope and fear as we discuss the possibility of getting it down." And then there is the capture: "then come contrivances and efforts,—pole after pole is cut and tied together with the cords which the forest-climbers afford. At length the plant is reached, and pushed off, and triumphantly bagged" (*Romance*, p. 257). But this collected object leads to another in the profusion of nature, for "lo! while examining it, some elegant twisted shell is discovered with its tenant snail, crawling on the leaves." And this moment of discovery is rapidly succeeded by yet another, since

> scarcely is this boxed, when a gorgeous butterfly rushes out of the gloom into the shade, and is in a moment seen to be a novelty; then comes the excitement of pursuit; the disappointment of seeing it dance over a thicket out of sight; the joy of finding it reappear; the tantalising trial of watching the lovely wings flapping just out of reach; the patient waiting for it to descend; the tiptoe approach as we see it settle on a flower; the breathless eagerness with which the net is poised; and the triumphant flush with which we gaze on its loveliness when held in the trembling fingers. (*Romance*, pp. 257–258)

This small incident is emblematic of the thrill of natural history: the discovery of a novel form, the appreciation of its beauty, its pursuit and possession—all while the naturalist's emotions fluctuate wildly from excitement to disappointment, to joy, to tantalization, to breathless eagerness, to the final "flush" of triumph. In Gosse's experience, nature is kaleidoscopic: dazzling, colorful images that shift continuously, one giving way to the next. As a writer, he brilliantly captures the mesmerizing beauty of such flickering images—now orchid, now snail, now butterfly—and the emotions they ignite. Gosse's natural history writing amply fulfills every requirement of the genre. Presented in his "aesthetic fashion," natural history truly is the "feasting of the eager eyes as they gloat over the novelties" of nature (*Romance*, p. 258).

Notes

1. Stephen E. Whicher and Robert E. Spiller, eds., *The Early Lectures of Ralph Waldo Emerson, Volume I: 1833–1836* (Cambridge: Harvard Univ. Press, 1959), p. 6.

2. Edmund Gosse, *Father and Son: A Study of Two Temperaments* (New York: W. W. Norton and Company, 1963), p. 233.

3. Alan C. Jenkins, *The Naturalists: Pioneers of Natural History* (New York: Mayflower Books, Inc., 1978), p. 159.

4. See Douglas L. Wertheimer, "Philip Henry Gosse: Science and Revelation in the Crucible" (Ph.D. Diss. Univ. of Toronto, 1977).

5. Edmund Gosse, *Father and Son*, p. 88.

6. James D. Woolf, *Sir Edmund Gosse*, (New York: Twayne Publishers, 1972), p. 19.

7. Edmund Gosse, *Father and Son*, p. 96.

8. Edmund Gosse, *Father and Son*, p. 109. Further page citations are made within the text.

9. C. M. Yonge, "British Marine Life," in *A Treasury of English Wild Life*, ed. W. J. Turner (New York: Chanticleer Press, n.d.), p. 232.

10. Edmund Gosse, *The Life of Philip Henry Gosse, F.R.S.* (London: Kegan Paul, Trench, Trübner and Co., Ltd., 1890), p. 337. Further page citations are made within the text.

11. David Elliston Allen, *The Naturalist in Britain: A Social History* (London: Allen Lane, 1976), p. 129.

12. For a lively annotated bibliography of his works, see R. B. Freeman and Douglas Wertheimer, *Philip Henry Gosse: A Bibliography* (Folkestone, Kent: Dawson, 1980). Unfortunately, as far as I have been able to discover, none of Gosse's works is currently in print, save for one book reprinted as a regional period piece for the southern United States: *Letters from Alabama, Chiefly Relating to Natural History* (Mountain Brook, AL: Overbrook House, 1983). Edmund Gosse's fine *Life* of his father is also out of print, which is a pity, for P. H. Gosse exemplifies some quintessentially Victorian habits of mind, in addition to having known many influential scientists like Huxley, Darwin, E. Forbes, and T. Bell.

13. Freeman and Wertheimer, p. 62.

14. P. H. Gosse, *The Romance of Natural History* (New York: A. L. Burt Company, Publishers, 1902), p. iii. Further page citations are made within the text.

15. A sea serpent "craze" had "swept" London in 1848–1849, after a reputable sea captain had claimed to see one in the South Atlantic, and the idea of such a serpent maintained a strong hold on the public imagination, even after the redoubtable Richard Owen pooh-poohed it. Richard D. Altick, *The Shows of London: A Panoramic History of Exhibitions, 1600–1862* (Cambridge, MA: Belknap Press-Harvard Univ. Press, 1978), p. 305.

16. Stanley Edgar Hyman, *The Tangled Bank: Darwin, Marx, Frazer, & Freud as Imaginative Writers* (New York: Grosset and Dunlap, 1966), p. 16.

17. James G. Paradis, *T. H. Huxley: Man's Place in Nature* (Lincoln: Univ. of Nebraska Press, 1978), p. 59.

18. Philip Henry Gosse, *Evenings at the Microscope* (New York: P. F. Collier and Son, 1901), p. 43. Further page citations are made within the text.

9

Charles Kingsley and the Wonders of the Shore

To the natural philosopher, the descriptive poet, the painter, and the sculptor, as well as to the common observer, the power most important to cultivate, and, at the same time, hardest to acquire, is that of seeing what is before him. Sight is a faculty; seeing, an art. The eye is a physical, but not a self-acting apparatus, and in general it sees only what it seeks. Like a mirror, it reflects objects presented to it; but it may be as insensible as a mirror, and it does not necessarily perceive what it reflects. It is disputed whether the purely material sensibility of the eye is capable of improvement and cultivation. It has been maintained by high authority, that the natural acuteness of none of our sensuous faculties can be heightened by us, and hence that the minutest details of the image formed on the retina are as perfect in the most untrained, as in the most thoroughly disciplined organ. This may well be doubted, and it is agreed on all hands that the power of multifarious perceptions and rapid discrimination may be immensely increased by well-directed practice.[1]

GEORGE PERKINS MARSH, 1864

Charles Kingsley, unlike Philip Henry Gosse, is not unknown to literary scholars. Indeed, Kingsley (1819–1875) claims attention as the author of novels such as *Yeast* and *Alton Locke*. His historical novels and works for children also endure to some extent: *Hypatia, Westward Ho!, The Heroes*, and *The Water-Babies*. But Kingsley is perhaps best known as a prominent Victorian intellectual and cleric, particularly as the keeper of the Anglican faith who clashed with Newman's Catholicism. Passionately committed to social reform, sanitation and public health, and spiritual

215

growth, Kingsley stands as an archetype of the earnest, dedicated, hard-working, serious-minded Victorian.

Like so many well-educated Victorians, Kingsley took a keen interest in the issues of his day, which included the progress of science. In spite of his piety, Kingsley promoted science with gusto. And like so many of his contemporaries, he was an amateur naturalist as well. Yet this aspect of him, Kingsley the naturalist and popularizer of science, fades all too readily from his official portrait. Like Darwin, Kingsley had a taste for fieldwork in science instilled in him when he was a child. Kingsley's father trained him especially well in botany, among other fields of natural history. In previous chapters, I have pointed out instances of overlap between scientific study and painting; in this light it is interesting that Kingsley's father excelled at landscape painting, passing this enthusiasm on to his son.[2] As a novelist, Kingsley would excel at "word-pictures" of landscapes,[3] while his skill as an illustrator would hold him in good stead when he took up lecturing on popular science. Like Agassiz and Philip Gosse, Kingsley embellished his science instruction with good chalk drawings.

Kingsley had, in fact, the kind of direct, natural education that Herbert Spencer advocated: learning to abstract and generalize from particular natural facts, specific rocks and flowers. Always fond of botany, Kingsley intensified his taste for geology at Cambridge by attending Adam Sedg-wick's Field Lectures. In later years, when he was Canon of Chester, Kingsley would turn geology teacher, leading very popular field excursions, armed with a geologist's hammer and botanical specimen box. At Chester his botany lectures blossomed as well. Like Philip Gosse's attempts to hold microscopical *conversaziones* in *Evenings at the Microscope*, Kingsley organized a *conversazione* in the Chester Town Hall in 1871. This makeshift museum boasted collections of fossils and shells, drawings, and an exciting Microscopical Exhibition.[4]

Besides botany and geology, Charles Kingsley fancied marine biology, an avocation greatly encouraged by his friendship with Philip Gosse. The two of them spent time together on happy dredging expeditions off Torquay in 1858. In his father's biography, Edmund Gosse recalls one such expedition. Kingsley was a good sailor, he remembers, while he himself and his father were less confident, but "when the trawl came up, and the multitudinous population of the bottom of the bay was tossed in confusion before our eyes, we forgot our qualms in our excitement."[5] Edmund most distinctly was impressed by "the hawk's eyes of Kingsley peering into the trawl."

The Kingsley-Gosse friendship, involving aquarium stocking and specimen exchange, stimulated Kingsley to write his only work of pure natural history. *Glaucus; or, the Wonders of the Shore* originated as an article in the *North British Review* in 1854, which Kingsley then expanded into a "little book." He intended this book to be in part a manual of instruction for his children. *Glaucus* owes a great debt to P. H. Gosse, being inspired by Gosse's congenial seaside guides. Because of Gosse's direct influence, *Glaucus* serves as a nice companion piece to *The Romance of Natural History* and *Evenings at the Microscope*, but it has its own virtues, too. For several reasons, *Glaucus* is important to a study of Victorian natural history. First, it displays many of Kingsley's—and general Victorian—attitudes about science, many of which infiltrate his other books as well, particularly *The Water-Babies*. Kingsley is well aware of scientific issues such as evolution, specialized terminology, and, especially, the limitations of the scientific method as a means of comprehending the world. Second, *Glaucus* contains a wealth of information about Victorian natural history—its pleasures, principles, and educational values. Kingsley wryly documents its ascendance and its popular manifestations, such as the trade in mounted specimens of seaweed and, of course, collecting. Finally, the descriptive set-pieces in *Glaucus* sparkle with the characteristic motifs of natural history discourse: microscopic images, visual images of all kinds, concrete and sensuous diction, the language of changing scale, and the preoccupation with "opening up" new worlds by falling through one reality into another.

Kingsley's staunch support of science colors much of his work. Unlike Gosse, Kingsley experienced no difficulty in reconciling religion and natural selection, and evolutions of one sort or another pervade his books. The famous evolutionary dream of the tailor in *Alton Locke* (chapter 36, "Dreamland"), in which he progresses from madrepore to crab to remora to mylodon, is one example. *The Water-Babies*, too, recounts the evolution, physical and spiritual, of Tom the sweep; one critic of the book, in fact, dubs the book "an evolutionary fantasy."[6] When he turned seriously to geology, Kingsley published a series of lectures (those given at Chester) as a volume called *Town Geology*, which at times approaches a Huxleyan metaphorical intensity.

Other signs of science are the natural history enthusiasts that appear in Kingsley's novels. These amateur naturalists signal his deep interest in the subject. There is the doctor-protagonist of *Two Years Ago*, fond of his microscope and of marine biology. There is Lancelot Smith, hero of *Yeast*, who had gone to college "with a large stock of general information, and a particular mania for dried plants, fossils, butterflies, and sketching."[7] To Kingsley, Lancelot Smith exemplifies both the good and bad aspects of natural history. To the good is concrete pleasure in the world of nature; but such pleasures may lead to mere materialism. Believing only in the material world, Lancelot undergoes a crisis of faith: "he had gradually, in fact, as we have seen, dropped all faith in anything but Nature; the slightest fact about a bone or a weed was more important to him than all the books of divinity."[8] By the end of the novel, Smith is redeemed from his lack of faith, reconciling the spiritual and the material worlds—something Kingsley demands that one do. Quintessentially Victorian in his attraction to and fear of materialism, Kingsley worries that science fosters a materialistic attitude. But in his works of natural history and popular science, he consistently advocates using the material world as a window into the spiritual: nature as God's display. Even *The Water-Babies*, a book for children, brims with caustic criticism of science that is too mechanistic, dissecting, materialistic, that denies the existence of things it cannot see—like water-babies, or gods.

The naturalist can find God in nature and at the same time heighten his enjoyment of the common and concrete. Alton Locke, the Cockney poet, who at one point in his eponymous novel has the "daily task of arranging and naming objects of natural history,"[9] especially lavishes praise on Tennyson, because Tennyson points out mundane objects in nature, and thereby makes them beautiful. Much as a naturalist would, teaching while on a field expedition, Tennyson calls one's attention to "trivial everyday sights and sounds of nature": this is "the revelation of the poetry which lies in common things" (*Alton Locke*, pp. 95–96). Locke is particularly impressed by the creeks where the dying swan floated and the "silvery marsh mosses by Mariana's moat," because these are ordinary settings made special, not settings originally sublime or picturesque. As Kingley's protagonist puts it, Tennyson

> has learnt to see that in all nature, in the hedgerow and the sandbank, as well as in the Alp peak and the ocean waste, is a world of true sublimity—a minute infinite—an ever fertile garden of poetic images, the roots of which are in the unfathomable and the eternal, as truly as any phenomenon which astonishes and awes the eye. (p. 95)

The "minute infinite"—the phrase picks up on one of the most earnestly repeated and cherished ideas in all of Victorian natural history. And if that is what Tennyson does, then he is approaching the world like a naturalist, like Philip Gosse looking through his brazen tube. The minute infinite is a secret world in small compass, which astonishes and awes the eye.

Still, Kingsley is Kingsley, and as a devout man he always hastens to append a spiritual goal to nature studies. In *Glaucus*, Kingsley exhaustively details the qualities needed by a good naturalist. The naturalist must be "like a knight of old,"[10] physically strong, athletically skilled with rod and gun, gentle, courteous, brave, enterprising; he must fiercely desire to advance knowledge and be free from the "perturbations of mind," such as laziness and melancholy, which would interfere with his mission. (This daunting ideal Kingsley recommends as a model for children, to be urged upon them by their parents. In effect, Kingsley seems to advocate that a budding naturalist become a sort of intrepid Boy Scout for nature; his rod-and-gun-toting model offers scant scope for girls.) Shaped by these noble qualities, the naturalist will remember always to give "Nature credit for an inexhaustible fertility and variety" (*Glaucus*, p. 44). He will then find himself

> wondering at the commonist, but not surprised by the most strange; free from the idols of size and sensuous loveliness; able to see grandeur in the minutest objects, beauty in the most ungainly; estimating each thing not carnally, as the vulgar do, by its size or its pleasantness to the senses, but spiritually, by the amount of Divine thought revealed to him therein; holding every phenomenon worth the noting down; believing that every pebble holds a treasure, every bud a revelation; making it a point of conscience to pass over nothing through laziness or hastiness, lest the vision once offered and despised should be withdrawn; and looking at every object as if he were never to behold it again.

All objects for Kingsley are manifestations of "Divine thought." But they are objects still—to be looked at long and lovingly. Even in this religious context, where nature embodies the Divine, the familiar natural history themes recur: focus on the minute, natural epiphany (or revelation), and the primacy of vision.

Kingsley maintains, as do so many others, that naturalists learn to see truly what is before them. Burroughs and Ruskin would certainly agree with Kingsley that the "highest faculty" is the "Art of Seeing" (*Glaucus*, p. 42). Naturalists, with their keen eyes, find the world "an inexhaustible treasure of wonder" (p. 17). Kingsley declares confidently that "happy, truly, is the naturalist" (p. 14). Happy because his vision, literal and imaginative, leads him to see in all of nature "significances, harmonies, laws, chains of cause and effect endlessly interlinked." With such vision, "the Earth becomes to him transparent." As a result, to the discerning naturalist no landscape is mundane. Wherever he wanders, whether over familiar or new terrain, the naturalist sees and understands so much that he finds himself transported to "a new world" (*Glaucus*, p. 15). Mastery of the Art of Seeing both unveils physical nature, and reveals its metaphysical significance.

Kingsley always assumes that what one can see of nature is but the fringe. One ought never to discount the possibility of further wonders. In part Kingsley displays the usual exuberant confidence of Victorian naturalists. After all, were they not privy to greater secrets with each passing day? The torrid pace of exploration and discovery continually brought new natural oddities to light (sometimes literally so, as in the case of the light microscope); there was no sign of slackening. But Kingsley also takes for granted the maxim that spiritual forms buttress the material: no form of creation is impossible to God. With this in mind, for Kingsley natural history becomes a spiritual quest.

A passage from *The Water-Babies* illustrates Kingsley's determination to see nature as endlessly varied, endlessly creative. Little Tom the chimney sweep, newly made aware that he is dirty and well aware that he is miserable, after a series of adventures is captured by fairies and turned into a water-baby. Slyly the author of the tale pokes fun at overzealous scientific quantification and pompous scientific nomenclature, informing his readers that as a water-baby Tom is "3.87902 inches long" and has "round the parotid region of his fauces a set of external gills" (chapter 2).[11] Then Kingsley admonishes any of his readers who may doubt that there are such things as water-babies, or fairies for that matter. One should not say a water-baby is "contrary to nature," because even the wisest man knows only the tiniest corner of nature. Don't say that water-babies cannot be, for

> you do not know what nature is, or what she can do; and nobody knows; not even Sir Roderick Murchison, or Professor Owen, or Professor Sedgwick, or Professor Huxley, or Mr. Darwin, or Professor Faraday, or Mr. Grove, or any other of the great men whom good boys are taught to respect. They are very wise men; and you should listen respectfully to all they say: but even if they should say, which I am sure they never would, "That cannot exist. That is contrary to nature," you must wait a little, and see; for perhaps even they may be wrong. (*Water-Babies*, p. 45)

After all, it seems impossible that seeds should grow into trees; even the nature one takes for granted is amazing. Nature can do anything—except, Kingsley hedges, run contrary to mathematical truth.

Kingsley's perception that nature is capable of the most amazing things is endemic among Victorian naturalists. Water-babies are possible in the world of nature; or, if they do not exist, something just as wonderful surely does. Henry Walter Bates, for example, expressed much the same idea after watching a hummingbird bathing itself in a small tropical stream. This "little pygmy belonging to the genus *Phaethornis*" is far more complex than any imaginary creature that a human might invent to populate the woodlands: "I thought, as I watched it, that there was no need for poets to invent elves and gnomes whilst Nature furnishes us with such marvellous little sprites ready to hand."[12] Or as Margaret Gatty pointed out in a story called "A Lesson of Faith," who could imagine that "butterflies' eggs are caterpillars, and that caterpillars leave off crawling and get wings, and become butterflies"?[13] But of course they do. And if that can happen in nature, then who is to say what else might not be possible? As one of Gatty's characters says looking at nature: "I see so many wonderful things, I know no reason why there should not be more."

The list of eminent Victorian scientists and the parody of their terminology in *The Water-Babies* amuses, but Kingsley's point goes beyond social satire. When Tom changes from a boy into a water-baby, he undergoes a "transformation," just as Gatty's caterpillar does in becoming a butterfly, as the seed does in becoming a tree, or as adults do in growing up from infants. Not only the forms of nature are wondrous, but also the fluidity of those forms. Jellyfish, goose barnacles, butterflies—all achieve a multiplicity of manifestations, so that nature is not only inexhaustible, but dynamic. And Kingsley likens this transformational quality in nature to the growth of a human soul—especially after death, the final transformation. Natural history and science alike should serve to keep one alert to such possibilities.

Worth noting at this point is the fact that *The Water-Babies*, although still hailed as a classic for children (Queen Victoria is said to have read it to hers), is in reality no more childish a book than *Alice in Wonderland*. Kingsley's classic exists today in two forms: the 1863 original and a drastically pruned version from 1928. Most adults today who read *The Water-Babies* in childhood encountered the abridged version. Twentieth-century editing excised the topical, satirical, adult sections from the book. This lost material is precisely what interests the Victorian scholar and historian of science, because Charles Kingsley, both in the original *Water-Babies* and in *Glaucus*, shows himself to be a veritable sponge of science. Famous scientists, theories, discoveries, fads, and gadgets—all make appearances at one time or another in these works. In fact, most of the prominent features of Victorian natural history take a bow on Kingsley's stage. One appreciative reader of the uncut *Water-Babies* comments on its scientific all-inclusiveness and notes that it contains all these treasures: "plants fresh-water and sea, . . . water-flies, dear to an old fisherman, and especially the gorgeous dragon-fly, . . . fish, birds, and shells . . . species, gorillas, specific gravities, latitudes, and longitudes, minute computations, philosophers."[14]

In addition to all the scientists listed in the passage above, Kingsley manages to include references to Lamarck, Paul du Chaillu (African explorer and discoverer of the gorilla), Bewick (eighteenth-century nature illustrator), and the British Association for the Advancement of Science (specifically, the hippocampus controversy). He mentions vivariums and the technical exhibits at the Crystal Palace. He spoofs pharmacy and medicine. After telling one fantastic tale, Kingsley says tongue-in-cheek, "And, if that is not all, every word, true, then there is no faith in microscopes, and all is over with the Linnaean Society" (*Water-Babies*, p. 119). The implication is obvious: all reasonable Victorians put their trust in microscopes. And what more impeccable standard of truth could there be than Linnaeus, the mighty systematizer himself? So impressed with the magical powers of science is Kingsley that he dubs it "the great fairy," one "likely to be queen of the fairies for many a year to come" (*Water-Babies*, p. 56).

Kingsley shrewdly caricatures both scientists and naturalists. He revels in his creation of Professor Ptthmllnsprts, who holds the daunting title of Chief Professor of Necrobioneopalaeonthydrochthonanthropopithekology (*Water-Babies*, p. 93). The scientific analysis practiced by this esteemed professor limits itself to the obvious and thus fails to perceive Tom, the water-baby. Medical doctors of this ilk, called upon to examine the captive Tom, diagnose him in melancholy tones as having this dire syndrome: "subanhypapsosupernal anastomoses of peritomoses of peritomic diacellurite in the encephalo digital region," producing the "interexclusively quadrilateral and antinomian diathesis" known, in short, as "Bumpsterhausen's blue follicles" (*Water-Babies*, p. 100). Here is Victorian professional science at its most pompous extreme. Kingsley's gibes at polysyllabic classification probably sounded funny to children, but his satire makes more sense to adults.

On the same distinctly adult level resides the giant-sized collector who is equipped with all the naturalist's requisite paraphernalia:

> He had a great pair of spectacles on his nose, and a butterfly-net in one hand, and a geological hammer in the other; and was hung all over with pockets, full of collecting boxes, bottles, microscopes, telescopes, barometers, ordnance maps, scalpels, forceps, photographic apparatus, and all other tackle for finding out everything about everything, and a little more too. (*Water-Babies*, p. 187)

A tidier précis of the Victorian naturalist/scientist would be difficult to imagine. This larger-than-life naturalist busily pounces on specimens of dubious importance. Recalling the thrilled tones of Alfred Wallace in possession of the rare butterfly, the giant exclaims: "An entirely new *Oniscus*, and three obscure *Podurellae*! Beside a moth which M. le Roi des Papillons (though he, like all Frenchmen, is given to hasty inductions) says is confined to the limits of the Glacial Drift." Ah, trills the collector, "This is most important!" Needless to say, the reader hardly inclines to agree. Kingsley had his doubts about the validity of species-chasing; in *Glaucus* he directly states his disapproval of the hubris involved in seeking a new species of animal or plant, just so it may bear one's name. But had the species mania not been so thoroughly pervasive in Victorian society, Kingsley would not have commented on it. His humorous disparagement of natural history highlights its popularity. (Similarly, his collector's comment about M. le Roi des Papillons betrays the prevalent English attitude toward French science: mingled envy and scorn. The English were very conscious of having lagged badly behind Continental science during the late eighteenth century.)

Natural history and science did breed excesses. But especially for the amateur, natural history obviously had great charms. Clearly, from the evidence of *Glaucus*, Kingsley was well aware of them; *Glaucus*, no less than *The Water-Babies*, is a veritable compendium of natural history practices in England. He several times refers to the natural history groundswell as a phenomenon that had developed during the previous twenty years. Overstating the case somewhat, he claims that in the eighteenth century naturalists were viewed with "contempt" (*Glaucus*, p. 9); at best the amateur naturalist was seen as an eccentric who stalked bugs because he lacked the manliness to hunt foxes (p. 7). Some English precursors stood out—Bewick, White, Ray—but they were lonely beacons, he implies, compared to the hordes of amateur naturalists active in England in 1854. Kingsley's perception underscores the fact that natural history achieved broad popularity only in Victorian times, although it certainly had adherents during the eighteenth century. Throughout his book, Kingsley offers much corroborative evidence for the stature natural history had attained by the middle of the nineteenth century. For one thing, as I mentioned in Chapter 2, he paints a deft portrait of young ladies obsessed with Pteridomania, or fern-collecting. Also, like Philip Gosse, Kingsley talks about the somewhat furtive practice of sugaring trees for moths.

Several of the collecting activities that Kingsley advocates benefited from the fact that specimens or materials for them were already widely available in shops. When he talks about collecting sponges, for example, Kingsley notes that one of the most beautiful and exotic of them, the Venus flower-basket of the Philippines, can be readily acquired. "Twenty years ago there was but one specimen in Europe," he says, but "now you may buy one for a pound in any curiosity shop" (*Glaucus*, p. 86). For displaying it, Kingsley recommends a glass case—another recent innovation—wherein it will repose, "a delight to your eyes, one of the most exquisite, both for form and texture, of natural objects." If one cares to investigate the variety of seaweeds, one can make a start by buying at a shop "some thirty pretty kinds, pasted on paper, with long names (probably misspelt) written under each" (*Glaucus*, p. 151). Such ready-made displays might serve as playthings for children, although characteristically Kingsley warns that by no means do they constitute a truly adequate collection. Better to collect seaweeds for oneself, prepare and mount them using recommended techniques, such as those given in domestic handbooks (see Chapter 1).

As a friend and admirer of Philip Gosse, Kingsley devotes much space in *Glaucus* to praising his invention, the aquarium (pointing out the other people involved in its discovery as well). For technical details of its construction, Kingsley refers his readers to Gosse's book, *The Aquarium*, but he does provide his own set of simplified instructions for a small jar-aquarium. If one lives inland and cannot acquire from a chemist's shop a package of Gosse's artificial sea salts, a freshwater collection will do. Fortunately, to pond-mud and gravel one can easily add specimens of two water-plants, *Vallisneria spiralis* and *Anacharis alsinastrum*—easily because, although they are North American species, they can be bought "at any good shop in Covent Garden" (*Glaucus*, p. 205).

That curiosity shops across England would stock such items as Philippine glass sponges, dried and labeled seaweeds, and American duckweeds testifies to the popularity of natural history study. Perhaps even more telling, however, is the bibliography that Kingsley summarizes within the final pages of his book. How could *Glaucus* "end more usefully than in recommending a few books on Natural History?" (p. 213). During the recent twenty-year triumph of natural history, Kingsley says, a "swarm" of "manuals and popular works" has appeared—"almost beyond counting" (*Glaucus*, p. 222).[15] In his endeavor to recommend natural history to young people, Kingsley names no fewer than forty-four titles and authors. As a social reformer, he takes special pleasure in praising books by "simple working men" turned naturalists, such as Hugh Miller, or Richard Shield, author of this imposing work: *Practical Hints Respecting Moths and Butterflies, forming a Calendar for Entomological Opera-*

tions (*Glaucus*, p. 220). Kingsley names Darwin, G. H. Lewes, Forbes, Harvey, Reverend Wood, St. John, and Waterton, along with a host of minor writers, several of them ladies. Ranked highest among them all, however, is Philip Henry Gosse. Gosse excels at "bringing out the human side of science," at including "little touches of pathos and humor," writing with a "playful and genial spirit," and with "a brilliant power of word-painting" (*Glaucus*, p. 214). In my estimation, Kingsley did not overpraise his friend.

Besides books and collectibles, Kingsley points out that serials and clubs offer other avenues of entry into natural history. Any amateur naturalist can find voluminous lists of manuals and equipment in the advertising columns of popular periodicals. And natural history clubs, whether they be Field Clubs or Microscopic or Geological Societies, "form a most pleasant and hopeful new feature in English Society" (*Glaucus*, p. 224). These clubs, like the one Kingsley was later to lead at Chester, recommend themselves particularly because they are egalitarian: they bring all classes together in healthful, useful, dutiful pursuits. With the rise of such clubs, Kingsley optimistically foresees a new sort of educational brotherhood bound by the love of natural facts, a "new freemasonry of Natural History" (*Glaucus*, p. 225). Here the sanguine Victorian hope emerges—that people from any class could improve themselves through hard work, dedication, and preference for "rational amusements" over dissipation and sin. And as a rational amusement, natural history, with its inherent educational rewards, rated very high.

Beyond providing ample evidence for the mid-century English craze for natural history, Kingsley's *Glaucus* displays several of the guiding motifs that characterize it. Most striking are those having to do with the Art of Seeing. Like so many other naturalists, Kingsley is fascinated by technological advances that act as eyes or lenses and open up, or see into, new worlds. One of these is deep-sea dredging. Kingsley, as I mentioned earlier, was fond of accompanying P. H. Gosse on dredging excursions in Torquay's relatively shallow waters. In *Glaucus* he touts dredging as a means to acquire specimens one would never find on the beach. Like Frank Buckland's water telescope, dredging can increase "the amusements of a water-party," combining as it does the delights of fair weather sailing with the always enjoyable "discovery of new objects" (*Glaucus*, p. 159). But Kingsley was even more intrigued with the recent innovation of dredging live objects up from the great ocean depths, previously thought barren. Edward Forbes (whose "Song of the Dredge" I quoted in Chapter 2) pioneered the technique. And C. Wyville Thomson's book about it, *The Depths of the Sea*, had just appeared when Kingsley revised the fifth edition of *Glaucus*. In addition to mentioning, and lauding, Thomson's book, Kingsley encourages his readers to seek out the deep-sea specimens housed at the British Museum, particularly the crinoids (so-called sea lilies). He also urges them to look for notices of new discoveries made by H.M.S. *Challenger*, as written up in the columns of *Nature* (*Glaucus*, p. 84).

The voyages of the deep-sea dredger, H.M.S *Challenger*, took place in 1873 and 1876, and were reported by C. Wyville Thomson in his book *The Voyage of the "Challenger"* (1877). When Thomson wrote of the abyssal depths in *The Depths of the Sea* (1873), he covered dredging expeditions by other ships during 1868, 1869, and 1870. Kingsley took note of all this activity when expanding *Glaucus* for a fifth edition in 1873, even borrowing some of Thomson's illustrations. Given his predilection for metaphors of "opening up" nature's secrets, it is not surprising that Kingsley, along with many other naturalists, found the dredging results exciting.

Deep-sea dredging captured Kingsley's imagination, as it did the public's, because it fulfilled a dream of being able to look into the depths of the ocean—depths peopled since antiquity with fantastic forms of life. In fact, Kingsley's fantasy about being able to enter the ocean and look around ties in with an ancient Greek myth, from which his book takes its name. Beachcombing for natural history, Kingsley often finds tantalizing fragments of wave-battered objects. They come from deeper water, "the riches of which have to be seen, alas! rather by the imagination than the eye" (*Glaucus*, p. 146). The dredge hauls up some of these treasures, albeit at random, and the imagination, like Gosse's when descending along the coral reef, can fill in some of the missing details. Thus the dredge is, in effect, a kind of water-telescope, but it can give just "mere hints to us of what the populous reality below is like." Kingsley wishes for more. He wishes, like the charmed Frenchman he cites who has some scuba-like device for underwater breathing or like the lucky Captain Nemo in his *Nautilus*, to walk into the water without drowning and see what is under it:

> Often, standing on the shore at low tide, has one longed to walk on and in under the waves, as the water-ousel does in the pools of the mountain burn, and see it all but for a moment. (*Glaucus*, p. 146)

This, incidentally, is exactly what Kingsley manages to do, although still only in the imagination, in *The Water-Babies*—where Tom sports under the waves with sunfish and sharks, porpoises and lobsters.

Contemplating the lucky ouzel, Kingsley finds its human counterpart in a mythic Greek fisherman named Glaucus, who always threw back some of his catch, giving each fish a special herb to restore its strength. Upon eating some of the herb himself, Glaucus was "seized on the spot with a strange longing to follow them under the waves" (*Glaucus*, p. 147). Like Thomson and other dredgers, Kingsley is a modern disciple, he says, of Glaucus, "who, enamoured of the wonders of the sea, plunged into the blue abyss once and for all" (*Glaucus*, p. 86). But Kingsley tries not to envy Glaucus too much. After all, he muses, the wonders of the shore alone are various enough for a lifetime.

If the dredge can open up the wonders of the sea, so the microscope can open up "The Wonders of the Little." (Kingsley was so fond of this "wonders of" phrasing that at one point in *Glaucus* he only half-jokingly urges the fishermen of England to join together in creating a science of "The Wonders of the Bank.") The microscope is a boon to naturalists because, as Kingsley believes much like Gosse, Burroughs, Ruskin, and others, nature is "not only 'maxima in minimis'—greatest in her least, but often 'pulcherrima in abditis'—fairest in her most hidden works" (*Glaucus*, p. 88). One Radiate, with "his extraordinary feeding mill, . . . is enclosed within an ever-growing limestone castle" (p. 127). To appreciate the intricacy of this little sea-egg, one must

> conceive a Crystal Palace, (for the mere difference in size, as both the naturalist and the metaphysician know, has nothing to do with the wonder,) whereof each separate joist, girder, and pane grows continually without altering the shape of the whole. (*Glaucus*, p. 128).

The Crystal Palace is a wonderful structure indeed, but its dynamic tiny analogue is equally amazing. With his focus on the minute and the hidden, Kingsley joins countless other naturalists who take delight in squeezing themselves through optical or imaginative apertures into worlds of tiny scale. Looking through his "diamond lens," O'Brien found enchanted gardens (of mildew; see Chapter 5); Kingsley finds a Crystal Palace.

Fortunately, Kingsley reports, the value of the microscope in ferreting out the hidden beauties of nature has not gone unnoticed. Recently, he himself has made a happy "discovery of unsuspected microscopists" (*Glaucus*, p. 224), toiling away in small towns, enraptured by the view through the lens:

> Microscopy, meanwhile, and the whole study of "The Wonders of the Little," have made vast strides in the last twenty years; and I was equally surprised and pleased, to find, three years ago, in each of two dozen towns

of a few thousand inhabitants, perhaps a dozen good microscopes, all but hidden away from the public, worked by men who knew how to handle them, and who knew what they were looking at; but who modestly refrained from telling anybody what they were doing so well. (*Glaucus*, pp. 223–224)

Thanks to the work, and the descriptions, of such mute inglorious microscopists, the "zoophytes and microscopic animalcules which people every shore and every drop of water, have been now raised to a rank in the human mind more important, perhaps, than even those gigantic monsters whose models fill the lake at the Crystal Palace" (*Glaucus*, p. 32). Interestingly, this comment combines what Gosse would call the Minute and the Vast, with minute animalcules and vast dinosaurs pushing the limits of human consciousness and human wonderment outward at both ends of the scale of natural size. And in fact, in the imagination the animalcules do become huge, just as did the insects when Alfred Wallace showed them to the people of Aru through his magnifying lens.

Helping the reader to find the curious, the overlooked, the unsuspected is the aim of *Glaucus*. To achieve his goal, Kingsley employs a typical rhetorical device of natural history prose: the second-person pronoun, which reaches right out from his pages to startle the reader into action. He begins with a witty anecdote about the impending boredom that awaits one on a typical six-weeks' vacation at "some watering-place along the coast." Riding along in the railway coach, Kingsley says,

You foreknow your doom by sad experience. A great deal of dressing, a lounge in the club-room, a stare out of the window with the telescope, an attempt to take a bad sketch, a walk up one parade and down another, interminable reading of novels, over which you fall asleep on a bench in the sun. (*Glaucus*, pp. 1–2)

The list of stultifying holiday activities goes on and on. Even walking on the beach will be valueless if there is no specific motivation for it. To forestall the holiday's ennui, one must learn to have "an object in every walk" (*Glaucus*, p. 54); otherwise, it will be "utterly nil." What goal can one embrace? Why, marine biology—which Kingsley describes within a single page as having "allurement," "marvels," "wonder," and "romance" quite sufficient to "feed the play of fancy" (p. 39). Sensitized to the wonders of marine biology, one can not only have an object for every walk, but, even better, *acquire* objects on every walk.

"You cannot deny," Kingsley says, "that there is a fascination" in natural history (*Glaucus*, p. 5). No small part of that fascination is discovery—whether of a species new to science or one only new to you.

Like Philip Gosse, Kingsley sees the purest moments of pleasure in nature as epiphanies or, to use his term, "beaconpoints" (*Glaucus*, p. 29), which burn brightly in everlasting memory. "There is a mysterious delight in the discovery" of a new natural form, a delight derived in part from a renewed sense of nature's autonomy, as well as variety. Some readers of *Glaucus*

> can recollect, at their first sight of the Alpine Soldanella, the Rhododendron, or the black Orchis, growing upon the edge of the eternal snow, a thrill of emotion not unmixed with awe; a sense that they were, as it were, brought face to face with the creatures of another world; that Nature was independent of them, not merely they of her. (*Glaucus*, p. 28)

The thrill is of entering another world, perhaps because one feels a touch of weariness at human society. This conceit, of finding a world elsewhere, of transporting oneself there, intoxicated Victorian naturalists. The naturalist, seeking the wonders of the shore, can leave human society behind, finding in "the grating roar/Of pebbles which the waves draw back, and fling" not melancholy human analogues (such as Matthew Arnold heard at "Dover Beach"), but purely *other* objects, nonhuman, existing in their own fecund realm of endless possibility. From a human perspective, Arnold was disappointed by the "vast edges drear/And naked shingles of the world," but to a naturalist like Kingsley, the world really *does* "lie before us like a land of dreams, so various, so beautiful, so new."

The "beaconpoints" in Kingsley's prose often involve surprises, descriptions of unprepossessing objects that, when touched or uncovered, suddenly display unexpected complexity. One such incident involves "a great boulder" lying at "the extreme low-water mark" near the Torquay pier. Even the upper, visible side displays "a whole forest of sea-weeds, large and small." Far from being monotonous, this miniature forest would, "if you examined it closely," turn out to be "as full of inhabitants as those of the Amazon or the Gambia" (*Glaucus*, p. 113). (Note how the Amazon forests, in keeping with their status as sites of exotic discovery in the nineteenth century, rank here as the epitome of natural profusion.) But the "dense cover" atop the boulder hides its creatures all too well, whereas if the rock can be turned over, they will be exposed to view.

Kingsley is tantalized by what may lurk beneath the boulder, for as he says, "we can see dark crannies and caves beneath," and the site is "such a one as sea-beasts love to haunt" (*Glaucus*, p. 114). A lever becomes the key to this kingdom:

> Now the crowbar is well under it; heave, and with a will; and so, after five minutes' tugging, propping, slipping, and splashing, the boulder gradually tips over, and we rush greedily upon the spoil.
>
> A muddy dripping surface it is, truly, full of cracks and hollows, uninviting enough at first sight: let us look round it leisurely, to see if there are not materials enough there for an hour's lecture. (p. 114)

And of course there are more than enough. (Kingsley gives no thought to the havoc he may be wreaking on this little habitat; to him, as to most of his contemporaries, nature seemed unassailable, indestructible, without limits.) "The first object which strikes the eye" is a rather unappealing group of "milk-white slugs" (p. 114), with nothing visible at their anterior ends except a "yellow dimple" (p. 115). But the slugs have hidden splendors, for, if captured and "settled" in a jar of saltwater, "each will protrude a large chocolate-coloured head, tipped with a ring of ten feathery gills . . . of the loveliest white and primrose" (p. 115). Even sea-slugs can produce "elegant plumes."

Next to the slugs on the upturned boulder, Kingsley discovers some madrepores, *Caryophyllia Smithii.* He does not simply describe them, but rather writes as if his readers are standing right beside him, confronted with the dripping rock, making the discoveries on their own. As in the case of Lewes or Gosse, such a narrative technique adds drama to the account, the excitement of the chase:

> Next, what are those bright little buds, like salmon-coloured Banksia roses half expanded, sitting closely on the stone? Touch them; the soft part is retracted, and the orange flower of flesh is transformed into a pale pink flower of stone. (pp. 116–117)

And if the readers/adventurers wish to witness yet another amazing transformation of the little flowers of stone, they can

> drop them into this small bottle of sea-water, and from the top of each tower issues every half-second—what shall we call it?—a hand or a net of finest hairs, clutching at something invisible to our grosser sense. (p. 117)

These "tiny casting nets" belong to miniature barnacles that live right "on the lip" of the madrepore. Living there unsuspected, and seemingly wholly insignificant, the minute barnacles in fact are extremely complicated creatures. Kingsley points out that they swim free as infants, until like any self-respecting adult they transform themselves, "settle down," and build "a good stone house" to live in (p. 118). Kingsley's description of how the barnacles clutch "at something invisible to our grosser sense" beautifully suggests the activities of natural history. Like the barnacle, the naturalist hopes to capture something heretofore invisible and trusts that one can transcend the grosser senses to reach something fine, something never before revealed. The naturalist has what one acquaintance said Tennyson had: "a deep reverence . . . for the Unseen, the Undiscovered, the as yet Unrevealed."[16]

The effect of Kingsley's boulder passage is similar to many I have cited from Gosse and others: successive veils of nature's mystery are parted, revealing ever-smaller beautiful forms nested one inside the other. For Kingsley, too, the world becomes a wonderful set of Chinese boxes, an intricate puzzle, an immense mosaic. Like Gosse, Kingsley employs a rhetorical tactic that both pulls the reader inside nature's secrets and assumes that the reader is already an eager devotee: the first-person plural. Surely the reader is as impatient as Kingsley is to open the next box. So "we" find the boulder, "we" turn it over, "we" drop the barnacles into vials. We are all in this adventure together.

Even the most unprepossessing objects in nature hold secrets and unsuspected treasures, as Kingsley shows in his description of the spider-crab, *Maia Squinado*. Dredged up from the bottom and installed in an aquarium, the crab at first appears downright ugly—an unlikely source of wonder. Kingsley vividly personifies *Squinado* while conveying his quintessentially crustacean character:

> There he sits, twiddling his feelers (a substitute, it seems, with crustacea for biting their nails when they are puzzled), and by no means lovely to look on in vulgar eyes;—about the bigness of a man's fist; a round-bodied, spindle-shanked, crusty, prickly, dirty fellow, with a villainous squint, too, in those little bony eyes, which never look for a moment both the same way. (*Glaucus*, p. 180)

The crusty character, however, more than redeems himself, in Kingsley's eyes, by the service he performs as one of nature's scavengers; nothing could be dearer to Kingsley's heart than an efficient sanitary engineer. Once through with his pitch for health reform, though, Kingsley moves on to the examination of the crab's carapace. With the help of a "hand-magnifier" (p. 180), both "an animal forest" and a "vegetable" one (p. 182) can be discerned growing on the crab. "His whole back is covered with a little grey forest of branching hairs, fine as a spider's web," and each of these hairs reveals further complexities on it, "each branchlet carrying its little pearly ringed club," and "each club its rose-coloured polype" (p. 181). The miniature panorama continues to unfold when Kingsley examines the legs of *Squinado*, for on that leg grows, amid another copse of the grey polypes, a delicate straw-coloured Sertularia, branch on branch of tiny double combs, each teeth of the comb being a tube containing a living flower; on another leg another Sertularia, coarser, but still beautiful; and round it again has trained itself, parasitic on the parasite, plant upon plant of glass ivy, bearing crystal bells, each of which, too, protrudes its living flower; on another leg is a fresh species, like a little heather-bush of whitest ivory, and every needle leaf a polype cell—let us stop before the imagination grows dizzy with the contemplation of those myriads of beautiful atomies. (pp. 181–182)

The inexhaustibility of these "myriads of beautiful atomies" is indeed dizzying. The effect of Kingsley's description is to make readers feel as though they are falling through one level of reality, down a chute to another level, and then another—like Alice down the rabbit hole. Down from the crab to its leg, down to the Sertularia on its leg, down to the glass ivy on the Sertularia. Again, in Kingsley as in Gosse, the predominant tone is euphoric; nature is so vast, so inventive, so attentive to detail that one can never come to the end of it.

Ultimately, *Squinado*, that "crusty, prickly, dirty fellow," turns out to be beautiful in his own way. If Kingsley had been repelled by the crab's crusty appearance, he never would have discovered the delicate flora and fauna growing on its legs. But Kingsley welcomes any natural object, whether lovely in the traditional sense or not. Squeamish fastidiousness never hampers him in his investigations; he is relentlessly tactile, willing to poke and prod and grab. In fact, he positively delights in unearthing nature's "dirty, slimy" creations, and then showing how even they have their glories.

Perhaps the best known episode from *Glaucus* involves one such unattractive creature, a black slimy worm encountered on the beach whose true form is not apparent at first. When discovered, it appears to be merely a "black, shiny, knotted lump among the gravel, small enough to be taken up in a dessert spoon" (p. 136). But when picked up, the unimpressive lump expands enormously, to become a worm some nine feet long, although exceedingly slim. Kingsley urges the reader to place this specimen in an aquarium:

> Is it alive? It hangs, helpless and motionless, a mere velvet string across the hand. Ask the neighboring Annelids and the fry of the rock fishes, or put it into a vase at home, and see. It lies motionless, trailing itself across the gravel; you cannot tell where it begins or ends; it may be a dead strip of seaweed, . . . or even a tarred string. So thinks the little fish who plays over and over it, till he touches at last what is too surely a head. In an instant a bell-shaped sucker mouth has fastened to his side. (pp. 136–137)

With a great sense of drama, Kingsley details the fish's fate, how "the black lips" (p. 138) of the worm expand and draw the fish downward into "his cave of doom." With its dinner ingested, the worm, that "black murderer, slowly contracts again into a knotted heap, and lies, like a boa with a stag inside him, motionless and blest" (p. 138).

Certainly this black sea-boa is no conventionally pretty bit of nature, not beautiful in color or form, nor a stimulus to human sentimentality. It lacks all the charms of a robin or rhododendron. But to a naturalist like Kingsley, it is nonetheless quite miraculous, an example of "infinitely more marvellous Nature" (p. 138n). The worm is wonderful because it is complex and surprising, because Kingsley "saw it with [his] own eyes" (p. 138n), and because its ordinary actions can be described in dramatic terms. Kingsley injects anthropomorphism into his description by calling the worm a "murderer," but "murder" seems here to be a fairly neutral term for the process of killing what amounts to its dinner, since, after all, when satiated the worm is called "blest." God would appear to value the worm no less than any other animal, no matter how it makes its living. And looking at God's creatures, the naturalist, too, comes to cherish them all.

Kingsley, Canon of Chester and Anglican stalwart, makes frequent references to God in *Glaucus*. Arguing from Design and assuming that God is the fountainhead of all nature, Kingsley also continually emphasizes that the "boundless realms of beauty," the "fairy gardens of life and birth" (p. 133) in nature, exist apart from human concerns. This autonomy of nature he finds refreshing and even reassuring, since it frees him from the suffocating claustrophobia of egocentrism—an ailment often suffered by personae in Victorian poems. Victorian poets might be plagued by doubt, but by and large Victorian naturalists were a cheerful lot. God was in his heaven, and all seemed right in the natural world. Divine designs are amazing—never mind such niggling questions as how they came to be, and why some were no more. As Kingsley points out, if not made simply for God's own pleasure,

why are those strange microscopic atomies, the Diatomaceae and Infusoria, which fill every stagnant pool; which fringe every branch of sea-weed which form banks hundreds of miles long on the Arctic sea-floor, and the strata of whole moorlands; which pervade in millions the mass of every iceberg, and float aloft in countless swarms amid the clouds of the volcanic dust;—why are their tiny shells of flint as fantastically various in their quaint mathematical symmetry, as they are countless beyond the wildest dreams of the Poet? (pp. 132–133)

The self-replenishing profusion of nature provides for the naturalist an antidote to "vanity and self-interest" (p. 3), a spur to the imagination, an adjunct to faith. Drawn out of himself, the naturalist cannot fail to be entranced and cheered by the independent "multitudinous nations of the sea!" (p. 141). God seemed to enjoy the world; why should not we?

To my mind, Charles Kingsley is not the equal of Philip Henry Gosse as a natural history writer. Certainly Gosse devoted himself more extensively to natural history studies, and the body of Gosse's prose is far larger. But Kingsley finds many of the same rewards as Gosse in the close study of nature—heightened vision, an awareness of microscopic complexity, and natural profusion, and the pleasures of acquisition. And in *Glaucus, The Water-Babies*, and *Town Geology* as well, Kingsley succeeds in communicating his enthusiasm to the reader. In *Glaucus*, he quotes Gosse as saying that the "most interesting parts, by far, of published Natural History are those minute, but graphic particulars, which have been gathered up by an attentive watching of individual animals" (p. 190), and Kingsley adds his own hoard of particulars to the pile. *Glaucus; or, the Wonders of the Shore* is the vivid testament of a man "alive and awake in every pore to the beauty, the marvels of nature,"[17] the record "of happy evenings spent over the microscope and the vase, in examining, arranging, preserving, and noting down in the diary the wonders and labours of the happy day."[18]

Notes

1. George Perkins Marsh, *Man and Nature*, The John Harvard Library, ed. David Lowenthal (Cambridge, MA: Belknap Press-Harvard Univ. Press, 1965), pp. 15–16.

2. Brenda Colloms, *Charles Kingsley: The Lion of Eversley* (London: Constable, 1975), p. 25. On Kingsley the naturalist, see also Una Pope-Hennessy, *Canon Charles Kingsley* (New York: The Macmillan Company, 1949), chapter 10, "Marine Biology and the Crimean War."

3. Colloms, p. 194.

4. Colloms, p. 326.

5. Edmund Gosse, *The Life of Philip Henry Gosse F.R.S.* (London: Kegan Paul, Trench, Trübner and Co., Ltd., 1890), p. 289.

6. Larry K. Uffelman, *Charles Kingsley* (Boston: Twayne Publishers, 1979), p. 67.

7. Charles Kingsley, *Yeast: A Problem* (London: Macmillan and Co., 1888), p. 3.

8. Kingsley, *Yeast*, p. 126.

9. Charles Kingsley, *Alton Locke: Tailor and Poet*, ed. Herbert Van Thal (London: Cassell, 1967), p. 178.

10. Charles Kingsley, *Glaucus; or, the Wonders of the Shore* (London: Macmillan and Co., Ltd., 1903), p. 44. The text in this edition was revised and slightly expanded by Kingsley in 1873. The 1855 text is available in Charles Kingsley, *The Water-Babies and Glaucus* (London: J. M. Dent and Sons, 1908). Further *Glaucus* page references, to the *Glaucus; or, the Wonders of the Shore* edition, are made within the text.

11. Charles Kingsley, *The Water-Babies and Glaucus* (London: J. M. Dent and Sons, 1908), pp. 43–44. Further page references to this edition of *The Water-Babies* are made within the text.

12. Henry Walter Bates, *The Naturalist on the River Amazons* (London: John Murray, 1864; rpt. Berkeley, CA: Univ. of California Press, 1962), pp. 99–100.

13. Margaret Gatty, *Parables from Nature* (London: G. Bell & Sons Ltd., 1914), p. 4.

14. Quoted in the Introduction to Kingsley, *Water-Babies*, p. xi.

15. The twenty-year period to which Kingsley refers is from approximately mid-century to 1873, the time at which he wrote his fifth edition of *Glaucus*. His list of natural history books in the 1873 edition is far larger than it was in the 1855 original, attesting to the truth of his assertion that natural history had grown tremendously in popularity. There are hints, however, that its very popularity already had contributed to its eventual decline; too many nature-collectors had begun to ravage habitats, destroying the very thing they loved. In the 1855 edition, Kingsley says that one can find on the beach a species of shellfish, the Red Capsicum, in the "tens of thousands." By 1873, Kingsley had amended this prediction to "hundreds." *The Water-Babies and Glaucus* (London: J. M. Dent and Sons, 1908), p. 249; *Glaucus; or, the Wonders of the Shore* (London Macmillan and Co., Limited, 1903), p. 65.

16. Norman Page, ed., *Tennyson: Interviews and Recollections* (Totowa, NJ: Barnes & Noble Books, 1983), p. 50.

17. Dean Stanley, quoted in the Introduction to Kingsley, *Water-Babies*, p. ix.

18. Quoted in the Introduction to Kingsley, *Water-Babies*, p. viii.

10

Hugh Miller
and Evocative Geology

Where can be seen an intenser delight than that of children picking
up new flowers and watching new insects, or hoarding pebbles and
shells? . . . Every botanist who has had children with him in the
woods and the lanes must have noticed how eagerly they joined him
in his pursuits, how keenly they searched out plants for him, how
intently they watched while he examined them, how they over-
whelmed him with questions. . . . Having gained due familiarity with
the simpler properties of inorganic objects, the child should by the
same process be led on to a like exhaustive examination of the things
it picks up in its daily walks, the less complex facts they present being
alone noticed at first: in plants, the color, number and forms of the
petals and shapes of the stalks and leaves; in insects, the numbers of
the wings, legs, and antennae, and their colors. As they become fully
appreciated and invariably observed, further facts may be successively introduced.[1]   HERBERT SPENCER, "Education:
                                   Intellectual, Moral, and Physical," 1861

In the natural history prose of Philip Henry Gosse and Charles Kingsley,
several common traits display themselves repeatedly: particularity of
details, fascination with natural facts, vivification of nature whether
organic or not, imaginative journeys through apertures of scale, and joy
in nature's boundless variety. But the two naturalists were friends, and
both took much of their pleasure at the seaside. Is it merely for those
reasons that their works exhibit definite stylistic similarities? On the
contrary, the language used by Gosse and Kingsley expresses common
Victorian responses to natural history. They are not isolated eccentrics,
but type specimens of the naturalist species. Their natural history discourse is thoroughly representative. This becomes clear if one looks at
other writers completely outside the Gosse-Kingsley mold.

For example, *The Old Red Sandstone: or, New Walks in an Old Field*, by the Scots geologist Hugh Miller (1802–1856), takes its natural history rambles in an entirely different realm from that treated by *The Romance of Natural History*, *Evenings at the Microscope*, or *Glaucus*. Nevertheless, within what at first appears to be an unpromising area of inquiry— one dusty stratum or formation of ancient rock—Miller discovers many of the same rewards that lured Gosse and Kingsley to marine biology and microscopy. And in its prose, although somewhat more scientific and theoretical than Gosse's or Kingsley's, *The Old Red Sandstone* exploits many of the same motifs and devices.

Miller's book is worth looking at, first of all, simply as a cultural phenomenon. Published in 1841 (in book form), *The Old Red Sandstone* became a best-seller almost immediately. Lynn Barber, who devotes a chapter of her natural history survey to Miller, declares that after 1841 "Miller's name was known in every Victorian parlour."[2] She quotes Archibald Geikie, the geologist, as saying that Miller's books "were to be found in the remotest log-hut of the Far West, and on both sides of the Atlantic ideas of the nature and shape of geology were largely drawn from them."[3] Certainly references to Miller abound in the books by other naturalists; indeed, he takes on the status of a sort of Olympian god of natural history. Charles Kingsley mentions Miller several times in *Glaucus*, praising *The Old Red Sandstone* as the best possible example of "induction learnt from a narrow field of objects."[4] And Herbert Spencer, while maintaining in 1861 that "science excites poetry rather than extinguishes it," cites Miller as a prime practitioner of poetic science.[5]

Hugh Miller rose to such prominence for several reasons. First, he was a self-taught, working-class geologist who learned the science while toiling away at hard labor in stone quarries; such successes of working-class diligence of course appealed to the Victorians. (Recall how fond Kingsley and Samuel Smiles were of praising self-taught naturalists, such as Smiles' biographical subjects, Thomas Edward and Robert Dick.) Second, Miller, curiously enough, was a devoted Christian naturalist, just like Gosse and Kingsley. His was a geology wholly consistent with Christian doctrine. In the disturbing world of post-Lyellian geology, Miller's *Old Red Sandstone* "charmed everyone with the beauty and vigor of its knowledgeable creationist assertions," long after most geologists had renounced creationist ideas.[6] Two other Miller works were even more reassuring: *Footprints of the Creator* (1849) and *The Testimony of the Rocks* (1857). Third, Hugh Miller, the humble Scotsman, inherited the mantle of geologic glory from Charles Lyell, keeping geology before the public during the 1840s.[7] This was the decade when Adam Sedgwick became influential and when Ruskin advocated the study of geological landscapes in *Modern Painters*; these were "years of triumph" for geology.[8] Busily opening up vistas of vanished worlds, geologists, or more specifically paleontologists, were creating a sensation for the reading public. As Charles Kingsley maintained in *Glaucus*,

> it is a question whether Natural History would have ever attained its present honors, had not Geology arisen, to connect every other branch of Natural History with problems as vast and awful as they are captivating to the imagination.[9]

Miller's fame rode on just such "vast and awful" speculations.

Finally, Hugh Miller became one of the most beloved of Victorian naturalists because of the power of his style. Among his peers, the naturalists and geologists of his day, Miller was held in high esteem, both for the thoroughness of his knowledge and for the gracefulness of his descriptions. Roderick Murchison called his style "beautiful and poetical," and William Buckland claimed that he "would give his left hand to possess such powers of description as this man."[10] Twentieth-century critics who deal with Miller agree. Lynn Barber calls Miller's style "lucid," full of apt similes,[11] and Julian M. Drachman goes so far as to proclaim that Miller "was one of the very finest literary masters who have ever undertaken to write on scientific subjects."[12]

It is true that in some sections of *The Old Red Sandstone* Miller's style is gripping; some of his descriptions of landscape are Ruskinian in intensity, and his imaginative recreations of past eras are vivid. But frankly, for the modern reader, *The Old Red Sandstone* is a daunting book. Packed with lengthy notes, figures, lists, and technical details of fossil fish anatomy, Miller's book makes for heavy slogging. I cannot agree with Lynn Barber, who says that "reading it today, one can still understand why" *Sandstone* "was a bestseller."[13] On the contrary, I find it difficult to picture large numbers of people enjoying many sections of the book. The really interesting question about *The Old Red Sandstone* is not why the descriptive set-pieces appealed to people, but why even the seemingly tedious technical portions appealed. I would suggest this explanation: that the exhaustive technical descriptions in chapter after chapter of the book, those that to a modern eye seem numbing in their detail, were embraced by Victorian readers as a fabulous treasure-store of material facts. *The Old Red Sandstone* captivated the Victorian imagination, in part, because it fairly bristled with particulars.

In the context of nineteenth-century natural history, of course, ever-multiplying particulars were a never-ending source of delight. To Lewes,

Gosse, Kingsley, and so many others, particulars were the emblems of nature's unlimited bounty, best appreciated by the sharp, focused eye, the eye of literal or figurative microscopic vision. Miller, in fact, employs this aid, saying of the ichthyolites in his favorite formation that it does not "lessen the wonder that their nicer ornaments should yield their beauty only to the microscope."[14] And, like other naturalists of his time, Miller made a conscious attempt to refine his sight. He reports that after some practice he has "now learned to look at rocks with another eye" (p. 129), and notes also how, in making collections of rock, "the eye becomes practised in such researches" (p. 132), making his labors pay off. Like other naturalists, Miller becomes obsessed with the multiplicity of nature—that close examination of nature will yield more and more details that can be brought to light. When Miller realizes that nodules within the Old Red Sandstone formation have fossils inside them, he breaks open all he can find, until they are, in his words, "laid open":

> I set myself carefully to examine. The first nodule I laid open contained a bituminous-looking mass, in which I could trace a few pointed bones and a few minute scales. The next abounded in rhomboidal and finely-enamelled scales, of much larger size and more distinct character. I wrought on with the eagerness of a discoverer entering for the first time a *terra incognita* of wonders. Almost every fragment of clay, every splinter of sandstone, every limestone nodule, contained its organism,—scales, spines, plates, bones, entire fish . . . (p. 130)

Here is the same sense of wonder, and the same delight in minuteness, that one finds in Gosse and so many other Victorian naturalists.

Since Miller perceives dusty rocks as a wonderful *terra incognita*, he takes the value of all he finds within that land for granted. Each fragment, each splinter, each outline and angle and pattern is important. And all these minute details are reported at length—resulting in passages that I think are detailed to a fault. Collecting specimens until "half my closet walls are covered with the peculiar fossils of the Lower Old Red Sandstone" (p. 57), Miller reports on every characteristic of them. Fossil fish scales, somewhat incredibly, are painstakingly described:

> Each scale consists of a double plate,—an inner and an outer. The structure of the inner is not peculiar to the family or the formation: it is formed of a number of concentric circles, crossed by still minuter radiating lines,—the one described, and the other proceeding from a common centre. . . . All scales that receive their accessions of growth equally at their edges exhibit internally a corresponding character. The outer plate presents an appearance less common. It seems relieved into ridges that drop adown it like

sculptured threads, some of them entire, some broken, some straight, some
slightly waved . . . (p. 99)

The effect of page after page of such description can well be imagined.
Two points should be made about the passage quoted above. The first
is that, obviously, structural examination of fish scales belongs more to
the province of science than to that of natural history. *The Old Red
Sandstone* is a mixture of both. Far more than *Glaucus* or *The Romance
of Natural History*, Miller's book aims to understand the laws governing
its subject. It is often quite theoretical, speculating about geological
causes and effects: Why did this species disappear? How did this come to
be so well fossilized? In fact, Miller's book survives today mostly for
geologists who appreciate its contribution to the geological understanding of an important stratigraphic member.[15]

The second point to be made about the passage is that Miller's technical descriptions frequently metamorphose into evocative descriptions.
Far from being a dispassionate scientist, Miller displays an appreciation
for the aesthetic features of minutiae that rivals even that of Gosse or
Kingsley. Thus Miller's work, as its emphasis on microscopic vision and
collecting indicates, also fits within the definition of natural history I
have suggested.

While seeking to comprehend them, Miller nonetheless sees the fossils
as quite beautiful, and portrays them as such. And although the quoted
passage is mostly technical and devoid of emotion, toward the end it
begins to exhibit Miller's sense of beauty, expressed in his typical figurative language. The outer plate of the scale has ridges "like sculptured
threads," the implication being that they are not only minutely detailed—
some straight and some wavy—but also that they are finely wrought, like
tiny works of art. Other passages from *The Old Red Sandstone* make
more explicit Miller's perception of beauty. One fossil fish, *Diplacanthus*,
has "spines" on its fins, which "are of singular beauty" (p. 112). Besides
their singularity, so esteemed in Victorian natural history, they each
resemble "a bundle of rods, or rather, like a Gothic column, the sculptured semblance of a bundle of rods." Again, these curious objects are
perceived as valuable natural works of art.

Another fish, the *Osteolepis*, turns up in the sandstone breathtakingly
preserved as fossils that are also works of art. (Yet while giving the reader
an aesthetic appreciation of the fossils, Miller is equally concerned with
giving accurate scientific details, such as correct species names—often
obtained in consultation with other experts, such as Agassiz or Murchison.) *Osteolepis* is a completely armored fish, sporting "plaited mail" on

its head, "scaly mail" on its body, and fins with "mail of parallel and jointed bars" (p. 115). Likening the scales to armored mail is one Gossean touch, but Miller goes even further, stating that the "entire suit glittered with enamel." And that striking enamel is rife with detail, since "every plate, bar, and scale, was dotted with microscopic points." These points, or dots, remind Miller of the "circular perforations in a lace veil," an exquisite example of artistry.

Moving on to the next type of fish, the *Cheirolepis*, Miller finds that "an entirely different style obtains" (p. 115). In these fossils, Miller finds that

> the enamelled scales and plates glitter with minute ridges, that show like thorns in a December morning varnished with ice. Every ray of the fins presents its serrated edge; every occipital plate and bone its sculptured prominences; every scale its bunch of prickle-like ridges.

Whereas the first species of fossil presented, to the magnified vision, an effect "of lightness and beauty," the *Cheirolepis* appears more formidable. Miller succeeds at imbuing the primitive, ancient creature with a savage life; one can vividly imagine this glittering armored fish swimming in mysterious seas. And significantly, every detail of the fossil, if examined closely, generates more details: the fin has rays, which in turn have serrated edges, and so on.

The joyful discovery of particularities within particularities runs throughout *The Old Red Sandstone*. Learning to see ever more precise details of rocks and fossils has a scientific point, since the details facilitate classification and therefore understanding, but compiling them partakes of the old-fashioned pleasures of natural history. And since nature's variety is endless, there is always more to see. For example, while poking around in broken rock that contains the fossil fish, *Cephalaspis*, Miller notes that

> some of the specimens which exhibit this creature are exceedingly curious. In one a coprolite still rests in the abdomen; and a common botanist's microscope shows it thickly speckled over with minute scales, the indigestible exuviae of fish on which the animal had preyed. In the abdomen of another we find a few minute pebbles, . . . which had been swallowed by the creature attached to its food. (p. 77)

In part, these details are "wonderful" because they enable "us" (like Gosse, Kingsley, and so many other Victorian naturalists, Miller uses the first-person plural pronoun as a means of including the reader and dramatizing the hunt) to understand how these ancient fish lived. But the

minute scales inside the coprolite, inside the stomach, inside the abdo-
men, inside the *Cephalaspis*, again reveal the naturalist's pleasantly dizzy
sensation of confronting details that recede to infinity.

Geology and paleontology (or "oryctology," the older name that Miller
uses, p. 136) add the dimension of *time* to the naturalist's contemplation
of objects scattered throughout *space*, and for this reason, Miller says,
"geology, of all the sciences, addresses itself most powerfully to the
imagination" (p. 57). What Miller calls the "wonders of geology" appeal
to us because they "exercise every faculty of the mind,—reason, memory,
imagination" (p. 119). God's infinite variety in nature, where truth is
always more wonderful than fiction, is revealed to the geologist in layers
of time, each containing objects infinitely individuated. Miller at one
point in his researches worries that the teeth of one fish he describes are
too bizarre to be believed. His colleague Louis Agassiz reassures him:

> Do not be deterred, if you have examined minutely, by any dread of being
> deemed extravagant. The possibilities of existence run so deeply into the
> extravagant, that there is scarcely any conception too extraordinary for
> nature to realize. (p. 78)

This is the faith of the naturalist: optimism about nature's endless extravagance.

Miller always keeps before the reader the motif of discovery. He speaks
of himself as a "sort of Robinson Crusoe of geology" (p. 137). In part,
he means that he was cut off from professional contacts for years,
because of his class, but Miller is a Robinson Crusoe of geology also
in the sense that he has a whole new world to explore in the layers
of the Old Red Sandstone. What he finds in that world is, invariably,
an "amazing multiplicity of being" (p. 227), "myriads" of creatures
and forms that are "innumerable" and "multitudinous." The realm that
he has stumbled upon is rich beyond comprehension: one two-mile
section of shoreline bounded by the Old Red Sandstone is so complex
that "years of examination and inquiry would fail to exhaust it" (p. 209).
Since the lost world now represented by the Old Red Sandstone is
dauntingly intricate, Miller opens his account of it with a personal
anecdote that shows how he came to it in all innocence and ignorance
and gradually learned about it. The lesson—quite overtly stated—is that
the reader can, too.

The opening chapter of Miller's book invites one to begin a voyage of
discovery. The very first sentence is Miller's "advice to young working
men desirous of bettering their circumstances"; they should not bother
with what "is misnamed pleasure" (presumably drinking and the like) but

rather pursue "study" (p. 33). Putting faith in the chimera of Chartism in hopes of gaining the right to vote, says Miller, is a waste of time. How much better to "learn to make right use of your eyes: the commonest things are worth looking at,—even stones and weeds, and the most familiar animals." Heeding this familiar naturalist's injunction will lead to happiness. Miller can attest to that with a "simple narrative" (p. 35) of his own life. Twenty years ago he had gone off to work in a stone quarry, fearful about the rigors of such a life. Almost immediately, however, this healthful outdoor labor opens Miller's eyes to the world around him. He notices birds, the "prospect" around him, clear air, a waveless bay, and pleasant wooded slopes.

Most important of all, Miller discovers what is hidden inside some of the rocks being quarried:

> In the course of the first day's employment I picked up a nodular mass of blue limestone, and laid it open by a stroke of the hammer. Wonderful to relate, it contained inside a beautifully finished piece of sculpture—one of the volutes, apparently, of an Ionic capital. (p. 39)

Amazed, he wondered: "Was there another such curiosity in the whole world?" He soon realizes that the entire area of sedimentary deposits around the quarry is "a richer scene of wonder than I could have fancied in even my dreams" (p. 40). The layers of rock are, Miller realizes, like leaves in a book or "a herbarium," with "the pictorial records of a former creation in every page" (p. 40). Paging through this book of nature, the incipient geologist finds himself

> lost in admiration and astonishment, . . . my very imagination paralysed by an assemblage of wonders that seemed to outrival in the fantastic and the extravagant even its wildest conceptions. (p. 41)

Brought face to face with this "assemblage of wonders," Miller embarks on a voyage of discovery through time and space. Unlike Wallace or Bates, Miller did not need to journey to remote jungles of Malaysia or the Amazon to encounter natural curiosities; they are amply entombed in the rock beneath his feet. He thinks of himself ever after as a typical rambling naturalist, picking up flotsam from the shore, saying of his life: "I have been an explorer of caves and ravines, a loiterer along sea-shores, a climber among rocks, a labourer in quarries. My profession was a wandering one" (p. 42). Interestingly, when Miller finds his first belemnite fossil (part of an extinct cuttle-fish), he compares it to a strange stone brought home by a relative from Java; both are exotic curios, but Miller's exotic locale is the ordinary landscape of Britain.

After opening thus on a personal note, *The Old Red Sandstone* proceeds to the enumeration of countless scales, ribs, prickles, tubercules, spines, fins, and bones of vanished fish. Chapter after chapter catalogues these features, but they are enlivened by similes and fresh metaphors— spines that "run deep into the body, as a ship's masts run deep into her hulk" (p. 113), a *Coccosteus* shaped either like "a boy's kite" or like an "ancient one-sided shovel which we see sculptured on old tombstones" (p. 74), or the head-plates of a fish that are "burnished like ancient helmets" (p. 98). Along with the details of specimens, Miller includes extremely precise descriptions of geological strata and rock types, since they are the sets against which the fish—the *"dramatis personae"* (p. 65) of the story—come alive. Miller himself realizes that the thoroughness of his report may overwhelm the unsuspecting reader: "I am particular, at the risk, I am afraid, of being tedious, in thus describing the geology of this northern country" (p. 56). He continues to be particular because the truth of his subject only exists in particulars. Only if one can amass all the facts can one discover the truth about them.

The facts—fragments of fish, plants, and other organisms—are strewn throughout the Old Red Sandstone and its attendant rocks like pieces of a puzzle. Miller is fond of telling stories of how those pieces have been reconstructed, and their meaning deciphered. He applauds Cuvier as a master of the craft of reconstructing bits of bone; they were to him clear "signs," though "incomprehensible to every one else" (p. 153). The current master of the art, though, is the ichthyologist whom Miller unabashedly reveres: Louis Agassiz. Miller tells the dramatic story of how Agassiz daringly reconstructed "the huge crustacean of Balruddery." Murchison, Buckland, and several other authorities had been baffled by the collection of "fragments of scaly rhombs, of scaly crescents, of scaly circles, with scaly parallelograms attached to them." No one would "hazard a conjecture" about their nature (p. 154).

Agassiz, however, "glanced over the collection" with a masterful eye. One strange specimen stood out; "his eye brightened as he contemplated it" (p. 154). Miller dramatically recounts Agassiz's revelation:

> "I will tell you," he said, turning to the company,—"I will tell you what these are,—the remains of a huge lobster." He arranged the specimens in the group before him with as much apparent ease as I have seen a young girl arranging the pieces of ivory or mother-of-pearl in an Indian puzzle. A few broken pieces completed the lozenge-shaped shield; two detached specimens placed on its opposite sides furnished the claws; two or three semi-rings with serrated edges composed the jointed body; the compound figure, which but a minute before had so strongly attracted his attention,

furnished the terminal flap; and there lay the huge lobster before us, palpable to all. (pp. 154, 156)

The scene radiates the joy of discovery and conveys the incredible sensation of having an extinct and hardly even suspected animal loom up suddenly, "palpable to all." Agassiz solves the puzzle with exceptional skill, but Miller's description of the problem as being an "Indian puzzle" is not unusual. Like most Victorian naturalists, he perceives nature as a mosaic made up of infinite pieces, which fit together in surprising ways. Miller finds such surprises everywhere he looks, albeit usually without such theatrical fanfare. Who but Miller, or another Victorian naturalist perhaps, would take the trouble to count, and then recount for a reader, how many fossil organisms reside in "a single cubic inch" of shale from the Eathie Lias? Miller had the patience to tally there "about eighty molluscous organisms, mostly ammonites, and minute striated scallops" (p. 194).

Gradually, Hugh Miller shifts his focus away from the particularities of the fish and other fossils and toward the longer view—the scenery, or, as he calls it, the "physiognomy" (p. 201) of landscape. At this point, especially in chapter XI, Miller demonstrates his formidable descriptive powers for scenery. Very much like the Ruskin and Gosse passages with which I ended Chapter 6, Miller's descriptions of scenery depend on a hypothetical traveler who walks through the varying countryside. One long passage illustrates how differing rock types affect the manifestation of terrain. At first, "the traveller passes through a mountainous region of gneiss" (p. 201). Here the hills are "bulky" but "shapeless," and somewhat somber: they "raise their huge backs so high over the brown dreary moors" that stretch away at their feet. The traveler then "pursues his journey" and

> enters a district of micaceous schist. The hills are no longer truncated, or the moors unbroken: the heavy ground-swell of the former landscape has become a tempestuous sea, agitated by powerful winds and conflicting tides. The picturesque and somewhat fantastic outline is composed of high sharp peaks, bold craggy domes, steep broken acclivities, and deeply serrated ridges; and the higher hills seem as if set round with a framework of props and buttresses, that stretch out on every side like the roots of an ancient oak. (p. 202)

Noteworthy here, as in the selections from Gosse and Ruskin, is the energy invested in the landforms. They seem almost to have life—the gneiss hills raising their backs and the mica hills moving as if agitated by inner anxiety. The animation of the landscape is accompanied by formal precision; Miller is careful to tell that the ridges are "deeply serrated," and that the acclivities are "steep" and "broken."

From the mica landscape, the traveler "passes on, and the landscape varies" (p. 202). At times the hills become "naked skeletons," sterile and foreboding. Other rocks shape the landscape into soft, swelling forms, over which streams "linger." These differences Miller characterizes as "styles" (p. 202) of scenery, each with its own "peculiarities" (p. 204). Miller's schema is reminiscent of Ruskin in *Modern Painters*; Miller also notes the slaty crystalline rocks and then looks at the resultant landscapes with a painter's eye. It is even reminiscent of Ruskin's attempts, in *The Poetry of Architecture*, to link human societies and their styles with landscape.

Later in this scenery chapter, Miller guides the geological novice on an exploration of a certain "rocky trench" (p. 210) cut into the sandstone. "Will the reader," he asks, be willing to devote just a few minutes to walking about in this "solitary recess"? The answer is—of course. "We pass onwards," then, into the "denuded hollow" (p. 210). The stream-cut ravine is a window into geological time, but Miller equally appreciates the natural profusion of forms that live along the rock. In a passage that would do Ruskin justice—one that Millais would be proud to capture in paint, perhaps as a background for Ophelia's downstream glide—Miller views the undergrowth with an artist's eye:

> We enter along the bed of the stream. A line of mural precipices rises on either hand,—here advancing in ponderous overhanging buttresses, there receding into deep damp recesses, tapestried with ivy, and darkened with birch and hazel. A powerful spring, charged with lime, comes pouring by a hundred different threads over the rounded brow of a beetling crag, and the decaying vegetation around it is hardening into stone. The cliffs vary their outline at every step, as if assuming in succession all the various combinations of form that constitute the wild and picturesque; and the pale hues of the stone seem, when brightened by the sun, the very tints a painter would choose to heighten the effect of his shades, or to contrast most delicately with the luxuriant profusion of bushes and flowers that wave over the higher shelves and crannies. (p. 211)

This is a natural tangle that seems an example of Carlylean "Natural Supernaturalism," because every element within the description seems alive or sensitive, in most cases fairly bursting with energy. The spring is "powerful," "charged," and does not merely flow but "comes pouring" over the rock. The buttresses "advance" and "overhang" the visitor. The crag has a "brow" like a face, and it "beetles" overhead.

Besides being vibrant, the seemingly small slice of scenery is visually crowded and complex. The stream moves through a "hundred" little channels, the cliffs constantly "vary their outline," and overlapping, changeable hues of dappled light and shade cover the stone. The cliff face is riddled with crannies, in which grow countless bushes and flowers. Miller continues his artist's metaphors, since the precipices seem to him "murals" and the luxuriant vegetation forms "tapestries." The very stone itself has chosen the exact "tints a painter would choose." How like Ruskin—who, in a famous "word painting" passage from *Modern Painters IV* (part V, chapter XI, section 6), notes how in one scene "on the broken rocks of the foreground . . . the mosses seem to set themselves consentfully and deliberately to the task of producing the most exquisite harmonies of colour in their power." The mosses "gather over" the rock "in little brown bosses, like small cushions of velvet made of mixed threads of dark ruby silk." Ruskin, too, looks at nature and sees a preexistent work of art, here mosses forming a beautifully "embroidered" cushion.

Miller continues his description, keeping it charged with a nearly personified energy. The banks become "steeper and more inaccessible," and the dell "wilder and more deeply wooded." The stream, restless, "frets and toils at our feet" (p. 211). Flowers multiply in an even "richer profusion . . . a thick mantling of ivy and honeysuckle." And the water unceasingly churns "foam, which, flung from the rock, incessantly" revolves in the stream's eddy (p. 212). Just when the rambler begins to feel claustrophobic, even slightly threatened by nature's demonstrated relentless fecundity, Miller changes tactics. "Mark now the geology of the ravine" (p. 212), he instructs. For this lush abundance of nature extends not only throughout the present—in space—but also backwards, throughout time. The rocks themselves, on close inspection, are found to be "a place of sepulture . . . where the dead lie by myriads" (p. 212). The river "brawls along," but Miller finds that

> it is through a vast burial-yard that it has cut its way,—a field of the dead so ancient, that the sepulchres of Thebes and Luxor are but of the present day in comparison,—resting-places for the recently departed, whose funerals are just over. These mouldering strata are charged with remains, scattered and detached as those of a churchyard, but not less entire in their parts,—occipital bones, jaws, teeth, spines, scales,—the dust and rubbish of a departed creation. (pp. 217–218)

To the consideration of these departed multitudes Miller now turns.

As he opens chapter XII, Miller shifts from the present to the past, attempting to pass "from the dead to the living" (p. 219), and reanimate the fossils now quiescent in the rock. From "consideration of the Old Red Sandstone as it exists in *space*," Miller changes to the description of the rock in previous "*time*,—during the succeeding periods of its formation, and when its existences lived and moved as the denizens of primeval oceans" (p. 219). In this imaginative sweep, the geologist encompasses what Tennyson calls the "terrible Muses,"[16] terrible to think about: the wastes of time and space. Literary Victorians frequently dwelled upon such vastness, as did Carlyle who spoke of the "two grand fundamental world-enveloping Appearances, SPACE and TIME." Miller proves himself especially adept at invoking the power of time. In the most famous and most vivid passages of *The Old Red Sandstone* Miller achieves what Carlyle hoped for in *Sartor Resartus*: a magician's hat that would enable one to travel backward in time (chapter VIII, book III). As Herr Teufelsdröckh says, "Had we but the Time-annihilating Hat, to put on for once only, we should see ourselves in a World of Miracles."

A world of miracles, most assuredly, is what Hugh Miller finds. In his mind's eye, the beautiful but static fossils come alive again. For Miller, successive geologic eras become acts within a play; when each is over, the "curtain rises, and the scene is new" (p. 245). Amazingly, with Miller as a guide, the reader is invited to imagine himself walking through the forests of the past, breathing in "the rank stream of decaying vegetation" that "forms a thick blue haze" of "carbonic acid gas" (p. 257). Through the "ancient forest," Miller confidently says, "we pursue our walk" (p. 249). It is indeed, as Barber maintains, "precisely as a field naturalist setting out on an exploring expedition that he enters the geological past."[17]

The ancient geologic scenes in Hugh Miller's imagination exhibit the same qualities of particularity and boundless variety found in his contemporary landscapes. His assemblage of Silurian organisms is especially striking. These creatures lived in the period before the Old Red Sandstone fish appeared, the period so thoroughly documented by Sir Roderick Murchison in his 1838 scientific tome, *The Silurian System*. Rocks from the Silurian era show life to have existed on "four distinct platforms," all of them teeming with multifarious creatures. Miller scans each story of Siluria:

> Life abounded on these platforms, and in shapes the most wonderful. The peculiar encrinites of the group rose in miniature forests, and spread forth their sentient petals by millions and tens of millions amid the waters; vast ridges of corals, peopled by their innumerable builders,—numbers without number,—rose high amid the shallows; the chambered shells had become abundant,—the simpler testacea still more so; extinct forms of the graptolite or sea-pen existed by myriads. (p. 221)

Here no less than in the "denuded hollow" of the stream's ravine, nature teems with wonderfully autonomous forms. Petals are "sentient," and coral skeletons are "peopled" with living tenants. Everywhere Miller looks, nature is without limits: curious and strange organisms swim and wave by "millions," "myriads," "numbers without number." Life abounds. And even better, nature in its endless multiplication creates enduring monuments, works of meticulous beauty, "in shapes the most wonderful": chambered shells, vast ridges of coral, miniature petrified forests.

But these creatures pass away, and the history of the Old Red Sandstone period opens, Miller surmises, like the first scene in *The Tempest*— "amid thunders and lightnings, the roar of the wind" (p. 224). Fish take command of the seas, "which literally swarmed with life," including "miniature forests of algae, and . . . waters darkened by immense shoals of fish" (p. 226). Mysterious catastrophes at times overtake the ichthyolites. Miller envisions one such period, of disease or volcanic upheaval, and its aftermath:

> The period of death passed, and over the innumerable dead there settled a soft muddy sediment, that hid them from the light, bestowing upon them such burial as a November snowstorm bestows on the sere and blighted vegetation of the previous summer and autumn. For an unknown space of time, represented in the formation by a deposit about fifty feet in thickness, the waters of the depopulated area seem to have remained devoid of animal life. A few scales and plates then begin to appear. (p. 231)

These dreary, almost incomprehensible wastes of time and death Miller finds awesome to contemplate. The stretches of time are not entirely wastes, however, for nature continues its generation. With the naturalist's faith in variety, as well as the Christian's in God, Miller summarizes the process:

> The process went on. Age succeeded age, and one stratum covered up another. Generations lived, died, and were entombed in the ever-growing depositions. Succeeding generations pursued their instincts by myriads, happy in existence, over the surface which covered the broken and perishing remains of their predecessors. (p. 233)

Not only does God experiment, quite joyously it seems, with "an inexhaustible variety of design expatiated freely within the limits of the ancient type" (p. 233), but the animals themselves, although doomed to perish, enjoy themselves while alive. Like Gosse's microscopic animalcules, they are "happy in existence."

The assumption of happy fulfillment on the part of each minute creature rescues Miller's contemplation of the ages from despair. The spectacle can continue with its pageantry of form:

> The curtain rises, and the scene is new. The myriads of the lower formation have disappeared, and we are surrounded, on an upper platform, by the existences of a later creation. There is sea all around, as before; and we find beneath a dark-coloured muddy bottom, thickly covered by a dwarf vegetation. . . . Forms of life essentially different career through the green depths, or creep over the ooze. Shoals of *Cephalaspides*, with their broad arrow-like heads and their slender angular bodies, feathered with fins, sweep past like clouds of cross-bow bolts in an ancient battle. We see the distinct gleam of scales, but the forms are indistinct and dim. . . . A huge crustacean, of uncouth proportions, stalks over the weedy bottom, or burrows in the hollows of the banks. (p. 245)

Again, the paleontological panorama is graphically animated and convincing, thanks to Miller's characteristic devices: subjective plurality ("we see"), figurative language ("like clouds of cross-bow bolts"), and active, concrete diction. Within a sensory setting, of ooze, a weedy bottom, green light, and gleaming scales, mysterious fish and other creatures "career," "sweep," and "stalk."

With such charged description, Miller succeeds in evoking an air of portentous mystery. Readers feel irresistably drawn into the remote geological past, as they might be drawn into the jungle of the present by Darwin or Wallace or Bates. In the final few pages of his book, Miller rises to a crescendo of detail and drama, as he imagines the sea receding to make way for the thick vegetable riot on land that will eventually compact into coal. The transition from sea to land Miller achieves by projecting himself into a boat that approaches the shore. He thus conflates a change of time with one of space:

> The water is fast shallowing. Yonder passes a broken branch, with the leaves still unwithered; and there floats a tuft of fern. Land, from the mast-head! land! land!—a low shore thickly covered with vegetation. Huge trees of wonderful form stand out far into the water. There seems no intervening beach. A thick hedge of reeds, tall as the mast of pinnaces, runs along the deeper bays, like water-flags at the edge of a lake. A river of vast volume comes rolling from the interior, darkening the water for leagues with its slime and mud. (p. 255)

Here the panoply of botanical forms, on a gigantic scale, is comparable only to deliberate works of art. Trees have "bright and glossy stems" that "seem rodded like Gothic columns," and their leaves are ranged in tiers, each resembling "a coronal wreath or an ancient crown."

As usual in Miller's scientific fantasies, the sheer quantity—not to mention diversity—of natural forms astonishes. Like the cubic inch of shale packed with mollusks, the jungle of bygone eons is crammed with curious specimens. The growth of the "vegetable kingdom" displays "amazing luxuriance" (p. 257). Organisms appear, "strangely-formed" (p. 256). Especially odd is one that swoops suddenly into view:

> But what monster of the vegetable world comes floating down the stream,—now circling round in the eddies, now dancing on the ripple, now shooting down the rapid? It resembles a gigantic star-fish, or an immense coach-wheel divested of the rim. (p. 256)

This truly bizarre plant, set off well by Miller's interrogative introduction, looks like some Rotifer or diatom that Philip Gosse might have sighted, but enlarged to monstrous size. Like a gigantic Rotifer, it displays ingenious appurtenances—cylinders, prickles, and "lance-like shoots."

In fact, one of the most interesting features of Miller's culminating sequence is his mention of the microscope. In O'Brien's story "The Diamond Lens," the protagonist longed to enter the microscopic world, temporarily deluded into thinking that the beautiful creatures there were compatible with his own size. Likewise, in the example I cited previously from Alfred Russel Wallace, the Malay people became terrified when looking through a microscope, assuming that the insects there illuminated had actually grown gigantic. For Hugh Miller, too, the wonders of nature on a microscopic scale can seem as tangible as those on a normal human scale. Size ranges are even interchangeable:

> And then these gigantic reeds!—are they not mere varieties of the common horse-tail of our bogs and morasses, magnified some sixty or a hundred times? Have we arrived at some such country as the continent visited by Gulliver, in which he found thickets of weeds and grass tall as woods of twenty years' growth, and lost himself amid a forest of corn fifty feet in height? The lesser vegetation of our own country,—reeds, mosses, and ferns,—seems here as if viewed through a microscope: the dwarfs have sprung up into giants. (p. 256)

Since the "lesser vegetation" of England did spring up, figuratively, into giants during the Fern Craze, it is appropriate that Miller points out how they literally reigned as giants in the past. The change of scale from gigantic to microscopic actually did take place in this instance. As Kingsley would say, nothing is impossible to nature.

As the author of such powerful passages as these, Hugh Miller captivated Victorian readers. They followed his geological narratives with rapt attention. They were willing even to follow him through the minute intricacies of serrated fish scales, if they were presented as astonishing particularities. So beloved did Miller become that his legions of admirers were stunned to learn that he had died by his own hand. In 1856, the last year of his life, Miller became increasingly agitated and fearful that robbers would break into and despoil his collections. He began to have hallucinations. After one especially terrifying vision, Hugh Miller scribbled a note to his wife saying that he could not bear the horror of his dream; what the horror was, he did not say. Then he shot himself.[18] Perhaps all the sepulchral imagery of his geology books presaged his embrace of death. In any case, the circumstances created a most difficult situation for his admirers: suicide was a sin. A public outcry insisted that Miller be spared that stigma. Was it not unthinkable that such a hero could have deliberately killed himself? Indeed it was. Miller was declared temporarily insane at the time of his death and granted Christian burial.

Hugh Miller advanced the science of geology by his patient research and careful speculation. But he advanced the cause of natural history as well, since geology, his chosen science, was for him preeminently an aesthetic and evocative study. Miller's widow remarked on this in her introduction to his posthumous volume, *Popular Geology*: "My dear husband, did, indeed, bring to his science all that fondness, while he found in it much of that kind of enjoyment, which we are wont to associate exclusively with the love of art."[19] Miller himself, puzzling about the antagonism sometimes found between science and poetry, unequivocally declared them brothers. Along with its particularities of crinoid and fish scale, geology can claim the evocative sweep—the poetry—of nature's variety in time. Just before his own death, Miller thought about that terrible Muse of poetry:

> The stony science, with buried creations for its domains, and half an eternity charged with its annals, possesses its realms of dim and shadowy fields, in which troops of fancies already walk like disembodied ghosts in the old fields of Elysium, and which bid fair to be quite dark and uncertain enough for all the purposes of poesy for centuries to come.[20]

Firm in his conception of the poetry of the "stony science," Hugh Miller garnered a wide audience for his works, an audience appreciative of this clear thinker whose "relation to nature and the knowledge of nature" was yet "above all a personal and emotional one."[21] Personal, artistic, emotional responses to rocks and fossil fish—these mark Miller as a naturalist, and *The Old Red Sandstone* as natural history discourse.

Notes

1. Herbert Spencer, "Education: Intellectual, Moral, and Physical," in *The Humboldt Library of Popular Science Literature*, Nos. 1–12 (New York: The Humboldt Publishing Co., n.d.), p. 284.

2. Lynn Barber, *The Heyday of Natural History: 1820–1870* (Garden City, NY: Doubleday and Company, Inc., 1980), p. 230.

3. Barber, p. 236.

4. Charles Kingsley, *Glaucus; or, the Wonders of the Shore* (London: Macmillan and Company, Limited, 1903), p. 218.

5. Spencer, p. 271.

6. Dennis R. Dean, "'Through Science to Despair': Geology and the Victorians," in *Victorian Science and Victorian Values: Literary Perspectives*, ed. James Paradis and Thomas Postlewait, Annals of the New York Academy of Sciences, vol. 360 (New York: The New York Academy of Sciences, 1981), p. 120.

7. Barber, p. 225.

8. Dean, p. 120.

9. Kingsley, *Glaucus*, p. 11.

10. Both quoted in Barber, p. 230.

11. Barber, p. 231.

12. Julian M. Drachman, *Studies in the Literature of Natural Science* (New York: The Macmillan Company, 1930), p. 131.

13. Barber, p. 231.

14. Hugh Miller, *The Old Red Sandstone; or, New Walks in an Old Field* (London: J. M. Dent and Co., n.d.), p. 114. Further page citations are made within the text.

15. A selection from *The Old Red Sandstone* is among those anthologized in one recent collection of geological literature, *Language of the Earth*, ed. Frank H. T. Rhodes and Richard O. Stone (New York: Pergamon Press, 1981). Miller's selection, however, is included not for its scientific value, but rather in the section "Geologists Are Also Human," pp. 36–41.

16. Noted in Dean, p. 115. Try as I might, I have been unable to track down the source of this particular quotation. However, Tennyson was fascinated by astronomy and geology, and recollections of the poet by those who knew him prove that he often mused on the vastness of geological time. For example, William Allingham quotes Tennyson as exclaiming: "Look at that hill (pointing to the one before the large window), it's four hundred millions of years old;—think of that!" In Norman Page, ed., *Tennyson: Interviews and Recollections* (Totowa, NJ: Barnes & Noble Books, 1983), p. 53. Another acquaintance reported of the poet: "This led him to speak of prehistoric things, and of the wonders which geology had brought to light. He referred to the period of the Weald, when there was a mighty estuary, like that of the Ganges, where we then stood; and when gigantic lizards, the iguanodon, etc., were the chief of living things." In Page, p. 180.

17. Barber, p. 231.

18. Carroll Lane Fenton and Mildred Adams Fenton, *Giants of Geology* (Garden City, NY: Doubleday & Company, Inc., 1952), p. 212.

19. From the Introductory Résumé to Hugh Miller, *Popular Geology: A Series of Lectures Read Before the Philosophical Institution of Edinburgh, With Descriptive Sketches from a Geologist's Portfolio* (Boston: Gould and Lincoln, 1859), p. 12.

20. Miller, *Popular Geology*, p. 127.

21. Drachman, p. 132.

Conclusion

During this summer [Philip Gosse] occasionally brought up to the Cottage his microscope or some natural history objects, and gave a familiar lecture on them. Some young friends were staying with us, and we all benefited by his interesting and cheerful remarks. These occasional visits were looked forward to by us all with great pleasure. The party sometimes accompanied him to the beach at Oddicombe or Babbicombe, when he always took great pains to show his mode of collecting, and sometimes brought out new and curious and lovely creatures, when we gathered around and exclaimed, in our ignorance of such matters, "How beautiful! how wonderful!"[1] ELIZA GOSSE

Naturalists, George Henry Lewes had pronounced, could practice their hobby wherever they pleased, and never come to the end of it. The objects of nature were everywhere; curiosity would never slacken. The natural history that captivated Lewes and so many Victorians was a personal, evocative, aesthetic science, a science that transmuted natural objects into texts. Unlike a pure scientist, a naturalist does not look at the objects of nature primarily in order to understand them. A scientist marshals them into categories, attaches labels that announce relationships and connections. But to the naturalist, all of nature's creations are like snowflakes: no two exactly alike. A naturalist looks at the objects of nature—just to *look* at them, whether in isolation or in pleasing arrangement. Shells, fish scales, fossils, butterfly wings, or fern spores: when intently seen, they intoxicate the eye. They amaze with their complexity. They tantalize with shapes, colors, textures; patterns and ridges and whorls. And more important, with their concrete qualities, they enliven language. The discourse of natural history glories in diversity, finding nature beautiful because it is multitudinous. Full of wonders, replete with marvels gleaned perhaps during a ramble, or a leisurely evening at the microscope, nature can always surprise with its singularity. And the singular specimen—captured, possessed, displayed, described—is the naturalist's beckoning lure.

Why, during the nineteenth century, was the lure so irresistible? In part, the popularity of natural history was a beneficiary of the prestige of other sciences. Histology, cell biology, organic chemistry, paleontology, physics—their advances of understanding and transformations of human life loomed large. Applied science had obvious power, and so scientific terminology and metaphors soon permeated Victorian thinking: science itself became a "norm of truth."[2] Reverence for the scientific method cast its glow over natural history, although the pursuit itself was not a rigorous one. Rambling and even dilatory, the amateur Victorian naturalist was nonetheless engaged in a fashionable science of sorts, with Latinate nomenclature to prove it. Naturalists put their own twist on technical Latin diction. Satisfyingly specific, names like *Melicerta* and *Squinado, Opuntia* and *Eudorina* and *Cheirolepis* became pleasurable verbal analogues for the novelty and strangeness of the creatures they identified. Even though such names classified and thus standardized nature, they rolled off the tongue like orotund verbal objects; to amateur naturalists, they became specimens themselves.

The Victorian passion for quantification, classifying, and naming also gave a boost to natural history. One could fearlessly face the oddities of the natural world by measuring them, taming them, making them comprehensible and delimited. Measurement is a form of possession. Like Latin tags, the numbers attached to nature could be a source of pleasure in themselves. For example, when a purported fossil whale skeleton was exhibited in 1837 at the Cosmorama in London, a handbill summed up its features in this way: "The wonderful remains of an enormous head, 18 feet in length, 7 feet in breadth, and weighing 1,700 pounds. The complete eighty-eight bones were discovered in excavating a passage for the purpose of a railway, at a depth of 75 feet from the surface of the ground, in Louisiana, and at the distance of 160 miles from the sea."[3]

The acme of such Victorian quantification, according to one observer, occurred in the 1910 edition of the *Encyclopedia Britannica*. There the supreme culmination (and perhaps last great expression) of nineteenth-century materialism can be found in a "penchant for lists" and in the endless cataloguing of the "natural world in those numbingly detailed statistics of miles, inches, degrees, and cubic feet that some of us may remember from our childhood reading of Jules Verne."[4] Verne's scientific characters embodied a powerful Victorian urge: go forth and appraise the world. Once you have taken its measure, it is yours.

Victorian determination to quantify the earth created a niche for the naturalist to continue on an ever-wider scale the eighteenth-century activity of acquiring and describing natural objects. Naturalists enumerated the features of the earth; biologists or geologists of more theoretical bent could explain them. Thus naturalists could ally themselves with science, and even, as in the case of P. H. Gosse, perform a valuable scientific service, while still being motivated primarily by aesthetic and emotional pleasure. Science stamped natural history with the imprimatur of respectability. Natural theology elevated it to a devotional exercise. And the British energy for exploration served as its accomplice. England might perhaps have seemed tame by the nineteenth century, not worth investigating in minute detail, but an infusion of tropical life forms fired an interest in its natural history.

In fact, the Victorian mystique of the tropics—of hot, fecund habitats—cannot be overstated. Africa, Malaysia, the Amazon Basin, all blended into one powerful metaphor of nature as a riot of invention, like Darwin's famous tangled bank. In considering Darwin, Loren Eiseley talks about the different effects of British and tropical nature. Eiseley contrasts Darwin to a young naturalist initially hampered by his provincialism. Edward Blyth (1810–1873) "saw about him the hedge-constricted, precision-cultivated English landscape." Unable to think in any other terms, Blyth saw nature as static and limited. On the other hand, after the *Beagle* voyage Darwin "brought back with him the memories of foreign weeds invading the new world, of introduced animals overrunning the indigenous products of oceanic islands. For Darwin, fresh from the wild lands, the boundaries of life seemed less rigid and sharp."[5] Nature for Darwin, as for Lewes and Kingsley, was dynamic, transformative, endlessly creative. The discovery of thousands of new species in tropical habitats reinforced the idea of nature's creative plenitude, while biochemical investigations of the cell created an awareness that all these life forms were intimately related—all "Life," which gave naturalists yet another incentive to seek out obscure organisms.

Nineteenth-century natural history took advantage of, indeed depended on, these new horizons. Like Darwin, Wallace, and Bates, many naturalists ventured to the torrid zone before returning to England with tales that found a voracious audience. With their captured orchids and burnished butterflies, they "enlarged the limits of the possible." Intimations of boundless diversity, "fresh from the wild lands," spurred new interest in what might be lurking in the tame land of England. Lewes, Harvey, Gosse, Kingsley, and battalions of followers turned up hitherto unsuspected wonders of the British shores, while the Fern Craze turned over new leaves, if you will, of botanical recluses, vegetable wonders hidden deep in English forests. Trawling with a naturalist's dredge revealed the hidden complexities of the ocean floor. And Gosse, Wood, Lewes, and countless others brought the brazen tube of the microscope to bear on ordinary ditch water, with spectacular results.

Realms of wonder, pleasurable paraphernalia, grateful objects, outdoor exercise, the exhilaration of a boundless creation—these amply rewarded the amateur naturalist. With such powerful inducements, natural history attracted legions of acolytes. Enthusiasts abounded, not only on England's beaches and in the pages of natural history books, but also in the characterizations of Victorian novelists. Literature is thus a good gauge for assessing the hold of natural history upon the Victorian imagination. Thackeray, to give one example, in *Vanity Fair* counts "a ladylike knowledge of botany and geology" (chapter 12) among poetry and music as a typical young woman's attainments. Trollope, in *Barchester Towers*, includes a female amateur naturalist as a minor character: "a lady very learned in stones, ferns, plants and vermin, and who had written a book about petals" (chapter 10). Mrs. Gaskell, who described the working-class naturalists of Oldham (see my Chapter 2), seems particularly attuned to the natural history craze. In *Wives and Daughters* (1866), she, too, mentions a genteel woman botanizer. When a gentleman brings her a rare plant as a present, she exclaims: "Mamma, look! this is the *Drosera rotundifolia* I have been wanting so long" (chapter 1). Note how readily the Latin name rolls off her tongue.

In addition to testifying to the apparent popularity of natural history among young ladies with this brief portrayal, Mrs. Gaskell also provides in this novel a perceptive longer sketch of a naturalist. In chapter 6, Gaskell describes the natural history hobbies of Roger Hamley, who will later go on to delve seriously into evolutionary biology:

> Roger knows a good deal of natural history, and finds out queer things sometimes. He'd have been off a dozen times during this walk of ours, if he'd been here: his eyes are always wandering about, and see twenty things where I only see one. Why! I've known him bolt into a copse because he saw something fifteen yards off—some plant, maybe, which he'd tell me was very rare, though I should say I'd seen its marrow at every turn in the woods.

The speaker pokes at a spider web on a leaf, and continues:

> If we came upon such a thing as this, . . . why, he could tell you what insect or spider made it, and if it lived in rotten fir-wood, or in a cranny of good sound timber, or deep down in the ground, or up in the sky, or anywhere.

It's a pity they don't take honours in Natural History at Cambridge. Roger would be safe enough if they did.[6]

Along with its echo of the Victorian science-education controversy, this passage neatly summarizes the skills of the typical naturalist. Self-taught, Roger knows a great deal about how animals live—that is, has some biological curiosity and understanding—but even more important, Roger has incredibly keen powers of sight. What he knows, he knows by direct observation.

This is the primacy of vision I have pointed to in Victorian natural history: the primacy of vision that naturalists craved and writers exalted. Burroughs and Ruskin would applaud Roger's trained, intensified eyesight, his eyes "always wandering about," able to seize upon an obscure object whose beauties and rarity would otherwise, literally, be overlooked. For a naturalist, or even for a Pre-Raphaelite painter, what greater goal could there be, or pleasure, than to "see twenty things" where the careless can only see one?

With keen eyesight and a zest for novelty, anyone could dash into the macroscopic thickets of nature and seize its minute treasures. Natural history was a technique, a trope, a metaphor for opening up new realms, for seeing more deeply, keenly, and intently. Worlds within worlds—that is what naturalists saw when peering at a specimen: the glass ivy that grows on the sertularia, that grows on the polyp, that grows on the crab. To the naturalist, peering at nature piecemeal, the world was a mosaic, the "most elaborate, and the most perfect that can be conceived" (as Gosse said of the butterfly's wing), composed of infinite details, nested one within the other. Revealing them, unveiling them became a wondrous game of opening a series of Chinese boxes, each with a surprise within. In search of surprises, the imaginative naturalist could venture in three directions: along the axis of space, along the axis of scale, or along the axis of time. A window into nature could be simply a threshold of space across which the naturalist stepped, like Bates traveling from England to the River Amazons. More exciting, perhaps, it could be an aperture of scale, as when Gosse peered into the playground of Rotifers and diatoms, or an aperture of time, as when Miller looked back at the armored fish lurking in prehistoric seas.

Especially when clambering through the lens of time, naturalists like Miller sometimes felt a shiver of evanescence, a tremble at the temporality of all existence, including their own. But still the imaginative potential of opening up such worlds was enormous, its joys unexcelled. That is one reason why natural history lent itself so well to expression in prose. The discourse of natural history mirrored its subject: visual, dialectical, emotional. It reveled in multiplicity and singularity, in panorama and particularity, and exhibited clear, focused vision, a love of concrete objects, a mania for the minute, and an aesthetic appreciation of intricate forms. It was science endowed with literary qualities, style, personal vision. Victorian natural history writing, unlike scientific prose, was not goal oriented but rather discursive—a gathering up, or collection, of disparate observations acquired on rambles or jaunts.

Zoophytes and ferns, seaweeds and beetles, corals and fossil fish are tokens of mysterious climes: the tropics, the microscopic realm, the remote geological past. They are keepsakes of adventures, harbingers of ones to come. Concrete, complex, sensuous, held in the hand, natural history specimens are in a sense wonder itself, reified. Specimens were the reward naturalists sought; particulars what natural history discourse thrived on. For the Victorians, particularity had its dangers, but also such seductive rewards that it became a demonstrable goal in art forms from poetry to fiction to painting to photography. Both the activity and the prose of the natural history vogue fueled the preoccupation with clearly delineated, concrete particulars in art.

Two dominant motifs of Victorian natural history sum up its attractions: the cabinet and the microscope. In filling a cabinet, one enjoys possession: having parts of nature for one's own. One creates an assemblage of particular objects; they can be endlessly studied, admired, rearranged, contemplated. Juxtaposing stones and beetles and bones in a cabinet is a creative act analogous to sketching them—in an *étude*—or recounting them, one by one, in natural history prose. The cabinet, like Pre-Raphaelite art or photography, creates meaning by means of a new syntax of capture and juxtaposition.

The cabinet can become, in effect, one's own personal museum, a chosen miniaturization of the natural world. It can become—and for the Victorian naturalist did become—the physical representation of one's mental diorama. Much more than just a wooden case of shelves and little drawers, the cabinet is an object full of other objects, a beautiful arrangement of beauties, compressed and selected from the multiplicity of nature, then framed. The cabinet served also as a metaphor for personal consciousness of nature—consciousness or remembrance. For Edmund Gosse, the cabinet as metaphor was so familiar, so ingrained, that it expanded to include curiosities other than seashells and cocoons. As a naturalist's son, steeped in the Victorian ethic of collecting, Edmund quite naturally employed this motif when looking back into memory. In a telling phrase, Edmund spoke of his father, Philip Gosse the naturalist, as being forever enshrined "in my mind's cabinet."[7]

Finally, as both tool and metaphor, the microscope is the most important device of Victorian natural history. For amateur microscopists, it was magical, a window into other worlds. As in O'Brien's story, the microscope became a "diamond lens" of purest clarity, of marvelous revelatory powers. Revealing unexpected complexity in nature, the lens invited the naturalist to squeeze through amazing apertures of scale, to become minute, in effect, while microscopic animals became gigantic, kicking and twisting and going about their lives in an unexpected alien panorama. Under the microscope, nature disported itself—boundless, startling, endlessly detailed. If one but held a feather or an insect under the potent lens, one particularity would generate another, and another.

In an 1883 manual appropriately titled *The Microscope and its Revelations*, William B. Carpenter testified to the instrument's popularity and its powers:

> To such as feel inclined to take up the use of the Microscope as a means of healthful and improving occupation for their unemployed hours, the Author would offer this word of encouragement,—that, notwithstanding the number of recruits continually being added to the vast army of Microscopists, and the rapid extension of its conquests, the inexhaustibility of Nature is constantly becoming more and more apparent; so that no apprehension need arise that the Microscopist's researches can ever be brought to a stand for want of an object![8]

Victorian microscopists marched forth like a conquering army; armed with the microscope, any amateur naturalist could, with a heady sense of personal imperialism, find a little kingdom to explore and rule. This device was the key to a visual and vast domain. As the Reverend J. G. Wood put it, "There is this great advantage in the microscope, that no one need feel in want of objects as long as he possesses his instrument and a sufficiency of light."[9] Inexhaustible objects, jeweled and bathed in light—who could resist the appeal of natural history, with its promise of aesthetic riches?

Late in the twentieth century, with rainforests ravaged, nature despoiled, the environment threatened and fragile and finite, such confidence is impossible to feel. But that was the glory of Victorian natural history: all nature lay open before one. If one could be receptive, train one's instrument of sight, then natural history would be in the highest sense transformational, "unveiling endless beauties"[10] in the most humble settings, exalting common objects whether at the seaside, in the jungle, or along the garden path. Nature's revelations had no prospect of an end; curiosity and collection knew no bounds. To the doubting, world-weary, or skeptical Victorian, natural history offered a discourse of joyous particularity, a metaphor of plenty, a sacrament of sight. Never did the naturalist lack an object.

Notes

1. Quoted in Edmund Gosse, *The Life of Philip Henry Gosse F.R.S.* (London; Kegan Paul, Trench, Trübner and Co., Ltd., 1890), p. 356.

2. Susan Faye Cannon, *Science in Culture: The Early Victorian Period* (New York: Dawson and Science History Publications, 1978), chapter 1.

3. In "London Whales," L. R. Brightwell, ed. *Buckland's Curiosities of Natural History: A Selection* (London: The Batchworth Press, 1948), p. 89.

4. Hans Koning, "Onward and Upward with the Arts: The Eleventh Edition," *The New Yorker*, 2 March 1981, pp. 77, 73.

5. Loren Eiseley, *Darwin and the Mysterious Mr. X: New Light on the Evolutionists* (New York: E. P. Dutton, 1979), p. 57.

6. Mrs. Gaskell, *Wives and Daughters* (London: Dent/Everyman's Library, 1966), p. 82.

7. Edmund Gosse, *Father and Son: A Study of Two Temperaments* (New York: W. W. Norton and Company, 1963), p. 52.

8. William B. Carpenter, *The Microscope and its Revelations*, 6th ed. (New York: William Wood and Company, 1883), p. vii.

9. J. G. Wood, *Common Objects of the Microscope* (London: George Routledge and Sons, n.d.), p. 3.

10. Wood, p. 3.

BIBLIOGRAPHY

For the convenience of the reader, I have divided this list of sources into three parts. Appearing first is an annotated list of the major critical works most relevant to the subject of Victorian natural history (or science) and its connection to literature or art. These are the works on which I have most relied. Next, primary sources from the nineteenth century appear together, followed by a list of other useful secondary sources.

MAJOR SOURCES

Allen, David Elliston. *The Naturalist in Britain: A Social History.* London: Allen Lane, 1976. Covers the social aspects of natural history, including fashions and taste, from the seventeenth century to the present day, with especially insightful treatment of nineteenth-century elements: science, religion, collecting, field clubs, books, specialized disciplines, equipment, and most important, attitudes toward nature.

————. *The Victorian Fern Craze: A History of Pteridomania.* London: Hutchinson and Co., Ltd., 1969. A brief but revealing study of one intense expression of the Victorian love for hitherto ignored natural objects. Allen covers Wardian Cases, fern books, articles, collecting, designs, and other motivations and results of the fashion.

Altick, Richard D. *The Shows of London: A Panoramic History of Exhibitions, 1600–1862.* Cambridge, MA: Belknap Press-Harvard Univ. Press, 1978. An awesomely detailed social history of every kind of exhibition and public spectacle popular in London, including natural history cabinets and museums, zoos, panoramas and dioramas, microscopes, menageries, technical and mechanical exhibits, the British Museum, and the Crystal Palace.

Ball, Patricia M. *The Science of Aspects: The Changing Role of Fact in the Work of Coleridge, Ruskin and Hopkins.* London: Univ. of London Athlone Press, 1971. An examination of how these three writers view natural objects, moving from more subjective (Coleridge) to more objective, taking into consideration the effects of Romanticism, pathetic fallacy, science, and the visual arts.

Barber, Lynn. *The Heyday of Natural History: 1820–1870.* Garden City, NY: Doubleday and Company, Inc., 1980. The best overall survey of the natural history craze, profusely illustrated. Covers Owen, Murchison, Miller, the Darwin-Wallace-Huxley controversies, Gosse, Agassiz, Frank Buckland, Waterton, Audubon, and numerous other figures, as well as collecting, museums, classification, and various popular natural history fads.

Christ, Carol T. *The Finer Optic: The Aesthetic of Particularity in Victorian Poetry.* New Haven, CT: Yale Univ. Press, 1975. An examination of the artistic uses of particular versus universal truths; specifically how Victorians such as Tennyson, the Pre-Raphaelites, Browning, and Hopkins crowded their poems with particular concrete details, while fearing that looking at the world with a "microscopic eye" could preclude a larger, coherent understanding.

Cosslett, Tess. *The "Scientific Movement" and Victorian Literature.* Sussex: The Harvester Press, 1982. An analysis of "the scientific world view" prevalent in the latter half of the nineteenth century, involving ideas of scientific truth, natural laws, kinship and interrelatedness of all nature, and scientific imagination, as found in Tennyson, George Eliot, Meredith, and Hardy.

Dance, Peter S. *The Art of Natural History: Animal Illustrators and Their Work.* Woodstock, NY: The Overlook Press, 1978. A historical survey of animal art, from prehistory on, lavishly illustrated; with special attention given to the "Nineteenth Century Background," the "Lithographic Revolution" of the nineteenth century, microscopic illustration, and pictures in popular books.

Knight, David. *The Age of Science: The Scientific World-view in the Nineteenth Century.* New York: Basil Blackwell, 1986. A good exploration of British and Continental science in its social context, including the growth of scientific education and research, major theoretical syntheses, the role of jargon, and the importance of "discourse in pictures."

Knoepflmacher, U. C., and G. B. Tennyson, eds. *Nature and the Victorian Imagination.* Berkeley: Univ. of California Press, 1977. An anthology of essays on many facets of Victorian attitudes toward nature, although not natural history as such; from cottages, nature decor, and gardens, to the "Arctic Sublime," the Alps, and rainbows as images, to essays on chemistry, biology, and physics, Romantic nature, landscape painting, and Pre-Raphaelitism.

Paradis, James, and Thomas Postlewait, eds. *Victorian Science and Victorian Values: Literary Perspectives.* Annals of the New York Academy of Sciences, Vol. 360. New York: The New York Academy of Sciences, 1981; rpt. New Brunswick, NJ: Rutgers Univ. Press, 1985. A collection of 14 articles ranging widely on the meaning of science (Darwin, astronomy, geology, and so on) for literary figures (Dickens, Ruskin, Eliot, Carlyle, among others).

Scourse, Nicolette. *The Victorians and Their Flowers.* London: Croom Helm; Portland, OR: Timber Press, 1983. A profusely illustrated and charming compendium of exhaustive information about Victorian gardens and glass-houses, botanical fashions, floral designs, flowers as emblems of morality and sentiment (the Language of Flowers), botanical collecting, classification, and "the passion for detail."

NINETEENTH-CENTURY SOURCES

Bates, Henry Walter. *The Naturalist on the River Amazons*. London: John Murray, 1864; rpt. Berkeley: Univ. of California Press, 1962.

Belt, Thomas. *The Naturalist in Nicaragua*. Original edition, 1874; Chicago: Univ. of Chicago Press, 1985.

Buckland, Frank. *Buckland's Curiosities of Natural History: A Selection*. Ed. L. R. Brightwell. London: The Batchworth Press, 1948.

———. *Natural History of British Fishes; Their Structure, Economic Uses, and Capture by Net and Rod*. London: Society for Promoting Christian Knowledge, n.d.

Buckley, Arabella B. *Life and Her Children: Glimpses of Animal Life from the Amoeba to the Insects*. Original edition, 1880; rpt. London: Macmillan & Co. Ltd., 1957.

———. *A Short History of Natural Science*, 4th ed. New York: D. Appleton and Co., 1888.

Burroughs, John. *The Complete Nature Writings of John Burroughs*. New York: Wm. H. Wise and Co., 1871; rpt. New York: Wm. H. Wise and Co., 1913.

———. *The Writings of John Burroughs*, 20 vols. Boston: Houghton Mifflin Company, 1904–1919.

Carpenter, William B. *The Microscope and its Revelations*, 6th ed. New York: William Wood and Company, 1883.

Chambers's Miscellany of Instructive and Entertaining Tracts, rev. ed. London and Edinburgh: W. and R. Chambers, n.d.

Clifford, William Kingdon. *Lectures and Essays*. Ed. Leslie Stephen and Frederick Pollock. London: Macmillan and Co., 1886.

Colling, James K. *Art Foliage, For Sculpture and Decoration; with an Analysis of Geometric Form, and Studies from Nature, of Buds, Leaves, Flowers, and Fruit*. London: Published by the author, 1865.

Collingwood, Cuthbert. *Rambles of a Naturalist on the Shores and Waters of the China Sea: Being Observations in Natural History During a Voyage to China, Formosa, Borneo, Singapore, Etc*. London: John Murray, 1868.

Cook, Edward T., and Alexander Wedderburn, eds. *The Complete Works of John Ruskin*, 38 vols. London: George Allen, 1903–1912.

Darwin, Charles. *The Autobiography of Charles Darwin*. Ed. Nora Barlow. New York: W. W. Norton and Company, Inc., 1958.

———. *Journal of Researches into the Geology and Natural History of the Various Countries visited by H.M.S. Beagle, Under the Command of Captain Fitzroy, R.N., from 1832 to 1836*. London: Henry Colburn, 1839; New York: Hafner Publishing Company, 1952.

————. *On the Origin of Species*. London: John Murray, 1859; Intro. Ernst Mayr. Cambridge, MA: Harvard Univ. Press, 1964 (facsimile edition).

————. *The Voyage of the Beagle*. Intro. H. Graham Cannon. London: Dent/ Everyman's Library, 1959.

Dowden, Edward. "The Scientific Movement and Literature." In *Studies in Literature: 1789–1877*, 6th ed. London: Kegan Paul, Trench, Trübner and Co., Ltd., 1892.

du Chaillu, Paul. *Explorations and Adventure in Equatorial Africa*. New York: Harper and Brothers, Publishers, 1867.

————. *Wild Life Under the Equator*. New York: Harper and Brothers, Publishers, 1869.

Forbes, Edward. *A History of British Starfishes, and Other Animals of the Class Echinodermata*. London: John Van Voorst, 1841.

Gaskell, Mrs. *Wives and Daughters*. London: Dent/Everyman's Library, 1966.

Gatty, Margaret. *Parables from Nature*. London: G. Bell & Sons Ltd., 1914.

Gosse, Edmund. *Father and Son: A Study of Two Temperaments*. New York: W. W. Norton and Company, 1963.

————. *The Life of Philip Henry Gosse F.R.S.* London: Kegan Paul, Trench, Trübner and Co., Ltd., 1890.

Gosse, Philip Henry. *Evenings at the Microscope*. New York: P. F. Collier and Son, 1901.

————. *Letters from Alabama, Chiefly Relating to Natural History*. Mountain Brook, AL: Overbrook House, 1983.

————. *The Romance of Natural History*. New York: A. L. Burt Company, Publishers, 1902.

————. *Tenby: A Sea-Side Holiday*. London: John Van Voorst, 1856.

Haeckel, Ernst. *Art Forms in Nature*. New York: Dover Publications, Inc., 1974.

Harvey, W. H. *The Sea-Side Book; Being an Introduction to the Natural History of the British Coasts*. London: John Van Voorst, 1849.

Herschel, John, ed. *A Manual of Scientific Inquiry: Prepared for the Use of Officers in Her Majesty's Navy, and Travellers in General*, 5th ed. London: Eyre and Spottiswoode, 1886.

————. *A Preliminary Discourse on the Study of Natural Philosophy*. London: Longman, Rees, Orme, and Green, 1830; rpt. New York: Johnson Reprint Corporation, 1966.

Hooker, Worthington. *The Child's Book of Nature; for the Use of Families and Schools; Intended to Aid Mothers and Teachers in Training Children in the Observation of Nature*. New York: Harper & Brothers, 1883.

Humboldt, Alexander von. *Cosmos; A Sketch of a Physical Description of the Universe*. Trans. E. C. Otte. New York: Harper and Brothers, Publishers, 1863.

Huxley, Thomas H. *Discourses Biological and Geological: Essays*. New York: D. Appleton and Company, 1894.

————. *Science and Education: Essays*. New York: D. Appleton and Company, 1896.

Inquire Within Upon Everything. Original edition, 1856. New York: Farrar, Straus and Giroux, 1978.

Kingsley, Charles. *Alton Locke: Tailor and Poet*. Ed. Herbert Van Thal. London: Cassell, 1967.

————. *Glaucus; or, the Wonders of the Shore*. London: Macmillan and Co., Limited, 1903.

————. "Town Geology." *The Humboldt Library of Popular Science Literature*, Nos. 1–12. New York: The Humboldt Publishing Co., n.d.

————. *The Water-Babies and Glaucus*. London: J. M. Dent and Sons, 1908.

————. *Yeast: A Problem*. London: Macmillan and Co., 1888.

Knapp, John Leonard. *Country Rambles in England; or Journal of a Naturalist*. Buffalo, NY: Phinney and Co., 1853.

Lewes, George Henry. *Studies in Animal Life*. London: Smith, Elder and Co., 1862.

Lyell, Charles. *Principles of Geology*, 3 vols. London: John Murray, 1830–1833.

Lyell, Sir Charles. *Principles of Geology; or, The Modern Changes of the Earth and its Inhabitants*, 11th ed., 2 vols. New York: D. Appleton and Company, 1887.

MacGillivray, John. *Narrative of the Voyage of H.M.S. Rattlesnake*. London: T. & W. Boone, 1852.

Marsh, George Perkins. *Man and Nature*. The John Harvard Library. Ed. David Lowenthal. Cambridge, MA: Belknap Press-Harvard Univ. Press, 1965.

Michelet, Jules. *The Bird*. 1879. Trans. W. H. Davenport Adams. London: Wildwood House Limited, 1981.

Miller, Hugh. *My Schools and Schoolmasters; or, The Story of My Education*. Edinburgh: W. P. Nimmo, Hay, and Mitchell, 1893.

————. *The Old Red Sandstone; or, New Walks in an Old Field*. London: J. M. Dent and Co., n.d.

————. *Popular Geology: A Series of Lectures Read Before the Philosophical Institution of Edinburgh, With Descriptive Sketches from a Geologist's Portfolio*. Boston: Gould and Lincoln, 1859.

Murchison, Sir Roderick Impey. *Siluria: The History of the Oldest Fossiliferous Rocks and Their Foundations*, 3rd ed. London: John Murray, 1859.

Penn, Granville. *Conversations on Geology; Comprising a Familiar Explanation of the Huttonian and Wernerian Systems*. London: J. W. Southgate and Son, 1840.

A Scottish Naturalist: The Sketches and Notes of Charles St. John, 1809–1856. London: Andre Deutsch, 1982.

Smiles, Samuel. "Hugh Miller." *Brief Biographies*. New York: Hurst and Co., Publishers, n.d.

————. *Life of a Scotch Naturalist: Thomas Edward, Associate of the Linnaean Society*. New York: Harper & Brothers, 1877.

_____. *Robert Dick, Baker, of Thurso: Geologist and Botanist.* New York: Harper & Brothers, 1879.

Spencer, Herbert. "Education: Intellectual, Moral, and Physical." *The Humboldt Library of Popular Science Literature*, Nos. 1–12. New York: The Humboldt Publishing Co., n.d.

Swinburne, Algernon Charles. *Under the Microscope.* London: D. White, 1872; rpt. New York: Garland Publishing Inc., 1986.

Thomson, C. Wyville. *The Depths of the Sea: An Account of the General Results of the Dredging Cruise of H.M.S. Porcupine and Lightning During the Summers of 1868, '69 and '70*, 2nd ed. London: Macmillan, 1874.

Tyndall, John. *The Forms of Water in Clouds and Rivers, Ice and Glaciers.* New York: D. Appleton and Company, 1905.

_____. *Fragments of Science*, 2 vols. A Library of Universal Literature. New York: P. F. Collier and Son, 1901.

Verne, Jules. *Twenty-Thousand Leagues Under the Sea.* Trans. Walter James Miller. New York: Pocket Books, 1966.

Wallace, Alfred Russel. *The Malay Archipelago: The Land of the Orang-utan and The Bird of Paradise, A Narrative of Travel with Studies of Man and Nature.* London: Macmillan and Company, 1869; New York: Dover Publications, Inc., 1962.

Ward, The Hon. Mrs. *Microscope Teachings: Descriptions of Various Objects of Especial Interest and Beauty adapted for Microscopic Observation.* London: Groombridge, 1864.

Waterton, Charles. *Wanderings in South America.* London: Oxford Univ. Press, 1973.

Wood, J. G. *Common Objects of the Microscope.* London: George Routledge and Sons, n.d.

_____, ed. *The Natural History of Selborne.* By Gilbert White. London: Routledge, Warne, and Routledge, 1864.

Yonge, Charlotte M. *The Herb of the Field.* London: Macmillan and Co., 1887.

OTHER SOURCES

Adams, Alexander B. *Eternal Quest: The Story of the Great Naturalists.* New York: G. P. Putnam's Sons, 1969.

Albritton, Claude C., Jr. *The Abyss of Time: Changing Conceptions of the Earth's Antiquity after the Sixteenth Century.* San Francisco: Freeman, Cooper and Company, 1980.

Altick, Richard D. *Victorian People and Ideas.* New York: W. W. Norton and Company, Inc., 1973.

Amsler, Mark, ed. *The Languages of Creativity: Models, Problem-Solving, Discourse.* Studies in Science and Culture, Vol. 2. Newark: Univ. of Delaware Press, 1986.

Appleman, Philip, ed. *Darwin. A Norton Critical Edition*. New York: W. W. Norton and Company, Inc., 1970.

Arber, Agnes. *The Mind and the Eye: A Study of the Biologist's Standpoint*. Cambridge: Cambridge Univ. Press, 1954.

Armytage, W. H. G. *A Social History of Engineering*. Cambridge, MA: The MIT Press, 1961.

Augros, Robert M., and George N. Stanciu. *The New Story of Science: Mind and the Universe*. Chicago: Gateway Editions, 1984.

Basalla, George, William Coleman, and Robert H. Kargon. *Victorian Science: A Self-Portrait from the Presidential Addresses of the British Association for the Advancement of Science*. Garden City, NY: Anchor Books/Doubleday and Company, 1970.

Bates, Marston. *The Nature of Natural History*. New York: Charles Scribner's Sons, 1950.

Beach, Joseph Warren. *The Concept of Nature in Nineteenth-Century English Poetry*. New York: Russell and Russell, 1966.

Beer, Gillian. *Darwin's Plots: Evolutionary Narrative in Darwin, George Eliot and Nineteenth-Century Fiction*. London: Ark Paperbacks, 1985.

_____. "Origins and Oblivion in Victorian Narrative." *Sex, Politics, and Science in the Nineteenth-Century Novel*. Ed. Ruth Bernard Yeazell. Selected Papers from the English Institute, 1983–1984. New Series, No. 10. Baltimore: The Johns Hopkins Univ. Press, 1986.

Bergon, Frank, ed. *The Wilderness Reader*. New York: New American Library, 1980.

Blunt, Wilfred. *The Ark in the Park: The Zoo in the Nineteenth Century*. London: Hamish Hamilton, 1976.

Botting, Douglas. *Humboldt and the Cosmos*. London: Joseph, 1974.

Bowler, Peter J. *Fossils and Progress: Paleontology in the Nineteenth Century*. New York: Neale-Watson Academic Press, 1976.

Bradbury, S. *The Microscope: Past and Present*. Oxford: Pergamon Press, 1968.

Brent, Peter. *Charles Darwin: "A Man of Enlarged Curiosity."* New York: W. W. Norton and Company, Inc., 1981.

Briggs, A. *Iron Bridge to Crystal Palace: Impact and Images of the Industrial Revolution*. London: Thames, 1979.

_____. *Victorian People: A Reassessment of Persons and Themes, 1851–1867*. Chicago: Univ. of Chicago Press, 1955.

Bronowski, J. *The Common Sense of Science*. New York: Vintage Books, n.d.

_____. *The Identity of Man*, rev. ed. Garden City, NY: The Doubleday/Natural History Press, 1971.

_____. *Science and Human Values*, rev. ed. New York: Harper Torchbooks, 1965.

Brooks, Paul. *Speaking for Nature: How Literary Naturalists from Henry Thoreau to Rachel Carson Have Shaped America*. Boston: Houghton Mifflin Company, 1980.

Brown, Harcourt, ed. *Science and the Creative Spirit: Essays on Humanistic Aspects of Science.* Toronto: Univ. of Toronto Press, 1958.

Buckley, Jerome Hamilton. *The Victorian Temper: A Study in Literary Culture.* New York: Vintage Books, 1951.

Burgess, G. H. O. *The Eccentric Ark: The Curious World of Frank Buckland.* New York: The Horizon Press, 1967.

Burton, Elizabeth. *The Early Victorians at Home: 1837–1861.* London: Longman, 1972.

Buttman, Günther. *The Shadow of the Telescope: A Biography of John Herschel.* New York: Charles Scribner's Sons, 1970.

Canham, Stephen W. "From Spiritual Optics to Prismatic Lenses: Artistic Characters and Aesthetics in Selected Nineteenth Century Novels from Thackeray to Wilde." Ph.D. Diss., Univ. of Washington, 1977.

Cannon, Susan Faye. *Science in Culture: The Early Victorian Period.* New York: Dawson and Science History Publications, 1978.

Cassidy, Harold Gomes. *The Sciences and the Arts: A New Alliance.* New York: Harper and Brothers, 1962.

Chapman, Raymond. *The Victorian Debate: English Literature and Society 1832–1901.* London: Weidenfeld and Nicolson, 1968.

Clark, Kenneth. *Ruskin Today.* New York: Penguin Books, 1982.

Colbert, Edwin H. *The Great Dinosaur Hunters and Their Discoveries.* Original edition, 1968. New York: Dover Publications, Inc., 1984.

Coleman, William. *Biology in the Nineteenth Century: Problems of Form, Function, and Transformation.* London: Cambridge Univ. Press, 1977.

Collingwood, W. G. *The Life of John Ruskin.* London: Methuen and Co., 1905.

Colloms, Brenda. *Charles Kingsley: The Lion of Eversley.* London: Constable, 1975.

Cornelius, David K., and Edwin St. Vincent. *Cultures in Conflict: Perspectives on the Snow-Leavis Controversy.* Chicago: Scott, Foresman and Company, 1964.

Cosslett, Tess, ed. *Science and Religion in the Nineteenth Century.* Cambridge: Cambridge Univ. Press, 1984.

Cruse, Amy. *The Victorians and Their Reading.* Boston: Houghton Mifflin Company, n.d.

Curtis, Charles P., and Ferris Greenslet, eds. *The Practical Cogitator: The Thinker's Anthology,* 3rd ed. Boston: Houghton Mifflin Company, 1962.

Dampier, W. C. *A History of Science,* 4th ed. Cambridge: Cambridge Univ. Press, 1971.

Dawson, Carl. *Victorian Noon: English Literature in 1850.* Baltimore: The Johns Hopkins Univ. Press, 1979.

Dean, Dennis R. "'Through Science to Despair': Geology and the Victorians." *Victorian Science and Victorian Values: Literary Perspectives.* Ed. James Paradis and Thomas Postlewait. Annals of the New York Academy of Sciences, Vol. 360. New York: The New York Academy of Sciences, 1981.

DeLaura, David J. "Nature Naturing: Literary Natural History." *Victorian Studies*, 22, No. 2 (1979), 194.

Desmond, Adrian. *Archetypes and Ancestors: Paleontology in Victorian London 1850-1875*. Original edition, 1982. Chicago: Univ. of Chicago Press, 1984.

Dodd, Philip. "The Nature of Edmund Gosse's *Father and Son.*" *English Literature in Transition*, 22 (1979), 270-280.

Drachman, Julian M. *Studies in the Literature of Natural Science*. New York: The Macmillan Company, 1930.

Eiseley, Loren. *Darwin and the Mysterious Mr. X: New Light on the Evolutionists*. New York: E. P. Dutton, 1979.

———. *Darwin's Century: Evolution and the Men Who Discovered It*. Garden City, NY: Anchor Books/Doubleday and Company, 1961.

Elman, Robert. *First in the Field: America's Pioneering Naturalists*. New York: Van Nostrand Reinhold Company, 1977.

Fenton, Carroll Lane, and Mildred Adams Fenton. *Giants of Geology*. Garden City, NY: Doubleday & Company, Inc., 1952.

Fiedler, Leslie A., and Houston A. Baker, Jr., eds. *English Literature: Opening Up the Canon*. Selected Papers from the English Institute, 1979. New Series, No. 4. Baltimore: The Johns Hopkins Univ. Press, 1981.

Foote, George. "Science and Its Functions in Early Nineteenth Century England." *Osiris*, XI (1954), 438-454.

Ford, Boris, ed. *From Dickens to Hardy*. The New Pelican Guide to English Literature, Vol. 6. New York: Penguin Books, 1982.

Ford, George H. "'A Great Poetical Boa-Constrictor,' Alfred Tennyson: An Educated Victorian Mind." *Victorian Literature and Society: Essays Presented to Richard D. Altick*. Ed. James R. Kincaid and Albert J. Kuhn. Ohio: Ohio Univ. Press, 1984.

Foucault, Michel. *The Birth of the Clinic: An Archaeology of Medical Perception*. New York: Vintage Books, 1975.

Franklin, H. Bruce. *Future Perfect: American Science Fiction of the Nineteenth Century*, Rev. ed. New York: Oxford Univ. Press, 1978.

Freeman, R. B., and Douglas Wertheimer, eds. *Philip Henry Gosse: A Bibliography*. Folkestone, Kent: Dawson, 1980.

Galassi, Peter. *Before Photography: Painting and the Invention of Photography*. New York: The Museum of Modern Art, 1981.

Girouard, Mark. *Alfred Waterhouse and the Natural History Museum*. London: British Museum (Natural History), 1981.

Green, Martin. *Science and the Shabby Curate of Poetry: Essays about the Two Cultures*. London: Longmans, 1964.

Greene, Mott T. *Geology in the Nineteenth Century: Changing Views of a Changing World*. Ithaca, NY: Cornell Univ. Press, 1982.

Gunther, Albert E. *A Century of Zoology at the British Museum through the Lives of Two Keepers, 1815-1914*. London: Dowson's of Pall Mall, 1975.

Haley, Bruce. *The Healthy Body and Victorian Culture*. Cambridge, MA: Harvard Univ. Press, 1978.

Hanley, Wayne. *Natural History in America: From Mark Catesby to Rachel Carson*. New York: Quandrangle/The New York Times Book Co., 1977.

Harper, Roger J. "The Literary Reputation of American Nature Writers in Nineteenth-Century British Periodicals (1865-1910)." Ph.D. Diss., Green State Univ., 1976.

Hays, H. R. *Birds, Beasts, and Men: A Humanist History of Zoology*. Baltimore: Penguin Books, Inc., 1973.

Helsinger, Elizabeth K. *Ruskin and the Art of the Beholder*. Cambridge, MA: Harvard Univ. Press, 1982.

Hepburn, James. "Religion, Science, and Philip Henry Gosse." *Contemporary Review*, 233 (1978), 195-202.

Hewison, Robert. *John Ruskin: The Argument of the Eye*. London: Thames and Hudson, 1976.

Hicks, Philip Marshall. *The Development of the Natural History Essay in American Literature*. Thesis, Univ. of Pennsylvania, 1924. Philadelphia: privately printed, 1924.

Himmelfarb, Gertrude. *Darwin and the Darwinian Revolution*. New York: W. W. Norton and Company, Inc., 1962.

——. *Victorian Minds*. New York: Harper Torchbooks, 1970.

Hix, John. *The Glass House*. Cambridge, MA: The MIT Press, 1981.

Houghton, Walter E. *The Victorian Frame of Mind: 1830-1870*. New Haven, CT: Yale Univ. Press, 1957.

Hughes, Robert. "From the Dark Garden of the Mind." *Time*, 8 July 1974, p. 64.

Hunt, John Dixon. *The Wider Sea: A Life of John Ruskin*. New York: The Viking Press, 1982.

Huth, Hans. *Nature and the American: Three Centuries of Changing Attitudes*. Lincoln: Univ. of Nebraska Press, 1957.

Huxley, Aldous. *Literature and Science*. New Haven, CT: Leete's Island Books, 1963.

——. "Wordsworth in the Tropics." *Collected Essays*. New York: Harper Colophon Books, 1971.

Huxley, Anthony, J. P. M. Brenan, and Brenda E. Moon, eds. *A Vision of Eden: The Life and Work of Marianne North*. Exeter, England: Webb and Bower, 1980.

Hyman, Stanley Edgar. *The Tangled Bank: Darwin, Marx, Frazer and Freud as Imaginative Writers*. New York: The Universal Library, Grosset and Dunlap, 1966.

Hyman, Susan. *Edward Lear's Birds*. New York: William Morrow and Company, Inc., 1980.

Irvine, William. *Apes, Angels, and Victorians: Darwin, Huxley, and Evolution*. New York: McGraw-Hill Book Company, 1955.

James, Kenneth W. "'Damned Nonsense!'—The Geological Career of the Third Earl of Enniskillen." Ulster: The Ulster Museum, 1986.

Jenkins, Alan C. *The Naturalists: Pioneers of Natural History.* New York: Mayflower Books, Inc., 1978.

Johnson, Walter, ed. *Gilbert White's Journals.* Cambridge, MA: The MIT Press, 1970.

Jones, W. T. *The Sciences and the Humanities: Conflict and Resolution.* Berkeley: Univ. of California Press, 1967.

Jordanova, L. J., ed. *Languages of Nature: Critical Essays on Science and Literature.* New Brunswick, NJ: Rutgers Univ. Press, 1986.

Joseph, Gerhard. "Tennyson's Optics: The Eagle's Gaze." *PMLA*, 92 (1977), 420–428.

Kargon, Robert H. *Science in Victorian Manchester: Enterprise and Expertise.* Baltimore: The Johns Hopkins Univ. Press, 1977.

Kastner, Joseph. "The Runcible Life and Works of the Remarkable Edward Lear." *Smithsonian*, 12, No. 6 (1981), 107–116.

_____. *A Species of Eternity.* New York: E. P. Dutton, 1977.

Keith, W. J. *The Rural Tradition: A Study of the Non-Fiction Prose Writers of the English Countryside.* Toronto: Univ. of Toronto Press, 1974.

Knight, David M. *The Transcendental Part of Chemistry.* Folkstone, Kent: Dawson, 1978.

_____. *Zoological Illustration.* Folkstone, Kent: Dawson, 1977.

Koning, Hans. "Onward and Upward with the Arts: The Eleventh Edition." *The New Yorker*, 2 March 1981, pp. 67–83.

Kuhn, Thomas S. *The Structure of Scientific Revolutions*, 2nd ed. International Encyclopedia of Unified Science. Chicago: Univ. of Chicago Press, 1970.

Lang, Cecil Y., ed. *The Pre-Raphaelites and Their Circle.* Boston: Houghton Mifflin Company, 1968.

Layton, David. *Science for the People: The Origin of the School Science Curriculum in England.* New York: Science History Publications, 1974.

Leavis, F. R. "Two Cultures? The Significance of Lord Snow." In *Nor Shall My Sword: Discourses on Pluralism, Compassion and Social Hope.* London: Chatto and Windus, 1972.

Lerner, Laurence, ed. *The Victorians.* The Context of English Literature Series. New York: Holmes and Meier Publishers, Inc., 1978.

Levine, George, and William Madden. *The Art of Victorian Prose.* New York: Oxford Univ. Press, 1968.

Ley, Willy. *Dawn of Zoology.* Englewood Cliffs, NJ: Prentice-Hall, Inc., 1968.

Lindquist-Cock, Elizabeth. *The Influence of Photography on American Landscape Painting, 1839–1880.* New York: Garland Publishing, Inc., 1977.

Lloyd, Clare. *The Travelling Naturalists.* Seattle: Univ. of Washington Press, 1985.

Lurie, Edward. *Louis Agassiz: A Life in Science.* Chicago: Univ. of Chicago Press, 1960.

Marsden, Christopher. *The English at the Seaside.* London: Collins, 1947.

Marx, Leo. *The Machine in the Garden: Technology and the Pastoral Ideal in America.* Oxford: Oxford Univ. Press, 1972.

Mason, Stephen F. *A History of the Sciences*, rev. ed. New York: Collier Books, 1962.

Mathias, Peter, ed. *Science and Society, 1600–1900*. Cambridge: Cambridge Univ. Press, 1972.

Mayr, Ernst. *Principles of Systematic Zoology*. New York: McGraw-Hill Book Company, 1969.

McCartney, Jesse F. "The Pedagogical Style of T. H. Huxley in 'On the Physical Basis of Life.'" *Southern Quarterly*, 14 (1975–1976), 97–107.

McIntosh, James. *Thoreau as Romantic Naturalist: His Shifting Stance Toward Nature*. Ithaca, NY: Cornell Univ. Press, 1974.

McKinney, H. Lewis, ed. *Lamarck to Darwin: Contributions to Evolutionary Biology, 1809–1859*. Lawrence, KS: Coronado Press, 1971.

Medawar, Peter B. "Science and Literature." In *The Hope of Progress: A Scientist Looks at Problems in Philosophy, Literature, and Science*. Garden City, NY: Anchor Press/Doubleday, 1973.

Middleton, Dorothy. *Victorian Lady Travellers*. Chicago: Academy, 1982.

Miles, Josephine. *Pathetic Fallacy in the Nineteenth Century: A Study of a Changing Relation Between Object and Emotion*. New York: Octagon Books, Inc., 1965.

Miller, Edward. *That Noble Cabinet: A History of the British Museum*. Athens, OH: Ohio Univ. Press, 1974.

Mingay, Gordon E. *Rural Life in Victorian England*. London: Heineman; New York: Holmes and Meier, 1978.

Moorehead, Alan. *Darwin and the Beagle*. New York: Penguin, 1971.

Morton, Peter. *The Vital Science: Biology and the Literary Imagination, 1860–1900*. London: George Allen & Unwin, 1984.

Mulvey, Christopher. *Anglo-American Landscapes: A Study of Nineteenth-Century Anglo-American Travel Literature*. Cambridge: Cambridge Univ. Press, 1983.

Nash, Roderick. *Wilderness and the American Mind*, 3rd ed. New Haven, CT: Yale Univ. Press, 1982.

Newhall, Beaumont. *A History of Photography*. New York: The Museum of Modern Art, 1964.

Nicolson, Marjorie Hope. *Mountain Gloom and Mountain Glory: The Development of the Aesthetics of the Infinite*. New York: W. W. Norton and Company, Inc., 1959.

––––––. *Newton Demands the Muse: Newton's Opticks and the Eighteenth Century Poets*. Princeton: Princeton Univ. Press, 1946.

Nochlin, Linda. *Realism and Tradition in Art: 1848–1900*. Sources and Documents in the History of Art Series, ed. H. W. Janson. Englewood Cliffs, NJ: Prentice-Hall, Inc., 1966.

Owen, Harry G. "The Hon. Mrs Ward and 'A Windfall for the Microscope,' of 1856 and 1864." *Annals of Science*, 41 (1984), 471–482.

Page, Norman, ed. *Tennyson: Interviews and Recollections.* Totowa, NJ: Barnes & Noble Books, 1983.

Paradis, James G. *T. H. Huxley: Man's Place in Nature.* Lincoln: Univ. of Nebraska Press, 1978.

Parrinder, Patrick. *Science Fiction: Its Criticism and Teaching.* New York: Methuen, 1980.

Paul, Sherman. *Emerson's Angle of Vision.* Cambridge, MA: Harvard Univ. Press, 1952.

Peters, Robert L., ed. *Victorians on Literature and Art.* New York: Appleton-Century-Crofts, Inc., 1961.

Pope-Hennessy, Una. *Canon Charles Kingsley.* New York: The Macmillan Company, 1949.

Porte, Joel, ed. *Emerson in His Journals.* Cambridge, MA: Belknap Press-Harvard Univ. Press, 1982.

Porter, Roy. *The Making of Geology: Earth Science in Britain, 1660–1815.* New York: Cambridge Univ. Press, 1977.

Rehbock, Philip F. *The Philosophical Naturalists: Themes in Early Nineteenth-Century British Biology.* Madison: Univ. of Wisconsin Press, 1983.

Reingold, Nathan, ed. *Science in Nineteenth-Century America: A Documentary History.* London: Macmillan, 1966.

Reiser, Stanley Joel. *Medicine and the Reign of Technology.* Cambridge: Cambridge Univ. Press, 1981.

Rhodes, Frank H. T., and Richard O. Stone, eds. *Language of the Earth.* New York: Pergamon Press, 1981.

Richards, I. A. *Science and Poetry.* London: Kegan Paul, Trench, Trübner and Co., Ltd., 1926.

Ritterbush, Philip C. *The Art of Organic Forms.* Washington, D.C.: Smithsonian Institution Press, 1968.

Roderick, G. W., and M. D. Stephens. *Scientific and Technical Education in Nineteenth-Century England.* Newton Abbot: David and Charles, 1973.

Ross, Frederick R. "Philip Gosse's *Omphalos*, Edmund Gosse's *Father and Son* and Darwin's Theory of Natural Selection." *Isis,* 68 (1977), 85–96.

Rudwick, Martin J. S. *The Meaning of Fossils: Episodes in the History of Paleontology.* Original edition, 1972. Chicago: Univ. of Chicago Press, 1985.

Ruse, Michael. *The Darwinian Revolution: Science Red in Tooth and Claw.* Chicago: Univ. of Chicago Press, 1979.

Sambrook, James, ed. *Pre-Raphaelitism: A Collection of Critical Essays.* Chicago: Univ. of Chicago Press, 1974.

Sanford, Derek, ed. *Pre-Raphaelite Writing: An Anthology.* London: Dent, 1973.

Savory, Theodore H. *The Language of Science.* London: Andre Deutsch, 1967.

Sealts, Merton M., Jr., and Alfred R. Ferguson. *Emerson's "Nature"—Origin, Growth, Meaning.* New York: Dodd, Mead and Company, Inc., 1969.

Shaw, W. David. "The Optical Metaphor: Victorian Poetics and the Theory of Knowledge." *Victorian Studies*, 23 (1979–1980), 293–324.

Skipwith, Peyton. *The Great Bird Illustrators and Their Art, 1730–1930*. London: Hamlyn, 1979.

Smith, Edward. *The Life of Sir Joseph Banks*. New York: Arno Press, 1975.

Smith, Elton E. "Pre-Raphaelite and Darwinian: Some Thoughts on Passion for Detail and Longing for Form." *Journal of Pre-Raphaelite Studies*, 6 (1985), 42–46.

Snow, C. P. *The Two Cultures: And a Second Look. An Expanded Version of The Two Cultures and the Scientific Revolution*. Cambridge: Cambridge Univ. Press, 1964.

Stapleton, Laurence, ed. *H. D. Thoreau: A Writer's Journal*. New York: Dover Publications, Inc., 1960.

Stevenson, Catherine Barnes. *Victorian Women Travel Writers in Africa*. Boston: Twayne Publishers, 1982.

Stevenson, Lionel. *The Pre-Raphaelite Poets*. New York: W. W. Norton and Company, Inc., 1974.

Stewart, Susan. *On Longing: Narratives of the Miniature, the Gigantic, the Souvenir, the Collection*. Baltimore: The Johns Hopkins Univ. Press, 1984.

Sussman, Herbert L. *Victorians and the Machine: The Literary Response to Technology*. Cambridge, MA: Harvard Univ. Press, 1968.

Tatarkiewicz, Wladyslaw. *Nineteenth Century Philosophy*. Trans. Chester A. Kisiel. Belmont, CA: Wadsworth Publishing Company, Inc., 1973.

Tennyson, Hallam, ed. *Tennyson and His Friends*. London: Macmillan and Co., Ltd., 1912.

Thackray, Arnold, and E. Mendelsohn. *Science and Values: Patterns of Tradition and Change*. New York: Humanities Press, 1975.

Thomas, Allan. *Time in a Frame: Photography and the Nineteenth Century Mind*. New York: Schocken, 1977.

Thomas, Keith. *Man and the Natural World: A History of the Modern Sensibility*. New York: Pantheon Books, 1983.

Toulmin, Stephen. *The Philosophy of Science: An Introduction*. New York: Harper and Row, Publishers, 1960.

Turner, Frank M. "The Victorian Conflict between Science and Religion: A Professional Dimension." *Isis*, 69 (1978), 356–376.

Turner, W. J., ed. *A Treasury of English Wild Life*. New York: Chanticleer Press, n.d.

Turrill, W. B. *Joseph Dalton Hooker: Botanist, Explorer, and Administrator*. London: Thomas Nelson and Sons Ltd., 1963.

Uffelman, Larry K. *Charles Kingsley*. Boston: Twayne Publishers, 1979.

Walton, Paul H. *The Drawings of John Ruskin*. Oxford: Clarendon Press, 1972.

Watson, Francis. *The Year of the Wombat: England, 1857*. New York: Harper, 1974.

Wechsler, Judith, ed. *On Aesthetics in Science*. Cambridge, MA: The MIT Press, 1978.

Welland, D. S. R. *The Pre-Raphaelites in Literature and Art*. Freeport, NY: Books for Libraries Press, 1969.

Wertheimer, Douglas. "The Identification of Some Characters and Incidents in Gosse's *Father and Son*." *Notes & Queries*, 23 (1976), 4–11.

―――. "Philip Henry Gosse: Science and Revelation in the Crucible." Ph.D. Diss., Univ. of Toronto, 1977.

Whicher, Stephen E., and Robert E. Spiller, eds. *The Early Lectures of Ralph Waldo Emerson: Volume I, 1833–1836*. Cambridge, MA: Harvard Univ. Press, 1959.

White, Gilbert. *The Natural History and Antiquities of Selborne*. New York: E. P. Dutton, 1926.

Whitehead, Alfred North. *Science and the Modern World*. New York: Macmillan, 1925.

Williams, Raymond. *Marxism and Literature*. Oxford: Oxford Univ. Press, 1977.

Wilson, David B. "Victorian Science and Religion." *History of Science*, 15 (1977), 52–67.

Winsor, Mary P. *Starfish, Jellyfish and the Order of Life: Issues of Nineteenth Century Science*. New Haven, CT: Yale Univ. Press, 1976.

Woodring, Carl. "Nature and Art in the Nineteenth Century." *PMLA*, 92 (1977), 193–202.

Woolf, James D. *Sir Edmund Gosse*. New York: Twayne Publishers, 1972.

Worster, Donald. *Nature's Economy: The Roots of Ecology*. Garden City, NY: Anchor Books/Doubleday, 1979.

Yeo, Richard. "William Whewell, Natural Theology and the Philosophy of Science in Mid-Nineteenth Century Britain." *Annals of Science*, 36 (1979), 493–516.

Young, G. M. *Victorian England: Portrait of an Age*. New York: Oxford Univ. Press, 1964.

Young, Robert M. *Darwin's Metaphor: Nature's Place in Victorian Culture*. Cambridge: Cambridge Univ. Press, 1985.

Zuckerman, Solly, ed. *The Zoological Society of London, 1826–1976 and Beyond*. London: Academic Press, 1977.

Index